Why Do You Need This New Edition?

If you're wondering why you should buy this new edition of *Gaining Word Power* here are 6 good reasons!

1. New **Stories in Context** are at the beginning of every lesson in order to introduce you to the vocabulary words you will learn in that section.

2. **Extra Word Power** is included at the end of the Practices for the additional vocabulary practice you may need.

3. **Special Academic Words** are highlighted throughout the text to prepare you for your academic course areas.

4. **Vocabulary word choices have been updated** to reflect important new terms and concepts.

5. **Cartoons** have been updated to be current and interesting for your review and analysis.

6. The author continues to highlight the **reading-writing connection** to help prepare you for your college courses.

PEARSON

Longman

EIGHTH EDITION

Gaining
Word
Power

Dorothy Rubin

Professor Emerita, The College of New Jersey

PEARSON
Longman

New York Boston San Francisco
London Toronto Sydney Tokyo Singapore Madrid
Mexico City Munich Paris Cape Town Hong Kong Montreal

With love to my understanding and supportive
husband, Artie,
my precious daughters, Carol and Sharon,
my delightful grandchildren, Jennifer, Andrew,
Melissa, and Kelsey,
and my very special and charming sons-in-law,
Seth and Dan.

Acquisitions Editor: Kate Edwards
Marketing Manager: Tom DeMarco
Production Manager: Ellen MacElree
Project Coordination, Text Design, and Electronic Page Makeup: Nesbitt Graphics, Inc.
Cover Design Manager: John Callahan
Cover Designer: Kay Petronio
Cover Photo: iStock: Chad McDermott
Senior Manufacturing Buyer: Alfred C. Dorsey
Printer and Binder: Courier Corporation
Cover Printer: Courier Corporation

Library of Congress Cataloging-in-Publication data was unavailable at publication.

Visit us at http://www.ablongman.com

ISBN 13: 978-0-205-64228-1

ISBN 10:   0-205-64228-4

3 4 5 6 7 8 9 10—V013—11

C O N T E N T S

P R E F A C E

A vocabulary book for the year 2009 must continue to reflect the times. It must continue to generate a college-level vocabulary quickly, effectively, and pleasurably to help students become more effective and strategic readers.

Good readers use a number of strategies to help them figure out the meanings of words. It makes sense, therefore, that knowledge of context clues and combining forms is essential if students want to become good strategic readers.

There's no question that vocabulary is a key variable in reading comprehension and a key feature in most academic aptitude assessments. Poor readers almost certainly have a smaller vocabulary than good readers do.

Gaining Word Power, Eighth Edition, as in all other editions, not only presents information on context clues and combining forms but also includes approaches to vocabulary that are based on sound psychological principles. Also, since the emphasis in the twenty-first century is on accountability, *Gaining Word Power* includes practices that emphasize accountability.

Before I discuss the various features of this vocabulary book, please allow me to digress for a moment to share an incident that happened a long time ago that greatly influenced my continued involvement in vocabulary study.

Many years ago, I was teaching a summer vocabulary course to freshman college students who had been admitted to college because they showed potential but who lacked basic skills and in particular the vocabulary necessary for them to succeed at college. After class one day, a very tall, husky student approached me and said that he had great animosity toward me. Needless to say, when I heard this, I was shocked and upset because I thought he liked my class. I kept my "cool" and asked him why he had such animosity toward me. He replied that because what we were doing was helping him a lot. His answer made me suspect that the young man did not know the meaning of *animosity*. I asked him whether he used the word *animosity* in speaking to anyone else. He grinned and said, "Oh, yes, I use it a lot. I like the way it sounds. I just told my boss that I have great animosity toward him."

As diplomatically as I could, I explained to him that the word he used meant just the opposite of what he wanted to say. I had a feeling that because of his size, the others to whom he had used the term did not try to explain the meaning to him. He sheepishly apologized and thanked me profusely. He also said that he felt that the vocabulary course was helping him a lot. I thanked him and told him that if he wasn't sure of a meaning of a word, it was better not to use it.

This book is an outgrowth of over thirty years of helping college students and other adults to build and retain better vocabularies.

NANCY

NANCY reprinted by permission of United Feature Syndicate, Inc.

TEXT FEATURES

Gaining Word Power, Eighth Edition, still includes a number of approaches to vocabulary building. Words are presented systematically, and each lesson contains challenging practices with immediate knowledge of results for self-evaluation of progress.

This textbook has a distinct structure, and the emphasis continues to be on the **overlearning** of vocabulary words. (See the section on "Understanding the Term *Overlearning*" in Chapter 1.) Because student interest is of prime importance, this edition, like the last, presents a diversity of practices in each lesson, as well as a variety of activities at the end of each chapter. It includes a section on extra word power after the practices.

NEW TO THIS EDITION

The Eighth Edition of *Gaining Word Power* has been updated in the following ways to help develop vocabulary skills:

1. Stories in Context are at the beginning of the lesson to introduce vocabulary words.
2. Extra Word Power is included at the end of the practices for additional practice.
3. The Dictionary is presented at the beginning of the book in Chapter 1.
4. In Part One, each Lesson begins with a Story in Context and the vocabulary words to be learned. In Part Two, each lesson begins with a Story in Context and then combining forms.
5. The reading–writing connection is maintained.
6. Crossword Puzzles are still used and have been updated.
7. Some words have been replaced, and others have been added.
8. Cartoons, wherever possible, have also been changed.
9. Special Academic Words are highlighted to prepare for academic course areas.

ADDITIONAL SUPPLEMENTS

Longman is pleased to offer a variety of support materials to help make teaching reading easier on teachers and to help students excel in their coursework. Many of our student supplements are available free or at a greatly reduced price when packaged with a Longman reading or study skills textbook. Contact your local Longman sales representative for more information on pricing and how to create a package.

ACKNOWLEDGMENTS

I would like to give my heartfelt appreciation to Kate Edwards, my editor, for her kindness and support. I would also like to thank her assistant, Lindsey Allen. In addition, I would like to thank the following reviewers for their important comments: Charlene Aldrich, Trident Technical College; Alan Brown, University of West Alabama; Gertrude Coleman, Middlesex County College; Julie Jackson-Coe, Genesee Community College; Betty Raper, Pulaski Technical College; Ellen Shur, Middlesex County College; Joe Taylor, University of West Alabama; and Gary Zacharias, Palomar College.

Dorothy Rubin

Chapter 1 An Introduction to *Gaining Word Power*

Chapter 1 discusses the organization of this book and how one can best go about improving one's vocabulary. Let us begin by considering the importance of vocabulary growth.

THE IMPORTANCE OF VOCABULARY GROWTH

A good vocabulary and good reading go hand in hand. Unless you know the meaning of words, you will have difficulty in understanding what is read. And the more you read, the more words you will add to your vocabulary. Read the following statement:

The senator behaved as a misanthrope.

Do you understand it? Unless you know the meaning of *misanthrope* you are not able to read the statement. In order to *read*, you must know the *meanings* of words and the way words are used in sentences.

Acquiring word meanings is an important reading skill. Because of the importance of this skill, this entire text is dedicated to its presentation.

ORGANIZATION OF THE BOOK

As in previous editions, this edition of *Gaining Word Power* is divided into two parts. Even though both parts stress context clues, Part One emphasizes context clues more because the words are not as easily derived from combining forms. These words have been chosen because they are used often in lectures, textbooks, and newspapers. Part Two places special stress on word parts, which are called combining forms in this text. Combining forms will be explained at the beginning of Part Two.

HOW LESSONS ARE PRESENTED

In Part One, the lessons are presented in three steps.

Step I. *Story in Context.*
Step II. *Vocabulary Words in Context.*
Step III. *Practice.*

Extra word power

In Part Two, the lessons are presented in four steps because of combining forms.

Step I. *Story in Context*
Step II. *Presentation of new combining forms and their meanings.*
   A. Learn new combining forms with their meanings.
   B. Cover the meanings of the combining forms, read the combining forms, and try to recall their meanings. Check the answers immediately.
   C. Cover the combining forms, read the meanings, and try to recall the combining forms. Check the answers immediately.
   D. Cover the meanings of the combining forms again, read the combining forms, and write their meanings in the space provided.
Step III. *Presentation of vocabulary derived from combining forms in context.*
   Learn words with their meanings and other information as you see the words used in sentences. The words are based on the combining forms learned in Step II. (See the following section.)
Step IV. *Practice.*
   Use the words in several different practices to ensure overlearning.

END-OF-CHAPTER ACTIVITIES

For both Parts One and Two, after every three lessons, there are End-of-Chapter Activities. In Part One, these activities consist of the following: Fun with Cartoons, Special Academic Words, Chapter Words in a Paragraph, Gaining Word Power on the Internet, Crossword Puzzle, Analogies, Multiple-Choice Vocabulary Test, Chapter True/False Test, Scoring of Tests, and Additional Practice Sets. (Scoring scales are given so that you will know where you stand. If you score below a certain level, you are provided with Additional Practice Sets. In these **Additional Practice Sets,** you are directed to restudy only those words that you have missed. You are provided with the page numbers for all the words and with different practice exercises to help you to learn the words you have missed.)

In Part One, the End-of-Chapter Activities are quite similar to those in Part Two. However, Part One's End-of-Chapter Activities begin with Fun with Cartoons before Special Academic Words.

CARTOON PRACTICES AND FUN WITH CARTOONS

In Part Two, almost all of the first practices are a cartoon practice, whereas in Part One, the first end-of-chapter activity is Fun with Cartoons. Both the cartoon practice and Fun with Cartoons require you not only to state the meaning of the vocabulary word used in the cartoon but also to determine what makes the cartoon amusing.

HOW WORDS ARE PRESENTED

The combining forms and words presented are a base from which you can increase your vocabulary quickly and easily. Combining forms and words have been selected on the basis of how often they appear in novels, stories, poems, textbooks, other non-fiction books, newspapers, and magazines. Words that are commonly used in college lectures are also included.

Words are presented with the following information to help your understanding of the word:

1. Correct spelling and plural (abbreviated *pl.*). Only irregular plurals are shown.
2. Pronunciation. The phonetic (pronunciation) spelling of the word may differ from the regular spelling to describe the pronunciation of the word. For example: **biology** (bī · ol′ uh · jē). The syllabication and pronunciation aids are combined in one entry.
3. Kind of word it is: *v.* for verb, *n.* for noun, *adj.* for adjective, *adv.* for adverb, and *prep.* for preposition.
4. Meaning of the word.
5. Use of the word in a sentence. Only one sentence is given for each word even though the word may have more than one meaning.

Here is an example of the presentation of a word:

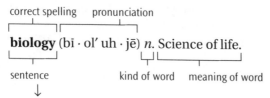

Because I intend to be a doctor, I am taking a course in **biology** *to learn about living things.*

SPECIAL NOTES

The Special Notes box in each lesson includes special information about words that might cause you unusual difficulty.

EXTRA WORD POWER

The combining forms presented in Extra Word Power are often used with thousands of words. For this reason, they are presented in a special boxed section. Extra Word Power will give additional help to your vocabulary growth.

UNDERSTANDING ANALOGIES

Analogy practice is presented after every three exercises. Analogies have to do with re-lationships. They are relationships between words or ideas. To make the best use of analogies, you must know not only the *meanings* of the words but also the relation-ship of the words or ideas to one another. For example, "*doctor* is to *hospital* as *minister* is to _____." Yes, the answer is *church*. The relationship has to do with spe-cialized persons and the places with which they are associated. Let's try another one: "*beautiful* is to *pretty* as _____ is to *decimate*." Although you know the meanings of *beautiful* and *pretty* and you can figure out that *beautiful* is more than *pretty*, you will not be able to arrive at the correct word to complete the analogy if you do not know the meaning of *decimate*. *Decimate* means "to reduce by one tenth" or "to destroy a considerable part of." Because the word that completes the analogy must express the relationship of more or greater than, the answer could be *eradicate* or *annihilate*, be-cause these words mean "to destroy completely."

Some of the relationships that words may have to one another are similar mean-ings, opposite meanings, classification, going from particular to general, going from general to particular, degree of intensity, specialized labels, characteristics, cause–effect, effect–cause, function, whole–part, ratio, and many more. The preceding rela-tionships do not have to be memorized. You will gain clues to these from the pairs that make up the analogies; that is, the words express the relationship. For example: "*pretty* is to *beautiful*"—the relationship is degree of intensity; "*hot* is to *cold*"—the re-lationship is one of opposites; "*car* is to *vehicle*"—the relationship is classification; "*sad* is to *unhappy*"—the relationship is one of synonyms; "*bell* is to *signal*"—the rela-tionship is function; "*chicken* is to *hen*"—the relationship is gender; "*word* is to *sentence*"—the relationship is part–whole; "*fire* is to *matches*"—the relationship is effect–cause.

PRONUNCIATION KEY

The simplified pronunciation key that is used in this book should help you quickly gain a good approximation of a word's pronunciation.[1] (It is important to note that pronunciations may vary from one region to another. [See "The Dictionary" on page 7.])

---

[1]A pronunciation key appears on the inside front cover of this text for easy reference.

To simplify pronunciation further, the author has given only long vowel markings (‾) and included only the primary accent mark (ʹ).

The accent mark (ʹ) is used to show which syllable in a word is stressed. This mark comes right after and slightly above the accented syllable. For example:

pilot (pīʹ lut)   **biology** (bī · olʹ uh · jē)

In the preceding two words, the syllables *piʹ* and *olʹ* are sounded with more stress and are called the accented syllables. The dot (·) is used to separate syllables. Note that no dot is used between syllables when the syllable is accented. Also note that the *o* in *pilot* and an *o* in *biology* have been changed to a *u* and an *uh*, the *y* in *biology* has been changed to an *ē*, and the *g* has been changed to a *j* to aid you in pronunciation.

The long vowel mark (‾) also helps to indicate pronunciation. A vowel that has a long vowel mark sounds like its letter name.

A slash through a letter means that the sound it stands for is silent. For example:

bāke̸   ē̸at   bīte̸   bō̸at   cūte̸

As another aid in pronunciation, the following key should be used.[2]

a (cat); **e** (less); **i** (sit); **o** (hot); **u** (but).

Words ending in *tion* and *sion* sound like *shun*, as in *nation.*
Words ending in *cian, tian,* and *sian* sound like *shin*, as in *Martian.*
Words ending in *cious* sound like *shus*, as in *delicious.*
Words ending in *ous* sound like *us*, as in *famous.*
Words ending in *ture* sound like *chur* as in *adventure, departure.*
Words ending in *cial* sound like *shul*, as in *special.*
Words ending in *ique* sound like ēk in lē̸ak, as in *critique, unique.*
Words ending in *le* preceded by a consonant usually sound like *ul* in *dull*, as in *bubble, crackle, sample.*
Words ending in *ce* sound like *s* in *safe*, as in *notice, sentence.*
Words ending in *c* sound like *k* in *like*, as in *picnic, traffic.*
Words beginning with *ce, ci,* or *cy* sound like *s* in *safe*, as in *cent, cease, citizen, city, cycle.*
Words beginning with *ca, cu,* or *co* sound like *k* in *like*, as in *cat, cut, cot.*
Words beginning with *au* sound like *aw* in *saw*, as in *author, autumn.*
Words beginning with *qu* sound like *kw*, as in *queen, quick.*
Words having *ph* sound like *f* in *fat, foot,* as in *phony, telephone.*

---

[2]In this book, *u* and *uh* are used in place of the schwa (ə), as in *visible* (vizʹ uh · bul).

UNDERSTANDING THE TERM *OVERLEARNING*

Although you may have at one time or another met many of the vocabulary words presented in this book, you may not be able to read or use the words because you have not *overlearned* them. Throughout this book, the emphasis is on the overlearning of vocabulary. *Overlearning* is not bad like *overcooking* the roast. Overlearning will help you to hold on to information over a long period of time. To overlearn the material, concentrate on the words to be learned, memorize them, and do all the exercises. Overlearning will take place only if practice is continued even after you think you have learned the information. The additional practice you engage in after you think you have mastered the material is called *overlearning*. Because practice is the key to overlearning, you will continue to meet many words that you have learned earlier in the practice sets of lessons later on.

SUGGESTIONS ON HOW TO STUDY VOCABULARY

1. You should choose a time that is best for you so that you do not feel pressured.
2. You should try to find a place that is free of things that may disturb your studying.
3. You shouldn't try to do all the lessons in one sitting. Studies have shown that you will remember your material better if you space your studying over a period of time. The thing to do is to find and work at a pace that is good for you.
4. *Recall*, which refers to how much you remember, is very important in learning. Recall is used as part of the teaching method in this book. After the presentation of the combining forms and their meanings, you are asked to cover the meanings to see if you can recall them.
5. When the entire lesson is completed, go over the words you have learned. In addition, take a few minutes before a new lesson to *review* the previous lesson.
6. To make you remember the vocabulary words, try to use them daily in your written work or speech. In addition, see how many times you meet those words in your classroom lectures and readings.

Reprinted by permission of King Features.

THE DICTIONARY

The dictionary, which is an important reference book for everyone, is filled with information about individual words, as well as other useful information. Even though the dictionary is a necessary tool, with which all students should be familiar, it should not be used as a crutch; that is, every time you meet a word whose meaning is unknown to you, you should first try to use your knowledge of combining forms and context clues to unlock the meaning. If these techniques do not help and the word is essential for understanding the passage, then you should look up the meaning.

To use the dictionary effectively, you should know that the purpose of dictionaries is not to prescribe or make rules about word meanings and pronunciations, but only to describe. Lexicographers use various methods to compile the words in the dictionary. One important method is based on citations of usage and research consulting older dictionaries. Another method involves choosing a group of people and recording the ways in which these subjects pronounce and use words. These then are recorded as the accepted standard spellings, definitions, and word usage.

Difficulties exist concerning pronunciation because persons in different parts of the United States often pronounce words differently. Pronunciation in the East is often different from that in the South or the Midwest. As a result, pronunciation of a word as given in the dictionary may not be in accord with your region's pronunciation of it.

Also, to compound this problem, different dictionaries may use different pronunciation keys. The pronunciation key is composed of words with diacritical marks. (Diacritical marks are the marks used with a letter to distinguish it from another and to help in pronunciation. Some examples are ă, ā, ȧ.) To know how to pronounce a word in a particular dictionary, you must familiarize yourself with the pronunciation key in that dictionary. For example, look at the way that six different dictionaries present a few similar words.

	WEBSTER'S NEW TWENTIETH CENTURY DICTIONARY	WEBSTER'S THIRD NEW INTERNATIONAL DICTIONARY	RANDOM HOUSE DICTIONARY OF THE ENGLISH LANGUAGE	THE AMERICAN HERITAGE DICTIONARY OF THE ENGLISH LANGUAGE	FUNK & WAGNALLS STANDARD COLLEGE DICTIONARY	OXFORD ENGLISH DICTIONARY
Word						
1. coupon	cöu′pon	′k(y)ü, pän	ko͞o′ pon	ko͞o′ pŏn	ko͞o′ pon	′kū·pon
2. courage	cŏur′ āġe	′kər·ij	kûr′ ij	kûr′ ĭj	kûr′ ij	′kʌr·idg
3. covet	cŏv′ et	′kəvəṫ	kuv′ it	kŭv′ ĭt	kuv′ it	′kʌv·it

If you had no knowledge of the pronunciation key of the specific dictionary, you would have difficulty in pronouncing the word. Pronunciation guides are generally found at the beginning of dictionaries. Many dictionaries also have a simplified pronunciation key at the bottom of every page.

Because this text will be used in various parts of the United States, this book uses a simplified pronunciation key, which is presented in the section "Pronunciation Key" on pages 4–5 and on the inside cover.

USES OF THE DICTIONARY

Before reading any further, list in the following space all the uses that you can think of for the dictionary.

_____

_____

_____

_____

_____

_____

_____

_____

_____

_____

Now compare your list with the following:

I. *Uses of the Dictionary*
   A. *Information Concerning a Word*
      1. Spelling.
      2. Definitions.
      3. Correct usage.
      4. Pronunciation.
      5. Syllabication.
      6. Antonyms.
      7. Synonyms.
      8. Parts of speech.
      9. Idiomatic phrases.
      10. Etymology—the history of the word.
      11. Semantics—the analysis of the word's meanings.
   B. *Other Useful Information*
      1. Biographical entries.
      2. Lists of foreign countries, provinces, and cities with their population figures.
      3. Charts of other geographical data.
      4. Air distances between principal cities.
      5. Listing of foreign words and phrases.

6. Complete listing of abbreviations in common use.
7. Tables of weights and measures.
8. Signs and symbols.
9. Forms of address.

Most people do not realize what an abundance of information can be gained from the dictionary. The kind of information that is presented varies according to the dictionary. Also, an unabridged dictionary usually presents more information than an abridged one.

DICTIONARY ACTIVITIES

Practice 1

Using your dictionary, answer the following questions:

1. What is a googol? _____

2. Is a montage a search engine? _____

3. Is *pre* a suffix? _____

4. Is a podiatrist a hand doctor? _____

5. Is *Miss.* an abbreviation for *Missus*? _____

6. Is haiku a type of poem? _____

7. Did Abraham Lincoln fight in the Civil War? _____

8. Is a statute a work of art? _____

9. Is a quadruped an extinct animal? _____

10. Is a centimeter a unit of measurement in the metric system? _____

Practice 2

Use your own dictionary to see how well you can answer the following questions. Answers may vary based on the dictionary you use.

1. On what page would the word *carrot* be found in your dictionary?

    _____

2. On what page would the word *affect* be found in your dictionary?

    _____

3. Between what two words in your dictionary would the word *immigrant* be found?

    _____

4. What is the abbreviation of *Honduras?* _____

5. What does *pyric* refer to? _____

6. What part of speech is *prose?* _____

7. What is a *Pollyanna?* _____

8. In what states is there a city named *Portland?* _____

9. What is the plural of *domino?* _____

10. Which syllable is accented in *favorite?* _____

11. Which syllable is accented in *portly?* _____

12. According to the pronunciation key in your dictionary, does a stress mark (accent mark) follow or precede the syllable being stressed? _____

13. Is a *heart* the same as a *hearth?* _____

14. What part of speech is *obtainable?* _____

15. Which word(s) in the pronunciation key in your dictionary is given as an example(s) of the long *a* sound? _____

16. Which word(s) in the pronunciation key is given as an example(s) of the short *a* sound? _____

17. What part of speech is *heartily?* _____

18. What part of speech is *hearty?* _____

19. What is a *polygon?* _____

20. Who was *Mozart?* _____

21. Where is the *Arabian Sea?* _____

22. How many syllables are there in *obtain?* _____

23. State two meanings for *light.* _____

24. In what Shakespeare play did *Portia* appear? _____

25. What is *posology* the scientific study of? _____

Answers to Dictionary Practice 2

1. Answers will vary.
2. Answers will vary.
3. Answers will vary.
4. *Hon* or *Hond.*
5. Fire.
6. Noun.

7. An excessively optimistic person.
8. Oregon and Maine.
9. *dominoes* or *dominos*.
10. The first syllable.
11. The first syllable.
12. Answers will vary.
13. No, a *hearth* is the stone or brick floor of a fireplace, often extending out into the room.
14. Adjective.
15. Answers will vary.
16. Answers will vary.
17. Adverb.
18. Adjective.
19. A many-sided figure.
20. An Austrian composer.
21. Between India and Arabia.
22. Two.
23. Not heavy; less than normal in amount.
24. *The Merchant of Venice.*
25. Drug dosages.

Vocabulary Derived Primarily from Context Clues

INTRODUCTION

In Part One, most of the words are not as easily derived from a knowledge of word parts (combining forms) as are those in Part Two. However, the words in Part One are used often, and you will meet them in your subject matter courses, in newspapers, in magazines, and so on. Lessons 1–9 consist of general vocabulary words. Because you will not have as much help from word parts (combining forms) to unlock word meanings, you should be especially aware of context clues. Remember, context refers to the words surrounding a particular word that can shed light on its meaning. Context clues are specific items of information that help us to gain the meaning of a particular word. When we refer to context clues, we mean clues that are given in the form of definitions, descriptions, examples, synonyms, antonyms, comparisons or contrasts, explanations, and so on.

Context Clues

Often, you can gain the meaning of a word from context clues. By *context,* we mean the words surrounding a word that can shed light on its meaning. For example, in the following sentence, see whether you can figure out the meaning of *hippodrome.*

> *In ancient times, the Greek people would assemble in their seats to observe the chariot races being held in the* hippodrome.

From the context of the sentence, you should realize that *hippodrome* refers to some arena (place) where races were held in ancient Greece.

Sometimes you can actually gain the definition of the word from the sentence or following sentences. For example:

> *The house had a cheerful atmosphere. At any moment, I expected* blithe *spirits to make their entrance and dance with joy throughout the house.*

From the sentences, you can determine that *blithe* refers to something joyful, gay, or merry.

A *context clue* is the specific item of information that helps the reader to figure out the meaning of a particular word. Context clues can be in the form of definitions, descriptions, comparisons, contrasts, examples, and so forth. The following examples display different kinds of context clues that writers frequently use.

Definition

Textbook writers often define key terms to make sure readers all learn their meanings. In this section, the terms *context* and *context clue* have been defined because they are key terms. Here are some other examples where the terms are directly defined.

EXAMPLES

An axis is a straight line, real or imaginary, that passes through the center of rotation in a revolving body at a right angle to the plane of rotation.

In geometry, a plane figure of six sides and six angles is called a hexagon.

Synonyms

Some writers give the meaning of the word by using a synonym (a word that has a meaning similar to that of another). This is a more indirect way of defining a word. However, it is an effective technique that makes the writing expressive and clear and avoids repetition.

EXAMPLES

Although Senator Hill is *candid* about his drinking problems, he is less frank about his investments.

The doctor said that the medication was *innocuous,* that is, it was harmless, merely a placebo.

Antonyms

Some writers use word opposites to help us learn the meaning of a word. Using an opposite, like using a synonym, is a more indirect way of giving a word meaning than directly defining it. However, it is an effective strategy that helps to make writing clearer and more expressive.

EXAMPLE

It seems peculiar that whenever Bill is *despondent,* his supposed friend Jason is always *lighthearted.* (From the context clues, you should realize that *despondent* and *lighthearted* are antonyms and that *despondent* must somehow mean "dejected" or "depressed.")

Contrast

Contrast is usually used to show differences between people, things, ideas, and so forth. (Antonyms are used to show contrast.)

EXAMPLES

He was impressed by the *ethereal* grace of Jane's walk rather than Ellen's heavy-footed one. (From the sentence you can determine that the meaning of *ethereal* is "light, airy.")

My sister Sara is always *optimistic*, but her boyfriend is always gloomy. (From the sentence, you can figure out that *optimistic* must mean "cheerful.")

Comparison

Comparison usually shows the similarities between people, ideas, things, and so on.

EXAMPLES

Maria was as *fickle* as a politician's promises before election. (In this sentence, *fickle* means "not firm in opinion" or "wavering." Because politicians try to court all their constituents [voters] before an election, they often are not firm in their opinions, make many promises, and are wavering. By understanding the comparison, you get an idea of the meaning of *fickle*.)

Paul is as *passive* as a bear in winter. (From the writer's comparison of Paul to a bear in winter, you can determine that *passive* means "inactive.")

Description

Writers often help us get the meaning of words by describing them for us.

EXAMPLES

Although my *diligent* friend works from morning to night, he never complains.

Interior paints no longer contain *toxic* materials that might endanger the health of infants and small children.

The *cryptic* message—which looks mysterious and secretive—is difficult to decode.

The *diffident* person, insecure and unsure, slowly approached the interviewer.

You could always tell when Lisa was getting ready to tell one of her famous *apocryphal* stories, stories that were beyond belief and verification. (From the sentence, you can figure out that an *apocryphal* story must be a fictitious story or one that cannot be authenticated, or proved true.)

Examples

Many times, a writer helps us get the meaning of a word by giving us examples illustrating the use of the word. An example is something that is representative of a whole or a group. It can be a particular single item, incident, fact, or situation that typifies the whole.

EXAMPLES

The lantern *illuminated* the cave so well that we were able to see the formations and even spiders crawling on the rocks. (From the sentence, you can determine that *illuminated* means "lit up.")

In the movie, the *mammoth* monster was able to reach the highest skyscraper, and it towered over all the apartment buildings. (From the sentence, you can determine that *mammoth* means "very large, huge.")

Good readers use all these context clues to help them to determine word meanings.

Words with Multiple Meanings

Context clues are especially important in determining meaning for words that have more than one meaning. For example, note the many uses of capital in the following sentences:

1. That is a *capital* idea.
2. Remember to begin each sentence with a *capital* letter.
3. The killing of police is a *capital* offense in some states.
4. Albany is the *capital* of New York State.
5. To start a business, you need *capital*.

Each of the preceding sentences illustrates one meaning for *capital*.

In sentence 1, *capital* means "excellent."
In sentence 2, *capital* means "referring to a letter in writing that is an uppercase letter."
In sentence 3, *capital* means "punishable by death."
In sentence 4, *capital* means "the seat of government."
In sentence 5, *capital* means "money or wealth."

Chapter 2 *College Life*

LESSON 1

Step I. Story in Context

DIRECTIONS: The following story contains several vocabulary words from this lesson. As you read the story, pay special attention to the vocabulary words in boldface type, and try to figure out the meaning of each of these words. Put the meanings in the blanks.

Joining a Fraternity

When we first came to college, there was a (1) **tacit** _____ agreement among my buddies and myself that we would not join a fraternity. Most of us felt that fraternities often tend to (2) **segregate** _____ people more than (3) **integrate** _____ them.

However, my buddy Jose said that he wanted to join one. He said that the rest of us were (4) **naive** _____ when it came to fraternities. I should tell you that Jose is a very (5) **inquisitive** _____ fellow who asks a lot of questions and checks everything out. He tends to be (6) **terse** _____ rather than (7) **verbose** _____ except when he cares strongly about something. He (8) **sustains** _____ his beliefs in spite of anything my friends or I could say. Once he makes up his mind, it is hard to change it. He is rather unsophisticated or (9) **naive** _____ about many things.

He told us that he was being quite (10) **candid** _____ about wanting to join a fraternity and that he was not (11) **frustrated** _____ by our efforts to talk him out of joining. We were disappointed that he had joined, but we did not (12) **terminate** _____ our relationship with him.

We therefore were not surprised when in Jose's sophomore year at school, he joined a fraternity.

When Jose joined the fraternity, he carefully read the by-laws. Jose is a young man who (13) **peruses** _____ everything. He does not like to leave anything to chance. He did notice that some guys at the fraternity were rather (14) **listless** _____. He wondered whether that was (15) **tentative** _____ or whether that was their permanent way of behaving.

STOP. Check answers at the end of the book (p. 328).

Step II. Vocabulary Words in Context

1. **candid** (kan′ did) *adj.* Honest; outspoken; frank. *You know that Franco is candid about his political views because he is so outspoken and open about everything.*
2. **ecstasy** (ek′ stuh · sē) *n.* Great joy. *Franco was in a state of ecstasy when the homecoming queen said that she would go to the dance with him.*
3. **frustrate** (frus′ trāte) *v.* To defeat; to bring to nothing. *adj.* (**frustrated**) Filled with a sense of discouragement and dissatisfaction as a result of defeated efforts, inner conflicts, or unresolved problems. *After a great amount of effort, they were able to frustrate the politician's plan, so that it was defeated.*
4. **inquisitive** (in · kwiz′ uh · tive) *adj.* Curious; given to asking many questions; unnecessarily or improperly curious; prying. *The inquisitive neighbor asked too many prying questions.*
5. **integrate** (in · tuh · grāte′) *v.* To unite; to make whole or complete by adding together parts. *When we integrated all the separate parts and saw the whole plan, we realized how good it was.*
6. **listless** (list′ less) *adj.* Spiritless; apathetic; indifferent; inactive. *Mrs. James was upset when her usually playful and energetic child behaved in such a listless and apathetic manner.*
7. **naive** (nī · ēve′) *adj.* Foolishly simple; childlike; unsophisticated. *Dennis is so naive that, like a child, he will believe anything you tell him.*
8. **peruse** (puh · rūze′) *v.* To read carefully; to inspect closely. *I will peruse the material at my leisure because I need time to go over it carefully.*
9. **segregate** (seg′ ruh · gāte) *v.* To set apart from others; to separate. *In school, some students tend to segregate themselves from others by forming special clubs that are not open for membership to everyone.*

10. **sustain** (sus · tāin′) *v.* To maintain; to keep in existence; to keep going; to uphold; to support. *Because the judge* **sustained** *the defense lawyer's objections, the prosecuting attorney had to resort to a different line of questioning.*
11. **tacit** (tas′ it) *adj.* Unspoken; not expressed openly but implied. *There seemed to be a* **tacit** *agreement because everybody knew how to behave even though no one said anything.*
12. **tentative** (ten′ tuh · tivé) *adj.* Not final; done on trial or experimentally; uncertain. *The arrangements we have made are only* **tentative** *ones because we want to see how well they work before we commit ourselves to something more permanent.*
13. **terminate** (tur′ muh · nāté) *v.* To end. *We decided to* **terminate** *our contract with that firm because it was always late in delivering our goods.*
14. **terse** (tursé) *adj.* Brief; concise. *Remember to be* **terse** *because the audience doesn't like long answers.*
15. **verbose** (vur · bōsé′) *adj.* Wordy. *Mia's speech is so* **verbose** *that the audience is becoming restless from listening to her.*

SPECIAL NOTES

1. The combining forms *tain, ten, tent* mean "hold". *Sustain* is derived from the combining form *tain*.
2. The combining form *greg* means "herd, flock, crowd, group." This combining form is found in the word *segregate*.

Step III. Practice

A **DIRECTIONS:** Sentences using vocabulary words from lesson 1 follow. Use the clues in the sentences to figure out the meaning of the underlined words. Write the meaning of each underlined word in the blank.

1. My parents are always <u>inquisitive</u> about my social life; they ask a lot of questions about my activities. _____

2. Mike was <u>ecstatic</u> when we were both accepted into a fraternity, but my emotions were less joyful and more mixed. _____

3. I have found that one of the hardest things for me to do as a college student is to <u>integrate</u> my social life with my schoolwork. _____

4. Before you sign the lease to your new apartment, <u>peruse</u> it carefully to make sure that all your <u>tacit</u> understandings are actually covered. _____ ;

_____

5. Alicia's plan to revolutionize campus life was <u>frustrated</u> when she failed in her bid to win the student body presidency. _____

6. Perhaps I was being <u>naive</u>, but I believed that it was important for me to be <u>candid</u> rather than guarded in my views about campus life in my sorority interview. _____ ; _____

7. I would have better feelings about this course if the teacher's introductory lecture had been shorter and less <u>verbose</u>. _____

8. Evan sometimes appears apathetic and <u>listless</u> in class, but he is actually paying close attention. _____

9. I decided to <u>terminate</u> my lease at the end of the school year so that I could leave the apartment and move back into student housing. _____

10. Even though Evie's first speech as student body treasurer was <u>terse</u> and to the point, she was able to explain her preliminary, <u>tentative</u> plan for eliminating the deficit. _____ ; _____

11. I got straight A's for the fall semester, but I'm not sure I'll be able to <u>sustain</u> that level of accomplishment in the spring. _____

12. I am not sure whether the purpose of a fraternity is to <u>segregate</u> members from other students or to encourage group solidarity. _____

STOP. Check answers at the end of the book (p. 328).

B DIRECTIONS: Each sentence contains a nonsense word. Choose a word from the word list that best replaces the nonsense word.

Word List

candid	inquisitive	naive	sustain	terminate
ecstasy	integrate	peruse	tacit	terse
frustrate	listless	segregate	tentative	verbose

1. Pedro tends to <u>elois</u> himself from others because he is a loner. _____

2. My <u>boible</u> friend Jana went to this guy's apartment to see his etchings, but he had other things on his mind. _____

3. It pays to be <u>lopple</u> most of the time; however, there are times when being outspoken can cause you a lot of grief. _____

4. The <u>proint</u> reporters continued to pry into the affairs of the government officials until they came up with the truth. _____

5. Many persons tried to <u>drepe</u> the reporters' attempts at discovering the truth.

_____

6. Ali prefers people who use as few words as possible rather than <u>croible</u> ones.

_____

7. In the film, the students had a <u>malon</u> agreement to bang their desks every time the teacher turned her back to write on the chalkboard. _____

8. Jana's answers are never <u>zelle</u> because she likes to elaborate on everything.

_____

9. In times of galloping inflation, it's difficult to <u>breable</u> a decent standard of living.

_____

10. When the two towns merge, they will <u>craim</u> their administrative staffs.

_____

STOP. Check answers at the end of the book (p. 328).

C DIRECTIONS: Write one sentence using at least two words from this exercise. The sentence must make sense. Try to illustrate the meanings of the words without actually defining them.

Example

Jose, who is usually *candid* and *terse,* gave a *verbose* speech that expressed his *frustration* at having to *terminate* his speech when the bell rang.

_____

_____

_____

_____

STOP. Check answers at the end of the book (p. 328).

EXTRA WORD POWER

y	Having; full of; tending to; like; somewhat. When *y* is added to the end of a word, it changes the word to an adjective. For example: *dirt— dirty*—full of dirt; *health—healthy*—full of health; *stick—sticky—* tending to stick; *wave—wavy*—like a wave; *horse—horsy*—like a horse; *salt—salty*—full of salt. How many more words with *y* can you supply?

LESSON 2

Step I. Story in Context

DIRECTIONS: The following story includes several vocabulary words from this lesson. As you read the story, pay careful attention to the vocabulary words in boldface type, and try to figure out the meaning of each of these words. Put the meanings in the blanks.

Life in the Fraternity

Jose was the only one of us who joined a fraternity. He said that he felt that we acted (1) **hostile** _____ to him because of it. We disagreed. We told him that it was all in his mind, that he was imagining it—it was (2) **fictitious.** _____ After all, he was free to do as he pleased. We would in no way (3) **curtail** _____ his desire to belong to a fraternity, even though before coming to college, we had all said that we would not join one.

Jose told us that he was surprised that he was voted into the fraternity of his choice because most of the members were quite (4) **affluent** _____, whereas he wasn't. Jose also told us that a few members of his fraternity had received (5) **amnesties** _____ from the college because of some shenanigans they had been involved in during pledge week.

It appears that these few members had behaved in a very (6) **covert** _____, that is, secret, rather than (7) **overt** _____ way during pledge season. They said that they were going to do one thing but did another.

What they did almost turned out to be (8) **fatal** _____ to a pledge. Fortunately for the fraternity brothers, the pledge did not drink the (9) **lethal** _____ dose he was given.

Jose told his friends that what had happened, or rather almost happened, to another pledge wasn't really (10) **relevant** _____ to him. We didn't want to sound like goody-goodies, but we thought that it did relate to him.

STOP. Check answers at the end of the book (p. 328).

Step II. Vocabulary Words in Context

1. **affluent** (af' flū · unt) *adj.* Having an abundance of goods or riches; wealthy; flowing freely. *Although Maria is very **affluent**, you would never know she has money from the way she acts.*
2. **amnesty** (am' nuh · stē) *n.* (*pl.* **ties**) A pardon from the government; act of letting someone off. *The government changed its policy on the granting of **amnesties** so that more persons would be able to receive pardons.*

3. **covert** (kō′ vurt) *adj.* Secret; concealed; covered over; sheltered. *The senator behaved in such a **covert** manner that everyone knew that he was trying to hide something.*

4. **crafty** (kraf′ tē) *adj.* Sly; cunning; skillful in deceiving. *I like trustworthy people who are aboveboard in everything they do rather than **crafty** ones.*

5. **curtail** (kur · tāil′) *v.* To shorten; to lessen; to cut off the end or a part; to cut back on; to reduce. *To **curtail** expenses, we are buying fewer clothes and not eating out as much as we did before.*

6. **fatal** (fā′ tul) *adj.* Resulting in or capable of causing death; deadly; bringing ruin or disaster; having decisive importance. *When someone has a **fatal** accident, his or her insurance company pays money to the beneficiaries.*

7. **fictitious** (fik · ti′ shus) *adj.* Imaginary; not real; made up; fabricated. *Janet's story was completely **fictitious** with no basis in fact.*

8. **hostile** (hos′ tilė) *adj.* Unfriendly; referring to an enemy. *The **hostile** audience did not applaud the speaker and behaved in a very unfriendly manner.*

9. **lethal** (lē′ thul) *adj.* Causing death; deadly. *The **lethal** blow caused his death.*

10. **overt** (ō′ vurt) *adj.* Open to view; public; apparent; able to be seen. *Because his actions were **overt**, nobody could accuse him of trying to hide anything.*

11. **relevant** (rel′ uh · vunt) *adj.* Applying to the matter in question; suitable; relating to. *Is what you are saying **relevant** to the issue, or does it apply to something else?*

SALLY FORTH

Reprinted by permission of King Features.

12. **temerity** (tuh · mer′ ut · ē) *n.* Rash boldness; foolhardiness. *What **temerity**! The driver had to pass four cars on a curve on a two-way road that had only one lane for each way.*

13. **tenet** (ten′ ut) *n.* Belief; any opinion, doctrine, principle, or dogma held as true. *One of my basic **tenets** is that hard work pays off.*

14. **tenure** (ten′ yurė) *n.* The right to hold or possess something; length of time something is held; status protecting an employee such as a teacher from being dismissed except for serious misconduct or incompetence. *After persons receive job **tenure**, it is very difficult to dismiss them, but it is possible to do so.*

15. **versatile** (ver′ suh · tilė) *adj.* Turning with ease from one thing to another; able to do many things well; many-sided; having many uses. *The **versatile** actor was able to play many different types of roles with ease.*

Step III. Practice

A DIRECTIONS: Here is a list of definitions. Choose the word that *best* fits the definition. There are more words in the list than you need. Some of the words are from Lesson 1.

Word List

affluent	curtail	lethal	sustain	tenure
amnesty	fatal	naive	tacit	terse
candid	fictitious	overt	temerity	verbose
covert	hostile	relevant	tenet	versatile
crafty				

1. Wordy   _____

2. Secret   _____

3. Deadly   _____

4. A pardon from
   the government   _____

5. Open to view   _____

6. To shorten   _____

7. Unfriendly   _____

8. Unsophisticated _____

9. Frank   _____

10. Suitable   _____

11. Imaginary   _____

12. Rashly bold   _____

13. Sly   _____

14. Belief   _____

STOP. Check answers at the end of the book (p. 328).

B DIRECTIONS: Ten sentences follow. Define the underlined words. Write your answers in the blanks.

1. Professor Ramirez received <u>tenure</u> last year after teaching for four years, getting excellent reviews from her students, and publishing her first book.

   _____

2. Rhona had the <u>temerity</u> to suggest to Mr. Wang that her grade on the midterm was

   too low. _____

3. Tom's desire to go out with Viv was quite <u>overt</u> and visible to all his friends.

   _____

4. Although Dan comes from a very <u>affluent</u> family, his parents neither bought him a car nor routinely give him any spending money. _____

5. Your essay was supposed to be factual, but I believe that what you have written is completely <u>fictitious</u>. _____

6. Because my mother was recently laid off from her job, my parents have had to cut back and <u>curtail</u> many expenses, including part of my allowance. _____

7. I think you should cut the third paragraph of your paper, because I don't think it's <u>relevant</u> to your topic. _____

8. Sally is a very <u>versatile</u> artist who is good at painting, drawing, and cartooning. _____

9. Raymonda's fatal action, which led to her bankruptcy, was borrowing too heavily against the value of her house. _____

10. I don't approve of Chi Lin's <u>covert</u> activities on behalf of her candidate, because I think campaigns should be conducted openly. _____

STOP. Check answers at the end of the book (p. 328).

C DIRECTIONS: Write one sentence using at least two words from this lesson. The sentence must make sense. Try to illustrate the meanings of the words without actually defining them.

Example

The *affluent* magnate said that he would *curtail* his *covert* dealings with the *hostile* forces.

_____

_____

_____

_____

STOP. Check answers at the end of the book (p. 328).

EXTRA WORD POWER

dom   State or condition of being; rank; total area of. *Dom* is added to the end of many words. For example: *Christendom*—the Christian world; *dukedom*—the rank or title of a duke; the area governed by a duke; *freedom*—condition of being free; *kingdom*—area controlled by a king; *stardom*—the status of being a star; *wisdom*—the state of having knowledge. How many more words that end in *dom* can you supply?

LESSON 3

Step I. Story in Context

DIRECTIONS: The following story includes several vocabulary words from this lesson. As you read the story, pay careful attention to the words in boldface type, and try to figure out the meaning of each of these words. Put the meanings in the blanks.

College Life

Living away at college has made me aware of how many things I have taken for granted. I don't want to sound (1) **nostalgic** _____ or (2) **sentimental** _____, but I actually miss being home, especially when it's time to eat or clean up. It's really a quite (3) **formidable** _____ task for me to attend to such (4) **mundane** _____ things as preparing food when I am (5) **famished** _____. Also, when I'm (6) **fatigued,** _____ there isn't anyone around to say, "Tanya, why don't you take a nap or at least rest while I prepare something for you to eat." Now I have no (7) **alternative** _____ but to prepare it myself or eat in the school cafeteria.

Actually, my friends and I are rather lucky because we were able to rent an apartment off campus. Consequently, we prepare most of our meals ourselves.

Sarita, who is our (8) **optimist** _____, always sees the bright side of things. Of course, she loves to cook. I, on the other hand, am more prone to be a (9) **pessimist** _____, so I usually expect doom and gloom. Also, I hate to cook, so when it's my turn, I usually moan and groan about it. In addition, no one talks to me or asks me any questions at that time because they know that I will be very (10) **concise** _____, that is, very terse, in answering them.

One of the biggest (11) **constraints** _____ I have has to do with money. I don't have very much. I tend to (12) **obfuscate** _____ everything I say when it comes to money. I am not very (13) **tactful** _____ when it comes to either cooking or money.

STOP. Check answers at the end of the book (p. 329).

Step II. Vocabulary Words in Context

1. **alternative** (awl · tur′ nuh · tivé) *n.* One or more things offered for choice; a choice between two or more things; a remaining choice; a choice. *adj.* Offering or providing a choice between two or more things. *Because the **alternative** to paying a fine was to go to jail, Lara chose the first penalty.*
2. **concise** (kun · sisé′) *adj.* Brief; terse. *Ali's **concise** statement was brief and to the point.*

3. **constraint** (kun · strāint') *n.* Confinement; a restriction; force; compulsion; coercion. *One of the constraints of the job was that I could not leave whenever I desired.*

4. **expedite** (ek' spuh · dīte) *v.* To hasten; to make easy the progress of; to speed up the progress of. *The buyer said that because he needs the order now, he wants the salesman to expedite the delivery of the goods.*

5. **famish** (fam' ish) *v.* To make or be very hungry; starve. *adj.* (**famished**) Very hungry. *I am so famished that I could eat almost anything.*

6. **fatigue** (fuh · tēgúe') *n.* Physical or mental tiredness; weariness. *v.* To tire out; to weary; to weaken from continued use. *I was so tired from working today that I was completely fatigued.*

7. **formidable** (for' mid · uh · bul) *adj.* Dreaded; causing awe or fear, hard to handle; of discouraging or awesome strength, size, difficulty, and so on. *That is such a formidable task that it may be too hard to handle.*

8. **mundane** (mun' dāne) *adj.* Referring to everyday things; referring to that which is routine or ordinary; referring to worldly things rather than more high-minded or spiritual things. *After listening to a lecture about the kinds of activities that archaeologists engage in, my tasks sounded mundane and ordinary.*

9. **nostalgic** (nuh · stal' jik) *adj.* Homesick; longing to go back to one's home, hometown, and so on; longing for something far away or long ago. *When I saw some of my childhood things, I became very nostalgic.*

10. **obfuscate** (ob · fus' kāte) *v.* To darken; to confuse; to obscure. *Every time he spoke, instead of clarifying the issue, he obfuscated it even more.*

11. **optimist** (op' tuh · mist) *n.* One who is hopeful; a cheerful person; one who tends to take the most hopeful view or expects the best outcome. *Carol always looks at the bright side of things because she is such an optimist.*

12. **pessimist** (pes' uh · mist) *n.* One who expects the worst to happen in any situation; one who looks on the dark side of things; a gloomy person. *George is such a pessimist that he seems to expect only bad things to happen.*

13. **sentimental** (sen · tuh · men' tul) *adj.* Marked by tenderness, emotion, feeling, and so on; influenced more by feeling or emotion than by reason; acting from feeling rather than from practical motives. *At my parents' fiftieth wedding anniversary, I behaved like a sentimental fool because I was so overcome with emotion.*

14. **tactful** (takt' ful) *adj.* Considerate; conscientiously inoffensive; skillful in dealing with people in difficult positions. *Because Alana does not like to hurt anyone's feelings, she is trying to think of a tactful way to tell Mrs. Brown that her son is a stupid oaf who is obnoxious to everyone.*

15. **variable** (var' ē · uh · bul) *adj. n.* Changeable; something that may or does vary. *Because the weather has been so variable, it's difficult to know what to wear.*

SPECIAL NOTES

The word *sentimental* may also mean "having or showing exaggerated or superficial emotion." This meaning is often used in literature.

Step III. Practice

A DIRECTIONS: Each sentence has a missing word. Choose the word from the list below that *best* completes the sentence. Write the word in the blank. Some words are from previous lessons.

Word List

alternative	expedite	mundane	segregate
amnesty	famish	nostalgic	sentimental
concise	fatigued	obfuscate	tactful
constraints	formidable	optimist	tenet
crafty	hostile	pessimist	variable

1. Even though Bill was guilty of dishonesty, the dean granted him _____ and allowed him to receive his diploma.

2. Your argument could perhaps be clearer, but your paper is so short that it could hardly be more _____.

3. Going to the spring formal made me feel _____ for senior year and the high school prom.

4. Because Victor is so _____ and considerate, he will do an excellent job greeting visitors to the admissions office.

5. My roommate's moods are highly _____, so I'll wait until her mood changes before asking to borrow her car this weekend.

6. Because I am an _____, I always think I will do well in all my courses.

7. Professor Emmanuel is such a poor speaker that everything he says tends to _____ things, instead of clarifying them as he intends.

8. Completing two papers and studying for a test within the next two days will be a _____ and challenging task.

9. Professor Clark has imposed many _____ on our choice of term paper topic; for example, no two students may write about the same author.

10. Your solution to the problem is certainly _____ but I am not sure that it is quite honest.

11. I would not have expected Dean Vernon to be _____ , but he certainly displayed an overflow of emotion at the college's fiftieth birthday commemoration.

12. After three hours of band practice and five hours of studying, I am so _____ that all I want to do is go to bed.

13. My campus job in the dean's office is not very exciting, but the everyday, _____ tasks I perform nevertheless help the college run smoothly.

14. I know you need your textbook as soon as possible, so I will do everything I can to _____ your order.

15. Susanna tends to be a _____, but in this case she says she doesn't see any reason why everything should not go well.

16. You say that you support me, but your actions certainly appear _____ to my candidacy.

17. I think that my only _____ is to keep my job until the end of the school year and look for a better one next year.

18. One of my most basic _____ is that if anything is worth doing, it is worth doing well.

STOP. Check answers at the end of the book (p. 329).

B **DIRECTIONS:** Some sentences that contain the meanings of vocabulary presented in Lesson 3 follow. Choose the word that *best* fits the word or phrase underlined in the sentence. More words are presented than you need.

Word List

alternative	famished	nostalgic	sentimental
concise	fatigued	obfuscate	tactful
constraint	formidable	optimist	variable
expedite	mundane	pessimist	

_____ 1. I become <u>overwhelmed with emotion</u> when I see things that relate to my early childhood.

_____ 2. After working all night on a paper, I was so <u>mentally and physically tired</u> that I collapsed.

_____ 3. Writing three themes in one week is <u>hard to handle</u>.

_____ 4. When I don't eat breakfast or lunch, I feel <u>starved</u> by dinner time.

_____ 5. Evita is a <u>person who always looks on the bright side of things</u>.

_____ 6. Jacob is a <u>person who always looks on the gloomy side of things</u>.

_____ 7. What is <u>routine or ordinary</u> to one person may not be for another.

_____ 8. We had no <u>choice</u> in the matter, so we let him go.

_____ 9. Answer the questions in a <u>brief</u> manner.

_____ 10. After being away from home, I started to have <u>homesick</u> feelings.

STOP. Check answers at the end of the book (p. 329).

C **DIRECTIONS:** Write one sentence using at least two words from this exercise. The sentence must make sense. Try to illustrate the meanings of the words without actually defining them.

Example

The *fatigued* and *famished* woman said that she had become a homeless person because she had no *alternative*.

_____

_____

STOP. Check answers at the end of the book (p. 329).

EXTRA WORD POWER

ful	Full of; characterized by; having the qualities of. When *ful* is added to the end of a word, it is spelled with only one *l*. In words ending in *y* after a consonant, the *y* changes to an *i* when *ful* is added. For example: *beauty—beautiful*—having the qualities of beauty; *joyful*—full of joy; *tearful*—full of tears; *peaceful*—characterized by peace. How many more words with *ful* can you supply?

!!! FUN WITH CARTOONS

State the meaning of the term *sustain*. Then explain why the cartoon is humorous.

WHY ARE YOU QUITTING THE PRESIDENTIAL RACE SO EARLY, SENATOR?

WELL, OUR POLLING INDICATED THAT ALTHOUGH WE HAVE WIDE SUPPORT IN MANY COMMUNITIES ACROSS AMERICA,

WE DID NOT HAVE THE DEPTH OF SUPPORT IN CRUCIAL AREAS NECESSARY TO SUSTAIN A SUCCESSFUL CAMPAIGN...

"WE'RE BROKE."

TRANSLATION

TRANSLATION

Reprinted by permission of Tribune Media Services.

STOP. Check answers at the end of the book (p. 329).

SPECIAL ACADEMIC WORDS

A **DIRECTIONS:** There are a number of words in this chapter that are used often in the social sciences. Without looking back at the chapter, see how well you can define them.

1. integration _____

2. segregation _____

3. amnesty _____

4. hostile _____

5. relevant _____

6. overt _____

7. covert _____

8. fictitious _____

9. tenet _____

10. crafty _____

B **DIRECTIONS:** Choose the answers to the riddles from the terms presented in the above Practice A.

1. I'm sly, so you never know what I really want. _____

2. I am always in the open. _____

3. I like to remain hidden. _____

4. You can believe in me. _____

5. I relate to you. _____

6. I don't like to be away from others. _____

7. I don't like to be with everyone. _____

8. I'm not real. _____

9. I'm too belligerent. _____

10. I desire a pardon. _____

STOP. Check answers at the end of the book (p. 329).

CHAPTER WORDS IN A PARAGRAPH

Write a paragraph on the given topic using at least two words from this chapter. The paragraph must make sense and be logically developed.

Topic: A Formidable Decision I Had to Make

STOP. Check answers at the end of the book (p. 329).

GAINING WORD POWER ON THE INTERNET

1. Choose a search engine. Write the name of the chosen search engine: _____

2. Do a search of the following two terms: *amnesty, optimist.*

3. Choose one site or reference generated by your search for each term. Try to select sites that help you gain a better understanding of the terms you are researching. Write the

   chosen site for each term: _____ _____

4. Write a three-sentence paragraph on the site information for each term.

5. Log onto the Web site that accompanies this textbook for extra practice exercises at [http://www.ablongman.com/vocabulary].

STOP. Check answers at the end of the book (p. 329).

CROSSWORD PUZZLE

The meanings of a number of words from Lessons 1 to 3 follow. Your knowledge of these words should help you solve the following crossword puzzle.

Across

1. Thirteenth letter of alphabet
2. Opposite of *stop*
3. Female pronoun
4. Brief
7. Roman numeral 100
8. Opposite of *happy*
11. Wordy
13. Abbreviation of Certificate of Deposit
14. Past tense of *send*
15. A dog and cat are household _____s
16. Unspoken
17. Indefinite article
18. A girl's name
20. Past tense of regular verbs
21. Homonym of *two*
22. Meaning of *fatigued*
25. Unsophisticated
27. Imitate someone
28. A cover
29. Abbreviation of pint
31. To turn around
32. Abbreviation of street
33. Same as #30 Down

Down

1. Pronoun referring to *self*
2. The Supreme Being
3. A plant used for seasoning in cooking
4. Outspoken; honest
5. Hidden; concealed
6. Arrange
7. Cut off
8. To accomplish what you wanted to
9. Employ
10. Meshed fabric used to catch fish
12. Someone who looks on the bright side
14. Noun plural
17. Abbreviation of *advertisement*
18. Unite
19. Infant's sound for *daddy*
22. You leave this for the waiter
23. Tenants _____ an apartment
24. Same as #20 Across
26. _____ and vigor
27. A woman's title
30. The twentieth letter of alphabet

STOP. Check answers at the end of the book (p. 330).

ANALOGIES

DIRECTIONS: Find the word from the following list that *best* completes each analogy. There are more words listed than you need.

Word List

amnesty	ecstasy	obfuscate	temerity
bad	expedite	optimist	tenacious
candid	famished	pathetic	tenet
changeable	good	posterior	tentative
clear	happiness	prying	term
commence	incredible	spiritless	terminate
concise	integrate	steady	termite
constraint	lucid	sustain	verbose
covert	mundane	tacit	vociferous
curtail	naive	tactful	voiced
defeat			

1. Fictitious : real :: sophisticated : _____.

2. Covert : overt :: segregate : _____.

3. Concede : surrender :: starved : _____.

4. Affluent : wealthy :: frustrate : _____.

5. Hostile : friendly :: clarify : _____.

6. Relevant : irrelevant :: unusual : _____.

7. Permanent : tentative :: variable : _____.

8. Lethal : deadly :: terse : _____.

9. Crafty : sly :: listless : _____.

10. Sentimental : unfeeling :: pessimist : _____.

11. Pat : strike :: joy : _____.

12. Dreaded : formidable :: foolhardiness : _____.

13. Positive : definite :: rear : _____.

14. Contemporary : ancient :: begin : _____.

15. Post : position :: pardon : _____.

16. Pacify : calm :: belief : _____.

17. Species : kind :: inquisitive : _____.

18. Archetype : model :: clamorous : _____.

19. Dormant : active :: lengthen : _____.

20. Animate : deaden :: spoken : _____.

STOP. Check answers at the end of the book (p. 330).

MULTIPLE-CHOICE VOCABULARY TEST

DIRECTIONS: This is a test on words in Lessons 1 to 3. Words are presented according to lessons. *Do all lessons before checking answers.* Underline the meaning that *best* fits the word.

Lesson 1

1. naive
   a. happy
   b. sophisticated
   c. childlike
   d. apathetic

2. segregate
   a. to unite
   b. regulate
   c. foolish
   d. to separate

3. sustain
   a. to help
   b. to maintain
   c. unnecessary
   d. to go

4. tacit
   a. to the point
   b. open
   c. unspoken
   d. friendly

5. terse
   a. unspoken
   b. brief
   c. frank
   d. a pardon

6. verbose
   a. quiet
   b. brief
   c. wordy
   d. friendly

7. candid
   a. happy
   b. frank
   c. cheerful
   d. to the point

8. frustrate
   a. to defeat
   b. anxious
   c. to separate
   d. foolish

9. integrate
   a. to separate
   b. to unite
   c. force
   d. race

10. inquisitive
    a. prying
    b. a quiz
    c. wise
    d. going before

11. ecstasy
    a. stars
    b. a stay
    c. great joy
    d. healthy

12. peruse
    a. to glance at
    b. to study carefully
    c. to read
    d. to write well

13. tentative
    a. sure of oneself
    b. temporary
    c. having to do with tents
    d. end

14. terminate
    a. end
    b. terms
    c. temporary
    d. lease

15. listless
    a. sleepy
    b. spirited
    c. a list of things
    d. spiritless

Lesson 2

16. overt
    a. closed
    b. relates to eyes
    c. open
    d. select

17. relevant
    a. friendly
    b. open
    c. secret
    d. relating to

18. fictitious
    a. story
    b. imaginary
    c. real
    d. unsophisticated

19. hostile
    a. friendly
    b. kill
    c. unfriendly
    d. hurt

20. lethal
    a. poison
    b. hurt
    c. dangerous
    d. deadly

21. affluent
    a. wealthy
    b. result
    c. secret
    d. cause

22. curtail
    a. curious
    b. cheerful
    c. to shorten
    d. inactive

23. covert
   a. open
   b. secret
   c. spy
   d. prying

24. amnesty
   a. wordy
   b. a pardon
   c. short
   d. honest

25. fatal
   a. causing death
   b. secret
   c. poison
   d. open

26. crafty
   a. mean
   b. witty
   c. sly
   d. relates to crafts

27. temerity
   a. rashly bold
   b. scared
   c. timid
   d. temporary

28. tenet
   a. a saying
   b. a belief
   c. a fool
   d. a word

29. versatile
   a. turning around
   b. refers to poetry
   c. turning
   d. able to do many things

30. tenure
   a. right to hold something
   b. able to do many things
   c. refers to teachers
   d. status

Lesson 3

31. alternative
   a. relating to
   b. choice
   c. imaginary
   d. unfriendly

32. mundane
   a. healthy
   b. ordinary
   c. uncaring
   d. friendly

33. nostalgic
   a. nosy
   b. homesick
   c. friendly
   d. noticeable

34. pessimist
   a. one who is a pest
   b. one who is sad
   c. one who is gloomy
   d. one who is cheerful

35. optimist
   a. one who is bad
   b. one who is friendly
   c. relating to kindness
   d. one who is cheerful

36. sentimental
   a. lacking feeling
   b. sentence
   c. emotional
   d. friendly

37. concise
   a. wordy
   b. long
   c. to cut off
   d. brief

38. famished
   a. tired
   b. long
   c. starved
   d. food

39. fatigued
   a. hungry
   b. starved
   c. tired
   d. asleep

40. formidable
   a. of discouraging difficulty
   b. inactive
   c. apathetic
   d. open

41. constraint
   a. fence
   b. a restriction
   c. closed
   d. open

42. obfuscate   a. to obscure   c. to open
                  b. to close   d. to fuse

43. expedite   a. to help   c. to close
                  b. to speed up the progress   d. to restrict

44. tactful   a. offensive   c. considerate
                  b. helpful   d. healthful

45. variable   a. refers to differences   c. changeable
                  b. refers to being open   d. refers to being closed

CHAPTER TRUE/FALSE TEST

DIRECTIONS: This is a true/false test on Lessons 1 to 3. Read each sentence carefully. Decide whether it is true or false. Put a *T* for *True* or an *F* for *False* in the blank. If the statement is false, change a word or words to make it true. The number after the sentence tells you in which lesson the word appears.

_____ 1. To *integrate* means to separate. 1

_____ 2. A *listless* person is energetic. 1

_____ 3. A person who is *frustrated* feels discouraged. 1

_____ 4. A *verbose* speech is too long. 1

_____ 5. *Tentative* means the same as "uncertain."

_____ 6. If you *peruse* a document, you skim it quickly.

_____ 7. Someone who is *hostile* is an enemy. 2

_____ 8. A *fictitious* character is not based on a real person. 2

_____ 9. Something that is *relevant* is unimportant. 2

_____ 10. A *fatal* shooting is one in which no one is killed. 2

_____ 11. A timid person is lacking in *temerity*. 2

_____ 12. *Overt* and *covert* are antonyms. 2

_____ 13. You feel *famished* right after you eat. 3

_____ 14. *Concise* is a synonym for brief. 3

_____ 15. Pens and paperclips are examples of *mundane* things. 3

_____ 16. To *obfuscate* means to clarify. 3

_____ 17. An *optimist* always expects the worst. 3

_____ 18. To have an *alternative* is to have a choice. 3

STOP. Check answers for both tests at the end of the book (pp. 330–331).

SCORING OF TESTS

Multiple-Choice Vocabulary Test	
Number Wrong	*Score*
0–2	Excellent
3–5	Good
6–8	Weak
Above 8	Poor
Score _____	

True/False Test	
Number Wrong	*Score*
0–1	Excellent
2–3	Good
4–5	Weak
Above 5	Poor
Score _____	

1. If you scored in the excellent or good range on *both tests,* you are doing well. Go on to Chapter 3.
2. If you scored in the weak or poor range on either test, look at the next page and follow directions for Additional Practice. Note that the words on the tests are arranged so that you can tell in which lesson to find them. This arrangement will help you if you need additional practice.

ADDITIONAL PRACTICE SETS

A **DIRECTIONS:** Write the words you missed on the tests from the three lessons in the space provided. Note that the tests are presented so that you can tell to which lessons the words belong.

Lesson 1 Words Missed

1. _____   6. _____
2. _____   7. _____
3. _____   8. _____
4. _____   9. _____
5. _____   10. _____

Lesson 2 Words Missed

1. _____   6. _____
2. _____   7. _____
3. _____   8. _____
4. _____   9. _____
5. _____   10. _____

Lesson 3 Words Missed

1. _____   6. _____

2. _____   7. _____

3. _____   8. _____

4. _____   9. _____

5. _____   10. _____

B **DIRECTIONS:** Restudy the words that you have written down on page 38 and this page. Do Step I for those you missed. Note that Step I is on the following pages:

Lesson 1—pp. 17–21
Lesson 2—pp. 22–25
Lesson 3—pp. 26–30

C **DIRECTIONS:** Do Additional Practice 1 on this page if you missed words from Lesson 1. Do Additional Practice 2 on page 40 if you missed words from Lesson 2. Do Additional Practice 3 on page 41 if you missed words from Lesson 3. Now go on to Chapter 3.

Additional Practice 1 for Lesson 1

DIRECTIONS: Ten sentences follow. Define the underlined word. Put your answer in the blank.

1. Sometimes it's best not to be so <u>candid</u> because people don't want to hear the truth. _____

2. Because I don't like nosy questions, I wish you wouldn't be so <u>inquisitive</u>.

   _____

3. How could you be so <u>naive</u> as to believe that Jacob wanted you to go to his apartment to look at his pictures? _____

4. Many school districts are trying to <u>integrate</u> their schools by combining groups of students from different neighborhoods. _____

5. At the party, try not to go off in a corner and <u>segregate</u> yourself from everyone else. _____

6. Jacob said that he doesn't know how he will be able to <u>sustain</u> himself on the salary that he has. _____

7. No one said anything, but there was a <u>tacit</u> agreement on what to do.
_____

8. Alfredo told his friends to remember to be <u>terse</u> when they give their reports so that they can leave early. _____

9. After working so hard on that plan, I am <u>frustrated</u> to learn that it has been defeated. _____

10. Some speakers are so <u>verbose</u> that they can go on for hours. _____

STOP. Check answers at the end of the book (p. 331).

Additional Practice 2 for Lesson 2

DIRECTIONS: Ten sentences that contain the meanings of vocabulary presented in Lesson 2 follow. Choose the word that *best* fits the word or phrase underlined in the sentence. All words are used.

Word List

affluent	curtail	hostile	overt
amnesty	fatal	lethal	relevant
covert	fictitious		

_____ 1. Since the Oliviers are so <u>wealthy</u>, money means nothing to them.

_____ 2. The <u>secret</u> activities of the government spies were finally uncovered.

_____ 3. All my business deals have to be <u>open and above board</u>.

_____ 4. We knew that the <u>decisive</u> hour would arrive soon.

_____ 5. As children, my friend and I used to make up lots of <u>imaginary</u> stories to tell to each other.

_____ 6. A <u>pardon</u> was given to a former spy who helped the government capture other spies.

_____ 7. If you <u>reduce</u> my funds any more, we won't have enough to live on.

_____ 8. Why are some people so <u>unfriendly</u>?

_____ 9. He accidentally drank a <u>deadly</u> dose of poison.

_____ 10. When you write your report, make sure that everything you put in it is <u>related</u> to your topic.

STOP. Check answers at the end of the book (p. 331).

Additional Practice 3 for Lesson 3

DIRECTIONS: Ten sentences follow. Define the underlined word. Put your answer in the blank.

1. We had no <u>alternative</u> but to concede that we were beaten. _____

2. When you give your answers on the final, be <u>concise</u> and to the point. _____

3. The task seemed so <u>formidable</u> to her that she didn't know whether she should undertake it. _____

4. I'm <u>famished</u> because I haven't eaten for almost 24 hours. _____

5. I'm so <u>fatigued</u> that I feel as though I could sleep for a week. _____

6. Every day, I have the same old <u>mundane</u> things to do. _____

7. When he saw his newborn child, he felt very <u>sentimental</u>. _____

8. Because I'm an <u>optimist</u>, I predict that we'll have a sunny day for our picnic tomorrow. _____

9. Because I'm a <u>pessimist</u>, I predict it will rain for our picnic tomorrow. _____

10. Every year during the spring, I become <u>nostalgic</u> about my former home with its garden and large lawn. _____

STOP. Check answers at the end of the book (p. 331).

Chapter 3 *Jose's Dilemma*

LESSON 4

Step I. Story in Context

DIRECTIONS: The following story includes several vocabulary words from this lesson. As you read the story, pay careful attention to the vocabulary words in boldface type, and try to figure out the meaning of each of these words. Put the meanings in the blanks.

Jose's Dilemma

Jose liked spending time with his friends. However, he also liked spending time with his fraternity brothers. However, he didn't have enough time to spend with both his friends and his fraternity brothers. Jose knew that he had a (1) **dilemma** _____. He didn't want to offend either his friends or his fraternity brothers. Yet he seemed to be doing just that.

His fraternity brothers nominated Jose to be their treasurer because he is a very (2) **diligent** _____ person. It seemed like a (3) **coincidence** _____ when his buddies with whom he shared an apartment also wanted him to be in charge of the household expenses. Jose couldn't be the treasurer and also in charge of household expenses. When Jose told his friends that he couldn't do what they wanted, his buddies were furious with him. They said that his behavior (4) **affirmed** _____ that he was a (5) **haughty** _____ person and that he looked upon them with (6) **disdain** _____ .

Jose felt that he was between a rock and a hard place, and his schoolwork was suffering. He just couldn't decide what to (7) **eradicate** _____ or (8) **delete** _____ from his life. Everything seemed (9) **pertinent** _____ to him. Jose thought that maybe if he (10) **isolated** _____ himself from his buddies and his fraternity brothers for a while, he could get a better view of things.

Jose needed to (11) **replenish** _____ his spirits. His friends thought that he had become (12) **arrogant** _____ . He felt that he hadn't. He needed a (13) **vestige** _____ of hope, that is, a sign that he was the same as he had been before he had joined the fraternity.

STOP. Check answers at the end of the book (p. 331).

Step II. Vocabulary Words in Context

1. **affirm** (uh · firm′) *v.* To declare or state positively; to say or maintain that something is true. *The auditor examined the bank accounts and **affirmed** that they were all in order with positively no problems.*

2. **arrogant** (ar′ uh · gunt) *adj.* Haughty; full of pride; overbearing; full of self-importance. *He is so **arrogant** that people try to avoid being in his presence because it's no fun being with someone who thinks he's so great.*

3. **coincidence** (kō · in′ suh · dense) *n.* The occurrence of things or events at the same time by chance. *What a **coincidence** to find Sanjay in Paris at the same time that I was there.*

4. **delete** (di · lēte′) *v.* To take out or remove a letter, word, and so on; to cross out; to erase. *After Ms. Johnson had dictated the letter to her secretary, she asked her to **delete** the whole last paragraph because it was not worded properly.*

5. **dilemma** (duh · lem′ uh) *n.* Any situation that necessitates a choice between equally unfavorable or equally unpleasant alternatives; an argument that presents two equally unfavorable alternatives. *Mr. Mfume's **dilemma** is a serious one because if he agrees to the transplant, he might die during the operation or from the effects of it; but if he doesn't have one, he might die also.*

6. **diligent** (dil′ uh · jent) *adj.* Applying oneself in whatever is undertaken; working in a constant effort to accomplish something; industrious. *He worked in such a **diligent** manner to complete his project that he didn't even stop for a break.*

7. **disdain** (dis · dāin′) *v.* To regard as unworthy; to despise. *n.* The feeling of scorn or of despisal; expression of scorn (contempt). *Joy was looked at with great **disdain** by all her fellow workers when they found out that she had been giving covert information about them to the boss.*

8. **eradicate** (uh · rad' uh · kāté) *v.* To destroy completely; to pull out by the roots; to wipe out; to exterminate. *The engineers wanted to **eradicate** all possible errors from their calculations before attempting to construct their new machine.*

9. **haughty** (haw' tē) *adj.* Having or showing great pride in oneself and contempt (disrespect) or scorn for others; overbearing; snobbish; arrogant. *Many **haughty** people are so egocentric and overbearing that they make others feel hostile toward them.*

10. **isolate** (ī' suh · lāté) *v.* To set apart from others; to place alone; to separate. *In the hospital, doctors **isolate** patients with contagious (catching) diseases in rooms by themselves so that they will not spread their germs to others.*

11. **pertinent** (pur' tuh · nunt) *adj.* Relevant; relating to or bearing upon the matter at hand; being to the point. *The witness said that he had **pertinent** information that could have a major effect on the case.*

12. **replenish** (ri · plen' ish) *v.* To supply or fill again. *Unless they **replenished** their stock immediately, they would run out of everything.*

13. **replete** (ri · plēté') *adj.* Well filled or supplied. *His words were **replete** with praise for his colleague, whom he admired.*

14. **thrifty** (thrif' tē) *adj.* Clever at managing one's money; economical; not spending money unnecessarily. *When you have a limited amount of money and many expenses, you have to be **thrifty**.*

15. **vestige** (ves' tijé) *n.* A trace, mark, or sign of something that once existed but doesn't exist anymore. *There was no **vestige** of woodland in this area, which had once been replete with trees.*

Step III. Practice

A DIRECTIONS: Sentences using vocabulary words from Lesson 4 follow. Use the clues in the sentences to figure out the meaning of the underlined words. Write the meaning of each underlined word in the blank.

1. I have always felt a proud <u>disdain</u> for people who cannot budget their time and money carefully, believing myself to be superior to them. _____

2. I have always believed that through <u>diligent</u> effort and continual struggle, a person can stay in control of his or her time and money. _____

3. I am afraid that my pride in my own efforts sometimes led me to feel <u>haughty</u> toward others or overconfident in myself. _____

4. However, something happened recently that I hope will completely do away with and <u>eradicate</u> those feelings forever. _____

5. Because of an unusual <u>coincidence</u>, I found myself with two very large bills to pay in the same month: I needed new brakes on my car and a new computer at the same time. _____

6. I found myself faced with a serious <u>dilemma</u>: I had to choose between emptying my small savings account, or, for the first time, going into debt. _____

7. I decided to empty my bank account to pay both bills and to save as much money as I could until I could once again <u>replenish</u> the account. _____

8. I lived in as <u>thrifty</u> a way as possible and saved wherever I could, but it still took me almost six months to restore my bank balance. _____

9. After going through this experience, I can certainly <u>affirm</u> how difficult it is to manage money; I would be willing to say this to anyone. _____

10. I can also state that my formerly <u>arrogant</u> feelings of pride have transformed into humility and understanding, because I now know how easy it is to fall into financial difficulties. _____

STOP. Check answers at the end of the book (p. 331).

B DIRECTIONS: Each sentence has a missing word. Choose the word that *best* completes the sentence. Write the word in the blank. All words are used.

Word List

affirm	dilemma	eradicate	isolate
coincidence	diligent	haughty	pertinent
delete	disdain		

1. It was a remarkable _____ that two scientists working separately in different countries discovered a cure for a disease at the exact same time.

2. You face a terrible _____ because either choice you make will have unfortunate consequences.

3. Make sure you report only _____ information and leave out anything that is not relevant.

4. We can both _____ that the evidence you have given is truthful.

5. _____ people, who are filled with pride and show disrespect toward others, are not well liked.

6. Because I had a contagious disease, the hospital had to _____ me from the other patients.

7. To _____ all the rats in the building, the exterminator used toxic materials that were lethal only to rats and other rodents.

8. Censors often _____ words from television programs because they feel that the words should not be presented to a family audience.

9. He looked with _____ at the man who was responsible for so many deaths because of his reckless driving.

10. As a(n) _____ worker, I always apply myself to whatever I do.

STOP. Check answers at the end of the book (p. 331).

C DIRECTIONS: Write one sentence using at least two words from this lesson. The sentence must make sense. Try to illustrate the meanings of the words without actually defining them.

Example

The *haughty* woman looked with *disdain* at the lawyer when the lawyer said that he had *pertinent* information that would *affirm* the truth of his witness's statements.

_____

_____

_____

STOP. Check answers at the end of the book (p. 331).

EXTRA WORD POWER

ante

Before. *Ante* is placed in front of many words and means "before." Do not confuse *ante* with *anti*. *Anti* means "against." Examples: *antebellum*—before the war; *anteroom*—waiting room, a lobby; *antedate*—to date before; *antecedent*—going before; *antediluvian*—relating to the period before the flood described in the Bible; *ante meridiem*—before noon (the abbreviation is A.M.).

LESSON 5

Step I. Story in Context

DIRECTIONS: The following story includes several vocabulary words from this lesson. As you read the story, pay careful attention to the vocabulary words in boldface type, and try to figure out the meaning of these words. Put the answers in the blanks.

Solving the Dilemma

Jose knew that he couldn't isolate himself from all his friends for too long. Even though Jose was rather (1) **reluctant** _____ to discuss his problem with his pals at work, he decided to do so. He looked upon his fellow workers as (2) **colleagues** _____ who would be unbiased in their views. He respected them because they were (3) **reliable** _____ and they never tried to (4) **interrogate** _____ him about his personal life.

You can imagine their surprise when Jose, who didn't like to discuss his private life with anyone, started to tell them (5) **intricate** _____ details about his life. (6) **Antecedent** _____ to Jose's problems, he had always been a very private person. There's no question that Jose was setting a (7) **significant** _____ (8) **precedent** _____ not only by sharing intimate details about his life but also by asking for advice.

Jose felt that he really had no choice if he wanted to (9) **persevere** _____ and be the fraternity treasurer and still be friends with his old buddies. Jose was willing to (10) **adapt** _____ himself to college life and all the experiences associated with it. He felt, however, that his old buddies didn't want to make any changes in their lives.

STOP. Check answers at the end of the book (p. 332).

Step II. Vocabulary Words in context

1. **adaptation** (ad · ap · tā′ shun) _n._ The act of fitting or suiting one thing to another; an adjusting to fit new conditions; a modification (a partial or slight change) for a new use. _As the story was too long for the kindergarten children, the teacher made an **adaptation** of it to suit the children's attention span._

2. **antecedent** (an · tuh · sēd′ unt) _adj._ Going before in time; prior; preceding; previous. _n._ The word, phrase, or clause to which a pronoun refers. _In writing, you must be careful that your pronoun refers to a definite **antecedent**._

3. **colleague** (kol′ ēg) _n._ A fellow worker in the same profession. _My **colleagues** and I are unhappy with our vocation because we work too hard._

4. **interrogate** (in · ter′ uh · gāte) _v._ To ask questions formally; to examine by questioning. _The police said that they would **interrogate** everyone who was anywhere near the location of the homicide to try to get some answers._

5. **intricate** (in′ tri · kit) _adj._ Complicated; difficult to follow or understand; complex. _The doctors said that my mother needed an **intricate** operation, which we didn't understand._

6. **persevere** (pur · suh · vēre′) _v._ To persist; to continue doing something in spite of difficulty. _Despite all hardships, some people are able to **persevere** and succeed in achieving their objectives._

7. **precedent** (pres′ i · dunt) _n._ Something done or said that may serve as an example; in law, a legal decision serving as an authoritative rule in future similar cases. _By doing that, you may have set a **precedent** for other people to follow._

8. **procrastinate** (prō · kras′ tuh · nāte) _v._ To postpone taking action; to put off doing something until a future date. _If you **procrastinate** all the time, you will never accomplish anything. You can put off doing things for just so long._

Reprinted by permission: Tribune Media Services

9. **prudent** (prū' dent) *adj.* Sensible; not rash; capable of using sound judgment in practical matters. *Consuela was always **prudent** rather than rash in dealing with difficult matters.*

10. **reliable** (ri · li' uh · bul) *adj.* Dependable, trustworthy. *As Jacob is so **reliable,** I know that we can depend on his doing the job diligently and well.*

11. **reluctant** (ri · luk' tunt) *adj.* Unwilling; opposed. *We were all **reluctant** to say that we would buy tickets to the show until we had more information about the cost.*

12. **satiate** (sā' shē · āté) *v.* To fill; to satisfy the appetite completely; to glut (overindulge). *Everyone was able to **satiate** his or her appetite at the banquet.*

13. **significant** (sig · nif' uh · kunt) *adj.* Having or expressing meaning; full of meaning; important. *The test results were so **significant** that the scientists knew that they had made a great breakthrough in medicine.*

14. **vindictive** (vin · dik' tivé) *adj.* Spiteful; revengeful in spirit. *It's difficult not to want **vindictive** punishment for killers who have murdered your loved ones.*

15. **virile** (vir' ulé) *adj.* Masculine; manly; forceful; able to procreate (to produce or reproduce). ***Virile** men usually don't have to prove their masculinity to anyone.*

SPECIAL NOTES

1. **precedent** *n.* Something done or said that may serve as an example.
2. **antecedent** *adj.* Going before in time. *n.* Word, phrase, or clause to which a pronoun refers. You have probably met the term *antecedent* in your English course. The word, phrase, or clause to which a pronoun refers is called the *antecedent*. For example, in the sentence "John Andretti was the judge who made that important decision," *judge* is the antecedent of *who*. In other words, *who* refers to *judge*. In "Jack lost his hat," *Jack* is the antecedent of *his*.

Step III. Practice

A DIRECTIONS: Sentences using vocabulary words from Lesson 5 follow. Use the clues in the sentences to figure out the meaning of the underlined words. Write the meaning of each underlined word in the blank.

1. This is a story of the importance of getting your work done on time rather than wait-ing until the last minute; in fact, the title of this paper might be "Don't Procrastinate!"

   _____

2. Dr. Wang, my computer science professor, assigned an intricate, complex, multi-part

   project and gave the class a month in which to complete it. _____

3. The prudent thing for me to do—what any sensible person would have done—was to review the project immediately, plan my topic, gather the resources I needed,

   and plan my time carefully. _____

4. Since Dr. Wang gave out the assignment a month in advance, I should have real-ized that it would take a significant amount of time to complete—in other words,

   it was not something I could toss off in a weekend. _____

5. Because I have a part-time job and carry a full class load, I should have realized that my schedule would need some adaptation to allow time for this big piece of

   work. _____

6. However, I was very reluctant to make any changes in my work or study time, and I was equally unwilling to give up any of my precious free time.

   _____

7. Besides, there was a precedent for my situation: I had recently completed a lengthy history assignment in just a few days, and I had gotten a decent grade for

   my work. _____

8. So I put off the project until the final weekend, but there was a big storm that made the college's Internet network, which is usually highly reliable, sporadic and

   undependable. _____

9. The end of my story is very clear from its antecedents: all the prior events led to

   the dismal climax and my failing grade on the assignment. _____

10. And the moral of the story is just as clear: students need to persevere—work steadily and continuously—rather than procrastinate. _____

STOP. Check answers at the end of the book (p. 332).

B **DIRECTIONS:** Each sentence has a missing word. Choose the word that *best* completes the sentence. Write the word in the blank. Not all words are used.

Word List

adaptation	interrogate	precedent	reliable	significant
antecedent	intricate	procrastinate	reluctant	vindictive
colleague	persevere	prudent	satiate	virile

1. My _____s and I held our biannual professional conference at the biologists' convention.

2. As there were no _____s to go by, the lawyers knew that they were dealing with a new legal area.

3. The mountain climbers said that they would allow nothing to get in the way of achieving their formidable task, and they would _____ at all costs.

4. Only the most _____ federal agents, who could be trusted, were used to guard former criminals who were giving evidence against top crime figures.

5. When we lost our passports in Europe, we were told by customs officials that they would have to _____ us to determine whether the passports had been stolen or lost.

6. I am always _____ to sign anything that I haven't first read.

7. The man in the commercial was trying to affirm that there was a(n) _____ difference between his product and a similar product produced by another manufacturer.

8. The directions to get to the picnic grounds were so _____ that we all had difficulty following them.

9. The newly elected official had many details to take care of _____ to taking office.

10. Have you ever seen a(n) _____ of an old movie in which the main story line is kept the same but the period in which the story takes place is changed?

STOP. Check answers at the end of the book (p. 332).

C **DIRECTIONS:** Write one sentence using at least two words from this lesson. The sentence must make sense. Try to illustrate the meanings of the words without actually defining them.

Example

At the *interrogation,* it looked as if the *reluctant* witness was not as *reliable* as we had thought.

_____

_____

_____

STOP. Check answers at the end of the book (p. 332).

EXTRA WORD POWER

ship

State, condition, or quality of; office, rank, or dignity; art or skill. *Ship* is added to the end of many nouns. For example: *kingship*—dignity or rank of king; *governorship*—rank or office of governor; *dictatorship*—office or rank of a head of government who has absolute control of the government; *citizenship*—state or quality of being a citizen; *friendship*—state of being a friend; *penmanship*—art or skill of handwriting; *leadership*—skill as a leader. How many more words with *ship* can you supply?

LESSON 6

Step I. Story in Context

DIRECTIONS: The following story includes several vocabulary words from this lesson. As you read the story, pay careful attention to the vocabulary words in boldface type, and try to figure out the meaning of each of these words. Put the answers in the blanks.

Money Matters

Juan had always considered himself a (1) **conservative** _____ rather than a (2) **liberal** _____ when it came to money matters, even though in relation to social issues, he was probably more of a (3) **liberal** _____.

Juan was quite (4) **frugal** _____ in regard to money, which he felt was an (5) **asset** _____. In other words, he was economically wise. He knew how to (6) **economize** _____. He didn't want the (7) **liability** _____ of owing people money. He also did not like to pay the exorbitant interest rates on some credit cards, so he very carefully (8) **allotted** _____ himself a certain amount of money for his needs. He did not exceed his careful budget.

Some of Juan's friends thought that he was overly concerned about money. However, he knew what it was like to be without, so he ignored them when it came to money matters. He came from a poor area of town and remembers how his mother and father struggled to earn enough money for all of them. He remembered the (9) **stagnant** _____ water near where he lived and how no one cleaned it up. He remembered the horrible odor from the water. He also remembered how he envied all those who went to college and made something of themselves. He remembered not only (10) **coveting** _____ what others had but also saying that one day he would (11) **modify** _____ his life and also have those things. He knew that changing his life was (12) **vital** _____. He also knew that (13) **castigating** _____ others for things he wanted wasn't (14) **laudable** _____.

STOP. Check answers at the end of the book (p. 332).

Step II. Vocabulary Words in context

1. **allot** (uh · lot′) _v._ To divide or distribute by lot; to distribute or parcel out in portions; to appoint. _The State Department of Education said that it would **allot** the money to school districts on the basis of a new formula, so that the money would be equally divided._

2. **asset** (as′ set) _n._ Anything owned that has value; any valuable or desirable thing that serves as an advantage. _Instead of being a problem and undesirable, he turned out to be an enormous **asset** to us._

3. **castigate** (kas′ ti · gāte) _v._ To rebuke; to correct or subdue by punishing; to criticize with drastic severity. _The judge **castigated** the parents for their behavior toward their children and warned the parents that next time he would take the children away from them._

4. **conservative** (kun · sur′ vuh · tive) _adj._ Tending to maintain established traditions and to resist or oppose any change in these; cautious; moderate; traditional in style or manner; avoiding showiness. _n._ One who clings to traditional or long-standing methods, views, ideas, and so on. _A **conservative** person is reluctant to see any change._

5. **covet** (kuv′ ut) _v._ To desire very much what another has; to crave; to long for. _In the Scriptures, it says that you should not **covet** another's wife._

6. **economize** (i · kon′ uh · mīze) _v._ To use or manage with thrift or prudence; to avoid waste or needless spending; to reduce expenses. _With everything costing so much, we will have to **economize** and curtail our spending._

7. **frugal** (frū′ gul) _adj._ Thrifty; not spending freely; avoiding waste. _When you have a fixed and limited income and when the price of everything is high, you must be **frugal**._

8. **laudable** (lawd′ uh · bul) *adj.* Commendable; worthy of praise. *What the students had done is highly **laudable**, and they should be praised for their efforts.*

9. **liability** (lī · uh · bil′ uh · tē) *n.* Something that is owed; a debt; legal obligation to make good any loss or damage that occurs in a transaction (a business deal); something that works to a person's disadvantage. *The officers of the corporation realized that the new company they had acquired was a **liability** to them because of its large losses.*

10. **liberal** (lib′ uh · rul) *adj.* Giving freely; generous; large or plentiful; tolerant of views differing from one's own; broad-minded; favoring reform or progress. *n.* A person who is open-minded or broad-minded. *As a very **liberal**-minded person, he is for reform and a great amount of personal freedom for individuals.*

11. **modify** (mod′ uh · fī) *v.* To change slightly or make minor changes in character, form, and so on; to change or alter; to limit or reduce; in grammar, to limit or restrict a meaning. *People usually **modify** their views as they get older because their ways of seeing things change.*

12. **sedate** (si · dāte) *adj. v.* Calm; composed; quiet; serene; sober; to put under sedation. *The sedative calmed him down so much that it was hard to believe that this **sedate** person had been so aggressive a few moments ago.*

13. **stagnant** (stag′ nunt) *adj.* Lacking motion or current; not flowing or moving; foul (dirty and bad-smelling) from lack of movement; lacking in activity; sluggish; dull. *The **stagnant** pond had a terribly bad odor because many of the aquatic plants in it were decaying.*

14. **vindicate** (vin′ di · kāte) *v.* To clear from criticism, accusation, or suspicion. *Although she was completely **vindicated** by the trial, some people treated her as though she were guilty.*

15. **vital** (vī′ tul) *adj.* Necessary to life; essential; energetic. *The doctor said that the operation was so **vital** that not having it would be fatal.*

SPECIAL NOTES

1. *Asset* has a special meaning when used in the plural: *assets.* The term *assets* is used in accounting to mean all the items on a balance sheet that show the property or resources (what an individual has) of a person or business, such as inventory (list of all goods in stock), cash, real estate, equipment, accounts and notes receivable, and so on.

2. When *liability* is used in the plural, it usually is referring to a debt such as accounts payable, capital stock, and losses. Accounts payable, losses, and capital stock are *liabilities* of a corporation.

3. When *modify* is used in grammar, it means "to limit or restrict in meaning." In the sentence "That is a huge dormitory," *huge* modifies *dormitory.* Adding the word *huge* to *dormitory* limits or restricts *dormitory.* You know that it is not a small dormitory. If *coed* is added to *huge dormitory,* you are limiting the meaning of *dormitory* even more. Words that limit or restrict another word are describing the word. That is, *huge* and *coed* are describing *dormitory.*

Step III. Practice

A **DIRECTIONS:** Each of the following sentences has a missing word. Choose the word from the list that *best* completes the sentence. Write the word in the blank. Not all words fit in.

Word List

allot	conservative	frugal	liberal	stagnant
assets	covet	laudable	modify	vindicate
castigate	economize	liability	sedate	vital

1. I believe that the investigation will _____ me from all suspicion that I plagiarized even a small part of my research paper.

2. Elena's general manner can best be described as pleasant but calm, cool, and

   _____ .

3. It is unusual for such a young person to be so _____ in his dress, manners, and opinions.

4. Professor Rubens strongly _____ the entire class for their poor performance on the midterm.

5. Given the cost of gas these days, I will have to _____ on many other things to continue to purchase enough for my daily commute.

6. It is of _____, even life-threatening importance that you make an appointment for a check-up right away.

7. I am not usually an envious person, but I admit that I do _____ your new designer shoes.

8. All of the company's _____, both cash and real estate, are being used to pay for the expansion of the factory.

9. I think that if I am very _____ in my spending for the next three months, I will be able to afford a vacation during spring break.

10. Your efforts to help the people who are homeless because of the storm are certainly _____, and I hope you receive all the praise you deserve.

11. It must be difficult for the Financial Aid Department to _____ a limited amount of scholarship money fairly among many needy students.

12. Now that I have heard both candidates speak, I will _____ my former statements in support of Senator Smith.

STOP. Check answers at the end of the book (p. 332).

B **DIRECTIONS:** Some sentences follow. Define the underlined word. Put your answer in the blank.

1. If I don't start to <u>economize</u> now, I won't have any money left at the end of the

   week. _____

2. My views are always contrary to my parents' views, and because they like everything to remain the same, I'm a <u>liberal</u>. _____

3. Consuela is so <u>frugal</u> that absolutely nothing is ever wasted by her. _____

4. As a young child, Juan was ridiculed about being so tall, but at college his height was an <u>asset</u> for the basketball team. _____

5. I <u>allot</u> myself a certain amount of time each week to spend reading books other than those assigned in class. _____

6. One of the political parties in our township is so <u>conservative</u> that it won't even let you change a meeting time. _____

7. I saw a film in which viewers know that conflict is going to take place because in the opening scene, a young cowhand wanders in and looks at the wife of the rancher, and immediately you know that he <u>covets</u> her. _____

8. The <u>stagnant</u> pond water smelled as bad as a sewer. _____

9. The city council members found that they would have to <u>modify</u> their plan if they wanted it to be accepted. _____

10. As a successful model, Tawana found that her height was an advantage to her rather than a <u>liability</u>. _____

STOP. Check answers at the end of the book (p. 332).

C **DIRECTIONS:** Write one sentence using at least two words from this lesson. The sentence must make sense. Try to illustrate the meanings of the words without actually defining them.

Example

Everyone was surprised when Jacob, a *frugal* person who always *economizes,* started to spend money very *liberally.*

_____

_____

_____

_____

STOP. Check answers at the end of the book (p. 332).

EXTRA WORD POWER

super

Above in position; over; above or beyond; greater than or superior to; extra; in the highest degree; in excessive degree. *Super* is found at the beginning of many words. You have probably met *super* in words such as *superior*, meaning "of higher degree"; *superb*, meaning "of the highest quality"; and *superlative*, meaning "of the highest degree." Following is a list of words in which *super* is added to the beginning of the word and changes the word meaning to include "in excessive degree" or "in the highest degree." *Supercritical*—highly critical; *supersafe*—safe in the highest degree; *supersweet*—sweet in the highest degree; *superabundance*—abundance in excess; *superacid*—excessively acid; *superpower*—excessive or superior power. Following is a list of words in which *super* is found at the beginning of the word, and it is a necessary part of the word; that is, if *super* were deleted from the word, the word would lose its meaning. *Supervision*—the act of overseeing others; *superintendent*—one who has charge of a department, building, institution, and the like; *superstitious*—having beliefs that are not consistent with the known laws of science. How many more words with *super* can you supply? Check your dictionary for a long list of *super* words.

!!! FUN WITH CARTOONS

State the meanings of the following words in each cartoon. Then explain what makes each cartoon humorous.

1.

BORN LOSER reprinted by permission of United Feature Syndicate, Inc.

1. **colleague** _____

_____

2.

ZITS

Reprinted by permission of King Features.

2. **procrastination** _____

_____

STOP. Check answers at the end of the book (p. 332).

SPECIAL ACADEMIC WORDS

A **DIRECTIONS:** Some words in this chapter that are used in business courses follow. Without looking back at the chapter, see how well you can define them.

1. economize   _____

2. allot   _____

3. thrifty   _____

4. asset   _____

5. liability   _____

B **DIRECTIONS:** Choose the answers to the riddles from the terms presented in Practice A.

1. Nobody wants me. _____

2. Everybody wants me. _____

3. You won't get much from me. _____

4. I'm divided up. _____

5. I'm not a big spender. _____

STOP. Check answers at the end of the book (p. 333).

CHAPTER WORDS IN A PARAGRAPH

Write a paragraph on the given topic using at least eight words from this chapter. The paragraph must make sense and be logically developed.

Topic: What I Would Change If I Could

STOP. Check answers at the end of the book (p. 333).

 ## GAINING WORD POWER ON THE INTERNET

1. Choose a search engine. Write the name of the chosen search engine: _____

2. Do a search of the following two terms: *liberal, conservative.*

3. Choose one site or reference generated by your search for each term. Try to select sites that help you gain a better understanding of the terms you are researching. Write the chosen site for each term: _____ _____

4. Write a three-sentence paragraph on the site information for each term.

5. Log onto the Web site that accompanies this textbook for extra practice exercises at [http://www.ablongman.com/vocabulary].

STOP. Check answers at the end of the book (p. 333).

CROSSWORD PUZZLE

DIRECTIONS: The meanings of a number of the words from Lessons 4 to 6 follow. Your knowledge of these words from Part One should help you solve this crossword puzzle.

Across

1. Way of saying father
2. Broadminded
3. Dependable
8. Opposite of down (pl.)
11. When your heart stops beating, you are_____.
12. When your heart stops beating, you have_____.
14. Homonym of *sew*
16. Same as #5 Down
17. Foul from not moving
21. Same as #4 Down
22. Part of the face
23. Choice between two equally bad alternatives
26. To ask formally
29. First person personal pronoun
30. Twenty-first letter of alphabet
31. Same as #29 Across
32. Twelfth letter of alphabet
33. Seventh letter of alphabet
34. Fourteenth letter of alphabet
35. Same as #29 Across
36. Eighteenth letter of alphabet
37. Makes many nouns plural
38. Twenty-fifth letter of alphabet

Down

1. A friend
2. Worthy of praise
4. *Much* _____ *about nothing*
5. Homonym of *bee*
6. Musical syllable
7. Ending for past tense of regular verbs.
9. _____ needles, which come from an evergreen tree
10. _____the table.
13. To despise; scorn
14. Important; full of meaning
15. Christian holiday in late March or April
18. Homonym of two
19. Without any; nothing left
20. Was in want; required
21. Verb that rhymes with "*ham*"
24. _____ of the valley; a flower
25. _____ shot; slang for picture of face
27. You do this when you are fatigued
28. The opposite of *off*

STOP. Check answers at the end of the book (p. 333).

ANALOGIES

DIRECTIONS: Find the word from the following list that *best* completes each analogy. There are more words listed than you need.

Word List

affirm	contagious	isolate	reply
alter	covert	manly	satiate
associate	covet	omission	save
blast	decisive	overt	scorn
bold	delete	persevere	sensible
broad-minded	diligent	postpone	sophisticated
build	eradicate	question	temerity
buy	fearful	rebuke	think
commendable	frugal	replenish	timid
conservative	intricate	replete	vital

1. Frank : candid :: virile : _____.

2. Positive : definite :: disdain : _____.

3. Parade : procession :: interrogate : _____.

4. Hostile : friendly :: liberal : _____.

5. Haughty : arrogant :: resupply : _____.

6. Stale : fresh :: deny : _____.

7. Dependable : reliable :: persist : _____.

8. Synonym : antonym :: simple : _____.

9. Frustrated : defeated :: colleague : _____.

10. Castigate : rebuke :: segregate : _____.

11. Thrifty : frugal :: laudable : _____.

12. Inferior : superior :: insert : _____.

13. Hate : animosity :: desire : _____.

14. Provisions : supplies :: prudent : _____.

15. Plump : corpulent :: modify : _____.

16. Pertinent : relevant :: industrious : _____.

17. Tepid : lukewarm :: essential : _____.

18. Modest : shy :: procrastinate : _____.

19. Alarm : warn :: bomb : _____.

20. Blanket : cover :: economize : _____.

STOP. Check answers at the end of the book (p. 333).

MULTIPLE-CHOICE VOCABULARY TEST

DIRECTIONS: This is a test on words in Lessons 4 to 6. Words are presented according to lessons. *Do all lessons before checking answers.* Underline the meaning that *best* fits the words.

Lesson 4

1. coincidence
   a. something that happens
   b. a chance happening
   c. occurrence of things at the same time by chance
   d. a happening

2. disdain
   a. a disagreement
   b. unequal choices
   c. to regard as unworthy
   d. to apply oneself

3. eradicate
    a. to take a word away
    b. to wipe out completely
    c. to despise
    d. to disagree with

4. haughty
    a. having a lot of pride in oneself
    b. applying oneself
    c. disagreeable
    d. hostile

5. isolate
    a. to harm
    b. to help
    c. to set apart
    d. to stay together

6. pertinent
    a. unrelated
    b. not appropriate
    c. appropriate
    d. set apart

7. delete
    a. to put in
    b. to take out
    c. to write
    d. to allow

8. affirm
    a. to deny
    b. to ask
    c. to question
    d. to state positively

9. dilemma
    a. a problem
    b. an argument
    c. something unpleasant
    d. a choice between two equally disagreeable things

10. diligent
    a. a choice
    b. a choice between equally disagreeable things
    c. applying oneself
    d. an argument

11. replenish
    a. to fill again
    b. full
    c. eat
    d. to finish

12. replete
    a. full moon
    b. well filled
    c. to fill again
    d. complete again

13. arrogant
    a. a problem
    b. an argument
    c. haughty
    d. speak

14. thrifty
    a. spend a lot
    b. spendthrift
    c. relates to economics
    d. economically wise

15. vestige
    a. a sign
    b. existing
    c. disappear
    d. a face

Lesson 5

16. adaptation
    a. act of adjusting to old situations
    b. a fitting outcome
    c. refers to adoption
    d. act of fitting one thing to another

17. antecedent
    a. going against
    b. going after
    c. going before
    d. going first

18. intricate
    a. complicated
    b. simple
    c. presenting a problem
    d. helpful

19. colleague
    a. a college buddy
    b. a friend
    c. an enemy
    d. a fellow worker in a profession

20. interrogate
    a. to speak
    b. to state
    c. to question
    d. to make a choice

21. persevere
   a. to help
   b. to persist
   c. to move
   d. to be active

22. precedent
   a. something that serves as an example
   b. an offense
   c. something unnecessary
   d. something that comes after

23. reliable
   a. helpful
   b. dependable
   c. hostile
   d. presenting an example

24. reluctant
   a. willing
   b. helping
   c. unwilling
   d. hostile

25. significant
   a. a sign
   b. a meaning
   c. helpful
   d. full of meaning

26. procrastinate
   a. do things immediately
   b. take action
   c. postpone
   d. to be cheap

27. prudent
   a. wise
   b. not using judgment
   c. rash
   d. a hope

28. satiate
   a. to satisfy
   b. not overindulge
   c. having sat
   d. to fill a well

29. virile
   a. spiteful
   b. revengeful
   c. manly
   d. unhealthy

30. vindictive
   a. forceful
   b. spiritual
   c. manly
   d. spiteful

Lesson 6

31. allot
   a. to donate
   b. to state an opinion
   c. to sell a lot
   d. to divide

32. asset
   a. to assess
   b. happy
   c. a valuable thing
   d. an opinion

33. conservative
   a. tending to like change
   b. tending to like differences
   c. tending to be broad-minded
   d. tending to like things to remain the same

34. covet
   a. to like things
   b. to dislike things
   c. to desire greatly things that others have
   d. to hope

35. frugal
   a. spending freely
   b. wise
   c. spends often
   d. thrifty

36. liability
   a. a gift
   b. legal
   c. a debt
   d. a feeling

37. economize
   a. to spend freely
   b. to spend money
   c. refers to economics
   d. to avoid waste

38. liberal	a. big b. broad-minded	c. remain the same d. helpful
39. modify	a. to change slightly b. to move	c. to dress d. to be modern
40. stagnant	a. flowing b. a male animal	c. foul d. moving
41. castigate	a. to judge b. to help	c. to beat d. rebuke
42. laudable	a. to praise b. to be able	c. loud d. not commendable
43. sedate	a. to give medication b. to excite	c. composed d. aggressive
44. vital	a. significant b. to move	c. aggressive d. energetic
45. vindicate	a. spiteful b. to clear from suspicion	c. a debt d. revenge

CHAPTER TRUE/FALSE TEST

DIRECTIONS: This is a true/false test on Lessons 4 to 6. Read each sentence carefully. Decide whether it is true or false. Put a *T* for *True* or an *F* for *False* in the blank. If the statement is false, change a word or words to make it true. The number after the sentence tells you in which lesson the word appears.

_____ 1. A haughty person is likely to show disdain for others. 4

_____ 2. A frugal person is likely to economize. 6

_____ 3. A vestige is a small remaining piece. 4

_____ 4. Both antecedents and precedents are things that come after something else. 5

_____ 5. A colleague is someone you live with. 5

_____ 6. A fact that is pertinent is one that is irrelevant. 4

_____ 7. To castigate is to perform an exotic dance. 6

_____ 8. An asset is the opposite of a liability. 6

_____ 9. To covet means to crave. 6

_____ 10. To satiate something is to complete it. 5

_____ 11. Something that is <u>intricate</u> is simple. 5

_____ 12. To <u>delete</u> is to eradicate. 4

_____ 13. If you are running out of something, you should <u>replenish</u> it. 4

_____ 14. To <u>isolate</u> is to separate. 4

_____ 15. To <u>interrogate</u> is to ask a single question. 5

_____ 16. A person who is <u>vindictive</u> is likely to be forgiving. 5

_____ 17. To be <u>vindicated</u> is to be proved guilty. 6

_____ 18. To <u>allot</u> is to give. 6

STOP. Check answers for both tests at the end of the book (pp. 333–334).

SCORING OF TESTS

Multiple-Choice Vocabulary Test	
Number Wrong	*Score*
0–2	Excellent
3–5	Good
6–8	Weak
Above 8	Poor
Score _____	

True/False Test	
Number Wrong	*Score*
0–1	Excellent
2–3	Good
4–5	Weak
Above 5	Poor
Score _____	

1. If you scored in the excellent or good range on *both tests,* you are doing well. Go on to Chapter 4.
2. If you scored in the weak or poor range on either test, look at the next page and follow directions for Additional Practice. Note that the words on the tests are arranged so that you can tell in which lesson to find them. This arrangement will help you if you need additional practice.

ADDITIONAL PRACTICE SETS

A **DIRECTIONS:** Write the words you missed on the tests from the three lessons in the space provided. Note that the tests are presented so that you can tell to which lessons the words belong.

Lesson 4 Words Missed

1. _____   6. _____
2. _____   7. _____
3. _____   8. _____
4. _____   9. _____
5. _____   10. _____

Lesson 5 Words Missed

1. _____   6. _____
2. _____   7. _____
3. _____   8. _____
4. _____   9. _____
5. _____   10. _____

Lesson 6 Words Missed

1. _____   6. _____
2. _____   7. _____
3. _____   8. _____
4. _____   9. _____
5. _____   10. _____

B **DIRECTIONS:** Restudy the words that you have written down on this page. Do Step I for those you missed. Note that Step I is on the following pages:

Lesson 4—pp. 42–46
Lesson 5—pp. 46–51
Lesson 6—pp. 51–56

C **DIRECTIONS:** Do Additional Practice 1 on this page and p. 66 if you missed words from Lesson 4. Do Additional Practice 2 on p. 66 if you missed words from Lesson 5. Do Additional Practice 3 on p. 67 if you missed words from Lesson 6. Now go on to Chapter 4.

Additional Practice 1 for Lesson 4

DIRECTIONS: Ten sentences with missing words follow. Underline the word that *best* fits the sentence. Two choices are given for each sentence.

1. Because he is such a (pertinent; diligent) worker, he will finish the job on time.
2. What a (dilemma; coincidence) to have to choose between two equally bad things.
3. My essay was too long; so I decided to (affirm; delete) some words.

4. Some rulers have tried to (eradicate; isolate) a whole group of people by murdering all of them.
5. This statement must be left in because it is (diligent; pertinent) to the report.
6. Because nations depend upon one another, it is difficult in contemporary times for nations to (affirm; isolate) themselves from others.
7. The witness said that he would again (affirm; delete) the statement he made before because it was correct and important.
8. What a (coincidence; dilemma) to have both of us doing the same thing at the same time.
9. I do not like to be with (diligent; haughty) people because they think that they are great and they look down on others.
10. When they heard that Ms. Jonas had betrayed their confidence, she was held in great (dilemma; disdain).

STOP. Check answers at the end of the book (p. 334).

Additional Practice 2 for Lesson 5

DIRECTIONS: Ten sentences containing the meanings of some vocabulary presented in Lesson 5 follow. Choose the word that *best* fits the word or phrase underlined in the sentence. All words are used.

Word List

adaptation	interrogate	precedent	reluctant
antecedent	intricate	reliable	significant
colleagues	persevere		

1. This play, which is based on a famous novel, is a perfect <u>modification</u> suited to the contemporary scene. _____

2. The plan we developed is so <u>involved and complicated</u> that it will probably take some time for the others to understand it. _____

3. The findings from your research are so <u>important and full of meaning</u> that they should be shared with the world. _____

4. My <u>fellow professional associates</u> are joining me at a special convention. _____

5. I am <u>unwilling</u> to go along with the rest of you because the idea does not sound workable to me. _____

6. As he is a very <u>dependable and trustworthy</u> person, I will vote for him. _____

7. The judge used <u>a former case as an example</u> on which to make his decision. _____

8. As a policewoman, I must always tell persons of their rights before I can <u>formally</u> <u>question</u> them. —————————————

9. When I have a hard job to do, I <u>persist</u> until I have finished it. —————————————

10. The invention of the train was <u>prior</u> to that of the airplane. —————————————

STOP. Check answers at the end of the book (p. 334).

Additional Practice 3 for Lesson 6

DIRECTIONS: Some sentences containing the meanings of some vocabulary presented in Lesson 6 follow. Choose the word that *best* fits the word or phrase underlined in the sentence. Not all words are used.

Word List

allot	covet	liberal	vindicate
asset	economize	modify	vital
castigate	frugal	sedate	
conservative	liability	stagnant	

1. Under the terms of the will, they will <u>divide</u> the money equally among the children. —————————————

2. A pleasant smile is <u>a valuable and desirable thing</u> to have. —————————————

3. We are <u>traditional</u> people, reluctant to have any change, and our group will oppose any changes that you attempt to make. —————————————

4. I am a <u>thrifty</u> person. —————————————

5. I <u>spend my money wisely</u> to avoid waste. —————————————

6. The major <u>debt</u> I have is my school loan. —————————————

7. Some people only <u>desire what other people have.</u> —————————————

8. When lake water is <u>without motion</u>, it can begin to have a bad smell. —————————————

9. My <u>broad-minded</u> friends are all very interested in reform and progress. —————————————

10. I am going to <u>change</u> my speech <u>slightly</u> so that it will appeal to more people. —————————————

STOP. Check answers at the end of the book (p. 334).

Chapter 4 *Jose's Dilemma Continues*

LESSON 7

Step I. Story in Context

DIRECTIONS: The following story includes several vocabulary words from this lesson. As you read the story, pay careful attention to the vocabulary words in boldface type, and try to figure out the meaning of each of these words. Put your answers in the blanks.

Jose's Dilemma at School

Since Jose had joined the fraternity at school, his friends from home behaved differently toward him. Jose thought that things would get better with time, but they seemed to get worse. At first, Jose thought that perhaps he had (1) **affronted** _____ his friends in some way. He did have an (2) **inclination** _____ to fly off the handle from time to time. But it was not (3) **characteristic** _____ of his friends to take offense at him. But Jose was really concerned when he heard from others that his friends had made some (4) **derogatory** _____ comments about him.

Jose was unhappy about his friends' (5) **attitude** _____ toward him. They really seemed to be quite (6) **antagonistic** _____ to him. When Jose approached them about their behavior toward him, they said that everything was "cool." Jose, however, didn't believe them. He felt that they were being (7) **hypocrites** _____ when they said that things were "cool." He noticed that whenever they were around him, they used lots of (8) **euphemisms** _____ and tried hard not to offend or (9) **intimidate** _____ him in any way. Also, since they knew that he enjoyed various (10) **aesthetic** _____ endeavors such as art and music, they would accompany him to art shows. However, after doing this, he heard from numerous other students at school that his supposed friends would joke about Jose and his tastes.

It reached a point at which Jose just didn't know what to think about his friends.

STOP. Check answers at the end of the book (p. 334).

Step II. Vocabulary Words in Context

1. **aesthetic** (ǽes · thet′ ik) *adj.* Referring to beauty; sensitive to art and beauty; showing good taste; artistic. *Sharon has a highly developed **aesthetic** sense because she is so sensitive to art and beauty.*

2. **affront** (uh · front′) *v.* To insult. *n.* An insult; an open and intentional insult. *That was a definite **affront** to me because I was the only one in the class not invited.*

3. **antagonize** (an · tag′ uh · nīzé) *v.* To make unfriendly; to make an enemy of; to oppose; to act against. *If you persist in behaving in this way, you will **antagonize** your boss and make him hostile toward you.*

4. **attitude** (at′ ti · tūdé) *n.* A way of feeling, acting, or thinking that shows one's disposition (one's frame of mind) or opinion; the feeling itself; posture. *It is very difficult to change **attitudes** because the way we feel about things comes to us from our past experiences and has been with us for some time.*

5. **characteristic** (kar · ik · tuh · ris′ tik) *adj.* Marking the peculiar quality or qualities of a person or thing; distinctive; special. *n.* A special trait, feature, or quality; individuality. *All mammals have certain **characteristics** in common.*

6. **corroborate** (kuh · rob′ uh · rāté) *v.* To confirm; to make more certain. *Philip **corroborated** our suspicions concerning Erin's guilt when he testified that she had tried to sell him the stolen goods.*

7. **derogatory** (di · rog′ uh · tor · ē) *adj.* Tending to make less well regarded; tending to belittle someone or something; disparaging; belittling. *The **derogatory** remarks were supposed to make us think less of Mr. Johansen, but on the contrary, they made us think less of the person who made them.*

8. **euphemism** (ǽu′ fuh · miz · um) *n.* The substitution of a word or phrase that is less direct, milder, or vaguer for one that is thought to be harsh, offensive, or blunt; a word or phrase that is considered less distasteful or less offensive than another. *"They are in their final resting place" is a **euphemism** for "They are dead."*

9. **exonerate** (ig · zon′ uh · rāte) *v.* To relieve of blame; to clear of a charge. *He was granted an amnesty by the government and **exonerated** of all charges made against him.*

10. **hypocrite** (hip′ uh · krité) *n.* A person who pretends to be what he or she is not; one who pretends to be better than he or she really is. *He is a **hypocrite** because he made us all feel guilty about asking for our share of the profits when he had already pocketed his share a long time ago.*

11. **inclination** (in · kluh · nā' shun) *n.* A personal leaning or bent; a liking; a bending, slanting, or sloping surface; a slope. *Whatever your **inclinations** are in this matter, you must try to be fair and not allow your personal leanings to get in the way of your decision.*

12. **intimidate** (in · tim' uh · dāte) *v.* To make timid; to cause fear; to scare; to discourage by threats or violence. *The reason many big crime figures are not convicted is that they **intimidate** witnesses so that the witnesses are afraid to say anything against them.*

13. **jeopardy** (jeøp' ur · dē) *n.* Peril; risk; danger. (*pl.* ies) *When the witness testified against a major crime figure, she knew that she was putting her life in **jeopardy.***

14. **repent** (ri · pent') *v.* To feel remorse; to feel sad or regret for something undone or done. *He **repented** the fact that he had not been kinder to his mother while she was still alive.*

15. **temperate** (tem' per · it) *adj.* Moderate; avoiding excesses. *Since Sarah is **temperate** in everything she does, you would not expect her to overeat or overdrink.*

SPECIAL NOTES

1. Note that *posture* and *attitude* are synonyms. Posture can mean "a mental position or frame of mind." Also, the way that one carries himself or herself or the position of the body can show an individual's attitude.
2. The phrase *strike an attitude* means "to assume a posture or pose for effect."

Step III. Practice

A DIRECTIONS: Each sentence has a missing word. Choose the word that *best* completes the sentence. Write the word in the blank. Not all words are used.

Word List

aesthetic	characteristic	exonerate	jeopardy
affront	corroborate	hypocrite	repent
antagonize	derogatory	inclination	temperate
attitude	euphemism	intimidate	

1. You can usually tell what a person's _____ toward something is by the way he or she behaves.

2. Because some people have a more developed _____ sense than others, they are more sensitive to art and beauty.

3. When you are insulted by someone whom you count as a friend, the _____ is even more painful.

4. The doctor asked the mother of the child whether she had noticed any special _____s that the child had.

5. As I don't like to have people hostile toward me, I try not to _____ others.

6. The hill's _____ was so steep that I had difficulty walking up the slope.

7. "She is pleasingly plump" is a(n) _____ for "she is fat."

8. Mary is a(n) _____ because she had us believing that she was going to help us when all along she had no intention of doing so.

9. They tried to _____ us by threats and insults, but we wouldn't change our story.

10. Politicians usually make _____ remarks about their opponents because they want to belittle them.

STOP. Check answers at the end of the book (p. 334).

B **DIRECTIONS:** Define the underlined word in each sentence. Write your answer in the blank.

1. You probably think that you are offering helpful criticism, but your <u>derogatory</u> remarks actually only make me feel bad about myself. _____

2. Mariko feels such a strong <u>inclination</u> toward Bruce that she has changed her mind about wanting to remain single until she turns thirty. _____

3. Carla's general <u>attitude</u> toward technology is to regard it as a useful tool, not as an object of fascination in itself. _____

4. I can appreciate your house in purely <u>aesthetic</u> terms, but in practical terms I think it might be inconvenient to live in. _____

5. I now think that I treated you very badly when we last met, and I <u>repent</u> the things I said to you. _____

6. It is <u>characteristic</u> of Erica to be sweet-tempered and thoughtful of others, so I am not surprised that you liked her so much. _____

7. Sometimes the expression, "But he's really good-looking" is just a <u>euphemism</u> for "He's boring and uninteresting." _____

8. Sharon is being a <u>hypocrite</u> when she says that she doesn't care about grades; she is miserable if she gets a B on a test or paper. _____

9. You know that your parents don't like Rita, so why did you <u>antagonize</u> them by talking about her all afternoon? _____

10. Carlo asked me to <u>corroborate</u> the fact that I was with him all afternoon, but I didn't like the idea of lying to his girlfriend. _____

11. Not inviting my parents, my brother, and me to the rehearsal dinner was a deliberate <u>affront</u> to our whole family. _____

12. After doing further research, Professor Li was able to <u>exonerate</u> Roger of the unfair charge of plagiarism. _____

STOP. Check answers at the end of the book (p. 334).

C **DIRECTIONS:** Write one sentence using at least two words from this lesson. The sentence must make sense. Try to illustrate the meanings of the words without actually defining them.

Example

It is not *characteristic* of Marisa to change her *attitude* so quickly and to be so *antagonistic* toward everyone.

_____

_____

_____

_____

STOP. Check answers at the end of the book (p. 334).

EXTRA WORD POWER

age

Condition; state of; action; collection of; place for. When *age* is added to the end of a word, it can mean "condition," "state of," "act of," "collection of," or "place for." For example: *haulage*—act of hauling; *foliage*—collection or mass of leaves; *marriage*—state of being wed; *passage*—act of passing; *wastage*—amount wasted; *salvage*—the act of saving; *acreage*—collection of acres; *orphanage*—place for orphans or collection of orphans; *advantage*—any condition, state, or circumstance favorable to success; *outage*—state of being interrupted; *wattage*—amount of electric power; total number of watts needed; *shrinkage*—act of shrinking; amount of decrease; *spillage*—amount spilled; the act of spilling. How many more words can you supply that end in *age*?

ure

Act; result of an action; agent of action; state of. *Ure* is found at the end of many nouns. For example: *legislature*—body of lawmakers; *exposure*—state of being exposed or laid open; *posture*—state of carriage (how one carries oneself); *rupture*—the act of something breaking apart; *torture*—act of causing severe pain; *temperature*—degree of hotness or coldness of something. How many more words that end in *ure* can you supply?

LESSON 8

Step I. Story in Context

DIRECTIONS: The following story includes several vocabulary words from this lesson. As you read the story, pay careful attention to the vocabulary words in boldface type, and try to figure out the meaning of each of these words. Put your answers in the blanks.

Jose's Problems with His Friends Increase

Jose started to become (1) **apprehensive** _____ about his relations with his buddies. He felt that they didn't trust him, and candidly speaking, nor did Jose trust them anymore. His friends used to be quite (2) **discreet** _____ about anything he told them in confidence. That was no longer the case. He tried to (3) **initiate** _____ discussions with them on safe, (4) **bland** _____ topics so that no one's nose would get out of joint. But most of the time, he felt as though he were walking on eggshells.

Jose realized that the break between himself and his old buddies was getting greater and greater when they had a party and didn't even tell him about it. Jose was upset about this (5) **omission** _____. He tried to (6) **scrutinize** _____, that is, investigate how this happened. However, when Jose asked them point blank whether the decision had been a (7) **unanimous** _____ one, his friends just looked blankly at him.

There were too many (8) **miscellaneous** _____ happenings that Jose knew he couldn't ignore. It bothered him that he was considered an outcast by his old friends because he had some new friends at school. After all, it's not as if his new friends were (9) **infamous** _____ criminals. Most of them were nice guys who did well in school. Actually, teachers usually liked having most of his new friends in their classes because of their (10) **docile** _____ behavior.

STOP. Check answers at the end of the book (p. 335).

Step II. Vocabulary Words in Context

1. **apprehensive** (ap · pri · hen' sive) *adj.* Fearful; expecting evil, danger, or harm; anxious. *The frightened witness was so **apprehensive** about his life that he refused to give evidence.*
2. **bland** (bland) *adj.* Mild; soft; gentle; balmy; kindly; soothing. *You should eat only **bland** foods after you have had an upset stomach because they are very gentle.*
3. **criterion** (krī · tir' ē · un) *n.* A standard of judging. (*pl.* **criteria**) (krī · tir' ē · uh) *The journal's staff decided on the **criteria** they would use to judge whether papers were acceptable for publication in their journal.*
4. **datum** (dā' tum) *n.* Information given; a premise upon which something can be argued (*pl.* **data**) (da' tuh). (Usually used in the plural.) *Because of insufficient **data**, the problem could not be solved.*

5. **discreet** (dis · krēét') *adj.* Careful about what one says or does; prudent; cautious. *The President's relatives should be* **discreet** *because if they are not careful about what they do or say, it can embarrass the President.*

6. **docile** (dos' ul) *adj.* Easy to teach; easy to discipline; obedient. *Teachers like to have* **docile** *students in their classes because they are easy to teach.*

7. **futile** (fū' tul) *adj.* Useless; ineffectual; unimportant. *The doctor's efforts to save the child who had consumed the toxic liquid were* **futile,** *because the dose consumed was a lethal one.*

8. **infamous** (in' fuh · møus) *adj.* Having a bad reputation; notorious. *Al Capone was* **infamous** *because he was well known for his bad actions.*

9. **initiate** (i · nish' ē · āté) *v.* To introduce by doing or using first; to begin; to bring into use or practice; to admit as a member into a fraternity, sorority, club, and so on, especially through the use of a secret ceremony. *I will* **initiate** *the program by having everyone introduce himself or herself to everyone else.*

10. **invincible** (in · vin' suh · bul) *adj.* Impossible to overcome; not able to be conquered. *The* **invincible** *army won every battle.*

11. **miscellaneous** (mis · uh · lā' nē · øus) *adj.* Mixed; consisting of several kinds; various. *The box contained a number of* **miscellaneous** *items, which were different things I had collected through the years.*

12. **omission** (ō · mish' un) *n.* Anything left out or not done; failure to include. *When it was discovered that the main speaker's name was left out of the program, an investigation was started to determine who was responsible for the* **omission.**

13. **scrutinize** (skrūt' un · īzé) *v.* To observe closely; to examine or inquire into critically; to investigate. *The police said that they would* **scrutinize** *the evidence very carefully to make sure that nothing escaped investigation.*

14. **unanimous** (ū · nan' uh · møus) *adj.* Agreeing completely; united in opinion; being of one mind; being in complete agreement. *As everyone was in agreement, the vote was* **unanimous.**

15. **valid** (val' id) *adj.* Sound; well grounded on principles or evidence; having legal force. *After the judge ruled that the will was* **valid,** *the lawyer for the estate called all the beneficiaries together for a reading of it.*

Step III. Practice

A DIRECTIONS: Each sentence has a missing word. Choose the word that *best* completes the sentence. Write the word in the blank. All words are used.

Word List

apprehensive	docile	miscellaneous	scrutinize
bland	infamous	omission	unanimous
discreet	initiate		

1. Spies must be _____ about what they do because they never know who is watching or listening to them.

2. People are _____ about walking alone late at night because it is so dangerous.

3. Not every school has students who are so _____ and obedient.

4. Although you are well known when you are _____, you are known because of the bad things that you have done.

5. I am on a(n) _____ diet because of my ulcer.

6. I am going to _____ that situation very carefully because it looks to me as if something is wrong.

7. Whenever a(n) _____ is made, we try to determine whether the item was left out on purpose or not.

8. At our meetings, it's almost impossible to get everyone to agree on anything, so we never have _____ agreements.

9. The _____ items were put on sale because the several things that were left were all one of a kind.

10. The fraternity decided not to _____ any members this year because of the fatal accident that occurred last year.

STOP. Check answers at the end of the book (p. 335).

B DIRECTIONS: Choose the vocabulary word from lesson 8 that best fits the underlined word or phrase in each sentence. Not all words are used.

Word List

apprehensive	discreet	initiate	scrutinize
bland	docile	invincible	unanimous
criterion	futile	miscellaneous	valid
datum	infamous	omission	

_____ 1. Sheila was <u>frightened</u> at the idea of making a speech before so many people.

_____ 2. My <u>standard for deciding</u> to take a course is whether or not I think I will enjoy it.

_____ 3. Peter likes spicy foods, but Carol prefers foods that are <u>mild flavored</u>, so it is difficult for them to choose a restaurant.

_____ 4. Dann's recent series of successes have made him feel <u>that he cannot lose</u>.

_____ 5. I still haven't packed a lot of <u>assorted</u> items.

_____ 6. Alan <u>checked carefully for errors</u> before submitting his report.

_____ 7. Our nominating committee was <u>in complete agreement</u> in recommending Natalie to be president.

_____ 8. Professor Smith said that the arguments I presented in my paper were <u>sound</u>.

_____ 9. Rea is such a(n) <u>notorious</u> flirt that no one wants to date her.

—————————————— 10. I have gathered all the <u>information</u> I need for my report and will now begin to write it.

—————————————— 11. I meant to call you but forgot; please forgive my <u>failure
to do so</u>.

—————————————— 12. Tomas is usually a very <u>obedient</u> child, but today he is
not behaving well.

STOP. Check answers at the end of the book (p. 335).

C DIRECTIONS: Write one sentence using at least two words from this lesson. The sentence must make sense. Try to illustrate the meanings of the words without actually
defining them.

Example

Sean was *apprehensive* when he was told to *scrutinize* his friend's report for any
significant *omissions*.

———

———

———

STOP. Check answers at the end of the book (p. 335).

EXTRA WORD POWER

ism	Act of, practice of, or result of; condition of being; action or quality of. *Ism* is used at the end of a great number of words. For example: *terrorism*—practice of terror; the use of fear to frighten or intimidate; *barbarism*—the condition of being primitive or brutal; *pauperism*—the condition of being very poor; *patriotism*—quality of being a pa-triot; *Americanism*—practice of values characteristic of Americans; *socialism*—the principle whereby the ownership and operation of the means of production are by society or the community rather than by private individuals, with all members of the community sharing in the work and products; *nationalism*—devotion to one's nation. How many other words with *ism* can you supply?
ive	Of; relating to; belonging to; having the nature or quality of; tending to. The word part *ive* is added to the end of many words. For example: *legislative*—relating to the body of lawmakers; *affirmative*—having the quality of a positive statement; *derogative*—tending to belittle; *native*—belonging to a country by birth; *creative*—tending to be able to create; *destructive*—tending to cause destruction or the tearing down of things; *massive*—having the quality of being very large. How many more words with *ive* can you supply?

LESSON 9

Step I. Story in Context

DIRECTIONS: The following story includes several vocabulary words from this lesson. As you read the story, pay careful attention to the vocabulary words in boldface type, and try to figure out the meaning of each of these words. Put your answers in the blanks.

Jose and His "Friends"

Jose was beside himself. He had known that things would be different at college, but he wasn't prepared for all the (1) **turmoil** _____ that he had encountered so far. He was a (2) **gregarious** _____ fellow who liked to have a good time and be with lots of people. He was used to being well-liked and not having (3) **adversaries** _____. He also couldn't ever imagine that his best friends from home would become his enemies. Jose at first tried to behave in a (4) **passive** _____ manner toward his former friends, but that didn't help. He told them that at spring break, he would go with them rather than with his fraternity brothers to the (5) **exotic** _____ island they were going to. That didn't help.

Finally, Jose told his friends that he was at his wit's end. He was (6) **adept** _____ at diplomacy, as they knew, but they obviously were so angry with him that whatever he did they would find fault with. He told them that it may sound (7) **trite** _____, but he had had it. He told them that what they had given him was the (8) **acquisition** _____ of anger. He felt that their anger was so (9) **contagious** _____ that he was walking around being angry all the time.

Jose then resorted to one last way to try to appease his former friends. He told them some (10) **anecdotes** _____ of when they were young children together. He felt that if anything would get them back on track, that would.

Do you think it did?

Write what you think happened to Jose and his friends.

STOP. Check answers at the end of the book (p. 335).

Step II. Vocabulary Words in Context

1. **abridge** (uh · brij′) *v.* To shorten; to curtail; to give the substance of in fewer words. *The kindergarten teachers decided to **abridge** some of the longer stories so that they would suit the younger children's attention spans.*
2. **acquisition** (ak · wi · zish′ un) *n.* The act of obtaining or acquiring; something obtained or gained as property, knowledge, and so on. *When the school population increased, the **acquisition** of another building was necessary to house all the students.*
3. **adept** (uh · dept′) *adj.* Highly skilled; proficient; expert. *I would call him an expert golfer because he is so **adept** at it.*
4. **adversary** (ad′ vur · ser · ē) *n.* One who opposes another, as in battle or debate; one who acts against something or someone; enemy; antagonist; opponent. *The politician said that the person running opposite him has been his **adversary** for years.*

5. **anecdote** (an′ ek · dōt*e*) *n.* A short, entertaining account of some happening, usu-ally personal or biographical. *The sailor told us many interesting **anecdotes** about his sea adventures.*

6. **attrition** (uh · trish′ un) *n.* A gradual wearing down or weakening; a rubbing out or grinding down. *When employees retired or quit their jobs, no new people were hired to take their places. The employers were not firing anyone; they were just letting the workforce become smaller through **attrition.***

7. **contagious** (kun · tā′ jus) *adj.* Spreading by contact; spreading or tending to spread from person to person. *Some diseases are very **contagious,** and you can catch them from persons if they sneeze or cough near you.*

8. **exotic** (eg · zot′ ik) *adj.* Foreign; not native; introduced from a foreign country; having the charm of the unfamiliar; strangely beautiful. *The florist imported some **exotic** plants from another country for one of his special customers.*

9. **gregarious** (gri · gar′ ē · øus) *adj.* Fond of the company of others; sociable; charac-teristic of a flock, herd, or crowd. ***Gregarious** people usually enjoy being in the company of other people.*

10. **imminent** (im′ uh · nunt) *adj.* About to happen. *The people were warned that an earthquake was **imminent** and they would have to leave their homes immediately.*

11. **paradox** (par′ uh · doks) *n.* Contradiction. *It is a **paradox** to say that you are here and not here at the same time.*

12. **passive** (pas′ siv*e*) *adj.* Not acting; acted upon; unresisting; not opposing; unen-thusiastic; inactive. *When you have no interest in something, you behave in a very **passive** manner.*

13. **phenomenon** (fi · nom′ uh · non) *n.* Any fact, circumstance, or experience that is apparent to the senses and that can be scientifically described; something ex-tremely unusual. (*pl.* **phenomena**) *An eclipse is a **phenomenon** of astronomy that has been observed and scientifically described.*

14. **trite** (trīt*e*) *adj.* Used so often as to be too common; made commonplace by rep-etition; lacking freshness or originality; commonplace. *It is easier to use **trite** phrases, which are ready-made and common, than to think of a more original way to say something.*

15. **turmoil** (tur′ moil) *n.* Confused motion or state; disturbance; tumult. *There was so much **turmoil** in the stores during the Christmas rush, with everyone dashing around in all different directions, that I became confused.*

SPECIAL NOTES

1. The word *contagious* usually refers to the spreading of disease, but it can also refer to the spreading of other things, such as laughter and sadness. For example:
   a. The *contagious* laughter spread throughout the whole class, and before long everyone was aching from laughing so much.
   b. The child's crying was so *contagious* that soon all the children in the kindergarten were crying.
2. The word part *greg* means "herd, flock, crowd, group." This combining form is found in the word *gregarious.*

Step III. Practice

A DIRECTIONS: Each sentence has a missing word. Choose the word from the list below that *best* completes the sentence. Write the word in the blank. Some words will not be used.

Word List

abridge	anecdote	gregarious	phenomenon
acquisition	attrition	imminent	trite
adept	contagious	paradox	turmoil
adversary	exotic	passive	

1. My assignment is to _____ this article by cutting unnecessary material.

2. Joelle is _____ at knitting but she is less skillful at crochet.

3. We observed an interesting _____ in chemistry lab this morning.

4. It is _____ but nevertheless true to observe that opposites attract.

5. Because flu is so _____, it is a good idea to get a flu shot every winter.

6. My journalism professor told us many fascinating _____ about his career as a foreign correspondent.

7. The announcement of the prize winners is _____, so everyone is continually checking e-mail.

8. Tina is extremely _____ and hates staying home by herself.

9. Because I had never met anyone from her country before, I thought that Tai was not only beautiful but also _____.

10. Professor Stein's announcement that the midterm would be moved up to this Friday threw the students into _____.

11. Some people think the purpose of college is the _____ of career skills, but I think this is the time to obtain knowledge.

12. It would be easier to figure out how to please you if you were not so _____.

STOP. Check answers at the end of the book (p. 335).

B DIRECTIONS: Ten sentences follow. Define the underlined word. Put your answer in the blank.

1. In the film, the main character's <u>adversary</u> was a powerful woman who would do anything to destroy her enemy. _____

2. Why don't you play a more active role in the convention elections rather than such a <u>passive</u> one? _____

3. As my brother can't stand any disturbances, we avoid any <u>turmoil</u>. _____

4. Many slang words are <u>trite</u> because they are used too often. _____

5. A Southern politician was known for the <u>anecdotes</u> he would tell concerning funny things that had happened to him. _____

6. When a number of people had a <u>contagious</u> disease, the doctors isolated these patients in a special wing of the hospital. _____

7. I like <u>exotic</u> things because they are rare. _____

8. Because Jack and Herb are very <u>gregarious</u>, they shine when they are with lots of people. _____

9. When the store ran out of necessary supplies, the manager was upset to learn that his order for the <u>acquisition</u> of new supplies had not yet been sent out. _____

10. A good secretary today should be <u>adept</u> at typing and be computer literate. _____

STOP. Check answers at the end of the book (p. 335).

C **DIRECTIONS:** Sentences using some vocabulary words from Lesson 9 follow. See whether you can figure out the meanings of the underlined words from the clues in the sentences. Sometimes the clue to help you figure out the word is in the next sentence or sentences. Blanks are provided for your estimates of the definitions. Check your meanings with those in Step II.

1. The <u>acquisition</u> of vocabulary is the objective of this book. If you have acquired knowledge of words and their meanings, this intention has been realized. _____

2. By this time, you should be more <u>adept</u> at figuring out words using context clues. As you have seen, to become an expert at something, you have to work diligently and persevere. _____

3. The words that have been presented in this book are neither <u>exotic</u> nor <u>trite</u>; that is, the words are neither so strange that you will hardly meet them nor so commonplace that they are used with almost no meaning. _____;

4. If you are a <u>gregarious</u> person who likes to be with a lot of people, you will find that being <u>adept</u> in vocabulary will help you in telling <u>anecdotes</u>. The more skilled you are in vocabulary, the more able you will be to make your stories exciting, interesting, and entertaining. _____; _____;

5. You will find also that you will become more active rather than <u>passive</u> in discussions _____

6. With your skill in words, you would probably be able to overcome your <u>adversary</u> in a debate. People would be reluctant to oppose you because of your <u>verbal ability</u>. _____

7. No more would your stomach be in a <u>turmoil</u> because you had to give a speech in a particular class. There is no need for feeling disturbed when you have "word power." _____

8. It is hoped that learning new vocabulary words will become a <u>contagious</u> "disease" from which you will not be cured. Not only will you continue acquiring new words, but you will also spread this enthusiasm for words to others. _____

STOP. Check answers at the end of the book (p. 335).

D **DIRECTIONS:** Write one sentence using at least two words from this lesson. The sentence must make sense. Try to illustrate the meanings of the words without actually defining them.

Example
When the *gregarious* man at the party told his *anecdote* about meeting an *exotic* woman who first became his *adversary* and then his wife, we had difficulty believing him.

_____

_____

_____

_____

STOP. Check answers at the end of the book (p. 335).

EXTRA WORD POWER

ish Belonging to; like or characteristic of; tending to; somewhat or rather; about. Many words end in *ish*. For example: *Spanish*—belonging to Spain; *Irish*—belonging to Ireland; *Danish*—belonging to Denmark; *devilish*—like or characteristic of a devil; *boyish*—like or characteristic of a boy; *bookish*—inclined to books; involved with books; *tallish*—rather tall; *bluish*—rather blue; *thirtyish*—about thirty. How many words with *ish* can you supply?

ic Relating to; like. *Ic* is added to the end of a great number of words. For example: *hyperbolic*—relating to a hyperbole or a great exaggeration; *heroic*—like a hero; *poetic*—like poetry; *tragic*—like a tragedy, in which something is very sad or there is disaster; *public*—relating to the public or people at large; *euphemistic*—relating to a euphemism or a milder way of saying something; *enthusiastic*—relating to enthusiasm or a lively interest in something; *toxic*—relating to poison; *epidemic*—relating to the rapid spread of a disease or something; *scientific*—relating to science; *historic*—relating to history, which is an account of what has happened; famous in history. How many words with *ic* can you supply?

FUN WITH CARTOONS

DIRECTIONS: State the meaning of the word *attrition* as it is used in the cartoon. Then explain what makes the cartoon amusing.

Reprinted by permission of Tribune Media Services.

_____

_____

_____

STOP. Check answers at the back of the book (p. 335).

SPECIAL ACADEMIC WORDS

A **DIRECTIONS:** Here are some words in this chapter that are used in criminal justice courses. Without looking at the chapter, see how well you can define them.

1. exonerate _____

2. corroborate _____

3. jeopardy _____

4. repent _____

5. discreet _____

6. antagonize _____

7. attitude _____

8. characteristic _____

9. intimidate _____

10. paradox _____

11. derogatory   _____

12. inclination   _____

13. unanimous   _____

14. infamous   _____

15. scrutinize   _____

16. valid   _____

17. adversary   _____

STOP. Check answers at the end of the book (p. 335).

CHAPTER WORDS IN A PARAGRAPH

Write a paragraph on the given topic using at least eight words from this chapter. The paragraph must make sense and be logically developed.

Topic: My Most Creative Endeavor

STOP. Check answers at the end of the book (p. 336).

www GAINING WORD POWER ON THE INTERNET

1. Choose a search engine. Write the name of the chosen search engine:

   _____

2. Do a search of the following two terms: *aesthetic, euphemism.*

3. Choose one site or reference generated by your search for each term. Try to select sites that help you gain a better understanding of the terms you are researching. Write

   the chosen site for each term: _____

4. Write a three-sentence paragraph on the site information for each term.

5. Log onto the Web site that accompanies this textbook for extra practice exercises at [http://www.ablongman.com/vocabulary].

STOP. Check answers at the end of the book (p. 336).

CROSSWORD PUZZLE

DIRECTIONS: The meanings of a number of the words from Lessons 7 to 9 follow. Your knowledge of these words from Part One should help you solve this crossword puzzle.

Across

1. Sound of surprise
4. You _____ the bell
6. Respectful address to men
7. Abbreviation of *discount*
10. Meaning of *ego*
11. Same as #8 Down
12. To stay or fall behind
13. He _____ with his eyes
15. Holds back water
18. Texas is a _____
21. Abbreviation of *South Carolina*
22. Able to be taught
24. Belittling; disparaging
27. Opposite of *he*
28. Personal pronoun
29. Fifteenth letter of alphabet
30. A _____ of film

Down

1. Abbreviation of *Arabic*
2. Opposite of *hers*
3. To make lively; to make alive
5. Sociable
7. Careful about what you say or do
8. Anger
9. You plant this
12. A drug that makes you erratic
14. Code signal for *help*
15. When your heart stops, you _____
16. Abbreviation of *Albert*
17. Homonym of *meat*
19. Homonym of *two*
20. *Me; I*
21. Feeling out of _____
23. Special trait
25. Indefinite article

32. Same as #25 Down
33. Rhymes with *cat*
34. Same as #14 Down
36. Exam
37. Faster than *walk*
39. To make an opening with a knife
40. Opposite of *present*
42. Past tense of *is*
43. A game called _____ ball
44. Same as #33 Down
45. You roll these in games of chance
46. Abbreviation of *period*
47. Something of value
50. Slang for *is not*
51. Refers to how old you are
52. Mixed; varied
55. Girl's name
56. Fifth letter of alphabet
57. Opposite of *yes*
58. Referring to *voice*
60. Abbreviation of *Rhode Island*

26. Opposite of *no*
31. Abbreviation of *lieutenant*
33. Indefinite article—rhymes with *man*
34. Synonym of *intimidate*
35. What you get when something is boiling
38. Employ
40. Opposite of *active*
41. A short, entertaining story
42. Opposite of *loser*
43. To ask for charity in a humble way
45. Abbreviation of *diameter*
46. Way of saying *father*
48. *Yes* in Spanish
49. *Docile* means "easy to _____"
50. Same as #16 Down
53. Abbreviation of United Nations
54. Homonym of *sew*
59. Opposite of *early*

STOP. Check answers at the end of the book (p. 336).

ANALOGIES

DIRECTIONS: Find the word from the following list that *best* completes each analogy. There are more words listed than you need.

Word List

active	commonplace	gregarious	risk
aesthetic	compliment	imminent	scrutinize
ally	disturbance	inclination	skilled
bland	euphemism	insult	spreading
careful	exonerate	jeopardy	standard
characteristic	exotic	notorious	terminate
commence	fearful	overindulgent	unmanageable
common	feeling	passive	unskilled

1. Convenient : unsuitable :: affront : _____.

2. Error : mistake :: apprehensive : _____.

3. Isolate : integrate :: initiate : _____.

4. Tenacious : stubborn :: trite : _____.

5. Corroborate : deny :: adept : _____.

6. Inanimate : alive :: opponent : _____.

7. Conceited : egotistical :: criterion : _____.

8. Custom : habit :: leaning : _____.

9. Boundary : limit :: contagious : _____.

10. Concede : resist :: docile : _____.

11. Attitude : feeling :: turmoil : _____.

12. Innate : inborn :: vindicate : _____.

13. Confuse : obfuscate :: mild : _____.

14. Abridge : curtail :: infamous : _____.

15. Bold : discreet :: domestic : _____.

16. Repentant : remorseful :: inactive : _____.

17. Lush : barren :: indiscreet : _____.

18. Inward : shy :: outgoing : _____.

19. Drizzle : downpour :: observe : _____.

20. Simmer : boil :: temperate : _____.

STOP. Check answers at the end of the book (p. 337).

MULTIPLE-CHOICE VOCABULARY TEST

DIRECTIONS: This is a test on words in Lessons 7 to 9. Words are presented according to lessons. *Do all lessons before checking answers.* Underline the meaning that *best* fits the word.

Lesson 7

1. aesthetic
   - a. referring to being poor
   - b. likes food
   - c. referring to beauty
   - d. a feeling

2. affront
   - a. an insult
   - b. a front
   - c. friendly
   - d. not friendly

3. antagonize
   - a. helpful
   - b. friendly
   - c. to make an enemy of
   - d. feeling

4. attitude
   - a. manner of feeling
   - b. unfriendly feeling
   - c. friendly feeling
   - d. happy feeling

5. characteristic   a. person   c. special trait
                        b. play   d. feeling

6. corroborate   a. to confirm   c. to deny
                        b. friendly   d. to feel happy

7. derogatory   a. a lot of   c. helpful
                        b. tending to belittle   d. talkative

8. euphemism   a. a wise saying   c. a saying
                        b. hold back   d. a less distasteful description of
                                                           something

9. exonerate   a. to blame   c. to free from blame
                        b. to free   d. to save

10. hypocrite   a. to frighten   c. to lean
                        b. to be friendly   d. one who pretends to be what
                                                         he or she is not

11. inclination   a. insult   c. frighten
                        b. a leaning   d. a saying

12. intimidate   a. to scare   c. to insult
                        b. to lean   d. to make unfriendly

13. jeopardy   a. to free from   c. to be dangerous
                        b. to score   d. danger

14. repent   a. to cry   c. to undo something
                        b. to feel regret   d. to be fearful
                             for something

15. temperate   a. moderate   c. to cry
                        b. to like to overeat   d. to like people

Lesson 8

16. apprehensive   a. mild   c. helpful
                        b. fearful   d. cheerful

17. bland   a. refers to sadness   c. mild
                        b. friendly   d. evil

18. criterion   a. a standard of judging   c. correct judgment
                        b. mild   d. an insult

19. datum   a. information   c. judgment
                        b. standard   d. a date

20. discreet   a. fearful   c. evil
                        b. friendly   d. careful

21. docile   a. active   c. noisy
                        b. easy to teach   d. frightened

22. futile
    a. important
    b. useless
    c. death
    d. useful

23. infamous
    a. well known
    b. happy
    c. a crook
    d. having a bad reputation

24. initiate
    a. to party
    b. to start
    c. to insult
    d. to frighten

25. invincible
    a. conquered
    b. task
    c. not able to be conquered
    d. invisible

26. miscellaneous
    a. mixed
    b. most
    c. one
    d. wrong

27. omission
    a. task
    b. skill
    c. trip
    d. anything left out

28. scrutinize
    a. able to see
    b. to watch someone
    c. to observe very closely
    d. to help

29. unanimous
    a. agreeing completely
    b. some
    c. several
    d. not any

30. valid
    a. a principle
    b. a standard
    c. truth-telling
    d. sound

Lesson 9

31. abridge
    a. lengthen
    b. shorten
    c. refers to bridges
    d. far away

32. acquisition
    a. curious
    b. inquisitive
    c. quiet
    d. the obtaining of something

33. adept
    a. helpful
    b. friendly
    c. skillful
    d. changing

34. adversary
    a. friend
    b. skilled
    c. one who opposes another
    d. hostile

35. anecdote
    a. something funny
    b. a note
    c. a joke
    d. a short, entertaining account of a happening

36. attrition
    a. attractive
    b. a weakness
    c. spreading
    d. wearing down

37. contagious
    a. germs
    b. referring to contact
    c. spreading from person to person
    d. unhealthy

38. exotic
    a. native
    b. foreign
    c. far away
    d. pretty

39. gregarious
    a. hostile
    b. helpful
    c. sociable
    d. strange

40. imminent   a. lively   c. spirit
                           b. about to happen   d. refers to mines

41. paradox   a. resisting   c. contradiction
                           b. unrest   d. unresisting

42. passive   a. enthusiastic   c. unresisting
                           b. lively   d. active

43. phenomenon   a. a science   c. something that can be
                           b. a fact   scientifically described
                                                  d. a description

44. trite   a. important   c. different
                           b. meaningful   d. commonplace

45. turmoil   a. movement   c. spirit
                           b. confused motion   d. lively

CHAPTER TRUE/FALSE TEST

DIRECTIONS: This is a true/false test on Lessons 4 to 6. Read each sentence carefully. Decide whether it is true or false. Put a *T* for *True* or an *F* for *False* in the blank. If the statement is false, change a word or words to make it true. The number after the sentence tells you in which lesson the word appears.

_____ 1. An <u>adversary</u> is the same as a supporter. 9

_____ 2. If something undergoes <u>attrition</u>, it gets weaker. 9

_____ 3. To <u>initiate</u> is to begin. 8

_____ 4. If an agreement is <u>valid</u>, it is illegal. 8

_____ 5. To <u>exonerate</u> is to clear of blame. 7

_____ 6. An <u>affront</u> is a kind of decoration. 7

_____ 7. <u>Jeopardy</u> is an antonym for "danger." 7

_____ 8. A <u>temperate</u> person would not overeat or get drunk. 7

_____ 9. To be <u>discreet</u> is to be careless. 8

_____ 10. A <u>futile</u> effort is a successful one. 8

_____ 11. To be <u>docile</u> is to be cooperative and quiet. 8

_____ 12. If you <u>scrutinize</u> a contract, you are likely to understand it. 8

_____ 13. A <u>paradox</u> is something that is easy to understand. 9

_____ 14. A <u>passive</u> person is likely to argue vehemently. 9

_____ 15. A <u>derogatory</u> remark is likely to be hurtful. 7

_____ 16. To <u>intimidate</u> is to purposely frighten. 7

_____ 17. A ramp is a kind of <u>inclination</u>. 7

_____ 18. You would base your judgment on a <u>criterion</u>. 8

_____ 19. To <u>abridge</u> is to expand. 9

_____ 20. A person who is <u>adept</u> at a skill is an expert. 9

_____ 21. A <u>trite</u> expression is one that is new and striking. 9

STOP. Check answers for both tests at the end of the book (p. 337).

SCORING OF TESTS

Multiple-Choice Vocabulary Test		*True/False Test*	
Number Wrong	*Score*	*Number Wrong*	*Score*
0–2	Excellent	0–1	Excellent
3–5	Good	2–3	Good
6–8	Weak	4–5	Weak
Above 8	Poor	Above 5	Poor
Score _____		Score _____	

1. If you scored in the excellent or good range on both tests, you are doing well. Go on to Chapter 5 in Part Two.
2. If you scored in the weak or poor range on either test, look below and follow directions for Additional Practice. Note that the words on the tests are arranged so that you can tell in which lesson to find them. This arrangement will help you if you need additional practice.

ADDITIONAL PRACTICE SETS

A **DIRECTIONS:** Write the words you missed on the tests from the three lessons in the space provided. Note that the tests are presented so that you can tell to which lessons the words belong.

Lesson 7 Words Missed

1. _____   6. _____

2. _____   7. _____

3. _____   8. _____

4. _____   9. _____

5. _____   10. _____

Lesson 8 Words Missed

1. _____   6. _____

2. _____   7. _____

3. _____   8. _____

4. _____   9. _____

5. _____   10. _____

Lesson 9 Words Missed

1. _____   6. _____

2. _____   7. _____

3. _____   8. _____

4. _____   9. _____

5. _____   10. _____

B **DIRECTIONS:** Restudy the words that you have written down on page 90 and this page. Do Step I for those you missed. Note that Step I is on the following pages:

> Lesson 7—pp. 68–72
> Lesson 8—pp. 73–76
> Lesson 9—pp. 77–81

C **DIRECTIONS:** Do Additional Practice 1 on this page and page 92 if you missed words from Lesson 7. Do Additional Practice 2 on pp. 92–93 and this page if you missed words from Lesson 8. Do Additional Practice 3 on p. 93 if you missed words from Lesson 9.

Additional Practice 1 for Lesson 7

DIRECTIONS: Some sentences containing the meanings of some vocabulary presented in Lesson 7 follow. Choose the word that *best* fits the meaning of the word or phrase underlined in the sentence.

Word List

aesthetic	attitude	euphemism	inclination
affront	characteristic	hypocrites	intimidate
antagonize	derogatory		

_____ 1. What an <u>insult</u> it was not to shake my hand in front of all my friends.

_____ 2. A person's <u>way of feeling</u> is very difficult to change.

_____   3. Can you think of a <u>milder phrase</u> for "the economy is terrible"?

_____   4. If anyone tries to <u>frighten</u> you so that you will not tell your story, go to the police.

_____   5. Jennifer has a certain <u>leaning</u> toward music.

_____   6. Every person should have at least one good <u>trait</u>.

_____   7. I dislike <u>those who pretend to be virtuous but who are not</u>.

_____   8. Korey doesn't like to <u>make an enemy of</u> anyone.

_____   9. You have an <u>artistic</u> appreciation of nature.

_____   10. No one is allowed to make <u>belittling</u> remarks about my friends in my presence.

STOP. Check answers at the end of the book (p. 337).

Additional Practice 2 for Lesson 8

DIRECTIONS: Ten sentences containing the meanings of some vocabulary presented in Lesson 8 follow. Choose the word that *best* fits the meaning of the word or phrase underlined in the sentence.

Word List

apprehensive	docile	miscellaneous	scrutinize
bland	infamous	omission	unanimous
discreet	initiate		

_____   1. The <u>leaving out</u> of his name from the guest list caused us a <u>lot</u> of embarrassment.

_____   2. Seth is such a <u>mild and kindly</u> gentleman.

_____   3. There were <u>various</u> items from which I could choose what I wanted.

_____   4. Our art teacher taught us to <u>observe very carefully</u> the subjects that we were painting.

_____   5. Everyone was in <u>complete agreement</u> that the meeting should have convened an hour ago.

_____   6. Throughout the land, he is <u>known for his bad actions</u>.

_____   7. I enjoy having <u>obedient</u> children in my class.

_____   8. He decided to <u>introduce</u> a new game among his friends.

_____ 9. Try to be careful about what you say because I don't want anyone to know that I'm seeing you.

_____ 10. I am rather fearful about telling my parents about what happened in school today.

STOP. Check answers at the end of the book (p. 337).

Additional Practice 3 for Lesson 9

DIRECTIONS: Ten sentences containing the meanings of some vocabulary presented in Lesson 9 follow. Choose the word that *best* fits the meaning of the word or phrase underlined in the sentence.

Word List

acquisition	anecdote	gregarious	trite
adept	contagious	passive	turmoil
adversary	exotic		

_____ 1. You always seem to use commonplace phrases rather than original ones.

_____ 2. The disturbance at the factory was due to the strike.

_____ 3. His opponent was very skillful.

_____ 4. Why are you always so unenthusiastic?

_____ 5. The disease was spreading from person to person so rapidly that the doctors feared there would soon be an epidemic.

_____ 6. Carol is a very sociable person.

_____ 7. Arthur is very skillful in fixing anything in the house.

_____ 8. The act of obtaining knowledge is not easy.

_____ 9. Some of the birds I saw in Africa were strangely beautiful.

_____ 10. The short, entertaining story told by Salima was very funny.

STOP. Check answers at the end of the book (p. 337).

PART TWO

Vocabulary Derived Primarily from Combining Forms

Combining Forms

As a means of helping you to use combining forms to increase your vocabulary, some terms should be defined. There are a great number of words that combine with other words to form new words with different but related meanings, for example, *grandfather* (*grand* + *father*) and *foolproof* (*fool* + *proof*)—both compound words. Many words are combined with a letter or group of letters—either at the beginning (prefix) or at the end (suffix) of the word—to form a new, related word, for example, *replay* (*re* + *play*) and *played* (*play* + *ed*).

In the words *replay* and *played, play* is a root, *re* is a prefix, and *ed* is a suffix. A *root* is the smallest unit of a word that can exist and retain its basic meaning. It cannot be divided further. *Replay* is not a root word because it can be divided into *re* and *play*. *Play* is a root word because it cannot be divided further and still keep a meaning related to the root word.

Combining forms are usually defined as roots borrowed from another language that join together or that join with a prefix, a suffix, or both a prefix and a suffix to form a word. Often, the English combining forms are derived from Greek and Latin roots. Because the emphasis in this book is on the building of vocabulary meanings rather than on the naming of word parts, prefixes, suffixes, English roots, and combining forms will *all* be referred to as combining forms. *Combining forms in this book are defined as any word part that can join with another word or word part to form a word or a new word*. Examples: *aqua* + *naut* = aquanaut (a word); *re* + *turn* = return (a new word); *aqua* + *duct* = aqueduct (a new word).

Care is taken not to present those combining forms that are similar in appearance in the same exercise.

Knowledge of the most common combining forms is valuable in helping you to learn the meaning of an unfamiliar word. For example, knowing that *pseudo* means "false" helps you to unlock *pseudoscience,* which means "false science." Knowing that *bi* means "two" and *ped* means "foot" helps you to determine the meaning of *biped* as a two-footed animal. Knowing that *bi* means "two," that *tri* means "three," and that *cycle* means "wheel" helps you realize that *bicycle* refers to a two-wheeled vehicle, whereas *tricycle* refers to a three-wheeled vehicle.

As an indication of the power of knowing a few combining forms, it has been estimated that with the knowledge of thirty combining forms (which are included in this text), one can unlock the meanings of as many as 14,000 words. Obviously, familiarity with a mere thirty forms is the quickest way to learning the largest number of words. It is also a method that, once learned, helps you to unlock new words all through your life.

SPECIAL NOTES

You should be aware that for a number of words especially two-syllable or more words, the dictionary definitions of the words are not exactly the same as the combining forms' definitions. For these words, you will have an approximation of the word. By using context clues however, you should be able to figure out the word. For example, the dictionary definition of *automobile* is usually "a four-wheeled automotive vehicle designed for passenger transportation"; however, the combining form definition of *automobile* is "able to be moved by self" or "self-moving."

Also, in this book, you will meet a number of words that are familiar to you, for example, *telephone* and *telegraph*. These familiar words help you to remember the meanings for the combining forms so that you can unlock unfamiliar words derived from similar combining forms.

Chapter 5

LESSON 10

Step I. Story in Context

DIRECTIONS: The following story includes several vocabulary words from this lesson. As you read the story, pay careful attention to the vocabulary words in boldface type, and try to figure out the meaning of each of these words. Put your answers in the blanks.

Mark's Dream

Mark, a (1) **bilingual** _____ person, has always dreamt of becoming a famous athlete. He imagined people vying for his (2) **autograph** _____. He also imagined not only many people writing (3) **biographies** _____ of his life but also being asked to write his own (4) **autobiography** _____. He imagined making lots and lots of money. Actually, as a famous athlete, if he could keep from getting injuries, he could play for a number of years. He then would make more money (5) **bimonthly** _____ and even (6) **biweekly** _____ than he could make his whole life in his present full-time job. Mark also dreamed of surprising his parents on their (7) **anniversary** _____ with a new house and car. His parents were (8) **pedestrians** _____ all their lives. They walked everywhere. Even though walking is good exercise, it hurt his heart when he saw them lugging groceries so many blocks to their house. He felt that it was amazing that they didn't need a (9) **podiatrist** _____. He loved giving presents to them.

He planned on giving them gifts (10) **annually** _____ and even (11) **biannually** _____ rather than merely (12) **biennially** _____. He also set up an (13) **annuity** _____ for them. However, he didn't want his friends to expect him to give them gifts just because they were (14) **bipeds** _____, that is, humans.

"Well," Mark thought to himself, "I'd better stop daydreaming and get back to work and continue practicing if I want to achieve my goal one day."

STOP. Check answers at the end of the book (p. 338).

Step II. Combining Forms

A **DIRECTIONS:** A list of combining forms with their meanings follows. Look at the combining forms and their meanings. Concentrate on learning each combining form and its meaning. Cover the meanings, read the combining forms, and state the meanings to yourself. Check to see whether you are correct. Now cover the combining forms, read the meanings, and state the combining forms to yourself. Check to see whether you are correct.

Combining Forms	Meanings
1. anni, annu, enni	year
2. aut, auto	self
3. bi	two
4. bio	life
5. graph	something written; machine
6. graphy	writing; drawing; writing in or on a specified subject or field; science
7. ped,[1] pod	foot

B **DIRECTIONS:** Cover the preceding meanings. Write the meanings of the following combining forms.

Combining Forms	Meanings
1. anni, annu, enni	_____
2. aut, auto	_____
3. bi	_____
4. bio	_____
5. graph	_____
6. graphy	_____
7. ped, pod	_____

---

[1]Only one meaning for the combining form *ped* is presented in Lesson 10. Another meaning will be presented in Lesson 20 in Chapter 8.

Step III. Vocabulary Words Derived from Combining Forms in Context

1. **anniversary** (an · ńuh · vur' suh · rē) *n.* (*pl.* **ries**). The yearly return of a date marking an event or occurrence of some importance. *adj.* Returning or recurring each year. *Mark celebrated the fifth **anniversary** of his high school graduation on June 10th.*

2. **annual** (an' ńū · ul) *adj.* Occurring once a year; yearly. *At the end of every year, Mark receives his **annual** rating from his boss.*

3. **annuity** (ań · nū' i · tē) *n.* A yearly payment of money; an investment yielding a fixed sum of money, payable yearly to continue for a given number of years or for life. *He receives such a sizable **annuity** each year from his investment that he retired at an early age.*

4. **autobiography** (aw · tuh · bī · og' · ruh · fē) *n.* (*pl.* **phies**) *Mark felt that at twenty-three, he had not lived enough to write his own **autobiography**.*

5. **autograph** (aw' tuh · graf) *n.* Signature. *adj.* Written by a person's own hand: *an **autograph** letter;* containing autographs: *an **autograph** album. v.* To write one's own name on or in. *Mark liked to get the **autographs** of famous people and compare their signatures with other signatures he had collected.*

6. **automaton** (aw · tom' uh · ton) *n.* Anything that can move or act by itself; a person or animal acting in a mechanical way. *The goose-stepping soldiers in Hitler's army looked like **automatons**.*

7. **autonomous** (aw · ton' uh · møus) *adj.* Self-governing; functioning independently of other parts. *Because education is not mentioned in the Constitution, each state is supposed to be **autonomous** in this area.*

8. **biannual** (bī · an' ńu · ul) *adj.* Occurring twice a year; (loosely) occurring every two years. *Mark feels that **biannual** block parties, which come twice a year, are lots of fun.*

9. **biennial** (bī · en' ńē · ul) *adj.* Occurring once every two years; lasting for two years. *Mark's vacation is a **biennial** event because he can afford a vacation only every two years.*

10. **bifocals** (bī · fo' kulz) *n.* A pair of glasses with two-part lenses, one for near and one for far. (*pl.*) *When my mother's eye doctor recommended **bifocals** for her, my mother felt that it was a sure sign that she was getting old.*

11. **bilateral** (bī · lat' uh · rul) *adj.* Two sides. *The two nations began **bilateral** talks, hoping to conclude a peace treaty between them.*

12. **bilingual** (bī · ling' gwul) *adj. n.* Having or using two languages equally well; a bilingual person. *In **bilingual** programs, students who speak a language other than English learn certain subjects in their native language.*

13. **bimonthly** (bī · month' lē) *adj.* Occurring every two months; occurring twice a month. *Mark feels that we should change our **bimonthly** meetings to monthly meetings because meeting every two months is not often enough.*

14. **binary** (bī' nuh · rē) *adj.* Twofold; relating to two parts; relating to base two. *The **binary** system of numbers is used with digital computers.*

15. **biography** (bī · og' ruh · fē) *n.* (*pl.* **phies**) An account of a person's life; a person's life story. *Mark expects to be famous one day, so he thinks people will write lots of **biographies** about him.*

16. **biped** (bī' ped) *n.* A two-footed animal. *Mark knows that humans, who are **bipeds,** are not the only two-footed animals.*

17. **biweekly** (bī · wēék′ lē) *adj.* Occurring every two weeks; occurring twice a week. *Mark's **biweekly** paycheck is always gone at the end of two weeks.*

18. **biopsy** (bī′ op · sē) *n.* In medicine, the cutting out of living tissue for examination. *To determine whether major surgery is necessary, the surgeon usually takes a **biopsy** of the organ in question.*

19. **graphic** (graf′ ik) *adj.* Marked by vivid and realistic detail. *His story of the brutal attack was so **graphic** that it left nothing to the imagination.*

20. **orthography** (or · thog′ ruh · fē) *n.* The art of writing words correctly; correct spelling. (*pl.* **ies**) *Spelling bee contestants are especially knowledgeable of the **orthography** of words.*

21. **pedestal** (ped′ es · tul) *n.* A base or bottom support; a position of esteem. *The newly acquired statue was placed on a special **pedestal** for all to view.*

22. **pedestrian** (puh · des′ trē · un) *n.* One who goes on foot. *Jose is a good **pedestrian** who obeys traffic laws when he crosses streets.*

23. **podiatrist** (puh · dī′ uh · trist) *n.* A foot doctor who specializes in the care and treatment of feet. *After I went on a ten-mile hike, my feet hurt so much that I needed to visit a **podiatrist.***

24. **podium** (po′ dē · um) *n.* A raised platform for the conductor of an orchestra; a dais; a low wall serving as a foundation. *When the conductor took his position on the **podium,** all eyes were directed toward him.*

SPECIAL NOTES

1. Note that *biannual* almost always means "occurring twice a year," but when *biannual* is used loosely, it can mean "occurring every two years." *Biennial* means "occurring every two years" or "lasting for two years." In botany, a biennial plant is one that lasts for two years.

2. Note that the meanings for *biweekly* and *bimonthly* may at times be almost the same, because *biweekly* can mean "occurring every two weeks" and *bimonthly* can mean "occurring twice a month." However, when a word has more than one meaning, the *sentence usually provides clues for the proper meaning.*

   a. **bimonthly.** Occurring once every two months; occurring twice a month. *The theater group decided to stop giving **bimonthly** plays because two months did not give them enough time to rehearse.*

   b. **biweekly.** Occurring once every two weeks; occurring twice a week. *The **biweekly** newspaper is very large because it comes out only every two weeks.*

3. Both *graph* and *graphy* mean "writing" or "something written"; however, they are presented separately because each combining form also has other meanings. *Graph* can also mean "machine" and *graphy* can mean "writing in or on a specified subject or field" and "science."

Step IV. Practice

A DIRECTIONS: Define autobiography and biography. State the difference between the two. Write an amusing commentary on autobiography and biography. Here are two cartoons on autobiography and biography.

1.

2.

Reprinted by permission of King Features.

1. _____

2. _____

STOP. Check answers at the end of the book (p. 338).

B DIRECTIONS: Here is a list of some words from this lesson. Fill in the blank with the word that makes the *best* sense. All words from the list are used.

Word List

anniversary	autobiography	biennial	biographies	biweekly
annual	autographs	bimonthly	biped	pedestrians

1. A famous athlete recently wrote his _____ because he was furious at what others had written about him.

2. He was very unhappy with people who had written _____ about him.

3. The biographers had claimed that he refused to give _____ to his fans.

4. The biographers also claimed that he liked to give large parties to celebrate the _____ of his divorce.

5. His biographers said that he had been married to a famous actress, but their marriage was filled with _____ battles. In other words, they fought at least twice a week.

6. It's not surprising then that they had _____ separations, that is, on average, they separated about every two months.

7. The athlete's biographers said that he was a(n) _____ whom the world would have been better off without.

8. His biographers portrayed him as a drunken person who once hit a(n) _____ with his car.

9. Have you noticed that every year someone else has written about another famous person? Actually, it seems to be more than a(n) _____ event.

10. It used to be that stories about others' lives were a(n) _____ event, in other words, something written about every two years.

STOP. Check answers at the end of the book (p. 338).

C **DIRECTIONS:** Define the underlined word in each sentence.

1. Schools used to emphasize basic skills, such as <u>orthography</u>, but now they devote little time to these important areas.

_____

2. Each November we attend the university's <u>annual</u> interfaith Thanksgiving celebration.

_____

3. I suggest that you omit some of the more <u>graphic</u> details when you describe your accident to your parents.

_____

4. So many people were on the <u>podium</u> receiving awards that there was not enough room for them all.

_____

5. I would prefer to be paid weekly than <u>bimonthly</u>, but I guess I will just have to learn to budget better.

_____

6. An ancient philosopher once famously defined human beings as the only featherless <u>bipeds</u>.

_____

7. Watch out for <u>pedestrians</u> when you drive on campus; students seem to think they can walk wherever they please!

_____

8. First thing in the morning, when I'm still sleepy, I go through my routine so mechanically that I act like an <u>automaton</u>.

_____

9. The new nation became <u>autonomous</u> when it elected a legislature and began making its own laws and treaties.

_____

10. My older sister needs separate eyeglass prescriptions for distance and reading, so she got <u>bifocals</u> instead of two pairs of glasses.

_____

11. Roland bought a beautiful antique <u>pedestal</u>, but he doesn't have anything to put on top of it!

_____

12. The <u>podiatrist</u> prescribed special inserts to put inside my running shoes to correct my foot pain.

_____

13. Keiko was born in Japan and lived there for the first two years of her life, but she is not <u>bilingual</u>, because she rarely has a chance to speak Japanese.

_____

14. The lab report about my father's <u>biopsy</u> showed that no cancer cells are present.

_____

15. My parents used some of their retirement money to buy an <u>annuity</u>, but left most of their funds invested in the stock market.

_____

STOP. Check answers at the end of the book (p. 338).

D **DIRECTIONS:** Write one sentence using at least two words from this lesson. The sentence must make sense. Try to illustrate the meaning of the words without actually defining them.

> ### Example
>
> At the *biweekly* meeting of our club, we discussed where we would hold our *annual* party.

_____

_____

_____

STOP. Check answers at the end of the book (p. 338).

EXTRA WORD POWER

re	Again; back. *Re* is found at the beginning of many words. For example: *rewrite*—to write again; *redo*—to do again; *recomb*—to comb again; *rerun*—to run again; *rework*—to work again; *repay*—to pay back; *return*—to go back. How many more words that begin with *re* can you supply?

LESSON 11

Step I. Story in Context

DIRECTIONS: The following story includes vocabulary words from this lesson. As you read the story, try to figure out the meaning of the words in boldface type. Write the meanings in the space provided.

Bashir's Sick Day

One Monday morning, Bashir woke up feeling terrible. He immediately picked up the (1) **telephone** _____ and called the university clinic to make an appointment with the doctor. He took his (2) **geography** _____ book with him, planning to study the landforms and climate of Asia while he was waiting. He felt so terrible that he couldn't study, however, and luckily he didn't have to wait very long.

When his turn came, a nurse listened to his chest with a (3) **stethoscope** _____. Then she asked him for a (4) **description** _____ of all his symptoms, including when he first started to feel bad. When Bashir told her that he had a terrible sore throat, she took his temperature and a throat culture. She explained, "We need to find out exactly what kind of (5) **microbes** _____ are making you sick. Different kinds of (6) **microorganisms** _____ require different types of medicine to treat them." She explained that the doctor would send the culture to a laboratory, where a technician would examine it with a (7) **microscope** _____ and send the doctor a report. Then the doctor would write a (8) **prescription** _____ for the correct kind of medicine. "I sure hope the doctor will print it rather than writing in (9) **script** _____," she joked. "You know how bad most doctors' penmanship is."

Bashir was planning to be a doctor. He loved studying about all kinds of living things, especially about human anatomy, in his (10) **biology** _____ classes. "I guess I'll have to develop a sloppy handwriting," he thought as he went home.

STOP. Check answers at the end of the book (p. 338).

Step II. Combining Forms

A **DIRECTIONS:** A list of combining forms with their meanings follows. Look at the combining forms and their meanings. Concentrate on learning each combining form and its meaning. Cover the meanings, read the combining forms, and state the meanings to yourself. Check to see whether you are correct. Now cover the combining forms, read the meanings, and state the combining forms to yourself. Check to see whether you are correct.

Combining Forms	*Meanings*
1. geo	earth
2. logy, ology	the study of; the science of
3. meter	measure
4. micro	very small
5. phon, phono	sound
6. scope	a means for seeing, watching, or viewing
7. scrib, scrip	write
8. tele	from a distance

B **DIRECTIONS:** Cover the preceding meanings. Write the meanings of the following combining forms.

Combining Forms   *Meanings*

1. geo   _____

2. logy, ology   _____

3. meter   _____

4. micro   _____

5. phon, phono   _____

6. scope   _____

7. scrib, scrip   _____

8. tele   _____

Step III. Vocabulary Words Derived from Combining Forms in Context

1. **biology** (bī · ol′ uh · jē) *n.* The science of life. **Biology** *helps students to learn about living things.*
2. **description** (di · skrip′ shun) *n.* An account that gives a picture of something in words. *Carol's* **description** *of the accident was so graphic that I could picture it clearly in my mind.*
3. **geocentric** (jē · ō · sen′ trik) *adj.* Relating to the earth as the center. *In ancient times, people thought that the universe was* **geocentric,** *that is, the earth rather than the sun was the center of the universe.*

4. **geography** (jē · og′ ruh · fē) *n.* A descriptive science that deals with the earth, its division into continents and countries, the climate, plants, animals, natural resources, inhabitants, and industries of the various divisions. *In **geography**, you learn about the earth's climate and about the plant and animal life there.*

5. **geology** (jē · ol′ uh · gē) *n.* Study of the earth's physical history and makeup. ***Geology** helps people learn about the makeup of the earth, especially as revealed by rocks.*

6. **geometry** (jē · om′ uh · trē) *n.* Branch of mathematics dealing with the measurement of points, lines, and planes among other things. *An engineer uses his or her knowledge of **geometry** to measure the land for the building of new roads.*

7. **inscription** (in · skrip′ shun) *n.* Something written or engraved on some surface; a brief dedication to someone in a book. *The **inscription** on the Statue of Liberty beckons all to our shores.*

8. **meter** (mē′ tur) *n.* In the metric system, a unit of length equal to approximately 39.37 inches; an instrument for measuring the amount of something; a measure of verse. *A **meter** is approximately 3.3 feet or 1.1 yards.*

9. **microbe** (mī′ krōbé) *n.* A very small living thing; a microorganism. *Doctors determine through tests what **microbes** in our bodies are causing our diseases.*

10. **microfilm** (mī′ kruh · film) *n.* Film on which documents, printed pages, and so forth are photographed in a reduced size. *Many of the older copies of newspapers that I needed for my report were on **microfilm** in the library.*

11. **micrometer** (mī · krom′ ut · ur) *n.* An instrument used to measure accurately very small distances, angles, etc. *Technicians use a **micrometer** with a telescope or microscope when measuring very, very small distances because it helps them to be as accurate as possible.*

12. **microorganism** (mī · krō · or′ gan · iz · um) *n.* An organism that is so small it can only be seen under a microscope; a microbe. *A virus is a **microorganism** that cannot be seen by the naked eye.*

13. **microscope** (mī′ kruh · skōpé) *n.* Instrument used to make very small things appear larger so that they can be seen. *The **microscope** has helped scientists to observe objects too small to be seen with the naked eye.*

14. **phonetics** (fuh · net′ iks) *n.* Study of speech sounds and their production. *Many actors and actresses take courses in **phonetics** to learn how to pronounce words better.*

15. **phonics** (fon′ iks) *n.* Grapheme (written)–phoneme (sound) relationships; study of relationship between letter symbols of a written language and the sounds they represent. *Children who are good in **phonics** are able to figure out the pronunciation of many words independently.*

16. **prescription** (pri · skrip′ shun) *n.* An order; rule; direction; a doctor's written directions for the use of medicine. *Many patients may endanger their health because they fail to follow their doctor's **prescription.***

17. **script** (skript) *n.* Writing that is cursive, printed, or engraved; a piece of writing; a prepared copy of a play for the use of actors. *The actors read from the **script** only for the first rehearsal, but after that, they could not depend on any writing to help them.*

18. **scripture** (skrip′ chur) *n.* The books of the Old and New Testaments or either of them; a text or passage from the Bible; the sacred writings of a religion. *There are*

*some lawyers who quote from the Holy **Scriptures** because they feel a reference to the Bible will gain the jury's sympathy.*

19. **stethoscope** (steth′ uh · skōpé) *n.* A medical instrument used in examinations. *The doctor used the **stethoscope** to listen to his patient's heartbeat.*

20. **telegraph** (tel′ uh · graf) *n.* Instrument for sending a message in a code at a distance. *v.* To send a message from a distance. *The **telegraph** is not used as much today as it used to be because there are now faster and simpler ways to send messages from a distance.*

21. **telephone** (tel′ uh · fōné) *n.* Instrument that sends and receives sound, such as the spoken word, over distance. *v.* To send a message by telephone. *I use the **telephone** when my girlfriend is away and I want to hear the sound of her voice.*

22. **telescope** (tel′ uh · skōpé) *n.* Instrument used to view distant objects. *Standing on the roof of the Empire State Building, he used the **telescope** to view the city.*

23. **transcript** (tran′ skript) *n.* A copy or reproduction of any kind; a written or typewritten copy of an original. *The lawyer asked for a **transcript** of a court case to review what had taken place during the trial.*

SPECIAL NOTES

1. Note that in the words *telescope* and *microscope* the meaning of the words includes the term *instrument*. A telescope is an instrument that is used to view distant objects. A microscope is an instrument that is used to make small objects appear larger.

2. The word *script* can refer to typed or printed matter and also to a piece of writing, especially a prepared copy of a play or dramatic role for the use of actors. For example: **a.** *This sentence is in **script.*** **b.** *The researchers were looking for the original ancient **script.*** **c.** *The **script** for the new play was not ready.*

3. The term ***scripture*** is used chiefly in the plural with "the" (and often "Holy") and has a capital letter when it refers to the books of the Old and New Testament or to either of them—in short, the Bible.

4. The combining forms *centr, centri,* and *centro* mean "center." *Centric* means "having (something specified) as its center." See *geocentric.*

5. A TelePrompTer is a device for unrolling an enlarged script in front of a speaker on television. *TelePrompTer* is capitalized because it is a trademark.

6. The terms *study of* and *science of* are often used interchangeably.

7. Note that *graphy* in *geography* means "science."

8. *Telecommunication* means "communication from a distance" and includes such forms as telephone, cellular phones, pagers, facsimiles, and e-mail via computer. The telegraph is also a form of telecommunication, but it is almost obsolete today.

Step IV. Practice

A DIRECTIONS: A story with missing words follows. Choose a word from the word list that *best* makes sense in the story. A word may be used once only. Not all words are used.

Word List

autobiography	microbe	phonics	scripture
biography	microscope	prescription	stethoscope
biology	phonetics	script	telescope
description			

My best friend is a famous singer who has overcome many hardships in his life. It is not surprising then that someone decided to write a(n) (1)_____ of him. Actually, my friend recently decided to write his own (2)_____. I thought that it was rather vain of him to do so. After all, he is only thirty years old. I asked him what he would put in his book. He said that his life story was so interesting that it would probably be made into a movie. "I bet my movie (3)_____ will be better than most. Think about it," he said, "I majored in (4)_____ in school, and I was the one who detected that I had a life-threatening illness. I actually saw the bug I had when I looked through the (5)_____. Consequently, I was able to give my doctors a pretty good (6)_____ of it. That's what saved my life. Once they knew what I had, they gave me medicine to kill it. When I was in the hospital, I used to look at the stars through my (7)_____. What singer do you know who can name all the star constellations?"

STOP. Check answers at the end of the book (p. 338).

B DIRECTIONS: A number of sentences with a missing word follows. Choose the word that *best* fits the sentence from the word list, and write it in the blank. Not all words from the word list are used. (Some words are from Lesson 10. Also, word forms may vary; that is, the answer may be in the plural [*scripts*], or a different form of the noun may be used [*biographer*], or a noun may be changed to a verb [*describe*].)

Word List

autobiography	geography	microscope	telegraph
biography	geology	script	telephone
description	geometry	scripture	telescope

1. The graphic _____ that the victim gave of the robber helped the police capture him.

2. This well-known _____ has just finished another book about the life of one of our presidents.

3. My _____ bill is making me broke because I love to hear the voice of my boyfriend.

4. Let's hope Mike doesn't become a sailor because he couldn't tell the difference between latitude and longitude in our _____ class.

5. Many people have written their _____ and revealed how badly they were treated as children.

6. Actors and actresses have to have good memories to be able to memorize such long _____.

7. The police said that the criminal they captured had a(n) _____ in his room that he used to spy on people.

8. The doctor said that the biopsy that they studied under the _____ did not reveal any disease.

9. I needed another mathematics course, so I took an advanced _____ course.

10. Our _____ teacher said that he has been studying rock formations for twenty years.

STOP. Check answers at the end of the book (p. 338).

C DIRECTIONS: Define the underlined word in each sentence.

1. A belief system that is <u>geocentric</u> not only places the earth at the center of the universe; it also tends to overemphasize the importance of humans.

_____

2. A knowledge of <u>geometry</u> can be useful in practical areas such as architecture, gardening, and landscape design, because they all deal with lines and shapes.

_____

3. A person who is two <u>meters</u> tall would tower over most other individuals.

_____

4. We gave my mother a locket for Mother's Day and had it engraved with an <u>inscription</u>.

_____

5. Before electronic storage devices were invented, old newspapers used to be preserved on <u>microfilm</u>.

_____

6. A knowledge of <u>phonetics</u> would help an actor learn to speak with an authentic-sounding accent.

_____

7. The <u>telescope</u> on top of the main building doesn't work too well because it is low-powered and there are too many lights all around.

_____

8. Eduardo writes so fast that his notes are almost as good as <u>transcripts</u> of the lectures.

   _____

9. Most religions have <u>scriptures</u> that describe how the world came to be and how humans should behave.

   _____

10. One of the last uses of the <u>telegraph</u> were the famous singing telegrams, but now they too are gone.

    _____

11. Reading specialists now believe in using a variety of approaches to teach children to read, including <u>phonics</u> to help them sound out new words.

    _____

12. I thought <u>geology</u> was just going to be a lot of boring lectures about rocks, but I'm finding all the information about the earth's history to be fascinating.

    _____

STOP. Check answers at the end of the book (p. 338).

D **DIRECTIONS:** Write one sentence using at least two words from this lesson. The sentence must make sense. Try to illustrate the meanings of the words without actually defining them.

   ### *Example*

   I enjoy courses that deal with the earth such as *geology, geography,* and *geometry* better than those that deal with the study of living things such as *biology.*

   _____

   _____

   _____

   _____

STOP. Check answers at the end of the book (p. 339).

EXTRA WORD POWER

ar
er
or

One who; that which. Note the three different spellings. When *ar, er,* or *or* is found at the end of a word, the word concerns a person or thing. For example, *biographer*—a person who writes biographies; *killer*—one who kills; *player*—one who plays; *author*—one who writes; *beggar*—one who begs; *captor*—one who holds someone a prisoner; *prisoner*—one who is kept in prison. How many more words that end in *ar, er,* or *or* can you supply?

LESSON 12

Step I. Story in Context

DIRECTIONS: The following story includes several vocabulary words from this lesson. As you read the story, pay careful attention to the vocabulary words in boldface type, and try to figure out the meaning of each of these words. Put your answers in the blanks.

A Soccer Team's Adventure

Last August, my buddies and I traveled across the (1) **universe** _____. Let me explain. We are all members of the school soccer team, and our (2) **union** _____ has made us the best in the state. In April, our school received a (3) **telegram** _____ from a school in a country located about 4,000 miles away. The school wanted our soccer team to play its team. It was a (4) **unique** _____ opportunity. All of us wanted to go. The country, however, is run by a (5) **dictator** _____ whose views are completely (6) **contrary** _____ to ours. To go there, we needed special permission from our government. After a great amount of letter writing involving the (7) **dictation** _____ of letters from one big shot to another and telecommunicating, we were told that we would be allowed to go. We were overjoyed.

In August, we left for what seemed like the ends of the earth. When we arrived at our destination, there were soldiers in (8) **uniform** _____ waiting to greet us and young children singing "God Bless America" in (9) **unison** _____ in English. We were surprised at their excellent (10) **diction** _____. It was a rather (11) **spectacular** _____ sight. Because we do not speak their language, we had brought a special (12) **dictionary** _____ with us. As soon as the song was over, two soldiers took us on a special bus to our hotel. As we rode in the bus, we were shocked at how bleak everything looked. The (13) **contrast** _____ between their country and ours is very great. You can imagine our surprise when we saw that our hotel was luxurious and thirty stories high. Our rooms were on the twenty-fifth floor. When Bill, who has a (14) **phobia** _____ of heights, heard this, he went into a shaking fit. We tried to calm Bill, but we seemed to make matters worse. We merely were making a (15) **spectacle** _____ of ourselves. Soon we had many (16) **spectators** _____ staring at us. We explained Bill's problem to a person who spoke English. There was (17) **universal** _____ agreement that we should have our rooms changed to the first floor. This worked. Throughout our visit, we felt that everything was a (18) **contradiction** _____. We thought things would be one way, but they turned out the opposite way.

STOP. Check answers at the end of the book (p. 339).

Step II. Combining Forms

A DIRECTIONS: A list of combining forms with their meanings follows. Look at the combining forms and their meanings. Concentrate on learning each combining form and its meaning. Cover the meanings, read the combining forms, and state the meanings to yourself. Check to see whether you are correct. Now cover the combining forms, read the meanings, and state the combining forms to yourself. Check to see whether you are correct.

Combining Forms	Meanings
1. contra	against; opposite
2. dic, dict	say; speak
3. gram	something written or drawn; a record
4. phob, phobo	fear
5. spect	see; view; observe
6. uni	one

B DIRECTIONS: Cover the preceding meanings. Write the meanings of the following combining forms.

Combining Forms	Meanings
1. contra	_____
2. dic, dict	_____
3. gram	_____
4. phob, phobo	_____
5. spect	_____
6. uni	_____

Step III. Vocabulary Words Derived from Combining Forms in Context

1. **acrophobia** (ak · ruh · fō′ bē · uh) *n.* Extreme fear of high places. *You would not expect to find a person with* **acrophobia** *at the top of the Empire State Building.*
2. **claustrophobia** (klaus · truh · fō′ bē · uh) *n.* Extreme fear of being confined. *How horrible to get stuck in an elevator when you have* **claustrophobia!**
3. **contradiction** (kon · truh · dik′ shun) *n.* Something (such as a statement) consisting of opposing parts. *If I answer yes and no to the same statement, I am making a* **contradiction.**
4. **contrary** (kon′ trer · ē) *adj.* Opposite. *We disagree because his opinion is* **contrary** *to ours.*
5. **contrast** (kon′ trast) *n.* Difference between things; use of opposites for certain results. *The black chair against the white wall makes an interesting* **contrast.**
6. **dictation** (dik · tā′ shun) *n.* The act of speaking or reading aloud to someone who takes down the words. *On Monday, Mr. Chertoff sometimes loses his voice because of the great amount of* **dictation** *he gives his secretary.*
7. **Dictaphone** (dik′ tuh · fōn) *n.* A machine for recording and reproducing words spoken into its mouthpiece. *Sometimes Mr. Chertoff used a* **Dictaphone** *to record his letters for his secretary.*
8. **dictator** (dik′ tā · tur) *n.* A ruler who has absolute power; a ruler who has complete control and say. *Stalin was a* **dictator** *who had complete control over his people.*
9. **diction** (dik′ shun) *n.* Manner of speaking; choice of words. *Mrs. Martinelli's* **diction** *is so precise that no one has any difficulty in understanding her speech.*

10. **dictionary** (dik′ shuh · ner · ē) *n.* A book for alphabetically listed words in a language, giving information about their meanings, pronunciations, and so forth. *Whenever I don't know the pronunciation or meaning of a word, I look it up in the* **dictionary.**
11. **dictum** (dik′ tum) *n.* Authoritative statement; a saying. *The union leaders impressed the strikers with their* **dictum** *of nonviolence.*
12. **grammar** (gram′ mur) *n.* Study of language that deals with the forms and structure of words and their arrangement in phrases and sentences. *A knowledge of* **grammar** *helps students understand their language better.*
13. **hydrophobia** (hī · druh · fō′ bē · uh) *n.* Extreme fear of water; rabies. *I know someone who developed* **hydrophobia** *after being thrown into the water as a child.*
14. **indictment** (in · dīct′ ment) *n.* A charge; an accusation. *The jury felt that the prosecutor had enough evidence to warrant an* **indictment** *against the defendant.*
15. **phobia** (fō′ bē · uh) *n.* Extreme fear. *My friend, who has a* **phobia** *about cats, is afraid to be in the same room with one.*
16. **spectacle** (spek′ ti · kul) *n.* Something showy that is seen by many (the public); an unwelcome or sad sight. *The drunken man made a terrible* **spectacle** *of himself for the crowd of people.*
17. **spectacular** (spek · tak′ ū · lur) *adj.* Relating to something unusual, impressive, exciting, or unexpected. *The* **spectacular** *rescue of the child from the burning house was widely applauded.*
18. **spectator** (spek′ tā · tur) *n.* An onlooker; one who views something, such as a spectacle. *There were many* **spectators** *at the fair who enjoyed looking at the sights.*
19. **speculate** (spek′ yuh · lāte) *v.* To think about something; to take part in a risky business venture. *I do not like to* **speculate** *in the stock market because I like only sure things.*
20. **telegram** (tel′ uh · gram) *n.* Message sent from a distance. *The* **telegram,** *which used to be sent when the message was important, has been replaced by more direct telecommunication.*
21. **uniform** (ū′ ni · form) *adj.* Being always the same; alike. *n.* A special form of clothing. *People in the armed forces wear* **uniforms** *that have been specially designed for them.*
22. **unify** (ū′ nuh · fī) *v.* To form into one. *After the strike, it was difficult to* **unify** *the different groups because there was still resentment against those who had crossed the picket lines.*
23. **unilateral** (ū · ni · lat′ er · ul) *adj.* One-sided; done by one only. *There is a tendency today in corporations toward consensus decisions by management rather than* **unilateral** *ones by individual executives.*
24. **union** (ūn′ yun) *n.* A joining; a putting together; something formed by joining. *A labor* **union** *is a group of people who have joined together because they have similar interests and purposes.*
25. **unique** (ū′ nēk) *adj.* Being the only one of its kind. *The ancient statue found in a cave was* **unique** *because there were no others like it.*
26. **unison** (ū′ ni · son) *n.* A harmonious agreement; a saying of something together; **in unison.** *adj.* Precise and perfect agreement. *Choral groups speak in* **unison** *when they recite.*
27. **universal** (ū′ · nuh · vur′ sul) *adj.* Applying to all. *It is very hard to give* **universal** *satisfaction to people because not everyone agrees on what is satisfactory.*

28. **universe** (ū′ nuh · versé) *n.* Everything that exists; all creation, all humankind. *With space exploration, humans have made but a small probe into the vast unknown region of the* **universe.**

SPECIAL NOTES

1. The term *phobia* is usually used to refer to an extreme fear of something. For example: *The doctors tried to help the man to overcome his* **phobia** *about heights.* There are a great many phobias. Here is a list of some of them:
   a. **agoraphobia** (ag′ uh · ruh · fō · bē · uh) an extreme fear of being in open spaces or fear of leaving one's house
   b. **ailurophobia** (ī · lur′ uh · fō · bē ·uh) an extreme fear of cats
   c. **arachnophobia** (uh · rak′ nuh · fō · bē · uh) an extreme fear of spiders
   d. **astraphobia** (as′ truh · fō · bē · uh) an extreme fear of lightning
   e. **cyberphobia** (sī′ bur · fō · bē · uh) an extreme fear of working with computers
   f. **cynophobia** (sin′ ō · fō · bē · uh) an extreme fear of dogs
   g. **scotophobia** (skuh · tō′ fō · bē · uh) an extreme fear of darkness
   h. **triskaidekaphobia** (tri · skī · dek · uh · fō′ bē · uh) an extreme fear of the number 13
   (See the "Peanuts" cartoon on p. 116 to find out what phobias poor Linus has.)
2. The term *Union,* which begins with a capital letter, refers to the United States as a national unit or to any other nation that is a unit made up of several parts.
3. The combining form *gram* means *something written; a record.* However, *gram* is also a noun that refers to a measurement of weight in the metric system.
4. The plural of *spectacle* (spectacles) can also refer to eyeglasses.
5. Do not confuse *contradiction* with *contrast.* A contradiction is something that is in disagreement with itself; it is logically incongruous. For example, you cannot be here and not here at the same time. Contrast, on the other hand, deals with the differences between persons, things, ideas, events, and so forth.
6. Note that the word *dictum* is pronounced (dik′ tum) and the word *Dictaphone* is pronounced (dik′ tuh · fōné), but the word *indictment* is pronounced (in · dīt′ ment). Unfortunately, in the English language, perfect uniformity of word pronunciation does not exist. It is possible to have two words that are spelled exactly the same but are pronounced differently. Many words are spelled the same but have different pronunciations and meanings.
7. *Dictaphone* (see Lesson 12) begins with a capital letter because it is a trademark. Trademarks, which are words or symbols that are developed by owners to identify their products and are legally reserved for their exclusive use, are capitalized.
8. The combining form *cyber* refers to computers, and it is being joined to other terms such as *space* (cyberspace) and *mate* (cybermate) to form new terms. Perhaps you can generate some new terms using *cyber,* for example, *cybernaut.*

Step IV. Practice

A DIRECTIONS: State the combining form from this lesson that is used in each of the following two cartoons. Then reread the first cartoon. State in your opinion what makes it humorous.

1.

Reprinted by permission of Tribune Media Services.

1. _____

_____

_____

_____

2.

PEANUTS reprinted by permission of United Feature Syndicate, Inc.

2. _____

_____

STOP. Check answers at the end of the book (p. 339).

B **DIRECTIONS:** Fill in each blank with a word from the word list that *best* fits. Not all words from the list are used. A word may be used once only.

Word List

contradiction	phobia	unify	unison
contrary	spectacular	unilateral	universal
dictator	speculate	union	universe
dictionary	uniforms	unique	

Music was everything to Kaleb. He had organized others who also claimed that they loved music, and they practiced very long every night. Lately, however, the other members of his group were rebelling about the need to practice so much. They called Kaleb a(n) (1)_____. They said that if they belonged to a(n) (2)_____, they wouldn't have to work so hard. They claimed that no one in the (3)_____ would blame them if they left. The group chose a spokesperson who told Kaleb that the band members said that they love music too and don't want to sound (4)_____, but they didn't have the time to practice so much. They said that they didn't have a(n) (5)_____ against hard work, but enough was enough. The spokesperson said that the group didn't feel it was a(n) (6)_____ to like music but not to like to practice so much. He then asked Kaleb to look up some words in relation to music in the (7)_____.

The spokesperson said that the group felt that what Kaleb had done was great—it was (8)_____. They also all knew that it was a(n) (9)_____ experience to work with him. In addition the spokesperson said that the group even liked the (10)_____ Kaleb had them wear. However, the spokesperson said that if Kaleb continued to expect them all to work so hard every night, each and every one of the other band members would quit.

STOP. Check answers at the end of the book (p. 339).

C **DIRECTIONS:** Define the underlined word in each sentence.

1. I found an old <u>Dictaphone</u> machine at a flea market and added it to my collection of antique office machines.

   _____

2. June has a mild case of <u>claustrophobia</u>, so she avoids riding in the elevator.

   _____

3. We painted the wall dark red to provide a strong <u>contrast</u> with the white mantelpiece.

_____

4. Your <u>diction</u> is so clear that I think you could earn extra money doing radio voiceovers.

_____

5. Rabies is sometimes called <u>hydrophobia</u> because one of the symptoms is avoidance of water.

_____

6. Jerisha has the <u>telegram</u> her grandfather sent home to announce his discharge from the army after World War II.

_____

7. Evinda <u>speculates</u> that Todd and Lea are likely to break up before the end of the semester.

_____

8. To learn a language well, you must master the <u>grammar</u> as well as the vocabulary.

_____

9. The grand jury did not issue an <u>indictment</u> against the mayor for misuse of campaign funds, but people still think she is guilty.

_____

10. Before everyone had a personal computer, secretaries were very skilled at <u>dictation</u> and at typing up what the person wrote later on.

_____

11. The <u>spectators</u> seemed to enjoy the show because the participants worked frantically to make it seem easy.

_____

12. My daughter has always had <u>acrophobia</u>, so we will not visit the Empire State building when we go to New York.

_____

STOP. Check answers at the end of the book (p. 339).

D **DIRECTIONS:** Write one sentence using at least two words from this lesson. Try to illustrate the meanings of the words without actually defining them.

Example

It was a _unique spectacle_ to see the people shouting in _unison_ for the overthrow of the cruel _dictator._

_____

_____

_____

_____

STOP. Check answers at the end of the book (p. 339).

EXTRA WORD POWER

ion _sion_ _tion_	State of; act of; result of. Note the three spellings. When _ion, sion,_ or _tion_ is found at the end of a word, it means that the word is a noun. For example: _diction_—the act of speaking in a certain manner; _dictation_—the act of speaking to someone who takes it down; _question_—the act of asking; _description_—the act of describing.

SPECIAL ACADEMIC WORDS

Some new combining forms follow:

Combining Forms	Meanings
osteo	bone
zo, zoo	animal; animal kingdom or kind
ec, eco	environment
hem, hema, hemo	blood

A **DIRECTIONS:** See how well you do in figuring out the following sciences.

Words	Meanings
1. osteology	_____
2. zoology	_____
3. ecology	_____
4. hematology	_____

B **DIRECTIONS:** Now, without looking back, see how many areas of study or sciences you can remember from this chapter.

1. _____

2. _____

3. _____

4. _____

5. _____

6. _____

7. _____

STOP. Check answers at the end of the book (p. 339).

Reprinted by permission of Tribune Media Services.

CHAPTER WORDS IN A PARAGRAPH

Write a paragraph on the given topic using at least five words from this chapter. The paragraph must make sense and be logically developed.

Topic: My Autobiography

STOP. Check answers at the end of the book (p. 339).

 ## GAINING WORD POWER ON THE INTERNET

1. Choose a search engine. Write the name of the chosen search engine: _____
2. Do a search of the following two terms: *microscope, phobia.*
3. Choose one site or reference generated by your search for each term. Try to select sites that help you gain a better understanding of the terms you are researching.

   Write the chosen site for each term: _____ _____
4. Write a three-sentence paragraph on the site information for each term.
5. Log onto the Web site that accompanies this textbook for extra practice exercises at [http://www.ablongman.com/vocabulary].

STOP. Check answers at the end of the book (p. 339).

CROSSWORD PUZZLE

DIRECTIONS: The meanings of many of the combining forms from Lessons 10 to 12 follow. Your knowledge of these combining forms will help you solve the crossword puzzle. Note that *combining form* is abbreviated as *comb. f.*

Across

1. A word ending meaning "one who"
3. Past tense of the verb *have*
5. Comb. f. for *foot*

Down

1. You make this sound when you are surprised
2. To tap; strike

Across

7. Comb. f. for *life*
9. Comb. f. for *from a distance*
11. Same as #1 Across
12. Roman numeral *100*
13. Comb. f. for *something written*
16. Opposite of *night*
18. Sliced pork meat
20. Pronoun
21. Comb. f. for *a means for seeing*
23. A car you can hire to drive you somewhere
26. Opposite of *off*
27. Word meaning "on"; "near"; "by"
28. Comb. f. for *self*
30. Opposite of *out*
31. What you hang clothes on
34. Same as #1 Down

Down

4. That which one owes
6. This happens when you stop breathing
8. Comb. f. for *the study of*
10. To make a mistake
12. You will do this to your lips when they are too dry
14. An indefinite article
15. Comb. f. for *sound*
16. Comb. f. for *say*
17. Same as #14 Down
19. A pronoun
21. Plural of nouns
22. Something to sleep on
24. Same as #14 Down
25. Money that is put up to release an arrested person from jail before his trial
27. Same as #14 Down
29. Comb. f. for *one*
32. Opposite of *yes*
33. A sound that means, "What did you say?"

STOP. Check answers at the end of the book (p. 340).

ANALOGIES

DIRECTIONS: Find the word from the following list that *best* completes each analogy. There are more words listed than you need. The symbol : means "is to," and the symbol :: means "as."

Example

Brutal is to savage as viewer is to spectator.
Brutal : savage :: viewer : spectator.

Word List

annually	biography	microbe	spectacular
autograph	biped	orthography	spectator
automatic	biweekly	pedestrian	telescope
automation	contradict	phobia	transcript
automaton	contrast	podium	uniform
bicyclist	hydrophobia	prescription	unique
biennial	indictment	spectacle	unite
bifocals			

1. Riding : walking :: motorist : _____.

2. Accessory : scarf :: instrument : _____.

3. Height : acrophobia :: water : _____.

4. Hear : racket :: view : _____.

5. Solo : duet :: weekly : _____.

6. Snow : blizzard :: interesting : _____.

7. Groomed : disheveled :: common : _____.

8. Hamper : hinder :: same : _____.

9. Arrest : stop :: dais : _____.

10. Primary : first :: signature : _____.

11. Automobile : vehicle :: robot : _____.

12. Pretty : beautiful :: fear : _____.

13. Smooth : wrinkled :: agree : _____.

14. Dress : gown :: spectacles : _____.

15. Hate : detest :: join : _____.

16. Structure : grammar :: spelling : _____.

17. End : beginning :: original : _____.

18. Advice : counsel :: charge : _____.

19. One : two :: annual : _____.

20. Rule : law :: microorganism : _____.

STOP. Check answers at the end of the book (p. 340).

MULTIPLE-CHOICE VOCABULARY TEST

DIRECTIONS: This is a test on words in Lessons 10 to 12. Words are presented according to lessons. *Do all lessons before checking answers.* Underline the meaning that *best* fits the word.

Lesson 10

1. biannual
   - a. lasting for two years
   - b. yearly
   - c. occurring twice a year
   - d. occurring once a year

2. biweekly
   - a. occurring every two weeks
   - b. occurring once a week
   - c. occurring every four weeks
   - d. occurring two weeks every year

3. bimonthly
   - a. occurring every two months
   - b. occurring every month
   - c. occurring four times yearly
   - d. occurring two times yearly

4. biped
   - a. feet
   - b. two socks for feet
   - c. two-footed animal
   - d. tame animal

5. pedestrian
   - a. one who goes on foot
   - b. a foot rest
   - c. a foot doctor
   - d. refers to two feet

6. biography
   - a. life story written by oneself
   - b. a science
   - c. life story written by another
   - d. some writing

7. autograph
   - a. life story
   - b. a machine that writes
   - c. some writing
   - d. signature

8. annual
   - a. month
   - b. occurring every year
   - c. occurring every two years
   - d. occurring twice a year

9. biennial
   - a. occurring every two years
   - b. occurring twice a year
   - c. celebration of birthday
   - d. occurring once a year

10. autobiography
    - a. life story
    - b. life story written by oneself
    - c. writing machine
    - d. science of writing

11. anniversary
    - a. refers to annual
    - b. occurring every two years
    - c. yearly return of a date marking an important event
    - d. a celebration

12. annuity
  a. year
  b. yearly payment of money
  c. yearly
  d. occurring yearly

13. bifocals
  a. glasses
  b. able to focus
  c. eyeglasses with two lenses
  d. two lenses

14. bilateral
  a. sides
  b. two-sided
  c. base two
  d. two lenses

15. orthography
  a. spelling
  b. an art
  c. correct spelling
  d. a science

16. binary
  a. twofold
  b. counting
  c. refers to binds
  d. digital computers

17. graphic
  a. vivid description
  b. imagination
  c. a graph
  d. something written

18. biopsy
  a. living tissue
  b. cutting of live tissue
  c. refers to tissues
  d. cutting of live tissue for examination

19. podiatrist
  a. doctor
  b. aching foot
  c. foot doctor
  d. foot care

20. pedestal
  a. any foundation or support
  b. foot care
  c. pride
  d. esteem

21. bilingual
  a. two-sided
  b. able to speak two languages equally well
  c. two languages
  d. two

22. automation
  a. moving by oneself
  b. self
  c. a monster
  d. refers to motion

23. podium
  a. a raised platform
  b. conductor
  c. a foot
  d. a wall

24. autonomous
  a. governing
  b. self-governing
  c. refers to self
  d. motion

Lesson 11

25. biology
  a. study of earth
  b. study of people
  c. study of life
  d. science

26. geography
  a. a branch of mathematics
  b. study of the earth
  c. study of the earth's physical makeup
  d. a science dealing with the earth and its division into continents and countries and its life

27. geometry
  a. study of earth's physical makeup
  b. study of earth's surface and life
  c. a branch of mathematics
  d. measurement

28. scripture
   a. refers to any writings
   b. the Bible
   c. refers to script
   d. refers only to the Old Testament

29. script
   a. a piece of writing
   b. a part in a play
   c. a writer
   d. the Bible

30. description
   a. an account that gives a picture of something in words
   b. some writing
   c. your signature
   d. a play script

31. geology
   a. science of life
   b. study of the world
   c. a science that deals with the earth and its division into continents and countries
   d. study of the earth's physical makeup

32. telegraph
   a. instrument used to see from a distance
   b. a machine used to send messages
   c. a machine that measures distance
   d. a message

33. microscope
   a. an instrument that makes things appear small
   b. an instrument used to make small objects appear larger
   c. an instrument that grows small things
   d. something small

34. telephone
   a. a sounding machine
   b. a recording machine
   c. an instrument that sends sound at a distance
   d. an instrument that measures sound at a distance

35. telescope
   a. an instrument used to view small objects
   b. an instrument used to see large objects
   c. an instrument used for viewing distant objects
   d. an instrument used to record sound

36. geocentric
   a. earth
   b. earth as center
   c. universe
   d. center of universe

37. inscription
   a. something written
   b. something enscribed on a surface
   c. act of writing
   d. a surface

38. meter
   a. part of metric system
   b. in metric system equal to 39.37 inches
   c. about 10 feet
   d. to measure

39. microbe
   a. a bug
   b. a small bug
   c. a microorganism
   d. any organism

40. microfilm   a. very small film   c. film on which printed
                b. material is reduced   material is reduced
                                                 d. small size

41. micrometer   a. distance   c. measures size
                b. measures distance   d. instrument that measures
                                                   very small distances

42. phonetics   a. study of speech sounds   c. speech
              b. study of sound relation-   d. a study
                ships

43. phonics   a. a study   c. study of sounds
             b. study of letters and the   d. written relationships
                sounds they represent

44. prescription   a. doctor's advice   c. rule
                b. written orders   d. preparation

45. stethoscope   a. medical instrument for   c. medical instrument
                examining the heart,   d. doctor's tool
                lungs, etc.
                b. lung and heart
                examination

46. transcript   a. a copy of an original   c. something written
             b. something typed   d. grades

47. telemeter   a. an instrument   c. measuring
              b. an instrument that sends   d. distance measurer
                information to a distant
                point

Lesson 12

48. contrast   a. difference between things   c. no agreement
            b. against someone   d. against everything

49. spectacle   a. one who views something   c. something showy seen by the
            b. glasses   public
                                               d. a place to see things

50. dictator   a. a ruler   c. a person who speaks
           b. a ruler without power   d. a ruler with absolute power

51. dictation   a. act of speaking   c. act of speaking to someone
           b. act of writing   who takes down the words
                                               d. a ruler with absolute power

52. diction   a. manner of speaking   c. act of writing
          b. a ruler   d. act of speaking to someone
                                               who takes down the words

53. contrary   a. no agreement   c. use of opposites for effect
          b. opposite   d. against someone

54. contradiction
   a. something (such as a statement) consisting of opposing parts
   b. something not in complete agreement
   c. use of opposites for effect
   d. against

55. telegram
   a. a message sent from a distance
   b. a machine used to send a message
   c. something from a distance
   d. a record

56. phobia
   a. a disease
   b. refers to hate
   c. extreme fear
   d. refers to sound

57. unique
   a. only one of its kind
   b. all
   c. the same
   d. joining together

58. union
   a. all
   b. refers to only one
   c. the act of putting together
   d. complete agreement

59. universal
   a. applying to none
   b. putting together
   c. applying to all
   d. only one of a kind

60. universe
   a. complete agreement
   b. similar
   c. everything that exists
   d. together

61. unison
   a. a saying of something together
   b. manner of speaking
   c. similar
   d. all

62. dictionary
   a. study of words
   b. a book on speech
   c. a book of alphabetically listed words in a language
   d. study of speaking

63. uniform
   a. joining together
   b. clothing
   c. special form of clothing
   d. all

64. spectator
   a. one who wears glasses
   b. one who views something
   c. a place for seeing
   d. something unusual

65. spectacular
   a. person who sees things
   b. one who wears glasses
   c. a shameful sight
   d. refers to something unusual

66. acrophobia
   a. fear of heights
   b. fear of being closed in
   c. high buildings
   d. fear

67. claustrophobia
   a. fear
   b. fear of heights
   c. fear of being closed in
   d. confined places

68. hydrophobia
   a. fear of water
   b. drinking
   c. fear
   d. fear of cats

69. dictum
   a. a saying
   b. needed for a computer
   c. an authority figure
   d. knowledge

70. indictment
   a. guilty charge
   b. a charge
   c. a saying
   d. found guilty

71. unify
   a. one
   b. to make uniform
   c. to form into one
   d. complete

72. unilateral
   a. one-sided
   b. to form into one
   c. to take sides
   d. to make the same

73. speculate
   a. risky
   b. a venture
   c. take part in any risky venture
   d. to avoid risky ventures

CHAPTER TRUE/FALSE TEST

DIRECTIONS: This is a true/false test on Lessons 10 to 12. Read each sentence carefully. Decide whether it is true or false. Put a *T* for *true* or an *F* for *false* in the blank. If the answer is false, change a word or part of the sentence to make it true. The number after the sentence tells you whether the word is from Lesson 10, 11, or 12.

_____ 1. When something is done in <u>unison</u>, it is done together. 12

_____ 2. In <u>geology</u> class, you learn about plants and animals. 11

_____ 3. When something is a <u>contradiction</u> of something else, it is in agreement with it. 12

_____ 4. A <u>biographer</u> would write your autobiography. 10

_____ 5. A <u>pedestrian</u> is one who goes on a bicycle. 10

_____ 6. When something is <u>unique</u>, it is the same for all persons. 12

_____ 7. If everyone were to agree, there would be a <u>universal</u> agreement. 12

_____ 8. If I receive interest <u>biennially</u>, I receive it twice a year. 10

_____ 9. Not all animals are <u>bipeds</u>. 10

_____ 10. The <u>telescope</u> helped me to get a better view of the one-celled animals. 11

_____ 11. If you had a <u>phobia</u> concerning water, you would fear going into deep water. 12

_____ 12. A <u>spectator</u> is one who watches others. 12

_____ 13. When something is <u>spectacular</u>, it is very exciting to observe. 12

_____ 14. <u>Scripture</u> refers to a play script. 11

_____ 15. When you give your <u>autograph</u>, you are giving your life story. 10

_____ 16. A <u>dictator</u> is not an <u>autonomous</u> ruler. 10, 12

STOP. Check answers for both tests at the end of the book (p. 341).

SCORING OF TESTS

Multiple-Choice Vocabulary Test	
Number Wrong	*Score*
0–3	Excellent
4–6	Good
7–9	Weak
Above 9	Poor
Score _____	

True/False Test	
Number Wrong	*Score*
0–1	Excellent
2	Good
3–4	Weak
Above 4	Poor
Score _____	

1. If you scored in the excellent or good range on *both tests*, you are doing well. Go on to Chapter 6.
2. If you scored in the weak or poor range on either test, look below and follow directions for Additional Practice. Note that the words on the tests are arranged so that you can tell in which lesson to find them. This arrangement will help you if you need additional practice.

ADDITIONAL PRACTICE SETS

A **DIRECTIONS:** Write the words you missed on the tests from the three lessons in the space provided. Note that the tests are presented so that you can tell to which lessons the words belong.

Lesson 10 Words Missed

1. _____   6. _____
2. _____   7. _____
3. _____   8. _____
4. _____   9. _____
5. _____   10. _____

Lesson 11 Words Missed

1. _____   6. _____
2. _____   7. _____
3. _____   8. _____
4. _____   9. _____
5. _____   10. _____

Lesson 12 Words Missed

1. _____   6. _____

2. _____   7. _____

3. _____   8. _____

4. _____   9. _____

5. _____   10. _____

B DIRECTIONS: Restudy the words that you have written on this page. Study the combining forms from which those words are derived. Do Step I and Step II for those you missed. Note that Step I and Step II of the combining forms and vocabulary derived from these combining forms are on the following pages:

Lesson 10—pp. 97–103
Lesson 11—pp. 104–110
Lesson 12—pp. 111–113

C DIRECTIONS: Do Additional Practice 1 on p. 129 if you missed words from Lesson 10. Do Additional Practice 2 on p. 129 if you missed words from Lesson 11. Do Additional Practice 3 on p. 130 if you missed words from Lesson 12. Now go on to Chapter 6.

Additional Practice 1 for Lesson 10

A DIRECTIONS: The combining forms presented in Lesson 10 follow. Match the combining form with its meaning.

_____ 1. aut, auto   a. something written; machine

_____ 2. graphy   b. self

_____ 3. bio   c. life

_____ 4. graph   d. foot

_____ 5. ped, pod   e. two

_____ 6. anni, annu, enni f. year

_____ 7. bi   g. writing; drawing; writing in or on a specified subject or field; science

STOP. Check answers at the end of the book (p. 341).

B DIRECTIONS: Some of the words presented in Lesson 10 follow. Match the word with its meaning.

_____ 1. biennial   a. yearly

_____ 2. biography   b. life story

_____ 3. autobiography   c. occurring every two years

_____ 4. autograph   d. one who goes on foot

_____ 5. bimonthly   e. signature

_____ 6. biweekly   f. yearly return of a date marking an event

_____ 7. pedestrian   g. two-footed animal

_____ 8. biped   h. occurring every two weeks; occurring twice a week

_____ 9. annual   i. occurring every two months; occurring twice a month

_____ 10. anniversary   j. life story written by oneself

_____ 11. biannual   k. occurring twice a year

STOP. Check answers at the end of the book (p. 341).

Additional Practice 2 for Lesson 11

A DIRECTIONS: The combining forms presented in Lesson 11 follow. Match the combining form with its meaning.

_____ 1. tele   a. a means for seeing, watching, or viewing

_____ 2. scope   b. sound

_____ 3. geo   c. very small

_____ 4. meter   d. earth

_____ 5. micro   e. write

_____ 6. scrib, scrip   f. measure

_____ 7. phon, phono   g. from a distance

_____ 8. logy, ology   h. the study of; the science of

STOP. Check answers at the end of the book (p. 341).

B DIRECTIONS: Some of the words presented in Lesson 11 follow. Match the word with its meaning.

_____ 1. telescope   a. instrument for sending a message in code at a distance

_____ 2. geology

_____ 3. microscope

_____ 4. geography

_____ 5. geometry

_____ 6. telegraph

_____ 7. scripture

_____ 8. telephone

_____ 9. script

_____ 10. description

b. a piece of writing

c. branch of mathematics dealing with the measurement of points, lines, and planes, among other things

d. science that deals with the earth's climate, natural resources, and life

e. instrument that sends sound at a distance

f. study of the earth's physical makeup

g. instrument used to make very small objects appear larger so that they can be seen

h. instrument used for viewing distant objects

i. Bible

j. an account that gives a picture of something in writing

STOP. Check answers at the end of the book (p. 341).

Additional Practice 3 for Lesson 12

A DIRECTIONS: The combining forms presented in Lesson 12 follow. Match the combining form with its meaning.

_____ 1. spect

_____ 2. uni

_____ 3. phob, phobo

_____ 4. gram

_____ 5. contra

_____ 6. dic, dict

a. against; opposite

b. say; speak

c. one

d. fear

e. something written or drawn; a record

f. see; view; observe

STOP. Check answers at the end of the book (p. 341).

B DIRECTIONS: Some of the words presented in Lesson 12 follow. Match the word with its meaning.

_____ 1. dictionary

_____ 2. spectator

a. manner of speaking

b. being the only one of its kind

_____ 3. telegram

_____ 4. phobia

_____ 5. uniform

_____ 6. unique

_____ 7. union

_____ 8. universe

_____ 9. universal

_____ 10. unison

_____ 11. contrary

_____ 12. contradiction

_____ 13. contrast

_____ 14. dictator

_____ 15. diction

_____ 16. dictation

_____ 17. spectacle

_____ 18. spectacular

c. the act of putting together

d. something (such as a statement) consisting of opposing parts

e. everything that exists

f. applying to all

g. message sent from a distance

h. being always the same

i. extreme fear

j. act of speaking to someone who takes down the words

k. a saying of something together

l. book of alphabetically listed words in a language

m. one who views something

n. referring to something unusual; exciting

o. opposite

p. difference between things

q. something showy

r. a ruler with absolute power

STOP. Check answers at the end of the book (p. 341).

Chapter 6

LESSON 13

Step I. Story in Context

DIRECTIONS: The following story includes several vocabulary words from the lesson. As you read the story, try to figure out the meaning of each word in boldface type. Write the meaning in the space provided.

The Twentieth Century

The changes that took place in the course of the twentieth **century** (1) _____ are truly astounding. If, in the year 1900, anyone had made up a story describing what actually happened, it would not have been **credible** (2) _____. The transformation in society, in technology, and in every aspect of human life was more **incredible** (3) _____ than all of the changes that occurred in the much longer span of the preceding **millennium** (4) _____.

Social change is most obvious if you consider the change in people's everyday **deportment** (5) _____. In fact, this word itself has almost become obsolete, because the kind of formal behavior it implies is neither taught nor expected from young people today. Instead, our social **creed** (6) _____ _____ might be summed up in the statement, "Be nice to everyone, and anything goes." And since another important social change is the **export** (7) _____ of American customs and manners to other countries throughout the world, it seems as if the entire planet is becoming informal and casual in its manners. American music, fashion, and slang seem to be our most **portable** products (8) _____ .

Technology is of course another very important change. In 1900 news traveled the world quickly by telegraph and telephone. Today it is transported in **nanoseconds** (9) _____ via the Internet. Originating less than three **decades** (10) _____ ago, in the early 1980s, the net and its more colorful offshoot, the World Wide Web, unite many **millions** (11) of people around the world. Many individuals **credit** (12) the Internet with giving their first taste of freedom and knowledge to people living in brutal dictatorships around the world. It is impossible to foresee how the Internet will have evolved by the time of its **centennial** (13) _____ in the 2080s.

STOP. Check answers at the end of the book (p. 341).

Step II. Combining Forms

A **DIRECTIONS:** A list of combining forms with their meanings follows. Look at the combining forms and their meanings. Concentrate on learning each combining form and its meaning. Cover the meanings, read the combining forms, and state the meanings to yourself. Check to see whether you are correct. Now cover the combining forms, read the meanings, and state the combining forms to yourself. Check to see whether you are correct.

Combining Forms	*Meanings*
1. cent, centi	hundred; hundredth part
2. cred	believe
3. dec, deca, deci	ten; tenth part
4. kilo	thousand
5. milli	thousand; thousandth part
6. port	carry
7. nano	one-billionth part

B **DIRECTIONS:** Cover the preceding meanings. Write the meanings of the following combining forms.

Combining Forms	*Meanings*
1. cent, centi	_____
2. cred	_____

3. dec, deca, deci _____

4. kilo _____

5. milli _____

6. port _____

7. nano _____

Step III. Vocabulary Words Derived from Combining Forms in Context

1. **accreditation** (aK · kred · i · tā′ shun) *n.* A vouching for; the act of bringing into favor; a giving authority to. *If a college does not have the proper **accreditation,** students might have difficulty in getting jobs or getting into graduate schools.*
2. **bicentennial** (bī · sen · ten′ n̄ē · ul) *adj.* Pertaining to or in honor of a two hundredth anniversary; consisting of or lasting two hundred years; occurring once in two hundred years. *n.* A two hundredth anniversary. *The United States celebrated its **bicentennial** in 1976.*
3. **centennial** (sen · ten′ n̄ē · ul) *adj.* Pertaining to a period of one hundred years; lasting one hundred years. *n.* A one hundredth anniversary. *The **centennial** celebration for the United States took place in 1876.*
4. **centimeter** (sent′ uh · mēt · ur) *n.* In the metric system, a unit of measure equal to $1/100$ meter (.3937 inch). *I measured the distance in **centimeters** because I needed to know it to the nearest hundredth of a meter.*
5. **centipede** (sent′ uh · pēde) *n.* An arthropod; a wormlike animal with many legs. *The **centipede** crawled along on its many feet.*
6. **century** (sen′ chuh · rē) *n.* (*pl.* **ies**) Period of one hundred years. *A person who is 110 years old has lived more than a whole **century.***
7. **credential** (kri · den′ shul) *n.* Something that entitles one to credit or confidence; something that makes others believe in a person; a document such as a degree, diploma, or certificate; *pl.* **credentials:** testimonials entitling a person to credit or to exercise official power. *Her **credentials** for the job were so good that everyone felt that she would do the work very well.*
8. **credible** (kred′ uh · bul) *adj.* Believable. *I doubt that anyone will believe you because that is not a **credible** story.*
9. **credit** (kred′ it) *n.* Belief in something; trust; faith; good name; a recognition by name of a contribution to a performance; something that adds to a person's reputation; praise or approval; in an account, the balance in one's favor; an amount of goods or money a person receives and pays for in the future; a unit of academic study. *v.* To supply something on credit to. *Because of Mr. Brown's strong financial position, he can receive as much **credit** as he needs from the bank.*
10. **creditor** (kred′ ut · ur) *n.* One to whom a sum of money or other things are due. *Savings and loan associations are more likely to be large **creditors** to the public through home purchase loans than are commercial banks.*

11. **creed** (krēėd) *n.* A statement of belief; principles; religious belief. *The* **creed** *"All men are created equal" is found in our Constitution.*
12. **decade** (dek' ādė) *n.* Period of ten years. *I can't believe that ten years have passed and that it's already been a* **decade** *since I last saw my married brother.*
13. **decameter** (dek' uh · mēt · ur) *n.* In the metric system, a measure of length containing 10 meters. *The metric system is used in Europe, so people there have to be familiar with such terms as* **decameter.**
14. **decimal** (des' uh · mul) *adj. n.* Numbered by tens; based on ten; a decimal fraction. *Most of the world's currency uses the* **decimal** *system, which divides the prime unit of money (such as dollars) into tenths or hundredths.*
15. **decimate** (des' uh · mātė) *v.* To destroy a tenth part of; to destroy but not completely. *If you have to lose a battle, it is better to be* **decimated** *than obliterated because in the former case, nine-tenths of your troops will survive.*
16. **decimeter** (des' uh · mēt · ur) *n.* In the metric system, a unit of length equal to $1/10$ meter. *A decimeter is approximately 4 inches, so it would take about 3* **decimeters** *to equal 1 foot.*
17. **deportment** (dē · port' ment) *n.* Conduct; behavior; the manner of conducting or carrying oneself. *Because his* **deportment** *has always been above question, everyone is confused by his present behavior.*
18. **export** (ek · sport') *v.* To carry away; to transport or send something to another country. *n.* Something that is exported. *The United States* **exports** *wheat to many nations.*
19. **import** (im · port') *v.* To carry in; to bring in goods from another country. *n.* Something that is imported. *The United States* **imports** *coffee from South America.*
20. **incredible** (in · kred' uh · bul) *adj.* Not believable. *It is not believable that you could have gotten yourself into such an* **incredible** *situation.*
21. **kilobyte** (kil' uh · bītė) *n.* A unit of storage capacity in a computer system; loosely 1,000 bytes. *Drew's computer has more* **kilobytes** *than mine, so he doesn't have to worry about storage capacity in his computer system.*
22. **kilometer** (kil' uh · mēt · ur) *n.* In the metric system, a unit of length equal to 1,000 meters. *There are approximately 1.6* **kilometers** *to a mile.*
23. **millennium** (mil · len' nė · um) *n.* (*pl.* **niums, nia**) Period of one thousand years; a one thousandth anniversary; a period of great happiness (the millennium). *When the* **millennium** *arrives, there will be great happiness on earth.*
24. **millimeter** (mil' uh · mēt · ur) *n.* In the metric system, a unit of length equal to $1/1,000$ meter. *Microorganisms are even smaller than a* **millimeter.**
25. **million** (mil' yun) *n.* One thousand thousands (1,000,000); a very large or indefinitely large number. *adj.* Being one million in number; very many; 1,000 thousands. *A* **million** *years equals ten thousand centuries.*
26. **nanosecond** (nan'ō · sek · und) *n.* One billionth of a second. *The term* **nanosecond** *is used a lot when people are exaggerating.*
27. **port** (port) *n.* Place to or from which ships carry things; place where ships may wait. *When a ship comes to* **port,** *its cargo is usually unloaded immediately.*
28. **portable** (port' uh · bul) *adj.* Can be carried; easily or conveniently transported. **Portable** *goods are those that can be easily taken from one place to another.*

SPECIAL NOTES

1. The combining forms *deci* meaning "tenth part," *centi* meaning "hundredth part," and *milli* meaning "thousandth part" are used in terms belonging to the metric system (*decimeter, centimeter, millimeter*).
2. The combining form *dec, deca* may also be spelled *dek, deka*.
3. The combining form *hect* or *hecto* means "hundred." In the metric system, *hectometer* is a unit of measure equal to 100 meters.
4. The combining form *giga* means "one billion."
5. A *bit* is a unit of computer information; one byte equals 8 bits of data; usually, 2 bytes equals one word.
6. A gigabyte equals approximately one billion bytes.
7. The term *cyber* refers to computers, and it is being joined to other terms such as *space* (cyberspace) and *mate* (cybermate) to form new terms. Perhaps you can generate some new terms using *cyber*, for example, *cybernaut*.

Step IV. Practice

A **DIRECTIONS:** State the meaning of the word *credit* as it is used in the cartoon. Also, explain what makes this cartoon humorous.

Reprinted by permission of Tribune Media Services.

STOP. Check answers at the end of the book (p. 341).

B **DIRECTIONS:** A few paragraphs with missing words follow. Fill in the blanks with the word that *best* fits. Words may be used more than once. Not all words are used.

Word List

centimeter	credit	decimeter	million
centipede	creed	export	nanosecond
credential	decade	import	port
credible	decameter	incredible	portable

As a reporter for a large newspaper, I am always looking for a good story. Approximately nine and one-half years ago, almost a whole (1)_____ ago, a lot of drugs were stolen right under the noses of the police. Only people with proper (2)_____s were allowed to deal with the drugs. It just did not seem possible that the drugs could be stolen. It seemed (3)_____. The amount of money that was involved was said to be thousands of dollars—over a(n) (4)_____ dollars.

Recently, (5)_____ for this (6)_____ robbery was given to insiders who had proper police (7)_____s. The informer's story about the robbery is a(n) (8)_____ one, and everyone seems to believe it. It seems that individuals with (9)_____s were able to get into the place where the drugs were stored. They placed the drugs on a(n) (10)_____ table and walked out with them. They replaced the drugs with a mixture of sugar and salt. The robbers then took the drugs to a(n) (11)_____, where they had a ship waiting for them. The drugs were (12)_____ed to another country. When things quieted down, the drugs were (13)_____ed to the United States and sold for (14)_____s of dollars.

STOP. Check answers at the end of the book (p. 341).

C DIRECTIONS: Write one sentence using at least two words from this lesson. The sentence must make sense. Try to illustrate the meanings of the words without actually defining them.

Example

The reporter said that the spectacular rescue was considered the most *incredible* in this *century.*

_____

_____

_____

_____

STOP. Check answers at the end of the book (p. 341).

EXTRA WORD POWER

able **ible**	Can do; able. When *able* or *ible* is found at the end of word, the word is an adjective meaning "able" or "can do." For example: *portable*—able to be carried; *incredible*—not able to be believed; *credible*—able to be believed; *manageable*—able to be managed; *laughable*—able to be laughed at; *enjoyable*—able to be enjoyed. How many more *able* or *ible* words can you think of ?

LESSON 14

Step I. Story in Context

DIRECTIONS: The following story includes several vocabulary words from this lesson. As you read the story, pay careful attention to the vocabulary words in boldface type, and try to figure out the meaning of each of the words. Put your answers in the blanks.

Carlos's Dream

Carlos had lived in an (1) **autocracy** _____ all his life. The (2) **monarchy** _____ in which he lived was ruled by a cruel and selfish (3) **autocrat** _____. The king had supreme power, and no one dared to defy him. The people lived in poverty while the king lived in a spectacular palace. Every week, the king gave speeches to the people. He would stir up their emotions and make it seem as though he were doing things for them. However, everyone knew that he was doing everything for his own selfish good. The king was a (4) **demagogue** _____. The people knew this, but they could do nothing. The king had complete control, and everyone was afraid to do anything. Also, the king had the people believing that if he were not in control, there would be (5) **anarchy** _____.

Carlos had heard stories of a country where people were free and ruled the government. The stories said that the people had a form of government called a (6) **democracy** _____. Carlos dreamed of one day leaving his small country and going there. He felt that it was better to be an (7) **alien** _____ than to live in your own country under such terrible conditions. Carlos talked about his feelings to his friends, but this (8) **alienated** _____ him from them. They were afraid to be seen with him. They told him that he had to stop talking the way he did. Even his family was afraid that Carlos would get them into trouble. They wanted Carlos to change his name, that is, to take an (9) **alias** _____. Carlos was not an (10) **atheist** _____, nor did he know much about (11) **theology** _____. However, he said that he was sure that God would not have wanted them to live the way they did. When people heard this, they said that he did not believe in God. Carlos was (12) **alienated** _____ even more from his friends and family. Centuries ago, this small country had been a (13) **theocracy**

_____, and the people were still very religious. They felt that things were the way they were because God willed it so. Carlos did not feel this way. One day he would show them.

STOP. Check answers at the end of the book (p. 342).

Step II. Combining Forms

A **DIRECTIONS:** A list of combining forms with their meanings follows. Look at the combining forms and their meanings. Concentrate on learning each combining form and its meaning. Cover the meanings, read the combining forms, and state the meanings to yourself. Check to see whether you are correct. Now cover the combining forms, read the meanings, and state the combining forms to yourself. Check to see whether you are correct.

Combining Forms	*Meanings*
1. agog, agogue	leading, directing, inciting
2. ali	other
3. arch, archy, cracy, crat	chief; ruler; rule; government
4. dem, demo	people
5. glot	language
6. mon, mono	one
7. olig, oligo	few
8. theo	God

B **DIRECTIONS:** Cover the preceding meanings. Write the meanings of the following combining forms.

Combining Forms	*Meanings*
1. agog, agogue	_____
2. ali	_____
3. arch, archy, cracy, crat	_____
4. dem, demo	_____
5. glot	_____
6. mon, mono	_____
7. olig, oligo	_____
8. theo	_____

Step III. Vocabulary Words Derived from Combining Forms in Context

1. **alias** (ā′ lē · us) *n.* (*pl.* **ses**) Another name taken by a person, often a criminal. *Persons who use* ***aliases*** *don't want others to know what their real names are.*
2. **alien** (ā′ lē · un) or (āl′ yun) *n.* A foreigner; a person from another country. *adj.* Foreign. *If* ***aliens*** *in the United States neglect to register as aliens, they may be deported to their country of origin.*

3. **alienate** (āl′ yun · āt*ē*) *v.* To make others unfriendly to one; to estrange (to remove or keep at a distance). *The politicians try not to* **alienate** *any voters.*

4. **anarchy** (an′ ar · kē) *n.* No rule; disorder; the absence of government; chaos. *In the West, years ago,* **anarchy** *existed in many towns because there were no laws.*

5. **apodal** (ap′ uh · dul) *adj.* Without feet. *The snake is an* **apodal** *animal.*

6. **archetype** (ar′ ki · tīp*ē*) *n.* The original pattern or model from which something is made or developed. *The Magna Carta, written in 1218 in England, is the* **archetype** *for the national and state constitutions of the United States.*

7. **atheist** (ā′ thē · ist) *n.* One who does not believe in the existence of God. *An* **atheist** *does not believe in the existence of God.*

8. **autocracy** (aw · tok′ ruh · sē) *n.* A form of government in which one person possesses unlimited power. *In any* **autocracy,** *the head of government has absolute control of the country.*

9. **autocrat** (aw′ tuh · krat) *n.* A ruler who has absolute control of a country. *The head of government who has absolute control in an autocracy is called an* **autocrat.**

10. **demagogue** (dem′ uh · gog*ē*) *n.* A person who stirs up the emotions of people in order to become a leader and achieve selfish ends. **Demagogues** *are usually highly persuasive speakers who play on the emotions of the crowds for their own ends.*

11. **democracy** (de · mok′ ruh · sē) *n.* A form of government in which there is rule by the people either directly or through elected representatives. *In a* **democracy,** *the people, through their voting power, have a say in who the leaders of the government will be.*

12. **demography** (de · mog′ ruh · fē) *n.* Statistical study of human populations, including births, deaths, and so on. *Demographers study the* **demography** *of a population to determine the trends of vital statistics.*

13. **monarchy** (mon′ ar · kē) *n.* A government or state headed by a single person, who is usually a king, queen, or emperor: called absolute (or despotic) when there is no limitation on the monarch's power and constitutional (or limited) when there is such limitation. *Although England is a* **monarchy,** *the king or queen does not exercise any power at all.*

14. **monoglot** (mon′ uh · glot) *n. adj.* A person who speaks and writes in one language only. *There are probably more* **monoglots** *in the United States than in Europe because Europe does not have a single dominant language.*

15. **monophobia** (mon · uh · fō′ bē · uh) *n.* Extreme fear of being alone. *I can't imagine a person who suffers from* **monophobia** *living alone in the mountains.*

16. **monopoly** (muh · nop′ uh · lē) *n.* (*pl.* **ies**) Exclusive control of commodity in a given market; control that makes possible the fixing of prices and elimination of competition. *Because the company had a* **monopoly** *on the grain market, they were able to charge whatever they wanted for grain.*

17. **monorail** (mon′ uh · rāil) *n.* A single rail serving as a track for cars suspended from it. *When you ride on the* **monorail** *at Walt Disney World, everything on the ground appears to be quite small.*

18. **monotone** (mon′ uh · tōn*ē*) *n.* Speech that has no change in pitch; speech in an unvaried tone. *When a lecturer speaks in a* **monotone,** *listeners have difficulty paying attention to what is being said.*

19. **monotonous** (mo · not′ uh · n*ø*us) *adj.* Dull; uniform; no variety; changeless. *Doing the same things over and over again is very* **monotonous.**

20. **oligarchy** (ol' uh · gar · kē) *n.* (*pl.* **ies**) A form of government in which a few rule. *Oligarchy, as a form of government, usually fails because each of the rulers generally competes with the others to try to gain more power for himself or herself.*
21. **theocracy** (thē · ok' ruh · sē) *n.* Government by a religious group. *A country ruled by the clergy (persons allowed to preach the gospel) would be called a **theocracy.***
22. **theology** (thē · ol' uh · jē) *n.* The study of religion. *Ministers, priests, and rabbis must take courses in **theology** to learn about religion.*

SPECIAL NOTES

1. The word *demagogue* is a little more difficult to define even though you know the meanings of the combining forms. A *demagogue* is a person who stirs the emotions of people to become a leader and gain selfish ends. A *demagogue* appeals usually to popular passion, especially by making extravagant promises or charges. This word is used to refer to leaders who use people for their own ends. *Hitler is probably one of the most hated demagogues of the twentieth century.*
2. The word *autocrat* means "a ruler in absolute control." An *autocrat* does not have to be a king or a queen. The word *autocracy* means "government by an autocrat." A *monarchy*, which is ruled by a monarch, be it a king, queen, or emperor, does not have to be an autocracy; that is, a country can have a king or a queen, but the king or queen does not necessarily have absolute control of the government. The king or queen usually gains his or her position by inheritance and retains it for life.
3. When the combining form *arch* is the final element of a word, it means "rule." When *arch* is used at the beginning of a word (such as *archbishop, archfiend*), it means "chief."
4. The combining form *crat* means "ruler" in the word *autocrat*. Crat also means "a participant or supporter of a form of government," as in *democrat*.

Step IV. Practice

A DIRECTIONS: Using the combining forms that follow, build a word from this lesson to fit the blank in each sentence.

Combining Forms

agog, agogue	glot
ali	mon, mono
arch, archy, cracy, crat	olig, oligo
dem, demo	theo

1. His real name is Jack Smith, but he often uses a(n) _____ such as Giacomo Fabricciatore.

2. Ever since Ali became chair of the membership committee, she has behaved like a(n) _____.

3. There are very few absolute _____ left in the world today.

4. Lady Macbeth is the _____ for all evil, domineering women in literature.

5. I have learned a great deal about the world's religions in my comparative _____ course.

6. Professor Ruiz gives very interesting lectures, but his assignments are all alike, so I find them to be _____.

7. A few strong rulers who vie with one another to take control can quickly turn a committee into a(n) _____.

8. Because we do not emphasize foreign languages in our schools, many Americans grow up to become _____.

9. It is often the case that a person whose parents are _____ and who grows up without any religion turns out to be very religious as an adult.

10. To avoid _____ her liberal friends, Marta tried to avoid talking about her new conservative views.

11. A(n) _____, moving on tracks high about the buildings, is a good way to provide transportation in a densely built central city.

12. Some people believe that anything is preferable to a state of _____, even a dictatorship.

STOP. Check answers at the end of the book (p. 342).

B **DIRECTIONS:** A number of sentences with missing words follow. Underline the word that *best* fits the sentence. Two choices are given for each sentence.

1. When there are no laws or government, a state of (autocracy, anarchy) usually exists.
2. Huey Long, a former governor of Louisiana, was known to be a(n) (autocrat, demagogue) because he was able to stir people's emotions to achieve his own selfish ends.
3. In a (monarchy, democracy), there is rule by the people directly or through elected representatives.
4. A monarchy that is also a(n) (theocracy, autocracy) is one in which the ruler has supreme and unlimited power.
5. A country that is headed by a king, a queen, or an emperor is called an absolute (democracy, monarchy) when there are no limitations on the ruler's powers.
6. A person who does not believe in the existence of God is called an (atheist, anarchist).

7. An (atheist, autocrat) is a ruler who has absolute power in his or her government.
8. Roberto used an (autograph, alias) when he didn't want people at the hotel to recognize his famous name.
9. Every year, (autocrats, aliens) living in the United States must register as citizens of another country.
10. Malik never (alienates, describes) anyone on purpose because he doesn't like to have enemies.
11. In a(n) (autocracy, theocracy), God is recognized as the ruler.

STOP. Check answers at the end of the book (p. 342).

C **DIRECTIONS:** Write one sentence using at least two words from this lesson. The sentence must make sense. Try to illustrate the meanings of the words without actually defining them.

> **Example**
> The *alien* used an *alias* when he discussed his leader who is an *autocrat* and a *demagogue*.

_____

_____

_____

STOP. Check answers at the end of the book (p. 342).

EXTRA WORD POWER

a	Without; not. *A* is used in front of some words and means "without" or "not." For example: *anarchy*—without rule; *atheist*—one who is without belief in God; *amoral*—without morals; without being able to tell right from wrong. *Those that bombed buildings filled with people are amoral because they do not know right from wrong.* The people in this sentence are *amoral*. An amoral person does not have a sense of right or wrong. However, an *immoral* person does know the difference between right and wrong but chooses to do wrong.

LESSON 15

Step I. Story in Context

DIRECTIONS: The following story includes several vocabulary words from this lesson. As you read the story, pay careful attention to the vocabulary words in boldface type, and try to figure out the meaning of each of these words. Put your answers in the blanks.

Marriage and State Legislatures

In our society, the state (1) **legislatures** _____ have passed many laws concerning marriage. For example, many states have outlawed the marriage of (2) **homosexuals** _____, that is, the marriage of people of the same sex. All states have outlawed the practice of having more than one spouse at the same time. (3) **Monogamy**_____, not (4) **bigamy** _____ or (5) **polygamy** _____, is legal. Some people joke about the many marriages and divorces of certain well-known people and claim that this is really legalized (6) **polygamy** _____. However, it isn't. These people do not have many spouses at the same time. Even though (7) **bigamy** _____ is not (8) **legal** _____, there are some people who do have more than one spouse at the same time. There have been a number of cases in which a person has been married to as many as a dozen spouses at the same time.

It's incredible that some of these people were able to get away with it for so long. You certainly can't call such a person a (9) **misanthrope** _____. The person's problem may be that he or she loves people too much. It is difficult to make a (10) **general** _____ statement about the people who are (11) **bigamists** _____. They are not a (12) **homogeneous** _____ group of people. For example, there was recently a case of a (13) **polygamist** _____ who was married to five women at the same time. When he was asked why he did this, he said that it made him feel good to make others happy. Another example is that of a woman who had studied (14) **anthropology** _____ all her life. She felt that if in other cultures people could have more than one spouse, she could too. She used the word "you" a lot and said that she was speaking in the (15) **generic** _____ sense. She also used (16) **homographs** _____ often. She seemed to be highly educated and verbal. Her husbands obviously found her quite attractive and interesting. When they found out that she was a (17) **polygamist** _____, each of them wanted to stay married to her.

STOP. Check answers at the end of the book (p. 342).

Step II. Combining Forms

A DIRECTIONS: A list of combining forms with their meanings follows. Look at the combining forms and their meanings. Concentrate on learning each combining form and its meaning. Cover the meanings, read the combining forms, and state the meanings to yourself. Check to see whether you are correct. Now cover the combining forms, read the meanings, and state the combining forms to yourself. Check to see whether you are correct.

Combining Forms	*Meanings*
1. anthrop, anthropo	man; human; mankind
2. gamy	marriage
3. gen, geno	race; kind; descent
4. gon	figure having (a specified number of) angles
5. heter, hetero	different, other
6. hom, homo[1]	same; man; human
7. leg, legis, lex	law
8. mis, miso[1]	hate; wrong
9. morph	form
10. morphic	having (a specified) form or shape
11. poly	many

B **DIRECTIONS:** Cover the preceding meanings. Write the meanings of the following combining forms.

Combining Forms   *Meanings*

1. anthrop, anthropo _____

2. gamy _____

3. gen, geno _____

4. gon _____

5. heter, hetero _____

6. hom, homo _____

7. leg, legis, lex _____

8. mis, miso _____

9. morph _____

10. morphic _____

11. poly _____

---

[1]When words combine with *mis* in this lesson, *mis* means "hate." When words combine with *homo* in this lesson, *homo* means "same." You will meet words with the other meanings for *mis* and *homo* in Lessons 17 and 18 in Chapter 7.

Step III. Vocabulary Words Derived from Combining Forms in Context

1. **anthropoid** (an′ thruh · poid) *adj. n.* A person resembling an ape either in stature, walk, or intellect; resembling man, used especially of apes such as orangutans and gorillas; suggesting an ape. *The gorilla, orangutan, and chimpanzee are* ***anthropoids.***

2. **anthropology** (an · thruh · pol′ uh · jē) *n.* The study of humankind; the study of the cultures and customs of people. *In* ***anthropology*** *we studied about a tribe of people who had an entirely different way of life from ours.*

3. **anthropomorphic** (an · thruh · pō · mor′ fik) *adj.* Giving human shape or characteristics to animals, objects, etc. *In Walt Disney films, all of the animals have* ***anthropomorphic*** *characteristics.*

4. **bigamy** (big′ uh · mē) *n.* Marriage to two spouses at the same time. *Because* ***bigamy*** *is not allowed in the United States, you will not find many persons who are married to two spouses at the same time.*

5. **bisexual** (bī · sek′ shū · ul) *adj. n.* Of both sexes; having male and female organs; is true in some plants and animals; a person sexually attracted by both sexes. *Because some plants are* ***bisexual,*** *they can fertilize themselves to reproduce the next generation.*

6. **genealogy** (jē · nē · al′ uh · jē) *n.* (*pl.* **ies**). A tracing of one's ancestors; the study of one's descent. *Mrs. Smith went to England to acquire certain documents that would help her in tracing the* ***genealogy*** *of her family.*

7. **general** (jen′ ur · ul) *adj.* Referring to all. *n.* In the U.S. Army and Air Force, an officer of the same rank as an admiral in the U.S. Navy. *The statement "All men are equal" is a* ***general*** *statement.*

8. **generate** (jen′ uh · rāte) *v.* To produce; to bring into existence. *Every animal* ***generates*** *its own species or kind.*

9. **generic** (juh · ner′ik) *adj.* Referring to all in a group or class. *When one uses the term* man *in the* ***generic*** *sense, one is referring to both males and females.*

10. **genus** (jē′ nus) *n.* A class, kind, or group marked by shared characteristics. (*pl.* **genera**) (jen′ uh · ruh) *In biology, when plants or animals are classified according to common characteristics, the name of the* ***genus*** *begins with a capital letter.*

11. **heterogeneous** (het · ur · uh · jē′ nē · us) *adj.* Mixed; consists of unlike things or ingredients. *I have always been in* ***heterogeneous*** *classes rather than homogeneous ones.*

12. **homogeneous** (ho · muh · jē′ nē · øus) *adj.* Being the same throughout; being uniform. *Alfredo feels that it is difficult to have a* ***homogeneous*** *group of students because students are not all the same.*

13. **homograph** (hom′ uh · graf) *n.* A word that is spelled the same way as another but has a different meaning and/or pronunciation. *Alfredo recognizes that the verb* saw *and the noun* saw *and the verb* refuse *and noun* refuse *are* ***homographs.***

14. **homosexual** (hō · muh · sek′ shū · ul) *adj.* Referring to the same sex or to sexual desire for those of the same sex. *n.* A homosexual individual. *A* ***homosexual*** *is one who prefers a relationship with an individual of the same sex.*

15. **legal** (lē′ gul) *adj.* Referring to law; lawful. *Although the deal was made between* ***legal*** *businesses, it did not sound lawful to me.*

16. **legislature** (lej′ is · lā · chur) *n.* Body of *people* responsible for lawmaking. *The **legislature** is the body of people who are given the power to write laws for a state or nation.*
17. **misanthrope** (mis′ an · thrōpé) *n.* Hater of humankind. *Although Alfredo does not like women, he is not a **misanthrope** because he doesn't hate all people.*
18. **misogamist** (mi · sog′ uh · mist) *n.* Hater of marriage. *Although Alfredo has never married, I do not think he is a **misogamist.***
19. **monogamy** (muh · nog′ uh · mē) *n.* Marriage to one spouse at one time. *In the United States, **monogamy** is practiced, so you can be married to only one spouse (husband or wife) at one time.*
20. **polygamy** (puh · lig′ uh · mē) *n.* Marriage to one spouses at the same time. *Because **polygamy** is allowed in some Middle Eastern countries, you will find some persons with many spouses in such countries.*
21. **polyglot** (pol′ ē · glot) *adj. n.* Speaking or writing many languages. *Linguists are generally **polyglots.***
22. **polygon** (pol′ ē · gon) *n.* A closed plane figure with several angles and sides. *In geometry, I always had difficulty solving problems involving **polygons** because they have so many angles.*

SPECIAL NOTES

1. The term *generic* means "general," "referring to all in a group or class." People use the word *generic* to make their statements more clear. For example: *I am speaking in the **generic** sense when I use the word* mankind *because* mankind *refers to both males and females.* When the word *chairman* is used, it is used in the *generic* sense; that is, a person can be chairman and be either a man or a woman. Today the word *chairperson* is used more often because it is more general.
2. A *homograph* is a word that is written the same way as another but has a different meaning and/or pronunciation. *General* and *general* are two words in this exercise that are homographs because they are spelled alike but have different meanings.
3. The word *homophone* is made up of the combining forms *homo* (same) and *phon* (sound). Homophones are words that are pronounced the same but have different spellings and meanings. For example, *to, too, two; pair, pear.*
4. There are two kinds of polygamy: *Polygyny* is the marriage of one man to two or more women at the same time, and *polyandry* is the marriage of one woman to two or more men at the same time. (You will meet the combining form *gyn,* meaning "woman," in Lesson 20 in Chapter 8.)
5. Bigamy is unlawful polygamy.
6. *Gon* will help you figure out many mathematical terms; for example, a *decagon* is a ten-sided figure with ten angles. (See "Special Academic Words" on p. 152 for more words with *gon.*)

Step IV. Practice

A **DIRECTIONS:** State the meaning of the word *generic* in the cartoon. Then explain why the cartoon is a good illustration of the term *generic*.

Reprinted by permission of Tribune Media Services.

_____

_____

_____

STOP. Check answers at the end of the book (p. 342).

B **DIRECTIONS:** Choose the word from the list below that best completes each sentence. Not all words will be used.

Word List

anthropology	general	heterogeneous	legislature
anthropomorphic	generate	homogeneous	misanthrope
bisexual	generic	homosexual	polyglot
geneology	genus	legal	

1. Men who are _____ often prefer to be referred to by the term "gay."

2. All three of these plants belong to the same _____ , but because they are different species, they look quite different.

3. Most flowering plants are dioecious, or in everyday terms, they have both male and female sex organs and are therefore _____ .

4. The science of _____ can be used to study not only so-called primitive people but also our own culture.

5. If our publicity campaign can _____ enough interest, we will show some interesting foreign films on Thursday nights.

6. Michael learns foreign language very easily, so he is becoming a real _____ .

7. Your ideas about taxes may be perfectly _____, but I don't think they are ethical.

8. My friends and I like the fact that we are a very _____ group, with many different backgrounds and interests.

9. People tend to attribute _____ feelings to their pets, believing their animal companions to be just like themselves.

10. More and more people are tracing their family _____ by learning as much as possible about their ancestors.

11. The state _____ passed a law allowing adult children to be covered by their parents' health insurance policies until the age of 25.

12. It is a _____ rule that people who have a great deal of power are reluctant to give it up.

STOP. Check answers at the end of the book (p. 342).

C DIRECTIONS: Write one sentence using at least two words from this lesson. The sentence must make sense. Try to illustrate the meanings of the words without actually defining them.

Example

The *polygamist* who has three wives is obviously not against marriage, and he certainly does not believe in *monogamy.*

_____

_____

_____

STOP. Check answers at the end of the book (p. 342).

EXTRA WORD POWER

ist

One who. When *ist* is found at the end of a noun, it means "one who" and changes the word to a certain type of person. For example: let's add *ist* to a number of words you have met: *geologist*—one who is in the field of geology; *biologist*—one who is in the field of biology; *anthropologist*—one who is in the field of anthropology; *bigamist*—one who is married to two spouses at the same time; *polygamist*—one who is married to many spouses at the same time; *monogamist*—one who believes in or practices monogamy; *anarchist*—one who believes that there should be no government; *podiatrist*—one who is in the field of podiatry. How many more words with *ist* can you add to this list?

SPECIAL ACADEMIC WORDS

Some new combining forms follow:

Combining Forms	Meanings
tri	three
tetra	four
penta	five
hexa	six
septa	seven
octa	eight

A DIRECTIONS: See how well you do in figuring out the following mathematical terms.

Words	Meanings
1. trigon	_____
2. tetragon	_____
3. pentagon	_____
4. hexagon	_____
5. septagon	_____
6. octagon	_____

B DIRECTIONS: Without looking back, see how many metric system terms you can remember from this chapter.

1. _____
2. _____
3. _____
4. _____
5. _____
6. _____

STOP. Check answers at the end of the book (p. 342).

CHAPTER WORDS IN A PARAGRAPH

Write a paragraph on the given topic using at least five words from this chapter. The paragraph must make sense and be logically developed.

Topic: Life in the Twenty-First Century: My View

STOP. Check answers at the end of the book (p. 342).

CROSSWORD PUZZLE

DIRECTIONS: The meanings of many of the combining forms from Lessons 13 to 15 follow. Your knowledge of these combining forms will help you solve the following crossword puzzle. Note that *combining form* is abbreviated as *comb. f.*

Across

1. A small word that refers to a position
3. A small word that means "in the same manner"
5. Comb. f. for *ten*
8. A monkey
9. A musical syllable
10. In poker, the stake put up before dealing the cards
11. Comb. f. for *kind* or *species*
13. Same as #9 Across
15. Refers to yourself
16. Part of a shoe
18. Comb. f. for *mankind*
24. Same as #8 Across
26. Twenty-first letter of the alphabet
27. Comb. f. for *one*
28. Opposite of *men*
30. Same as #7 Down

Down

1. Abbreviation for *advertisement*
2. Comb. f. for *from a distance*
3. Abbreviation for *apartment*
4. Meaning of *spect*
6. A container
7. Comb. f. for *without*
8. An indefinite article
10. Same as #7 Down
11. Word meaning *class; kind; group*
12. Fifteenth letter of the alphabet
13. Supports oneself against something
14. A high mountain
15. An informal way of referring to mother
16. Comb. f. for *man; same*
17. Fifth letter of the alphabet
19. Refers to an explosive
20. A greeting
21. Eighteenth letter of the alphabet
22. Sound made when you are hurt

31. A piece of wood that supports a sign
33. Opposite of *gain*
34. Refers to a kind of metal
37. Sound made to quiet someone
38. Comb. f. for *marriage*
41. Twentieth letter of the alphabet
42. Opposite of *yes*
43. Meaning of *uni* and *mono*

23. Comb. f. for *many*
25. What you do when you are hungry
26. Opposite of *down* (pl.)
29. The ending of *highest*
32. An exclamation of surprise
35. Opposite of *out*
36. A negative answer
38. Opposite of *stop*
39. Same as #8 Down
40. Same as #15 Across

STOP. Check answers at the end of the book (p. 343).

 GAINING WORD POWER ON THE INTERNET

1. Choose a search engine. Write the name of the chosen search engine: _____

2. Do a search of the following two terms: *democracy, millennium.*

3. Choose one site or reference generated by your search for each term. Try to select sites that help you gain a better understanding of the terms you are researching. Write the chosen site for each term: _____

   _____

4. Write a three-sentence paragraph on the site information for each term.

5. Log onto the Web site that accompanies this textbook for extra practice exercises at [http://www.ablongman.com/vocabulary].

STOP. Check answers at the end of the book (p. 343).

ANALOGIES

DIRECTIONS: Find the word from the following list that *best* completes each analogy. There are more words listed than you need.

Word List

alias	arch	centimeter	decade
alien	archetype	century	decameter
alienate	atheist	credential	decimal
anarchy	autocracy	credit	decimate
anthropoid	bigamy	creditor	export
anthropology	cent	deca	incredible

millennium	million	podiatrist	polygon
milli	penny	polyglot	reporter
millimeter	physician		

1. Scientist : biologist :: doctor : _____.

2. Mono : poly :: monoglot : _____.

3. Millimeter : centimeter :: meter : _____.

4. Vehicle : automobile :: writer : _____.

5. Pepper : spice :: hexagon : _____.

6. Milli : cent :: cent : _____.

7. Pedestal : base :: foreigner : _____.

8. Two : binary :: ten : _____.

9. Democracy : autocracy :: import : _____.

10. None : universal :: credible : _____.

11. Decade : century :: century : _____.

12. Beautiful : pretty :: obliterate : _____.

13. One : ten :: decade : _____.

14. Conduct : deportment :: disorder : _____.

15. Earth : geology :: man : _____.

16. Genus : kind :: model : _____.

17. Week : fortnight :: monogamy : _____.

18. Same : unique :: debtor : _____.

19. Glasses : spectacles :: separate : _____.

20. Suit : clothing :: degree : _____.

STOP. Check answers at the end of the book (p. 343).

MULTIPLE-CHOICE VOCABULARY TEST

DIRECTIONS: This is a test on words in Lessons 13 to 15. Words are presented according to lessons. *Do all lessons before checking answers.* Underline the meaning that *best* fits the word.

Lesson 13

1. accreditation
   a. refers to credit
   b. a vouching for
   c. an act
   d. believable

2. bicentennial
a. one thousand years
b. a two hundredth anniversary
c. one hundred years
d. period of great happiness

3. centennial
a. two thousand years
b. one thousand thousands
c. one thousand years
d. a hundredth anniversary

4. centimeter
a. in metric system
b. equal to 10 meters
c. to measure
d. equal to $1/100$ meter

5. centipede
a. an animal
b. a worm
c. wormlike animal
d. wormlike animal with many legs

6. century
a. a hundredth anniversary
b. period of one hundred years
c. period of ten years
d. period of one thousand years

7. credential
a. good name
b. owe money
c. something that entitles someone to credit or confidence
d. believable

8. credible
a. good faith
b. a balance
c. good name
d. believable

9. credit
a. balance in one's favor in an account
b. owe money
c. believable
d. something that gives someone authority

10. creditor
a. a lender
b. a buyer
c. one to whom money is due
d. a note of credit

11. creed
a. a religious belief
b. a religious person
c. a person of good faith
d. faith

12. decade
a. period of ten years
b. one hundred years
c. twenty years
d. one thousand years

13. decameter
a. ten meters
b. metric system
c. $1/10$ meter
d. to measure

14. decimal
a. refers to tenth
b. any fraction
c. based on ten
d. $1/10$ meter

15. decimate
a. to destroy but not completely
b. to completely destroy
c. to annihilate
d. to wipe out

16. decimeter
a. refers to metric system
b. 100 meters
c. ten meters
d. $1/10$ meter

17. deportment
a. conduct
b. manners
c. carrying things
d. washing oneself

18. export
a. carry in goods
b. carry out goods to other areas or countries
c. able to be carried
d. one who carries things

19. import
   a. able to be carried
   b. place where ships wait
   c. to carry out goods
   d. to carry in goods from other areas or countries

20. incredible
   a. believable
   b. not faithful
   c. not a good reputation
   d. not believable

21. kilobyte
   a. refers to computers
   b. refers to metric system
   c. 1,000 bytes
   d. storage

22. kilometer
   a. a unit of length
   b. 1,000 meters
   c. refers to the metric system
   d. 100 meters

23. millennium
   a. 1,000 thousands
   b. period of two thousand years
   c. period of great happiness
   d. a hundredth anniversary

24. millimeter
   a. refers to the metric system
   b. 1,000 meters
   c. a unit of length
   d. $1/_{1000}$ meter

25. million
   a. one thousand thousands
   b. period of one thousand years
   c. period of one hundred years
   d. period of great happiness

26. nanosecond
   a. refers to seconds
   b. one billionth of a second
   c. a small time period
   d. 1,000 seconds

27. port
   a. to carry out
   b. to carry in
   c. place where ships may wait
   d. able to be carried

28. portable
   a. carry in goods
   b. able to be carried
   c. carry out goods
   d. one who carries things

Lesson 14

29. monarchy
   a. rule by many
   b. rule by a few
   c. rule by king, queen, or emperor
   d. absolute rule

30. autocracy
   a. absolute rule
   b. rule by one
   c. rule by a few
   d. no rule

31. autocrat
   a. one who does not believe in rule
   b. absolute ruler
   c. ruler who shares power
   d. one who does not believe in God

32. anarchy
   a. without belief in God
   b. no rule
   c. absolute rule
   d. rule by one

33. atheist
   a. one who believes in no rule
   b. one who believes in absolute rule
   c. one who believes in rule by a religious group
   d. one who does not believe in God

34. demagogue
   a. ruler of people
   b. rule by the people
   c. leader who influences persons for own purposes
   d. leader of people

35. alias
   a. a foreigner
   b. unfriendly
   c. another name
   d. turns people away

36. alien
   a. another name
   b. a foreigner
   c. turns people away
   d. unfriendly

37. alienate
   a. make others unfriendly
   b. a foreigner
   c. another name
   d. makes friends

38. theocracy
   a. belief in God
   b. rule by a religious group
   c. the study of religion
   d. absolute rule

39. theology
   a. rule by a religious group
   b. belief in God
   c. absolute rule
   d. the study of religion

40. democracy
   a. absolute rule
   b. leader who influences persons for own purposes
   c. rule by the people
   d. the study of people

41. apodal
   a. refers to feet
   b. no feet
   c. a snake
   d. walking

42. archetype
   a. first
   b. original show
   c. first of its kind
   d. to model

43. demography
   a. refers to statistics
   b. refers to birth
   c. statistical study of populations
   d. the study of statistics

44. monoglot
   a. refers to language
   b. unvaried speech
   c. one speech
   d. refers to one language

45. monophobia
   a. fear of one
   b. fear
   c. fear of being alone
   d. fear of heights

46. monopoly
   a. refers to competition
   b. one thing
   c. control of commodity
   d. no variety

47. monorail
   a. a suspension system
   b. one rail serving as a track
   c. refers to transportation
   d. one rail

48. monotone
   a. one tone
   b. refers to speech
   c. speaking in unvaried tone
   d. speech

49. monotonous
   a. dull
   b. refers to one
   c. one tone
   d. refers to speech

50. oligarchy
   a. refers to a few
   b. a form of government
   c. refers to government
   d. government in which a few rule

Lesson 15

51. monogamy
    a. hater of marriage
    b. no belief in marriage
    c. marriage to one spouse at one time
    d. the study of marriage

52. bigamy
    a. something not lawful
    b. marriage to two spouses at the same time
    c. having been married twice
    d. marriage to one spouse at one time

53. polygamy
    a. marriage to many spouses at one time
    b. many marriages
    c. something not legal
    d. the study of many marriages

54. misanthrope
    a. hater of marriage
    b. married to a man
    c. hater of humankind
    d. the study of humankind

55. anthropology
    a. marriage to men
    b. the study of humankind
    c. a science
    d. hater of humankind

56. general
    a. referring to the same
    b. referring to all
    c. referring to a group of people
    d. referring to kinds of people

57. generic
    a. referring to all in a group or class
    b. referring to people
    c. referring to a group
    d. referring to generals in the army

58. anthropoid
    a. person resembling an ape
    b. human form
    c. walk
    d. giving human shape to apes

59. anthropo-morphic
    a. resembling an ape
    b. giving human shape to animals
    c. refers to apes
    d. animals

60. bisexual
    a. of both sexes
    b. attracted to two people
    c. sexually attractive
    d. plants and animals

61. genealogy
    a. refers to genes
    b. tracing of one's ancestors
    c. the study of genes
    d. a study or science

62. generate
    a. to cause
    b. exist
    c. to produce
    d. study of genes

63. genus
    a. a characteristic
    b. shared characteristic
    c. a class marked by shared characteristics
    d. a class

64. heterogenous
    a. other
    b. refers to a characteristic
    c. mixed kind
    d. one of a kind

65. misogamist
    a. marriage
    b. hater of marriage
    c. wrong marriage
    d. refers to hatred

66. polyglot
   a. refers to speech
   b. able to speak and write
   c. many languages
   d. speaking and writing many languages

67. polygon
   a. a closed plane figure
   b. a triangle
   c. closed plane figure with several sides and angles
   d. a rectangle

68. legal
   a. person responsible for law
   b. body of people responsible for lawmaking
   c. lawful
   d. a person who defends others

69. legislature
   a. lawful
   b. person responsible for laws
   c. body of people responsible for lawmaking
   d. persons who defend others

70. homosexual
   a. same kind
   b. referring to a man
   c. one who prefers relationships with the same sex
   d. one who prefers relationships with the opposite sex

71. homogeneous
   a. being of the same kind
   b. the same sex
   c. referring to man
   d. one who prefers relationships with the same sex

72. homograph
   a. the study of man
   b. the study of graphs
   c. the same word
   d. a word spelled the same as another but having a different meaning

CHAPTER TRUE/FALSE TEST

DIRECTIONS: This is a true/false test on Lessons 13 to 15. Read each sentence carefully. Decide whether it is true or false. Put a *T* for *True* or an *F* for *False* in the blank. If the statement is false, change a word or words to make it true. The number after the sentence tells you in which lesson the word appears.

_____ 1. A centipede is an animal that has scales and lays eggs. 13

_____ 2. A century is longer than a decade. 13

_____ 3. A centimeter is larger than a millimeter. 13

_____ 4. Demography is the study of democracy. 14

_____ 5. A speaker who talks in a monotone is monotonous. 14

_____ 6. The customs of a foreign country often seem alien to visitors. 14

_____ 7. A straight line is a kind of polygon. 15

_____ 8. The words "there," "their," and "they're" are <u>homographs</u>. 15

_____ 9. A <u>genus</u> is a larger grouping than a species. 15

_____ 10. A <u>legislature</u> decides whether something is <u>legal</u>. 15

_____ 11. A <u>misanthrope</u> would probably not be a very nice person. 15

_____ 12. A <u>demagogue</u> is likely to establish a <u>democracy</u>. 14

_____ 13. A constitutional <u>monarchy</u> places limits on the ruler's power. 14

_____ 14. A <u>monorail</u> runs on two tracks. 14

_____ 15. A <u>monopoly</u> has many competitors. 14

_____ 16. A <u>bicentennial</u> would occur one hundred years after a <u>centennial</u>. 13

_____ 17. The person who gets a job is usually the one with the best <u>credentials</u>. 13

_____ 18. A story that is believable is <u>credible</u>. 13

_____ 19. If you <u>credit</u> a report, you distrust it. 13

_____ 20. The United States <u>imports</u> goods to other countries. 13

_____ 21. A <u>misogamist</u> would probably have several spouses. 15

_____ 22. Apes and humans are <u>anthropoids</u>. 15

_____ 23. Both <u>bigamy</u> and <u>polygamy</u> are illegal. 15

_____ 24. A person who suffers from <u>monophobia</u> would be afraid of crowds. 14

STOP. Check answers for both tests at the end of the book (p. 344).

SCORING OF TESTS

Multiple-Choice Vocabulary Test	
Number Wrong	*Score*
0–3	Excellent
4–6	Good
7–9	Weak
Above 9	Poor
Score _____	

True/False Test	
Number Wrong	*Score*
0–1	Excellent
2–3	Good
4–5	Weak
Above 5	Poor
Score _____	

1. If you scored in the excellent or good range on *both tests,* you are doing well. Go on to Chapter 7.
2. If you scored in the weak or poor range on either test, look below and follow directions for Additional Practice. Note that the words on the test are arranged so that you can tell in which lesson to find them. This arrangement will help you if you need additional practice.

ADDITIONAL PRACTICE SETS

A **DIRECTIONS:** Write the words you missed on the tests from the three lessons in the space provided. Note that the tests are presented so that you can tell to which lessons the words belong.

Lesson 13 Words Missed

1. _____   6. _____
2. _____   7. _____
3. _____   8. _____
4. _____   9. _____
5. _____   10. _____

Lesson 14 Words Missed

1. _____   6. _____
2. _____   7. _____
3. _____   8. _____
4. _____   9. _____
5. _____   10. _____

Lesson 15 Words Missed

1. _____   6. _____
2. _____   7. _____
3. _____   8. _____
4. _____   9. _____
5. _____   10. _____

B **DIRECTIONS:** Restudy the words that you have written on this page. Study the combining forms from which those words are derived. Do Step I and Step II for those you missed. Note that Step I and Step II of the combining forms and vocabulary derived from these combining forms are on the following pages.

Lesson 13—pp. 134–140
Lesson 14—pp. 140–145
Lesson 15—pp. 146–151

C DIRECTIONS: Do Additional Practice 1 on this page and p. 164 if you missed words from Lesson 13. Do Additional Practice 2 on pp. 164–165 if you missed words from Lesson 14. Do Additional Practice 3 on pp. 165–166 if you missed words from Lesson 15. Now go on to Chapter 7.

Additional Practice 1 for Lesson 13

A DIRECTIONS: The combining forms presented in Lesson 13 follow. Match the combining form with its meaning.

_____ 1. cent, centi	a. thousand
_____ 2. dec, deca, deci	b. hundred; hundredth part
_____ 3. milli	c. believe
_____ 4. port	d. thousand; thousandth part
_____ 5. cred	e. ten
_____ 6. kilo	f. carry

STOP. Check answers at the end of the book (p. 344).

B DIRECTIONS: Sentences containing the meanings of some vocabulary words presented in Lesson 13 follow. Choose the word that *best* fits the meaning of the word or phrase underlined in the sentence.

Word List

bicentennial	credible	imports	port
centennial	credits	incredible	portable
century	decade	millennium	porter
credentials	export	million	reporter

_____ 1. It is <u>not believable</u> that you are able to do all that.

_____ 2. In <u>a period of one hundred years</u>, many changes have taken place in the United States.

_____ 3. What do you call <u>the place where a ship waits</u>?

_____ 4. <u>The one hundredth anniversary</u> of the first space capsule's landing on the moon will be 2069.

_____ 5. When complete peace comes to earth, a period of great happiness will exist.

_____ 6. That is a believable statement.

_____ 7. How many academic units have you earned toward your degree?

_____ 8. One thousand thousands is a large number.

_____ 9. The man's college degree and work experiences helped him to get the job.

_____ 10. I will meet you in a nanosecond.

_____ 11. My television set is on a movable table.

_____ 12. She is a person who gathers information and writes articles for the magazine.

_____ 13. When will you take the goods out of the country?

_____ 14. The year 1976 was the two hundredth anniversary of the United States.

_____ 15. Every year, the United States brings into the country many goods made by foreign countries.

_____ 16. In a ten-year period, clothing styles may change from one extreme to another.

STOP. Check answers at the end of the book (p. 344).

Additional Practice 2 for Lesson 14

A DIRECTIONS: The combining forms presented in Lesson 14 follow. Match the combining form with its meaning.

_____ 1. agog, agogue   a. chief; ruler; rule; government

_____ 2. arch, archy, cracy, crat   b. other

_____ 3. ali   c. God

_____ 4. dem, demo   d. leading, directing, inciting

_____ 5. mon, mono   e. few

_____ 6. theo   f. one

_____ 7. glot   g. people

_____ 8. olig, oligo   h. language

STOP. Check answers at the end of the book (p. 344).

B **DIRECTIONS:** A number of sentences with missing words follow. Fill in the blank with the word that *best* fits.

Word List

alias	anarchy	autocrat	monarchy
alien	atheist	demagogue	theocracy
alienate	autocracy	democracy	theology

1. You will _____ a lot of people by the way you are acting.

2. Because I did not want to be recognized when I traveled, I wore a disguise and used a(n) _____.

3. A(n) _____ is a person who belongs to another country.

4. In a(n) _____, a king or queen may be at the head of government but not necessarily have any power.

5. A(n) _____ has absolute power in his or her country.

6. I would not like to live in a(n) _____ because one does not have any freedom to disagree with the ruler.

7. The form of government in the United States is a(n) _____ whereby all persons age eighteen and over have the right to vote and the government is ruled by the people through elected representatives.

8. In a state of _____, there is confusion because there are no laws.

9. A(n) _____ would not be a churchgoer because he or she does not believe in the existence of God.

10. A(n) _____ existed in the Middle Ages when the Church ruled a large part of Europe.

11. Persons who study _____ are interested in religion.

12. Hitler is a good example of a(n) _____ because he could stir persons' emotions and get them to do what he wanted.

STOP. Check answers at the end of the book (p. 344).

Additional Practice 3 for Lesson 15

A **DIRECTIONS:** The combining forms presented in Lesson 15 follow. Match the combining form with its meaning.

_____ 1. mis, miso   a. figure having (a specified number of) angles

_____ 2. poly   b. different; other

_____ 3. gamy   c. kind; race, descent

_____ 4. hom, homo   d. having (a specified) form or shape

_____ 5. gen, geno   e. form

_____ 6. anthrop, anthropo   f. man; human; mankind

_____ 7. leg, legis, lex   g. same; man; human

_____ 8. heter, hetero   h. many

_____ 9. morph   i. law

_____ 10. gon   j. marriage

_____ 11. morphic   k. hate, wrong

STOP. Check answers at the end of the book (p. 344).

B **DIRECTIONS:** Some vocabulary words presented in Lesson 15 follow. Match the word with its meaning.

_____ 1. hater of mankind   a. misogamist

_____ 2. a high-ranking office in the army;   b. polyglot
          referring to all

_____ 3. marriage to many spouses at the same   c. monogamy
          time

_____ 4. marriage to one spouse at one time   d. generate

_____ 5. marriage to two spouses at the same   e. genealogy
          time

_____ 6. referring to all in a group or class   f. homogeneous

_____ 7. being of the same kind   g. misanthrope

_____ 8. lawful   h. homosexual

_____ 9. body of people who make laws   i. anthropoid

_____ 10. referring to sexual desire for the same sex j. anthropology

_____ 11. the study of humankind   k. genus

_____ 12. a word that is written in the same way   l. polygamy
          as another but has a different meaning

_____ 13. hater of marriage   m. bigamy

_____ 14. speaking and writing many   n. homograph
          languages

_____ 15. mixed kind   o.   heterogenous

_____ 16. person resembling an ape   p.   anthropomorphic

_____ 17. produce   q.   legislature

_____ 18. giving human shape to animals   r.   generic

_____ 19. a class marked by shared characteristics   s.   general

_____ 20. tracing of one's ancestors   t.   legal

STOP. Check answers at the end of the book (p. 344).

Chapter 7

LESSON 16

Step I. Story in Context

DIRECTIONS: The following story includes several vocabulary words from this lesson. As you read the story, pay careful attention to the vocabulary words in boldface type, and try to figure out the meaning of each of these words. Put your answers in the blanks.

Television and Criminals

There is an incredible show on television that is helping the police catch criminals. Last week, it featured a person who uses (1) **astrology** _____ to help police find needed (2) **evidence** _____ and wanted criminals. The astrologist, who reads the stars to forecast events, seems to have some special (3) **vision** _____. She has helped (4) **astronauts** _____ in trouble in space and (5) **aquanauts** _____ having difficulty underwater. She is often called in when the police feel (6) **impotent** _____. (7) **Science** _____ does not have an explanation as to why she has the

(8) **potential** _____ to do things that the police can't. The police call her their most (9) **potent** _____ weapon. Many people think that she is a quack, but it is (10) **evident** _____ that she does have the (11) **potential** _____ to find escaped or wanted criminals better than others. It is difficult to (12) **convene** _____ any meeting dealing with crime unless (13) **provisions** _____ have been made to have her as one of the speakers. She gives talks at numerous (14) **conventions** _____ and is seen often on television. You can see her at a time that is (15) **convenient** _____ for you because she is (16) **omnipresent** _____. This astrologist has also taken a number of (17) **astronomy** _____ courses to study the stars, planets, and space. She feels that this has helped her. She says also that she has always had an interest in (18) **aquatic** _____ animals. She claims that her large (19) **aquarium** _____ filled with exotic fish helps to calm her and sharpens her concentration. She learned certain secrets as a young child and can actually make things appear (20) **visible** _____ or (21) **invisible** _____ at will. The police feel fortunate that she is on their side.

STOP. Check answers at the end of the book (p. 344).

Step II. Combining Forms

A **DIRECTIONS:** A list of combining forms with their meanings follows. Look at the combining forms and their meanings. Concentrate on learning each combining form and its meaning. Cover the meanings, read the combining forms, and state the meanings to yourself. Check to see whether you are correct. Now cover the combining forms, read the meanings, and state the combining forms to yourself. Check to see whether you are correct.

Combining Forms	Meanings
1. aqua, aqui	water
2. astro	star
3. naut	sailor
4. omni	all
5. poten	powerful
6. sci, scio	know
7. ven, veni, vent	come
8. vid, vis	see

B **DIRECTIONS:** Cover the preceding meanings. Write the meanings of the following combining forms.

Combining Forms	*Meanings*
1. aqua, aqui	_____
2. astro	_____
3. naut	_____
4. omni	_____
5. poten	_____
6. sci, scio	_____
7. ven, veni, vent	_____
8. vid, vis	_____

Step III. Vocabulary Words Derived from Combining Forms in Context

1. **aquanaut** (ak′ wuh · nawt) *n.* One who travels underwater; a person trained to work in an underwater chamber. *Ocean explorer Jacques Cousteau had many **aquanauts** on his team who explored the wonders under the seas.*

2. **aquarium** (uh · kwar′ ē · um) *n.* A pond, a glass bowl, a tank, or the like, in which aquatic animals and/or plants are kept; a place in which aquatic collections are shown. *The aquatic plants and animals in my **aquarium** were specially chosen to make sure that they can live together.*

3. **aquatic** (uh · kwat′ ik) *adj.* Living or growing in or near water; performed on or in water. *The best swimmers performed in our **aquatic** ballet.*

4. **astrology** (uh · strol′ uh · jē) *n.* The art or practice that claims to tell the future and interpret the influence of the heavenly bodies on the fate of people; a reading of the stars. *There are a large number of people who believe in **astrology's** ability to predict their futures.*

5. **astronaut** (as′ truh · nawt) *n.* One who travels in space, that is, beyond the earth's atmosphere; a person trained to travel in outer space. *The Apollo **astronauts** shook hands with the Russian **astronauts** in space during a special space flight in 1975.*

6. **astronomy** (uh · stron′ uh · mē) *n.* The science that deals with stars, planets, and space. *When I studied **astronomy,** I used a very high-powered telescope to view the stars and planets.*

7. **convene** (kun · vēnė′) *v.* To come together; to assemble. *The members were waiting for everyone to arrive so that they could **convene** for their first meeting of the year.*

8. **convenient** (kun · vēn′ yent) *adj.* Well suited to one's purpose, personal comfort, or ease; handy. *The professional and political conventions are held in cities that have **convenient** hotels and halls to take care of a great number of people.*

9. **convention** (kun · ven′ shun) *n.* A formal meeting of members for political or professional purposes; accepted custom, rule, or opinion. *The teachers hold their **convention** annually to exchange professional views and learn about new things.*

10. **envision** (en · vizh′ un) *v.* To imagine something; to picture in the mind. *The ship-wrecked crew, who had been drifting on the raft for two days, deliriously **envisioned** a banquet.*

11. **evidence** (ev′ uh · densė) *n.* That which serves to prove or disprove something. *The **evidence** was so strong against the defendant that it didn't seem possible that he could prove his innocence.*

"I don't listen to the evidence. I like to make up my own mind."

Drawing by P. Barlow; © 1954, 1982 The New Yorker Magazine, Inc.

12. **evident** (ev' uh · dent) *adj.* Obvious; clearly seen; plain. *From everything that you have said, it is **evident** that he is lying about where he was on the night of the murder.*
13. **impotent** (im' puh · tent) *adj.* Without power to act; physically weak; incapable of sexual intercourse (said of males). *The monarch in England is politically **impotent** because he or she has hardly any power in the governing of the country.*
14. **invisible** (in · viz' uh · bul) *adj.* Not able to be seen. *In the film, the **invisible** man was able to appear in many prohibited places because no one was able to see him.*
15. **nautical** (nawt' i · kul) *adj.* Pertaining to seamen, ships, or navigation. *Because Jason has a **nautical** bent, he wants to become a sailor.*
16. **omnipotent** (om · nip' uh · tent) *adj.* All powerful. *No matter how much wealth, power, and prestige someone has, he or she is not **omnipotent.***
17. **omnipresent** (om · ni · prez' unt) *adj.* Being present everywhere at all times. *The **omnipresent** toothpaste commercial was annoying because it seemed to be on all the channels at the same time.*
18. **omniscient** (om · nish' ent) *adj.* All knowing. *With the rapid increase of knowledge, it is not possible for someone to be **omniscient.***
19. **potent** (pōt' ént) *adj.* Physically powerful; having great authority; able to influence; strong in chemical effects. *The drug was so **potent** that it actually knocked out Jossi, who is over 6 feet tall and weighs almost 200 pounds.*
20. **potentate** (pō' ten · tāté) *n.* A person possessing great power; a ruler; a monarch. *The ruler of that country is a **potentate** whom I would not want as my enemy.*
21. **potential** (puh · ten' shul) *n.* The possible ability or power one has. *adj.* Having force or power to develop. *The acorn has the **potential** to become a tree.*

22. **provision** (pruh · vizh' un) *n.* The act of being prepared beforehand; preparation; something made ready in advance; *pl.* **provisions:** needed materials, especially a supply of food for future needs; a part of an agreement referring to a specific thing. *The army was running out of necessary **provisions,** and the troops were beginning to complain that they did not have enough supplies to carry on their operations.*

23. **science** (sci' ense) *n.* Any area of knowledge in which the facts have been investigated and presented in an orderly manner. *New **sciences** develop as we learn more and more about the universe.*

24. **venture** (ven' chur) *n.* A risky or dangerous undertaking, especially a business enterprise in which there is danger of loss as well as profit. *The business **venture** involved a great amount of speculation; therefore I did not want to become a part of it.*

25. **visa** (vē' zuh) *n.* Something stamped on a passport that grants an individual entry into a country. *We need a **visa** to visit some countries.*

26. **visage** (viz' ije) *n.* The face; appearance of the face or its expression. *His wolfish **visage** warned me about what he might be thinking.*

27. **visible** (viz' uh · bul) *adj.* Able to be seen; evident; apparent; on hand. *On a clear day the skyline of the city is **visible.***

28. **vision** (vizh' un) *n.* The sense of sight. *Because the man's **vision** was blocked by the screen, he could not see what the spectators were looking at.*

29. **visionary** (vizh' un · er · ē) *n. (pl.* **ies**). A person who sees visions. *The leader of the newly formed religious group claims that he is a **visionary** who has seen visions of things to come.*

30. **visor** (vī' zor) *n.* The projecting front brim of a cap for shading the eyes. *Baseball players wear hats with **visors** because the game is often played in bright sunlight.*

SPECIAL NOTES

1. When the term *potential* is used, it refers to *possible ability*. This means that potential is something that a person may have within him or her, but it may or may not come out.

2. *Astrology* is concerned with the reading of the stars. Astrologists use the stars to try to predict the future of persons. Do not confuse astrology, which is a false science, with astronomy, which is the science that deals with the study of stars, planets, and space.

3. The term *television* comes from the combining forms *tele* and *vis*. It is an electronic system for the transmission of visual images from a distance.

4. Note that the term *study* is often used interchangeably with *science* because *science* is a branch of study that is concerned with observation and classification of facts.

Step IV. Practice

A DIRECTIONS: State the meaning of the word *evidence*. Then explain what would make a cartoon amusing using the term *evidence*.

_____

_____

_____

_____

_____

STOP. Check answers at the end of the book (p. 344).

B DIRECTIONS: A few paragraphs with missing words follow. Fill in the blanks with the words that *best* fit. Words may be used more than once. There are more words than you need. Not all words are from this lesson.

Word List

anniversary	convention	incredible	provision
aquanauts	decade	invisible	scientists
aquatic	envision	nautical	visa
astrologer	evidence	omnipresent	visage
astronauts	evident	potent	visible
convenient	impotent	potentate	visionary

As a reporter, I get to investigate and write stories. I especially remember one story I wrote about a(n) (1)_____ ago. I remember it was ten years ago because my wife and I were celebrating our first wedding (2)_____ with a special dinner when the phone rang. It was my boss. His excitement was clearly (3)_____. "Jason, did you see what just happened on television?" he asked. "No, we didn't have the television . . ." Before I could finish answering, he said, "Well, get down here immediately. I want you to cover a special story that just broke." Although it was not a(n) (4)_____ time for me, I went to meet him.

It seemed that a group of well-known (5)_____, such as biologists, geologists, and astronomers, were meeting at a national (6)_____ held in our city. At the (7)_____, there were exhibits of materials that (8)_____ had brought back from space. There were also special (9)_____ plants that (10)_____ had found underseas.

At about ten in the morning, a woman phoned the editor in the newspaper office. She said she was a(n) (11)_____ who could foretell the future. She told the editor to watch the (12)_____ exhibits that were being shown on television to people all over the country. She knew that something (13)_____ was going to take place shortly and that it would be (14)_____ to all who were watching. The editor felt that from the way the woman was talking, it was (15)_____ she was a "crackpot." He received many calls from people telling about things that would happen that never did. There are so many crackpots around that they seem to be (16)_____.

Well, at eight that night, in plain view of all who had their televisions tuned to the channel covering the exhibits, a(n) (17)_____ robbery took place. The people watching the robbery must have felt (18)_____ because they had no power to do anything about it.

People dressed as (19)_____ who were going on a space flight and as (20)_____ who were going to explore the ocean stole the priceless materials on display.

Nobody could figure out how they got into the special room. It was as if they were (21)_____ and at the proper moment they materialized and became (22)_____ for all to see. They seemed to have had all the (23)_____s they needed to carry out the robbery.

It was so well planned that no (24)_____ as to who they were or why they did it has ever been found.

STOP. Check answers at the end of the book (pp. 344–345).

C DIRECTIONS: Write one sentence using at least two words from this lesson. The sentence must make sense. Try to illustrate the meanings of the words without actually defining them.

Example

At the *convention*, a *scientist* said that he had *evidence* to prove that a drug on the market was dangerous and too *potent* for most people.

STOP. Check answers at the end of the book (p. 345).

D **DIRECTIONS:** Choose the word that *best* fits each sentence. You may have to change the form of the word (for example, astronomy, astronomer). Each word from the list below will be used no more than once, and not all words will be used.

Word List

aquanaut	envision	omnipotent
aquarium	evidence	omnipresent
astrology	evident	potential
astronomy	impotent	science
convenient	nautical	visionary

1. Since the time he received his first tiny _____ for his fifth birthday, Raul has always been fascinated with ocean plants and animals.

2. At an equally young age, his older brother Michael became entranced with the moon and planets and announced that he wanted to be a(n) _____.

3. When the two brothers got a little older, they _____ founding a society for the study of oceans on distant planets.

4. It was just a joke at the time, but Michael now points out that there is considerable _____ for the existence of oceans on several of Saturn's moons.

5. Today Michael, a college junior, has decided against becoming a _____ of any kind.

6. However, Raul, now a freshman, is still entranced with all things _____ and plans to become a Navy officer after graduating from college.

7. He hopes to become a Navy _____ and participate in underwater experiments and rescues.

8. Michael's interests now revolve around computers, which he believes have the _____ to transform society in many different ways.

9. He has many _____ beliefs about computers, such as a worldwide project that would encourage people of the future to develop and use open-source software.

10. It is _____ to Michael that this would give many more people access to computers and to the Internet.

11. Michael has unusual ideas about the power, even the _____, of computers to modern society.

12. He thinks that this power results from the way in which computers can interact with one another and with humans, not just from the fact that they are _____ in our society today.

STOP. Check answers at the end of the book (p. 345).

EXTRA WORD POWER

less	Without. When *less* is placed at the end of a word, it means "without." *Less* changes a noun into an adjective. For example: the word *mother* becomes *motherless*—without a mother; *father* becomes *fatherless*—without a father; *blame* becomes *blameless*—without blame; without fault; *harm* becomes *harmless*—without harm; without hurting. For example: *How lucky you are that you have both a mother and a father. Mary is a **motherless** child.* How many more words with *less* can you supply?
co *col* *com* *con* *cor*	Together; with. When *con* is placed at the beginning of some words, the *n* may change to an *l, m,* or *r.* The *n* in some words may be left out altogether. However, *con, com, cor, col,* and *co* all mean "together" or "with." Examples: *co-worker*—someone working with you; *convene*—come together; assemble; *convention*—a meeting where persons come together; *combine*—to join together; unite; *collect*—to gather together; *correspond*—to be equivalent; to write letters to one another.

LESSON 17

Step I. Story in Context

DIRECTIONS: The following story includes several vocabulary words from this lesson. As you read the story, pay careful attention to the vocabulary words in boldface type, and try to figure out the meaning of each of these words. Put your answers in the blanks.

A Student's Death

Last month, David a college student, fell from a ten-story building. The police did not know whether it was a (1) **suicide** _____, an accident, or a (2) **homicide** _____. The young men in the (3) **fraternity** _____ that David belonged to said that lately he had a lot of (4) **apathy** _____ toward everything; however, they didn't think he would kill himself. The police took David's (5) **corpse** _____ to the (6) **morgue** _____. Words cannot describe how David's parents felt when they had to view their son's body there. They couldn't believe that they would be contacting a (7) **mortician** _____ to handle their child's funeral.

When David's parents arrived on campus, everyone felt great (8) **sympathy** _____ for them. Of course, only those parents who have lost children in the same way could feel (9) **empathy** _____ for them. Needless to say, David's parents were in shock. They said that it couldn't be (10) **suicide** _____. They had been loving parents, and their son had been a good, moral, and religious person. It was against his religious beliefs to commit (11) **suicide** _____. David hated all violence. He didn't believe in either (12) **corporal punishment** _____ or (13) **capital punishment** _____. David would react very strongly when he read about such crimes as (14) **genocide** _____. He couldn't believe that dictators could try to wipe out a whole race or religious group of people. At the funeral, the priest said that David was a sensitive (15) **mortal** _____, and even though he was dead, his soul would be (16) **immortal** _____. The (17) **mortality** _____ of each person was certain, but David's death was too soon. His parents and friends sobbed uncontrollably. They kept saying that he had so much to live for. He was going to work in a large (18) **corporation** _____ or bank. He had studied about various economic systems and was very knowledgeable of our economic system, (19) **capitalism** _____. He had done very well in courses dealing with (20) **mortgages** _____ and finance. He had hoped one day to (21) **incorporate** _____ all his background and experiences and start his own firm. David's death was a tragedy.

STOP. Check answers at the end of the book (p. 345).

Step II. Combining Forms

A **DIRECTIONS:** A list of combining forms with their meanings follows. Look at the combining forms and their meanings. Concentrate on learning each combining form and its meaning. Cover the meanings, read the combining forms, and state the meanings to yourself. Check to see whether you are correct. Now cover the combining forms, read the meanings, and state the combining forms to yourself. Check to see whether you are correct.

Combining Forms	*Meanings*
1. capit	head
2. cide	murder; kill
3. corp, corpor	body
4. em, en	into; in
5. frater, fratr	brother
6. mors, mort	death
7. pathy	feeling; suffering
8. syl, sym, syn	same; with; together; along with

B **DIRECTIONS:** Cover the preceding meanings. Write the meanings of the following combining forms.

Combining Forms	Meanings
1. capit	_____
2. cide	_____
3. corp, corpor	_____
4. em, en	_____
5. frater, fratr	_____
6. mors, mort	_____
7. pathy	_____
8. syl, sym, syn	_____

Step III. Vocabulary Words Derived from Combining Forms in Context

1. **amortize** (am or · tiz*é*) *v.* The gradual extinction of a debt such as a mortgage. *The accountant **amortized** the plant's machinery on a twenty-year schedule.*
2. **apathy** (ap' uh · thē) *n.* Lack of feeling; indifference. *Rasheed had such **apathy** regarding the sufferings of people around him that he didn't care one way or the other what happened to the hurt people.*
3. **capital** (kap' uh · tul) *n.* City or town that is the official seat of government; money or wealth; first letter of a word at the beginning of a sentence. *adj.* Excellent. *The **capital** of the United States is Washington, D.C.*
4. **capitalism** (kap' uh · tul · iz · um) *n.* The economic system in which all or most of the means of production, such as land, factories, and railroads, are privately owned and operated for profit. *Because **capitalism** is practiced in the United States, individuals in this country privately own and operate their businesses for profit.*
5. **capital punishment** (kap' uh · tul pun' ish · ment) *n.* The death penalty. ***Capital punishment** has been outlawed in many countries because it is believed that the death penalty is a punishment too extreme.*
6. **capitulate** (kuh · pich' uh · lāt*é*) *v.* Surrender; to give up. *With the criminal gang surrounded by the police and having no possible means of escape, they had no choice but to **capitulate**.*
7. **caption** (kap' shun) *n.* The heading of a chapter, section, or page in a book; a title of a picture. *By reading chapter **captions**, I am able in a very short time to gain some idea about the chapter.*
8. **corporal punishment** (kor' puh · rul pun' ish · ment) *n.* Bodily punishment; a beating. *Because New Jersey is a state that outlaws **corporal punishment** in the schools, it is illegal for teachers to hit students.*
9. **corporation** (kor · puh · rā' shun) *n.* A group of people who get a charter granting them as a body certain of the powers, rights, privileges, and liabilities (legal responsibilities) of an individual, separate from those of the individuals making up the group. *We formed a **corporation** so that we would not individually be liable (legally responsible) for the others.*
10. **corpse** (korps*é*) *n.* Dead body. *After the detectives examined the **corpse**, they were told that there was another dead body in the next room.*

11. **corpulent** (kor′ pū · lent) *adj.* Fleshy, fat, obese. ***Corpulent** people usually eat a lot.*
12. **empathy** (em′ puh · thē) *n.* (*pl.* **ies**) The imaginative putting of oneself into another person's personality; ability to understand how another feels because one has experienced it firsthand or otherwise. *Michael felt **empathy** for the boy with the broken arm because that same thing had happened to him.*
13. **fraternity** (fra · tur′ nuh · tē) *n.* (*pl.* **ies**) A group of men joined together by common interests for fellowship; a brotherhood; a Greek letter college organization. *In college, I decided to join a **fraternity** so that I could make a lot of new friends.*
14. **fratricide** (frat′ ruh · sīde) *n.* Killing of a brother; may also refer to killing of sister. ***Fratricide** is an especially horrible crime because it involves the murder of a close relative.*
15. **genocide** (jen′ uh · sīde) *n.* The systematic and deliberate killing of a whole racial, ethnic, or religious group or a group of people bound together by customs, language, politics, and so on. *During World War II, Hitler attempted to commit **genocide** against the Jewish people because he wanted to wipe them out completely.*
16. **homicide** (hom′ uh · sīde) *n.* Any killing of one human being by another. *The spectator witnessed a horrible **homicide,** in which the victim was beaten to death.*
17. **immortal** (im · mor′ tul) *adj.* Referring to a being who never dies; undying. *n.* One who never dies. *Because human beings must eventually die, we are not **immortal.***
18. **incorporate** (in · kor′ puh · rāte) *v.* To unite; combine. *We decided to **incorporate** because by joining together, we could be a more potent company.*
19. **monosyllable** (mon′ uh · sil · uh · bul) *n.* A word consisting of one syllable. *The word made is a **monosyllable.***
20. **morgue** (morgue) *n.* Place where dead bodies (corpses) of accident victims and unknown people who are found dead are kept; for reporters, it refers to the reference library of old newspaper articles, pictures, and so on. *The police took the accident victim's body to the **morgue** because they could find no identification on it.*
21. **mortal** (mor′ tul) *adj.* Referring to a being who must eventually die; causing death; ending in death; very grave; said of certain sins; to the death, as mortal combat; terrible, as mortal terror. *n.* A human being. *Because he still advanced, after having been shot six times, everyone began to wonder whether he was a **mortal.***
22. **mortality** (mor · tal′ i · tē) *n.* The state of having to die eventually; the proportion of deaths to the population of the region, nation, and so on; death rate; death on a large scale, as from disease or war. *The **mortality** of children among all socioeconomic groups depends on the care that the children are given.*
23. **mortgage** (mor′ gij) *n.* The pledging of property to a creditor (one to whom a sum of money is owed) as security for payment. *v.* To put up property as security for payment; to pledge. *Most people who buy homes obtain a **mortgage** from a bank.*
24. **mortician** (mor · ti′ shin) *n.* A funeral director; undertaker. ***Morticians** are accustomed to handling corpses because their job is to prepare the dead for burial.*
25. **mortify** (mor′ tuh · fī) *v.* To cause to feel shame; to embarrass; to feel humiliation. *The minister was **mortified** that the people in his church had been involved in the riots.*
26. **suicide** (sū′ uh · sīde) *n.* The killing of oneself. *People who take their own lives often give many signs beforehand that they are thinking of **suicide.***
27. **syllable** (sil′ uh · bul) *n.* A vowel or group of letters with one vowel sound. *In the word* pilot, *which has two **syllables,** pi is the first **syllable,** and lot is the second **syllable.***

28. **symbol** (sim′ bul) *n.* Something that represents another thing; an object used to represent something abstract. *The dove is a **symbol** of peace, the cross is a **symbol** of Christianity, and the Star of David is a **symbol** of Judaism.*

29. **symmetry** (sim′ uh · trē) *n.* (*pl.* **ies**) Balanced form or arrangement; balance on both sides. *Melissa disliked the disorganized pattern because it lacked **symmetry.***

30. **sympathy** (sim′ puh · thē) *n.* (*pl.* **ies**) Sameness of feeling with another; ability to feel pity for another. *When Rolanda lost both her parents in an automobile accident, we all felt deep **sympathy** for her.*

31. **symphony** (sim′ fuh · nē) *n.* A large-scale musical composition for full orchestra; harmony of sound. *In the **symphony**, the instruments blended together in perfect harmony.*

32. **symptom** (simp′ tum) *n.* In medicine, a condition that results from a disease and as an aid in diagnosis; a sign or token that indicates the existence of something else. *The doctor said that the rash was a definite **symptom** of the disease and that there was a cure for it.*

33. **synthesis** (sin′ thuh · sis) *n.* (*pl.* **theses**) A putting together of two or more things; to form a whole. *Carmen, the architect, was told that her design must be a **synthesis** of everyone's ideas.*

SPECIAL NOTES

1. The term *homicide* is used in the generic sense. You met the term *generic* in an earlier lesson. *Generic* means "referring to all within a group." Therefore, when someone says that *homicide* is used in the generic sense, he or she means that the combining form *homo* (meaning "man" in the word *homicide*) refers to both men and women, not just to males.

2. Remember the term *misanthrope*? *Misanthrope* means "hater of humankind." When the meaning is given as "hater of mankind," it is being used in the generic sense in that *mankind* refers to both men and women.

3. There are a number of words that are derived from the combining forms *cide* with which you may be familiar. For example: *insecticide* means "an agent that destroys insects"; *germicide* means "an agent that destroys germs"; *herbicide* means "an agent that destroys or holds in check plant growth." *Patricide* is the murder of a father, and *matricide* is the murder of a mother.

4. Do not confuse *capital* with *capitol*. *Capitol* refers to the building in which a legislative body meets.

5. a. **empathy:** The imaginative putting of oneself into another in order to better understand the other; putting oneself into the personality of another. *When people feel **empathy** for another, they know how the other person feels because they have had the same experience or can imaginatively put themselves into the personality of the other.*

   b. **sympathy:** Sameness of feeling with another; ability to feel pity for another. *When you have **sympathy** for someone, you feel pity for him or her.*

You do not have to go through the same experience as the person. Empathy is a stronger feeling than sympathy. When you say that you *sympathize* with someone's views, it means that you have the same feeling about the views as the person.

6. **apathy.** Lack of feeling; indifference. *Kim felt complete apathy about the whole situation.* The term *apathy* means that someone has no feeling one way or another. Such a person is indifferent.

7. When an individual takes out a mortgage on a house, he or she uses the property as collateral. *Collateral* is the pledging of property by a borrower to protect the interests of the lender.

Step IV. Practice

A DIRECTIONS: Define the term *prediction*. Write an amusing commentary using the term *prediction*.

STOP. Check answers at the end of the book (p. 345).

B DIRECTIONS: Choose the word that *best* fits each sentence. You may have to change the form of the word (for example, apathy, apathetic). Each word from the list below will be used no more than once, and not all words will be used.

Word List

apathy	incorporate	mortify
capital	empathy	suicide
capitalism	fraternity	symbol
caption	incorporate	sympathy
corporation	mortality	symptom
corpse	mortgage	synthesis

1. Abib, a recent college graduate, went to work for a newspaper and was assigned to help cover events in the state _____.

2. At first he helped out in the newsroom, doing tasks such as writing photo _____, rewriting articles, and helping reporters with research.

3. One particularly interesting assignment was to assist a hugely _____ science reporter who needed to write a series of articles about exercise.

4. Abib, who had always been thin and athletic, had trouble _____ with the reporter, but he nevertheless helped him out all he could by trying out all the exercise regimens the man wrote about.

5. Another interesting assignment was to pose as a _____ brother at the state university campus.

6. His role was to gather information about the death, which many people believed was a _____, of a depressed student who was rejected by the Greek letter organization.

7. Many students reported that the student was shamed and _____ by the way the brothers treated him during pledge week.

8. Abib felt that the final article, which turned the dead student into a _____ of students' indifference to suffering, went too far.

9. In the course of his research, he talked to many students, including some members of the fraternity, who showed great _____ for the dead student's suffering.

10. Because he found the topic so upsetting, Abib was grad to be transferred to the business desk, where he helped write an article about a large banking _____ headquartered in the area.

11. The company was accused of making risky home _____ loans to customers with poor credit ratings.

12. Abib's research made him think that the company's shady loan practices were merely a _____ of a more widespread problem in the banking industry.

13. He began to believe that companies were able to continue their illegal practices because most people were _____ or indifferent, thinking that they themselves were not affected.

14. He suggested to the writer that she _____ some research he had found about indifference to other people's problems into the article about banking.

15. The writer took Abib's advice and wrote a series of prize-winning articles that

_____ Abib's research findings with her own information about the banking industry.

STOP. Check answers at the end of the book (p. 345).

C DIRECTIONS: Write one sentence using at least two words from this lesson. The sentence must make sense. Try to illustrate the meanings of the words without actually defining them.

Example
Did you hear that Mr. Ruggiero, who had been with our *corporation* for two decades, tried to commit *suicide* because he lost his job, his house, and all his *capital?*

_____

_____

_____

_____

STOP. Check answers at the end of the book (p. 345).

EXTRA WORD POWER

un

Not. When *un* is placed at the beginning of a word, it means "not." *Un* is used with a very great number of words. Examples: *unwed*—not married; *unaided*—not helped; *unloved*—not loved; *unable*—not able; *uncooked*—not cooked; *unclaimed*—not claimed; *uncaught*—not caught; *uncarpeted*—not carpeted. How many other words can you supply with *un*?

pre

Before. When *pre* is placed in front of a word it means "before in time" or "before in order." *Pre,* like *un,* is used with a very great number of words. Examples: *prehistoric*—referring to time before history was recorded; *pre-Christian*—referring to time before there were Christians; *prerevolutionary*—referring to time before a revolution; *preheat*—to heat before; *prejudge*—to judge or decide before; *prejudice*—an opinion or judgment made beforehand; *preunite*—to join together before; *preset*—to set before; *premature*—ripened before, developed before the natural or proper period; *predict*—to say before, to foretell, to forecast, to tell what will happen. See how many more words with *pre* you can supply. Use the dictionary to see the great number of words that begin with *un* and *pre*.

LESSON 18

Step I. Story in Context

DIRECTIONS: The following story includes several vocabulary words from this lesson. As you read the story, pay careful attention to the vocabulary words in boldface type, and try to figure out the meaning of these words. Put your answers in the blanks.

The Will

Not too long ago, there was a big court battle over the will of a very wealthy man. He owned a number of (1) **local** _____ (2) **factories** _____ that (3) **manufactured** _____ different things. In his (4) **factories** _____, everything was automated; nothing was done by (5) **manual** _____ labor. When the man died, he left all his money to his fifth wife; she was the sole (6) **beneficiary** _____ of his entire will.

Needless to say, the (7) **effect** _____ of this on his children was predictable. Their protests were certainly (8) **audible** _____; they were furious. They did not expect their father's young wife of only a few months to (9) **benefit** _____ from the will. They had expected that their father would (10) **allocate** _____ his wealth to them. They decided to contest the will. They felt that they had an (11) **effective** _____ case because of a (12) **manuscript** _____ they had found in their father's safe that was hidden in a special location on his boat. Even though the (13) **manuscript** _____ was signed with a different name, they felt that it was their father's; he had used a (14) **pseudonym** _____ before. They knew that their father often published things under another name.

In addition, the man's children received an (15) **anonymous** _____ letter from someone saying that he knew that their father had been under some big strain, which could have (16) **affected** _____ his judgment. The (17) **anonymous** _____ letter also stated that their father's latest wife was concerned about an (18) **audit** _____ of the companies' books. It said further that his latest wife had bought a lot of (19) **audiovisual** _____ equipment lately and had had an (20) **audition** _____ for a play. The writer seemed to know quite a bit about the wife. The writer said that she had performed as a go-go dancer in a certain (21) **auditorium** _____ for many different (22) **audiences** _____. The children didn't know what to make of the letter. The letter was unsigned and full of (23) **misnomers** _____, wrongly spelled (24) **homonyms** _____, and (25) **synonyms** _____ that were used as (26) **antonyms** _____ and vice versa. Clearly, the writer had it in for the wife. However, this was excellent ammunition for the children.

Most important, the (27) **manuscript** _____ that the children had found had a note in it from their father that said that he thought something strange was going on. He felt that he was slowly losing his mind. Also, he said that he intended to leave his entire fortune to his children and to his first wife, who had borne his children. He said that the other women he had been married to were more concerned about their (28) **manicures** _____ than about him. He did not want to be their (29) **benefactor** _____ because he knew that they had all married him for his money.

The children felt that their father had met with foul play. They went to the police with their evidence. The police dug up the body and did an autopsy. They found that he had died of a heart attack but that it had been brought on by a special drug. The drug had been given to him in small doses for a number of months. It turned out that his wife and her boyfriend had planned and carried out his murder.

STOP. Check answers at the end of the book (p. 345).

Step II. Combining Forms

A DIRECTIONS: A list of combining forms with their meanings follows. Look at the combining forms and their meanings. Concentrate on learning each combining form and its meaning. Cover the meanings, read the combining forms, and state the meanings to yourself. Check to see whether you are correct. Now cover the combining forms, read the meanings, and state the combining forms to yourself. Check to see whether you are correct.

Combining Forms	Meanings
1. aud, audi	hear
2. bene	good
3. cura	care
4. fac, fect, fic	make; do
5. loc, loco	place
6. man, manu	hand
7. nomin, onym	name
8. pseudo	false

B DIRECTIONS: Cover the preceding meanings. Write the meanings of the following combining forms.

Combining Forms	Meanings
1. aud, audi	_____
2. bene	_____

3. cura   _____

4. fac, fect, fic   _____

5. loc, loco   _____

6. man, manu   _____

7. nomin, onym   _____

8. pseudo   _____

Step III. Vocabulary Words Derived from Combining Forms in Context

1. **affect** (uh · fekt′) *v.* To act upon or to cause something; to influence; to produce an effect or change in. *Your poor study habits will definitely begin to **affect** your grades and cause them to go down.*
2. **allocate** (al′ uh · kāté) *v.* To set something apart for a special purpose; to divide up something; to divide and distribute something. *Each person was **allocated** a certain share of the profits according to the amount of time and work he or she had put into the project.*
3. **anonymous** (uh · non′ uh møus) *adj.* Lacking a name; of unknown authorship. *Because it is the policy of the newspaper to publish signed letters only, the **anonymous** letter was not published.*
4. **antipathy** (an · tip′ uh · thē) *n.* A dislike for someone. *Mary had great **antipathy** toward the people who had injured her brother.*
5. **antonym** (an′ tuh · nim) *n.* A word opposite in meaning to some other word. *The words* good *and* bad *are **antonyms** because they are opposite in meaning.*
6. **audible** (aw′ duh · bul) *adj.* Capable of being heard. *He spoke so softly that what he had to say was hardly **audible** to anyone.*
7. **audience** (aw′ dē · ensé) *n.* An assembly of listeners or spectators at a concert, play, speech, and so on. *The **audience** listened to the politicians' speeches to learn what their views were on the income tax.*
8. **audiology** (awd · ē · ol′ uh · jē) *n.* The study of hearing. *Selima decided to major in **audiology** in college because she wanted to help children who had hearing problems.*
9. **audiometer** (awd · ē · om′ ut · ur) *n.* An instrument used to measure hearing. *The doctor used the **audiometer** to determine whether John had a hearing problem.*
10. **audiovisual** (aw′ dē · ō · vizh′ ū · ul) *adj.* Of, pertaining to, involving, or directed at both hearing and sight. *Many teachers use **audiovisual** aids in the classroom because the added senses of seeing and hearing help in learning.*
11. **audit** (aw′ dit) *v.* To examine or check such things as accounts; to attend class as a listener. *n.* An examination of accounts in order to report the financial state of a business. *Every year, banks have their accounts **audited** to check whether everything is in order.*
12. **audition** (aw · dish′ un) *n.* A trial hearing, as of an actor or singer; the act of hearing. *v.* To try out for a part in an audition. *Carol's first **audition** for the part in the play was so successful that she was told there was no reason for them to listen to any other person.*
13. **auditorium** (aw · duh · tor′ ē · um) *n.* A building or hall for speeches, concerts, public meetings, and so on; the room in a building occupied by an audience.

*The school **auditorium** was so large that it was able to seat the entire graduating class and their parents.*

14. **benediction** (ben · uh · dik′ shun) *n.* A blessing; expression of good wishes. *At the end of the church service, the minister gave the **benediction.***

15. **benefactor** (ben′ uh · fak · tor) *n.* One who gives help or confers a benefit; a patron. *Many times, artists have **benefactors** who help to support them while they are painting.*

16. **beneficiary** (ben · uh · fish′ ē · er · ē) *n.* (*pl.* **aries**) One who receives benefits or advantages; the one to whom an insurance policy is payable. *Rachel, as the only **beneficiary** of her husband's insurance policy, did not know that she would receive all the money.*

17. **benefit** (ben′ uh · fit) *n.* That which is helpful; advantage; a payment; a performance given to raise funds for a worthy cause. *v.* To be helpful or profitable to; to receive benefit; to aid. *The actors gave a **benefit** to collect money for the needy children.*

18. **curator** (kūr · āt′ ur) *n.* Head of department in a museum; one in charge. *A good **curator** of a museum should know everything that is going on in the museum.*

19. **effect** (uh · fekt′) *n.* Something that is brought about by some cause; the result; consequence. *I told you what the **effects** of your not studying would be before the results were in.*

20. **effective** (uh · fek′ tiv) *adj.* Producing or having the power to bring about an intended result; producing results with the least amount of wasted effort. *His way of doing the job is much more **effective** than yours because it takes him so much less time to do the same amount of work.*

21. **emancipate** (i · man′ suh · pāt) *v.* To set free; to set free from slavery or servitude. *After enslaved people have been **emancipated,** they must learn how to live like free people.*

22. **facsimile** (fak · sim′ uh · lē) *n. v.* An exact copy; to make an exact copy; the transmission of graphic material by electronic means. *The police sent a **facsimile** of the mugger's face over the wire.*

23. **faction** (fak′ shun) *n.* Number of people in a group, government, party, organization, etc. having a common goal that is often self-serving and reckless of the common good. *There was a special **faction** in the union that was trying to gain power so that its members could further their own desires.*

24. **factory** (fak′ tuh · rē) *n.* (*pl.* **ies**) A building or buildings in which things are manufactured. *My mother and father work in a **factory** where automobiles are made.*

25. **homonym** (hom′ uh · nim) *n.* A word that agrees in pronunciation with some other word but differs in meaning and may differ in spelling. *The adjective* mean *and the verb* mean *are **homonyms** because they sound alike and are spelled alike but have different meanings.*

26. **local** (lō′ kul) *adj.* Referring to a relatively small area, region, or neighborhood; limited. *As a child, I always went to the **local** movie theater because it was close to where I lived.*

27. **location** (lō · kā′ shun) *n.* A place or site; exact position or place occupied; an area or tract of land; a place used for filming a motion picture or a television program (as in the expression *to be on location*). *The **location** of our picnic was perfect because it was such a scenic place.*

28. **manicure** (man′ uh · kūr) *n.* Care of the hands and fingernails. *v.* To provide care for hands and nails with a manicure; to cut closely and evenly. *Because I like my fingernails to look good, I give myself a **manicure** every week.*

29. **manipulation** (muh · nip′ yuh · lā · shun) *n.* Act of handling or operating; the act of managing or controlling skillfully by influence. *By his clever **manipulation** of all those around him, he was able to gain the position he desired.*

30. **manual** (man′ ū · ul) *adj.* Referring to the hand; made, done, or used by the hands. *n.* A handy book used as a guide or source of information. *Some people prefer **manual** labor because they like to work with their hands.*

31. **manufacture** (man · yuh · fak′ chur) *v.* To make goods or articles by hand or by machinery; to make something from raw materials by hand or machinery. *n.* The act of manufacturing. *Some very special and expensive items are still made by hand, but most goods are **manufactured** by machine on a large scale.*

32. **manuscript** (man′ yuh · skript) *adj.* Written by hand or typed; not printed. *n.* A book or document written by hand; a book written by hand or typed and usually sent for publication; style of penmanship in which letters are not joined together, whereas in cursive writing they are. *When an author sends a **manuscript** to a publisher, he or she hopes that the editor will like it.*

33. **misnomer** (mis · nō′ mur) *n.* A name wrongly applied to someone or something; an error in the naming of a person or place in a legal document. *It is a **misnomer** to call a spider an insect.*

34. **pedicure** (ped′ i · kūr∉) *n.* Care of feet, toes, and nails. *I always have a **pedicure** before I wear open sandals.*

35. **personification** (pur · son · uh · fuh · kā′ shun) *n.* A figure of speech in which human characteristics are given to non-living things. *"The clouds wept a torrent of tears that almost flooded the city," is an example of **personification**.*

36. **pseudonym** (pséū′ duh · nim) *n.* False name, especially used by an author to conceal his or her identity; pen name. *Samuel Clemens wrote under the name Mark Twain, his **pseudonym**.*

37. **pseudopodium** (pséū · duh · pō′ dē · um) *n.* (*pl.* **dia**) False foot. *Some one-celled animals have **pseudopodia**, which are used for taking in food and for movement.*

38. **pseudoscience** (pséū · dō · séí′ ens∉) *n.* A false science. *Astrology is a **pseudoscience** because it involves only the reading of the stars to foretell the future and is not based on rational principles.*

39. **synonym** (sin′ uh · nim) *n.* A word that has the same or nearly the same meaning as some other word. *The words* vision *and* sight *are **synonyms** because they have the same meaning.*

Reprinted by permission of NEA, Inc.

SPECIAL NOTES

1. Note that *alias* (a word from Lesson 14) and *pseudonym* are basically synonyms. However, the term *alias* is usually used when a criminal uses a name other than his or her own, whereas the term *pseudonym* is usually used when an author uses a name other than his or her own.

   Do not confuse *pseudonym* and *alias* with *misnomer*. The term *misnomer* refers to someone's using a wrong name or word accidentally, that is, *not on purpose*. When someone uses an *alias* or *pseudonym*, he or she is doing it *on purpose* and has not made a mistake.

   The term *anonymous* refers to someone who has not signed his or her name, so that the name of the person is unknown. When you see *anonymous* at the end of a poem or story, it means that the author is unknown.

2. *Affect* and *effect* are terms that are used a great deal. However, they are often used incorrectly. Note the way the words are used in the sentences that follow.

   a. **affect.** *v.* To act upon or to cause something; to influence. *You will probably affect your team's chances to win because you seem to have such a great influence on them.*

   b. **effect.** *n.* Something that is brought about by some cause; the result. *The effect on the team was that they won the game.*

3. *Homonym* and *homophone* are synonyms.

QUESTION: What homonym or homophone is Alex confusing with *locks?*

ALEX IN WONDERLAND   **by Bob Cordray**

© 1978 by Bob Cordray. Reprinted by permission of Bob Cordray.

ANSWER: lox (smoked salmon)

Step IV. Practice

A DIRECTIONS: State the meaning of the word *audible* in the cartoon. Then explain what makes the cartoon amusing.

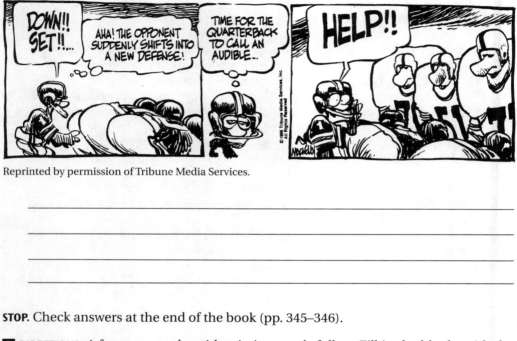

Reprinted by permission of Tribune Media Services.

_____

_____

_____

_____

STOP. Check answers at the end of the book (pp. 345–346).

B DIRECTIONS: A few paragraphs with missing words follow. Fill in the blanks with the word that *best* fits. Words may be used more than once.

Word List

audible	beneficiary	emancipate	manual
audience	benefit	factory	manufacture
audition	curator	local	pseudonym
benediction	effect	location	pseudoscience
benefactor	effective	manicure	

Because I enjoy making things and working with my hands, I don't mind (1)_____ labor even though I'm a woman. However, my parents want me to have lots of (2)_____s. They believe that the only way I can get the advantages they want me to have is by finishing college. To go to college, I work in a(n) (3)_____ in which clothing is (4)_____d on a large scale. I have no (5)_____ to help me, and I am not the (6)_____ of any rich old uncle's insurance policy.

This summer, the (7)_____ where I am working was used as the (8)_____ for a movie. It was very exciting! Every day, we had a large (9)_____ watch the making of the film. The spectators came from all over. The movie people were so (10)_____ in getting the (11)_____s they wanted for the film that very little time was wasted. When they worked, no outside sounds were (12)_____ because they told the spectators to be silent.

They were going to use a number of (13)_____ people in some of the mob scenes. Because I lived in the neighborhood, I was chosen for a(n) (14)_____. I was told that if they liked what they saw and heard, they would use me in the movie. Well, I tried to make myself look as glamorous as possible. I even decided to give my hands a(n) (15)_____.

When the day for my (16)_____ came, I was so excited that I could hardly talk. By the time I got to the (17)_____ where the test was being made, my voice was not (18)_____.

The director told all of us that we were supposed to be in a scene where we all fall into mud. Ugh! And for this, I had made myself glamorous and had given myself a(n) (19)_____! For this role, I would probably use a(n) (20)_____ rather than my real name.

STOP. Check answers at the end of the book (p. 346).

C DIRECTIONS: Write one sentence using at least two words from this lesson. The sentence must make sense. Try to illustrate the meanings of the words without actually defining them.

Example
As my grandfather's *beneficiary*, I will inherit his *local factory*, where he *manufactures* women's clothing.

_____

_____

_____

_____

STOP. Check answers at the end of the book (p. 346).

EXTRA WORD POWER

anti
Against; opposed to. *Anti,* meaning "against," is found at the beginning of a great number of words. For example: *antiwar*—against war; *antigambling*—against gambling; *antimachine*—against machines; *antimen*—against men; *antiwomen*—against women; *antilabor*—against labor. Note that *anti* changes into *ant* before words that begin with a vowel, as in *antacid*—something that acts against acid; *antonym*—a word opposite in meaning to some other word. As you can see, you can place *anti* at the beginning of a lot of words. Can you think of some words to which you might add *anti*? Use the dictionary to see the great number of words that begin with *anti*.

non
Not. When *non* is placed in front of a word, it means a simple negative or the absence of something. The number of words beginning with *non* is so large that the dictionary has them listed in a special section. Check your dictionary to see how many it has. Following are some words with *non: nonbeliever*—not a believer; *non-Arab*—not an Arab; *non-Catholic*—not Catholic; *noncapitalist*—not a capitalist; *non-Communist*—not a Communist; *noneffective*—not effective; *noncriminal*—not criminal; *non-English*—not English. How many more can you supply?

CROSSWORD PUZZLE

DIRECTIONS: The meanings of many of the combining forms from Lessons 16 to 18 follow. Your knowledge of these combining forms will help you to solve this crossword puzzle. Note that *combining form* is abbreviated *comb. f.*

Across

2. Roman numeral *five*
3. Comb. f. for *without*
4. A misanthrope is a _____ of mankind
8. Same as #1 Down
9. Squirrels eat these
12. Two-wheeler
15. Comb. f. for *place*
16. To be
17. Comb f. for *in*
18. An artificial waterway
19. Meaning of *vis; vid*
20. Comb. f. for *care*
23. Roman numeral *100*
24. Rhymes with *ham*
26. Opposite of *off*
27. Comb. f. for *hand*
30. Same as #3 Across
31. Word for *strong feeling against*
34. Same as #26 Across
35. Word for *written by hand*
41. Rhymes with *hit*
42. Comb. f. for *wrong; hate*
43. Comb. f. for *star*
45. To hand out something a little at a time
46. A period of time
48. Comb. f. for *from a distance*
50. You do this in a chair
51. Abbreviation for *advertisement*
52. A long slippery fish
53. Opposite of *friend*
54. Comb. f. for *sail*
55. Comb. f. for *powerful*
56. Comb. f. for *kill*
59. Comb. f. for *all*

Down

1. Comb. f. for *make; do*
2. Comb. f. for *come*
3. Comb. f. for *water*
4. A sound you make when you laugh
5. A monarch is a _____ of a monarchy
6. Comb. f. for *see*
7. Comb. f. for *good*
8. You put this around a picture
10. A homonym of *two*
11. Comb. f. for *know*
12. Marriage to two spouses at the same time
13. Opposite of *no*
14. Comb. f. for *without*
18. Something to sleep on
20. Comb. f. for *body*
21. Comb. f. for *not; lack of*
22. Word meaning *yearly*
23. Comb. f. for *head*
25. A way of saying *mother*
28. Comb. f. for *name*
29. Word meaning *to join*
30. Comb. f. for *hear*
31. Same as #3 Across
32. Past tense of *eat*
33. A farmer uses this tool
35. Comb. f. for *death*
36. A homonym of *sew*
37. You can do this when you put two hands together
38. When you do something again, you _____ it
39. A pronoun
40. He is a _____-ager
43. Same as #3 Across
44. Comb. f. for *same*
47. Comb. f. for *again, back*
49. Same as #15 Across
50. To be in appearance
57. Same as #39 Down
58. When you carry out an act, you _____ it

STOP. Check answers at the end of the book (p. 346).

SPECIAL ACADEMIC WORDS

Here are some of the business terms you met in this chapter:

amortized	corporation	manufacture
capital	factory	mortgage
capitalism	incorporate	

DIRECTIONS: A number of sentences with missing words follow. Choose the word that *best* fits the sentence. Put the word in the blank.

1. My family would like to buy a home, but they do not know whether they will be able to get a(n) _____.

2. I have relatives who work in a clothing _____.

3. They _____ coats there.

4. My friend, who is in business, said that he was going to _____ so that he would not have to worry about anyone suing him personally.

5. My friend said that he would be president of his _____.

6. My friend needed a lot of _____ to start his business, so he went to a bank.

7. Every time he makes a payment to the bank, his debt is _____.

8. My friend feels that _____ is the best economic system in the world.

STOP. Check answers at the end of the book (p. 346).

CHAPTER WORDS IN A PARAGRAPH

Write a paragraph on the given topic using at least eight words from this chapter. The paragraph must make sense and be logically developed.

Topic: My Goals in Life

STOP. Check answers at the end of the book (p. 346).

www GAINING WORD POWER ON THE INTERNET

1. Choose a search engine. Write the name of the chosen search engine: _____

2. Do a search of the following two terms: *astronomy, capitalism.*

3. Choose one site or reference generated by your search for each term. Try to select sites that help you gain a better understanding of the terms you are researching. Write the chosen site for each term: _____

4. Write a three-sentence paragraph on the site information for each term.

5. Log onto the Web site that accompanies this textbook for extra practice exercises at [http://www.ablongman.com/vocabulary].

STOP. Check answers at the end of the book (p. 346).

ANALOGIES

DIRECTIONS: Find the word from the following list that *best* completes each analogy. There are more words listed than you need.

Word List

affect	caption	facsimile	pedestrian
anonymous	convene	feel	potential
antipathy	convenient	genocide	pseudopodal
apathy	convention	homicide	pseudoscience
audible	corpulent	impotent	stars
audiology	creditor	love	suicide
audiometer	creed	mortify	sympathy
audition	deny	omnipotent	underwater
capital	effect	omnipresent	visage
capitulate	empathy	omniscient	

1. Astronaut : space :: aquanaut: _____.

2. Visible : evident :: everywhere: _____.

3. Incredible : credible :: potent: _____.

4. Mortal : immortal :: adjourn: _____.

5. Astronomy : science :: astrology: _____.

6. Snake : apodal :: amoeba: _____.

7. Incorporate : unite :: humiliate: _____.

8. Benediction : blessing :: heading: _____.

9. Pseudonym : alias :: face: _____.

10. Autograph : signature :: copy: _____.

11. Life : biology :: hearing: _____.

12. Vest : clothing :: fratricide: _____.

13. Deny : contradict :: fleshy: _____.

14. Symmetry : balance :: dislike: _____.

15. Assembly : meeting :: handy: _____.

16. Benefit : advantage :: indifference: _____.

17. Noise : clamor :: faith: _____.

18. Handbook : manual :: result: _____.

19. Location : site :: nameless: _____.

20. Anarchy : order :: resist: _____.

STOP. Check answers at the end of the book (p. 346).

MULTIPLE-CHOICE VOCABULARY TEST

DIRECTIONS: This is a test on words in Lessons 16 to 18. Words are presented according to lessons. *Do all lessons before checking answers.* Underline the meaning that *best* fits the word.

Lesson 16

1. potential
   a. the ability or power one may have
   b. refers to sex
   c. refers to males only
   d. refers to feeling

2. omnipresent
   a. referring to a gift
   b. referring to all
   c. referring to everyone
   d. being present everywhere at all times

3. invisible
   a. not able to be seen
   b. in disguise
   c. out of sight
   d. to view from inside

4. provision
   a. something made ready in advance
   b. something to see from a distance
   c. something to see
   d. to see for someone

5. evident
   a. obvious
   b. sense of sight
   c. able to see from a distance
   d. to view

6. evidence
   a. that which seems to prove or disprove something
   b. able to see clearly
   c. that which is seen from a distance
   d. that which shows something

7. science
   a. a knowing person
   b. able to know
   c. the sense of knowing
   d. area of ordered and investigated knowledge

8. vision
   a. able to be seen
   b. system for the transmission of visual images from a distance
   c. sense of sight
   d. easily recognized

9. visible
   a. sense of sight
   b. system for the transmission of visual images from a distance
   c. able to be seen
   d. not seen

10. convene
    a. something suitable
    b. a meeting
    c. to come together
    d. to call a special meeting

11. convention
    a. a friendly get-together
    b. a formal meeting of members for professional purposes
    c. something suitable
    d. to come together

12. convenient   a. suited to one's purpose   c. joining together
                  b. a get-together   d. a special meeting

13. potent   a. a drug   c. powerful
                  b. a perfume   d. refers to money

14. impotent   a. refers to sex   c. refers to power
                  b. without power   d. refers to males only

15. astrology   a. the study of heavenly   c. a true science
                     bodies   d. refers to stars
                  b. the reading of the
                     stars to foretell the
                     future

16. astronomy   a. the study of stars, planets   c. a true science
                     and space   d. refers to stars
                  b. the reading of the stars

17. astronaut   a. refers to space   c. one who travels underwater
                  b. refers to stars   d. one who travels in space

18. aquanaut   a. refers to undersea   c. refers to water
                  b. one who travels   d. refers to one who travels in
                     underwater   space

19. aquatic   a. referring to a water plant   c. referring to water
                  b. referring to a water flower   d. referring to undersea plants

20. aquarium   a. a water bowl   c. a globelike bowl or rectangular
                  b. refers to water   container for water plants and
                                         animals
                                         d. an area of study

21. nautical   a. ships   c. pertaining to sailors
                  b. sailors   d. pertaining to stars

22. envision   a. to see   c. to foretell events
                  b. to imagine   d. to tell what's on one's mind

23. omnipotent   a. all powerful   c. pertains to knowledge
                  b. all knowing   d. pertains to power

24. omniscient   a. all knowing   c. pertains to science
                  b. all powerful   d. pertains to studying

25. potentate   a. a person   c. someone who possesses
                  b. refers to great power   great power
                                         d. a ruler without power

26. venture   a. an enterprise   c. something dangerous
                  b. something always   d. a risky undertaking
                     profitable

27. visage   a. the face   c. a passport
                  b. your deportment   d. your sign

28. visa
   a. your passport
   b. stamped on passports
   c. something stamped
   d. stamped on passports that grants entry to a country

29. visor
   a. a cap
   b. front brim of cap
   c. a brim
   d. pertains to seeing

30. visionary
   a. pertains to vision
   b. entry to a country
   c. the front brim of a cap
   d. a person who sees visions

Lesson 17

31. homicide
   a. killing of a brother
   b. killing of oneself
   c. killing of one person by another
   d. killing of a whole group of people

32. mortal
   a. referring to death
   b. referring to a dead person
   c. referring to any dead animal
   d. referring to someone who must die

33. immortal
   a. referring to all living persons
   b. referring to all dead persons
   c. referring to death
   d. referring to a being who never dies

34. mortality
   a. dead persons
   b. death rate
   c. one who never dies
   d. one who must die

35. mortician
   a. a dead man
   b. one who must die
   c. a person who counts the dead
   d. an undertaker

36. suicide
   a. killing of oneself
   b. killing a whole group of people
   c. killing of a brother
   d. killing of one person by another

37. genocide
   a. killing of man
   b. killing of a whole racial, political, or cultural group
   c. killing of a brother
   d. killing of oneself

38. sympathy
   a. feeling sad
   b. ability to put oneself into the personality of another
   c. self-pity
   d. ability to feel pity for another

39. empathy
   a. ability to feel pity for
   b. ability to imaginatively put oneself into the personality of another
   c. self-pity
   d. feeling sad

40. apathy
   a. refers to pity
   b. self-pity
   c. lack of feeling
   d. feeling sad

41. fraternity
   a. a Greek letter college organization
   b. a brother
   c. killing of a brother
   d. refers to friends and relatives

42. capital punishment
   a. bodily harm
   b. head punishment
   c. death penalty
   d. beatings

43. capitalism
   a. refers to profit
   b. an economic system in which all or most of the means of production are privately owned
   c. an economic system in which all or most of the means of production are not privately owned
   d. an economic system in which all or most of the means of production are privately owned and operated for profit

44. capital
   a. an official seat of government
   b. relevant
   c. refers to an economic system
   d. refers to death

45. corpse
   a. a body
   b. a dead body
   c. a group of people
   d. refers to beatings

46. corporation
   a. men getting together
   b. group of people with a charter granting them certain powers, rights, and privileges of an individual
   c. a group of people with a charter granting them certain powers to rule supreme
   d. a business

47. incorporate
   a. to unite
   b. to join a club
   c. refers to a body
   d. men getting together

48. corporal punishment
   a. death penalty
   b. a beating
   c. refers to the body
   d. refers to punishment of an officer in the service

49. mortgage
   a. refers to death
   b. pledging property
   c. giving up your property
   d. pledging property to a creditor as security for payment

50. morgue
   a. refers to the dead
   b. place to keep all dead bodies
   c. an undertaker's office
   d. place where unidentified dead bodies are kept

51. caption
   a. a person's heading
   b. refers to heading
   c. a chapter
   d. the act of chopping off a person's head

52. corpulent
   a. refers to body
   b. a bodily function
   c. fleshy
   d. to give up

53. fratricide
   a. a killing
   b. may include sisters
   c. refers to a brother
   d. the killing of a brother

54. monosyllabic
   a. refers to syllables
   b. a one-syllable word
   c. refers to the number one
   d. a word

55. mortify
   a. death
   b. to be dead
   c. to feel shame
   d. to die

56. syllable
   a. any vowel
   b. a word with one vowel sound
   c. one sound
   d. a vowel or a group of letters with one vowel sound

57. symbol
   a. a sign
   b. a sound
   c. something representing another thing
   d. refers to an object

58. symmetry
   a. balanced form
   b. an arrangement
   c. refers to the metric system
   d. the same

59. symphony
   a. refers to sound
   b. a musical composition
   c. balanced sound
   d. refers to orchestra

60. symptom
   a. an aid
   b. a condition
   c. a sign that indicates the existence of something else
   d. refers to disease

61. amortize
   a. to die
   b. to become extinct
   c. gradual extinction of debt
   d. a mortgage

62. capitulate
   a. to surrender
   b. refers to capital
   c. to give
   d. to think

63. synthesis
   a. a form
   b. putting things together
   c. whole
   d. a theme

Lesson 18

64. audit
   a. to hear
   b. to examine accounts
   c. to examine
   d. to be a spectator

65. audition
   a. an examination of books
   b. an examination
   c. a hearing for a jury trial
   d. a trial hearing for an actor or singer

66. audiovisual
   a. instruction using books
   b. instruction using printed matter
   c. instruction using only television
   d. pertaining to hearing and seeing

67. local
   a. referring to a neighborhood area
   b. referring to a distant place
   c. referring to a place
   d. referring to a situation

68. location
   a. in the neighborhood
   b. a place or site
   c. a situation
   d. any place close

69. allocate
   a. to place
   b. to set
   c. to divide and distribute
   d. to put together

70. antonym
   a. a word similar to another in meaning
   b. a word opposite in meaning to another
   c. a word that is pronounced the same as another
   d. a word that is spelled like another

71. synonym
   a. a word similar in pronunciation to another
   b. a word opposite in meaning to another
   c. a word similar to another in spelling
   d. a word similar to another in meaning

72. effective
   a. producing no results after a while
   b. producing
   c. making something do
   d. producing results in a minimum of time

73. audible
   a. referring to hearing
   b. referring to a listener
   c. capable of being heard
   d. not heard

74. auditorium
   a. building in which things are made
   b. a special building
   c. a place for workers
   d. a place for speeches, concerts, and so on

75. audience
   a. a group of listeners or spectators at a play, concert, and so on
   b. spectacles
   c. people
   d. a building

76. manual
   a. referring to the hands
   b. referring to manly work
   c. referring to men
   d. referring to help

77. manicure
   a. refers to cure
   b. refers to hands
   c. the curing of hand problems
   d. the care of the hands and fingernails

78. manuscript
   a. a newspaper
   b. a role in a play
   c. written by hand
   d. a letter

79. manufacture
   a. to make machinery
   b. to store in a factory
   c. to make by hand or machine from raw material
   d. made to sell

80. factory
   a. a building
   b. a house
   c. a place for storing things only
   d. a place for manufacturing things

81. benefactor
   a. one who gets help
   b. one who gives help
   c. someone good
   d. a blessing

82. beneficiary
   a. one who gives help
   b. one who needs help
   c. one who gets help
   d. a blessing

83. benefit
   a. a performance for some charity or cause
   b. a blessing
   c. a performance
   d. charity

84. affect
   a. the result
   b. to bring
   c. an action
   d. to influence

85. effect
   a. to influence
   b. the result
   c. the action
   d. to bring something

86. homonym
    a. a word that is similar to another in spelling
    b. a word that is similar to another in pronunciation
    c. a word that is different from another in meaning and spelling but similar in pronunciation
    d. a word that is different in meaning from another

87. pseudonym
    a. wrong name
    b. same name
    c. lacking a name
    d. false name

88. misnomer
    a. false name
    b. lacking a name
    c. same name
    d. wrong name

89. anonymous
    a. wrong name
    b. false name
    c. lacking a name
    d. same name

90. antipathy
    a. a liking
    b. refers to feeling
    c. a feeling of distress
    d. a dislike for someone

91. audiology
    a. a science
    b. the study of hearing
    c. refers to hearing
    d. a study

92. audiometer
    a. an instrument
    b. used to measure something
    c. a measurement
    d. instrument to measure hearing

93. benediction
    a. a blessing
    b. refers to good
    c. saying something to make a person feel worse
    d. good thoughts

94. pedicure
    a. care of oneself
    b. care
    c. care of foot
    d. care of hands

95. personification
    a. refers to person
    b. human beings
    c. gives human characteristics to inanimate things
    d. gives characteristics to animals

96. pseudopodium
    a. found in most animals
    b. a place to rest feet
    c. refers to kinds of feet
    d. false foot

97. pseudoscience
    a. refers to science
    b. refers to false
    c. false science
    d. any science that isn't false

98. faction
    a. people
    b. people in the government
    c. a number of people in an organization having a common goal
    d. government

99. manipulation
    a. act of managing
    b. clever
    c. to change objects
    d. purposeful

CHAPTER TRUE/FALSE TEST

DIRECTIONS: This is a true/false test on Lessons 16 to 18. Read each sentence carefully. Decide whether it is true or false. Put a *T* for *True* or an *F* for *False* in the blank. If the statement is false, change a word or words to make it true. The number after the sentence tells you in which lesson the word appears.

_____ 1. Capitalism can only be practiced in capitals. 17

_____ 2. Affect is a verb, while effect is almost always a noun. 18

_____ 3. Anonymous is an antonym of *famous*. 18

_____ 4. A curator is someone who cures disease. 18

_____ 5. A computer manual tells you how to operate the computer. 18

_____ 6. To capitulate is to vanquish. 17

_____ 7. A homicide results in a corpse. 17

_____ 8. A symphony is usually performed in an auditorium. 17, 18

_____ 9. To convene a meeting is to end it. 16

_____ 10. An astronaut is someone who studies astronomy. 16

_____ 11. Visage means the same as *face*. 16

_____ 12. A visor might block a person's vision. 16

_____ 13. A venture is the opposite of an adventure. 16

_____ 14. The prefix omni means "opposite." 16

_____ 15. You might bump into something that was invisible. 16

_____ 16. To allocate is to take. 18

_____ 17. Audiovisual aids include both sight and sound. 18

_____ 18. To benefit is to harm. 18

_____ 19. To personify is to flatter. 18

_____ 20. To manipulate is to control. 18

_____ 21. Astrology is an example of a pseudoscience. 16, 18

_____ 22. A synonym for convenient is *comfortable*. 16

_____ 23. Impotent means even stronger than potent. 16

_____ 24. A corporation refers to a corpse. 17

_____ 25. The word morgue is a monosyllable. 17

_____ 26. A <u>mortgage</u> is a kind of death. 17

_____ 27. Something that is balanced is <u>symmetrical</u>. 17

_____ 28. <u>Capital punishment</u> is the same as <u>corporal punishment</u>. 17

STOP. Check answers for both tests at the end of the book (p. 347).

SCORING OF TESTS

Multiple-Choice Vocabulary Test		*True/False Test*	
Number Wrong	*Score*	*Number Wrong*	*Score*
0–4	Excellent	0–2	Excellent
5–10	Good	3–5	Good
11–14	Weak	6–7	Weak
Above 14	Poor	Above 7	Poor
Score _____		Score _____	

1. If you scored in the excellent or good range on *both tests,* you are doing well. Go on to Chapter 8.
2. If you scored in the weak or poor range on either test, go to the next page and follow directions for Additional Practice. Note that the words on the tests are arranged so that you can tell in which lesson to find them. This arrangement will help you if you need additional practice.

ADDITIONAL PRACTICE SETS

A DIRECTIONS: Write the words you missed on the tests from the three lessons in the space provided. Note that the tests are presented so that you can tell to which lessons the words belong.

Lesson 16 Words Missed

1. _____   6. _____

2. _____   7. _____

3. _____   8. _____

4. _____   9. _____

5. _____   10. _____

Lesson 17 Words Missed

1. _____   6. _____

2. _____   7. _____

3. _____   8. _____

4. _____   9. _____

5. _____   10. _____

Lesson 18 Words Missed

1. _____   6. _____

2. _____   7. _____

3. _____   8. _____

4. _____   9. _____

5. _____   10. _____

B **DIRECTIONS:** Restudy the words that you have written down on this page. Study the combining forms from which those words are derived. Do Step I and Step II for those you missed. Note that Step I and Step II of the combining forms and vocabulary derived from these combining forms are on the following pages:

Lesson 16—pp. 168–175
Lesson 17—pp. 176–183
Lesson 18—pp. 184–191

C **DIRECTIONS:** Do Additional Practice 1 on this page and on p. 206 if you missed words from Lesson 16. Do Additional Practice 2 on pp. 207–209 if you missed words from Lesson 17. Do Additional Practice 3 on pp. 209–211 if you missed words from Lesson 18. Now go on to Chapter 8.

Additional Practice 1 for Lesson 16

A **DIRECTIONS:** The combining forms presented in Lesson 16 follow. Match the combining form with its meaning.

_____   1. vid, vis   a. star

_____   2. sci, scio   b. all

_____   3. poten   c. see

_____   4. omni   d. come

_____   5. aqua, aqui   e. sailor

_____   6. astro   f. water

_____ 7. naut   g. powerful

_____ 8. ven, veni, vent   h. know

STOP. Check answers at the end of the book (p. 347).

B **DIRECTIONS:** Sentences containing the meanings of some vocabulary presented in Lesson 16 follow. Choose the word that *best* fits the meaning of the word or phrase underlined in the sentence.

Word List

aquanauts	astronomy	evident	potential
aquarium	convene	impotent	provisions
aquatic	convenient	invisible	science
astrology	conventions	omnipresent	visible
astronauts	evidence	potent	vision

_____ 1. If you are blind, you do not have your <u>sense of sight</u>.

_____ 2. In the film, a man played a ghost who was <u>not able to be seen</u>.

_____ 3. The sign was <u>able to be seen</u>, but I went past it.

_____ 4. We will take enough <u>supplies</u> for our trip.

_____ 5. I am studying astronomy, which is a <u>field of organized knowledge</u> concerning heavenly bodies.

_____ 6. The lawyer needed <u>something that would prove</u> that his client was innocent of the charges.

_____ 7. It is <u>plain</u> from the way you are acting that you want me to leave.

_____ 8. Some people believe that a <u>reading of the stars</u> will predict their futures.

_____ 9. What do you call <u>people who travel in space</u>?

_____ 10. What do you call <u>people who travel undersea</u>?

_____ 11. My favorite course is the <u>study of stars, planets, and space</u>.

_____ 12. I enjoy studying about <u>water</u> plants and animals.

_____ 13. I keep my water plants and animals in a <u>large tank</u> where I can watch them.

_____ 14. The judge said that the people in court should <u>come together</u> again at two in the afternoon.

_____ 15. I enjoy attending <u>formal professional meetings</u>.

_____ 16. Attending classes in the afternoon is not <u>suitable</u> for me because I work in the afternoon.

_____ 17. That is <u>powerful</u> medicine you are taking.

_____ 18. The person in charge was merely a figurehead who was <u>without power</u>.

_____ 19. If I knew what my <u>possible ability</u> was, I would try to do something with it.

_____ 20. The bandits seemed to be <u>present everywhere at all times</u>.

STOP. Check answers at the end of the book (p. 347).

Additional Practice 2 for Lesson 17

A **DIRECTIONS:** The combining forms presented in Lesson 17 follow. Match the combining form with its meaning.

_____ 1. cide   a. into; in

_____ 2. pathy   b. kill; murder

_____ 3. syl, sym, syn   c. death

_____ 4. frater, fratr   d. same; with; together; along with

_____ 5. mors, mort   e. brother

_____ 6. capit   f. feeling; suffering

_____ 7. corp, corpor   g. head

_____ 8. em, en   h. body

STOP. Check answers at the end of the book (p. 347).

B **DIRECTIONS:** Sentences containing the meanings of some vocabulary words presented in Lesson 17 follow. Choose the word that *best* fits the meaning of the word or phrase underlined in the sentence.

Word List

apathy	corporation	homicide	mortals
capital	corpse	immortals	mortgage
capitalism	empathy	incorporate	mortician
capital punishment	fraternity	morgue	suicide
corporal punishment	genocide	mortality	sympathy

_____ 1. More and more people are involved in the act of killing others.

_____ 2. Only a madman would attempt the destruction of a whole race of people.

_____ 3. I have the ability to understand how you feel because I had the same experience.

_____ 4. I have no feeling about that.

_____ 5. I have pity for the child who lost both parents in an accident.

_____ 6. The man resorted to the act of killing himself when he lost all his money.

_____ 7. I am joining a Greek letter college organization next semester.

_____ 8. My father's friends formed an association of a number of businesspeople, which took out a special charter granting it certain rights.

_____ 9. In the United States, we have an economic system based on private ownership and profit.

_____ 10. Are you and the other men going to join together to form a business?

_____ 11. All human beings must eventually die.

_____ 12. Undying beings do not exist on earth.

_____ 13. We found a dead body in the woods.

_____ 14. I wonder if the death penalty will return in my state.

_____ 15. Many persons believe that children should not be subjected to a beating in school.

_____ 16. Do you know the death rate of teenagers involved in automobile accidents?

_____ 17. Because it was unidentified, the body was taken to a special place where unidentified bodies are held until it could be claimed.

_____ 18. They had difficulty paying off the loan on their property because of other very large unexpected expenses.

_____ 19. She went to <u>an undertaker</u> to arrange for her father's funeral.

_____ 20. Do you have enough <u>money</u> to start such a business venture?

STOP. Check answers at the end of the book (p. 347).

Additional Practice 3 for Lesson 18

A DIRECTIONS: The combining forms presented in Lesson 18 follow. Match the combining form with its meaning.

_____ 1. man, manu   a. make; do

_____ 2. fac, fect, fic   b. place

_____ 3. loc, loco   c. hear

_____ 4. pseudo   d. care

_____ 5. bene   e. name

_____ 6. aud, audi   f. false

_____ 7. cura   g. good

_____ 8. nomin, onym   h. hand

STOP. Check answers at the end of the book (p. 347).

B DIRECTIONS: Some sentences containing the meanings of some vocabulary presented in Lesson 18 follow. Choose the word that *best* fits the meaning of the word or phrase underlined in the sentence.

Word List

affect	audit	faction	manuscript
allocate	audition	factory	misnomer
anonymous	auditorium	homonyms	pedicure
antipathy	benediction	local	personification
antonyms	benefactor	location	pseudonyms
audible	beneficiary	manicure	pseudopodium
audience	benefit	manipulation	pseudoscience
audiology	effect	manual	synonyms
audiovisual	effective	manufacture	

_____ 1. Consuela goes to the beauty shop for <u>the care of her fingernails.</u>

_____   2. We learned <u>the style of writing our letters without joining them together.</u>

_____   3. Consuela's husband works in <u>a building that makes furniture.</u>

_____   4. Many artists have <u>a person who supports them</u> so that they do not have to worry about money.

_____   5. <u>Hand</u> labor does not bother me.

_____   6. Consuela was just <u>capable of being heard.</u>

_____   7. When the auditors <u>examine the accounts,</u> they had better balance, or Consuela will be in trouble.

_____   8. There will be <u>a tryout</u> for the new play next week.

_____   9. Consuela's school uses a lot of <u>television, radio, tapes, and picture aids.</u>

_____   10. The method you have for studying is really <u>productive in getting results</u> for you.

_____   11. The concert is being held in <u>a large special room</u> that is used for such performances in the school.

_____   12. In this day and age, we <u>make goods by machinery</u> on a large scale in order to have enough available for so many people.

_____   13. What <u>result,</u> if any, did Consuela find?

_____   14. Consuela just found out that she is <u>the receiver of a large amount of money</u> that was left to her by an old uncle who recently died.

_____   15. What is the major <u>advantage</u> of going to college?

_____   16. <u>The group of listeners at the concert</u> was so quiet that you could hear a pin drop.

_____   17. Consuela is not going <u>to influence</u> her brother in any way.

_____   18. *Bear* and *bare* are <u>words that sound alike but are spelled differently and have different meanings.</u>

_____   19. *Corpulent* and *fat* are <u>words that are similar in meaning.</u>

_____   20. *Antonym* and *synonym* are <u>words that are opposite in meaning.</u>

_____   21. Some writers use <u>pen names or names other than their own names.</u>

_____   22. When Consuela used the term *misanthrope* to mean a hater of marriage, she was using a <u>wrong word</u>.

_____   23. The poem was <u>without an author's name</u>.

_____   24. Consuela shops only in <u>neighborhood</u> stores.

_____   25. The men will <u>set aside</u> a certain number of tickets for us.

_____   26. Consuela's house is in a lovely <u>place</u>.

_____   27. She cleverly <u>managed</u> people to do what she wants.

_____   28. Consuela's professors called astrology a <u>false science</u>.

_____   29. Consuela needs to take better <u>care of</u> her <u>feet</u>.

STOP. Check answers at the end of the book (p. 347).

Chapter 8

LESSON 19

Step I. Story in Context

DIRECTIONS: The following story includes several vocabulary words from this lesson. As you read the story, pay careful attention to the vocabulary words in boldface type, and try to figure out the meaning of each of these words. Put your answers in the blanks.

Writing Assignment

Writing has never been easy for me. Maybe I don't have a (1) **fertile** _____ brain; maybe I don't have the sitting power; maybe I can't (2) **transfer** _____ my thoughts very well to a blank sheet of paper that is staring at me. Whatever the reasons, and these may be (3) **infinite** _____, I (4) **suffer** _____ a great amount of anxiety when I have to write anything. You can imagine my state of mind when our professor, Dr. Percy, said that one of the class requirements was to write a short play and that this would count very heavily toward the (5) **final** _____ grade. My (6) **preference** _____ originally had been for a literature course, but it was full. My heart sank further as the professor's voice droned on with all the other requirements. We needed to include a (7) **prologue** _____ or introduction,

as well as an (8) **epilogue** _____. Dr. Percy wanted good (9) **dialogue**
_____, and the play had to develop in a (10) **logical**
_____ fashion. She also wanted us to write a paper on the type of play
we had chosen to write. She wanted us to use (11) **references** _____
and to read a number of plays by different playwrights and list them in a formal (12) **bibliography** _____.

Dr. Percy suggested that we become familiar with the computers in the library because
they had a (13) **catalogue** _____ of everything in the library. She said
also that she would have an individual (14) **conference** _____ with
each of us to discuss our progress. I couldn't believe my ears! I have only a (15) **finite**
_____ amount of time to work in this course. Dr. Percy must think
that her course is the only one that we are taking. In addition, she told us that during the
semester, we would be going to see three plays in the local theater. She showed us a (16) **diagram** _____ of it and said that the theater was very unusual because
it was round and the stage was in the center of the theater right on its (17) **diameter**
_____. She asked us to guess the (18) **circumference**
_____ of the theater. She then told us that the first play we would see
dealt with a couple's problems with (19) **fertilization** _____.

STOP. Check answers at the end of the book (p. 348).

Step II. Combining Forms

A **DIRECTIONS:** A list of combining forms with their meanings follows. Look at the combining forms and their meanings. Concentrate on learning each combining form and
its meaning. Cover the meanings, read the combining forms, and state the meanings
to yourself. Check to see whether you are correct. Now cover the combining forms,
read the meanings, and state the combining forms to yourself. Check to see whether
you are correct.

Combining Forms	*Meanings*
1. biblio	book
2. cata	down
3. dia	through
4. epi	upon; beside; among
5. fer	bring; bear; yield (give up)
6. fin	end
7. log, logo	speech; word
8. pro	before; forward

B **DIRECTIONS:** Cover the preceding meanings. Write the meanings of the following
combining forms.

Combining Forms	Meanings
1. biblio	_____
2. cata	_____
3. dia	_____
4. epi	_____
5. fer	_____
6. fin	_____
7. log, logo	_____
8. pro	_____

Step III. Vocabulary Words Derived from Combining Forms in Context

1. **affinity** (uh · fin′ uh · tē) *n*. Close relationship; attraction to another. *Ali knew that our relationship would grow into more than just being acquaintances because of the **affinity** we had for one another when we first met.*
2. **bibliography** (bib · lē · og′ ruh · fē) *n*. (*pl*. **phies**) A listing of books on a subject or by an author (the description includes author's name, title, publisher, date of publication, and so on). *The **bibliography** for Ali's paper was large because our teacher wanted us to list at least twenty books on the topic we were writing about.*
3. **catalogue** (kat′ uh · log) *n*. A listing of names, titles, and so on, in some order; a book containing such a list. *v*. To make a catalogue. *Even though the card **catalogue** in the library lists books in alphabetical order according to topics, authors, and titles, I prefer to use the library's computers to locate what I want.*
4. **circumference** (sur · kum′ fur · unsé) *n*. The distance around a circle; a boundary line of any rounded area. *When Ali speaks of the **circumference** of the globe, he is referring to the distance around the globe.*
5. **conference** (kon′ fur · unsé) *n*. A discussion or meeting on some important matter. *Because the dean wanted a **conference** with the students who were involved in the fight, he asked his secretary to call in the students for a meeting with him.*
6. **defer** (di · fur′) *v*. To postpone; to delay; to leave to another's opinion; to put off for a future time. *Ali will **defer** to my partner because he has studied the matter very closely.*
7. **deference** (def′ ur · unsé) *n*. Respect; a giving in to another's opinion. *In **deference** to Ali's age and position, the group decided to give him a chance to speak.*
8. **definitive** (di · fin′ uh · tivé) *adj*. Final; conclusive; most nearly complete or accurate. *The results from the studies are not **definitive** because there are too many different conclusions.*
9. **diagram** (dī′ uh · gram) *n*. An outline figure that shows the relationship among parts or places; a graph or chart. *The **diagram** showing the circulatory system of the body helped me to see the relationship between the veins and arteries.*
10. **dialect** (dī′ uh · lekt) *n*. A variety of speech; a regional form of a standard language. *It's evident that Tonya comes from the South because she speaks with a Southern **dialect**.*

11. **dialogue** (dī' uh · logúé) *n.* A conversation in which two or more take part; the conversation in a play. *Lee and Kelsey had such a good dialogue going that when the bell rang, they still continued their conversation.*

12. **diameter** (dī · am' uh · tur) *n.* A straight line passing through the center of a circle. *The diameter of a circle divides the circle in half because it passes through the center of the circle from one end to the other.*

13. **epilogue** (ep' uh · logúé) *n.* A short section added at the end to a book, poem, and so on; a short speech added to a play and given at the end. *We were very moved by the actor's epilogue at the end of the play.*

14. **fertile** (fer' tulé) *adj.* Able to produce a large crop; able to produce; capable of bearing offspring, seeds, fruit, and so on; productive in mental achievements; having abundant resources. *The land was so fertile that each year it produced a very large crop.*

15. **fertilization** (fer · tul · uh · zā' shun) *n.* The act of making something able to produce; in biology, the union of a male and female germ cell; impregnation. *Human fertilization takes place when a sperm cell and egg cell unite.*

16. **final** (fī' nul) *adj.* Conclusive; last; coming at or relating to the end. *Most instructors give a final examination at the end of the semester.*

17. **finale** (fuh · nal' ē) *n.* End; last part; the concluding movement of a musical composition. *The play's finale was completely unexpected on the basis of everything that had gone before.*

18. **finite** (fī' nīté) *adj.* Having a limit or end; able to be measured. *Because there are a finite number of places where the missing item can be, we'll find it.*

19. **inference** (in' fur · unsé) *n.* Something derived by reasoning; something not directly stated but implied or suggested; a deduction; a logical conclusion drawn from statements. *Although Marcus did not say so exactly, the inference I got was that he was quitting his job.*

20. **infinite** (in' fuh · nité) *adj.* Having no limit or end; not able to be measured. *If the universe is infinite, it has no beginning or end.*

21. **infinitesimal** (in · fin · i · tes' uh · mul) *adj.* Very small; too small to be measured. *The microorganism was almost infinitesimal in size because it could be seen only with the most high-powered microscope.*

22. **logical** (loj' uh · kul) *adj.* Relating to the science concerned with correct reasoning. *The arguments that you are giving are not very logical because the reasoning is faulty.*

23. **monologue** (mon' uh · logúé) *n.* A long speech by one person; a dramatic speech by an actor. *Ramon's monologue was so long that after a while, nobody was listening to what he was saying.*

24. **preference** (pref' ur · unsé) *n.* The choosing of one person or thing over another; the valuing of one over another; a liking better. *Rebecca's preference for science courses is obvious, for she chooses those over all others.*

25. **proficient** (pruh · fish' unt) *adj.* Knowing something very well; able to do something very well. *It is obvious that Andrew is a proficient skier because he is able to ski on the highest and steepest mountain trails with ease.*

26. **prologue** (prō' logúé) *n.* An introduction, often in verse (poetry), spoken or sung before a play or opera; any introductory or preceding event; a preface. *The prologue of the play comes at the beginning and sometimes introduces the characters or sets the mood for the play.*

27. **reference** (ref′ ur · unsĕ) *n.* A referring or being referred; the giving of a problem to a person, a committee, or an authority for settlement; a note in a book that sends the reader for information to another book; the name of another person who can offer information or recommendation; the mark or sign, as a number or letter, directing the reader to a footnote, and so on; a written statement of character, qualification, or ability; testimonial. *My biology and geology instructors said that they would give me good **references** for a job after college.*

28. **suffer** (suf′ fur) *v.* To feel pain or distress. *The woman who lost five sons in World War II must have **suffered** a great deal of pain and distress.*

29. **transfer** (trans′ fur) *v.* To carry or send from one person or place to another; to cause to pass from one person or place to another. *n.* An act of transferring or being transferred. *When my boss said that he would **transfer** me to another department, I was very pleased because I wanted to go to the other place.*

SPECIAL NOTES

1. *Prologue* and *preface* are both introductory statements. However, a prologue is usually found at the beginning of a play or poem but usually not in a book such as a novel or textbook. In a book, article, or speech, the introduction that is found at the beginning is usually called a *preface*. The preface sets forth the plan, purpose, and subject of the book, article, or speech.

2. **logical.** Relating to correct reasoning. A person who is *logical* is able to present arguments in a carefully thought out manner so that each statement correctly follows the other.

Step IV. Practice

A **DIRECTIONS:** Fill in the word that *best* completes each sentence. Two choices are given for each missing word.

1. The closets in this apartment are so small they can only be described as _____. (infinite, infinitesimal)

2. All the characters in the play except for Lola speak with a Latino _____. (dialect, dialogue)

3. Fred monopolized the conversation so completely that he turned it into a _____ (dialogue, monologue).

4. The _____ at the end of the play was spoken by the actor who played the Duke. (epilogue, prologue)

5. My_____ is that although you seem to be talking about the characters in the movie, you are really talking about your last breakup. (inference, reference)

6. Because your room is so small, there is only a(n) _____ number of places where your cellphone could be. (finite, infinite)

7. You would skate about a quarter mile if you went around the _____ of the entire rink. (circumference, diameter)

8. In _____ to all your previous experience, we want you to chair the committee. (deference, reference)

9. Tomas has a great _____ for languages and he always likes to learn new ones. (affinity, preference)

10. The _____ at the end of your paper should include the full name, author, and publishing information for every work you consulted. (bibliography, reference)

11. Dan is extremely _____ at identifying different species, so he should be a good field zoologist. (fertile, proficient)

12. The hero of the movie _____ greatly throughout, but she emerged triumphant in the end. (deferred, suffered)

13. I would like to work in an office that is closer to my dorm, so I will ask to _____ to the admissions office. (defer, transfer)

14. It is easier to understand complex geometric relationships if you draw a _____. (diagram, dialogue)

15. Many classical symphonies end with an elaborate _____ that restates all the principal themes of the work. (epilogue, finale)

STOP. Check answers at the end of the book (p. 348).

B DIRECTIONS: A number of sentences with missing words follow. Choose the word that *best* fits the sentence. Put the word in the blank. Some words are not used as answers. These words are from previous chapters.

Word List

affinity	diagram	finite	preference
alias	dialogue	inference	prologue
aquatic	diameter	infinite	pseudonym
bibliography	epilogue	infinitesimal	reference
catalogue	fertile	logical	suffer
circumference	fertilization	misnomer	transfer
conference	final	monologue	
defer	finale	potent	

1. At the beginning of some plays, there may be a(n) _____.

2. The _____ between the main characters in the play was interesting to listen to.

3. Some authors add a(n) _____ at the end of their books.

4. _____s have always helped me in learning something because I can understand something better when I see an outline picture of it.

5. Our instructor wants us to list at least twenty-five books for our topic and to make sure that we give the author, name of book, publisher, and date in the proper form for our _____.

6. As a senior, do you have to take _____s at the end of the semester?

7. Only a(n) _____ number of people can attend the jazz concert because there is limited seating.

8. The number system is _____ because you can go on counting numbers without end.

9. At the science convention, a group of scientists had _____s to discuss some important matters.

10. The _____ cuts a circle in half.

11. The boundary of a circle is called its _____.

12. I am going to _____ my funds from the State National Bank to the Security Bank because the Security Bank pays more interest.

13. Because your argument is full of holes, it is not very _____.

14. A file clerk has to _____ things in some order.

15. The soil in our garden is so _____ that we can grow practically anything.

16. I asked Professor Jones, from whom I received an A, if I could use his name as a(n) _____ for a job.

17. Because Melissa has a(n) _____ for certain kinds of clothing, I know exactly what she will choose.

18. Jim was willing to _____ and bear the pain of another operation if it meant that he would walk again.

19. In the process of sexual reproduction, the union of sperm and egg is called

_____.

STOP. Check answers at the end of the book (p. 348).

C DIRECTIONS: Write a sentence that makes sense using at least two words from this lesson. Illustrate the meanings of the words without actually defining them.

Example

The play had a *prologue*, too much *dialogue*, too many *references*, and an *epilogue*, but no real ending.

_____

_____

_____

STOP. Check answers at the end of the book (p. 348).

D **DIRECTIONS:** Fill in each blank with the word that matches the meaning. Some words are from other lessons.

1. Endless _____

2. A listing of books _____

3. Last _____

4. Killing of oneself _____

5. An introduction _____

6. Not believable _____

7. Not legal _____

8. Able to produce _____

9. Able to be measured; having an end _____

10. Relating to correct reasoning _____

11. A listing of names, titles, and so on, in some order _____

12. A conversation _____

13. The act of making something able to produce _____

14. The distance around a circle _____

15. A straight line passing through the center of a circle _____

16. A short section added to the end of a book _____

17. An outline figure that shows the relationships among parts _____

18. To feel pain or distress _____

19. A note in a book that sends the reader to another book _____

20. The choosing of one person or thing over another _____

21. A discussion or meeting of some important matter _____

22. To carry from one place to another _____

STOP. Check answers at the end of the book (p. 348).

EXTRA WORD POWER

il
im
in
ir

Not; into. Note that when *in* is placed at the beginning of a word, it can mean either "into" or "not." Note also that the *n* changes to an *m* when *in* is added to a word beginning with an *m, b,* or *p*. Example of *in* meaning "into": *inspection*—the act of looking into something. *The inspector gave the restaurant a careful* **inspection** *to see whether everything was in order.* Examples of *in* meaning "not": *infinite*—not ending; *ineffectual*—not being able to bring about results. *The lifeguard*
(continued)

il ***im*** ***in*** ***ir***	was ***ineffectual*** in his efforts to save the drowning child. Examples of *in* meaning "into" changing to *im*: *import*—to carry in; *important*— deserving of notice; of great value. *The materials being **imported** were so **important** that fifteen extra guards were hired to watch them as they came off the ship.* Examples of *in* meaning "not" changing to *im*: *imperfect*—not perfect; having a fault. Note that *in* meaning "not" and "into" also changes to *il* and *ir* when *in* is added to words beginning with *l* or *r.* For example: *illegal*—not legal; *irregular*—not uniform; not the same; *illustrate*—to make clear; *illuminate*—to light up; *irrigate*—to wet.
trans	Across; beyond; through; on the other side of, over. When *trans* is placed at the beginning of a word such as the following, it means "across," "beyond," "through," "on the other side of." For example: *transatlantic*—across the Atlantic; on the other side of the Atlantic; *transhuman*—beyond human limits; *transport*—to carry from one place to another; *transparent*—able to be seen through; *transfer*—to move from one place to another.

LESSON 20

Step I. Story in Context

DIRECTIONS: The following story includes several vocabulary words from this lesson. As you read the story, pay careful attention to the vocabulary words in boldface type, and try to figure out the meaning of each of the words. Put your answers in the blanks.

Eating in Contemporary Times

In (1) **contemporary** _____ times, life can be rather confusing. For example, it may sound (2) **ridiculous** _____, but I don't know what to eat anymore. Everything seems to have something (3) **toxic** _____ in it or too much fat or carbs. A (4) **pediatrician** _____ (5) **diagnosed** _____ my cousin's problem recently and said that it was due to what he was eating. He told his parents to make sure that they do not give their child anything that has artificial color in it because it makes him overactive. I don't think you can (6) **conceive** _____ of how many foods have artificial color in them. We are really (7) **captives** _____ of the food manufacturers. Just read some of the labels. Often, the advertisers try to (8) **deceive** _____ us into thinking that their foods are pure when they are not. The manufacturers package foods in such a way that we get a deceptive (9) **perception** _____ of the item.

Recently, my (10) **gynecologist** _____ told me that I should not drink coffee any more because it was bad for me; it could cause lumps in the breast. Also, since my cholesterol is very high, my family doctor suggested that I avoid beef and fatty foods. He also said that this should not be a (11) **temporary** _____ measure but a permanent one. He said that these foods are (12) **capable** _____ of clogging my arteries. Without (13) **exception** _____, there seems to be some food that is bad for you. When my friend broke out in hives, the (14) **dermatologist** _____ said that it was due to something he had eaten. I just do not feel that I am (15) **capable** _____ of figuring out what foods to buy anymore.

Have you ever noticed how most of the commercials deal with yummy junk food? Yet we live in a society in which everyone wants to be thin. Have you also ever noticed how on television shows, the people are always eating three full meals and going to fancy (16) **receptions** _____ and they still stay slim? Amazing! Have you also seen how television shows usually (17) **ridicule** _____ fat people?

I believe in the (18) **hypothesis** _____ that most of our ills are due to what we eat. I do not believe, however, in some people's (19) **prognosis** _____ that soon many of us, instead of eating, will just take various food (20) **capsules** _____ three times a day or give ourselves (21) **hypodermic** _____ injections that will have all the vitamins and nutrients that we require based on our body weight and height.

STOP. Check answers at the end of the book (p. 348).

Step II. Combining Forms

A **DIRECTIONS:** A list of combining forms with their meanings follows. Look at the combining forms and their meanings. Concentrate on learning each combining form and its meaning. Cover the meanings, read the combining forms, and state the meanings to yourself. Check to see if you are correct. Now cover the combining forms, read the meanings, and state the combining forms to yourself. Check to see if you are correct.

Combining Forms	Meanings
1. cap, cep	take, receive
2. derm, dermo	skin
3. gnosi, gnosis	knowledge
4. gyn, gyno	woman
5. hypo	under
6. ped, pedo	child
7. ri, ridi, risi	laughter
8. temp, tempo, tempor	time
9. tox, toxo	poison

B **DIRECTIONS:** Cover the preceding meanings. Write the meanings of the following combining forms.

Combining Forms	Meanings
1. cap, cep	_____
2. derm, dermo	_____
3. gnosi, gnosis	_____
4. gyn, gyno	_____
5. hypo	_____
6. ped, pedo	_____
7. ri, ridi, risi	_____
8. temp, tempo, tempor	_____
9. tox, toxo	_____

Step III. Vocabulary Words Derived from Combining Forms in Context

1. **agnostic** (ag · nos′ tik) *adj. n.* Professing uncertainty; one who is not for or against; one who doubts whether the existence of God is knowable. *Pat must be an* **agnostic** *because she believes that there is no way for anyone to know for sure about the existence of God.*
2. **antitoxin** (an · ti · tok′ sin) *n.* Something used against bacterial poison. *The doctor injected my brother with an* **antitoxin** *to prevent his getting a certain disease.*
3. **capable** (kā′ puh · bul) *adj.* Able to be affected; able to understand; having ability; having qualities that are able to be developed. *Although he is* **capable** *of many things, time will tell whether he will use all his abilities.*
4. **capsule** (kap′ sul) *n.* A small container made of gelatin (or other material that melts) that holds a dose of medicine; a special removable part of an airplane or rocket. *Each* **capsule** *contained the exact amount of medicine the doctor wanted my grandfather to take.*
5. **captive** (kap′ tiv) *n.* One who is taken prisoner; one who is dominated. *When the daughter of a wealthy man was held* **captive** *by dangerous criminals, one million dollars was paid to the criminals to release the girl.*
6. **conceive** (kun · sēiv′) *v.* To become pregnant with; to form in the mind; to understand; to think; to believe; to imagine; to develop mentally. *I cannot* **conceive** *of him as a scientist because the image I have of him is as a playboy.*
7. **contemporary** (kun · tem′ puh · rer · ē) *adj.* Belonging to the same age; living or occurring at the same time; current. *n.* (*pl.* **ies**) One living in the same period as another or others; a person or thing of about the same age or date of origin. *Even though they act like* **contemporaries,** *they are a generation apart.*
8. **deceive** (di · sēiv′) *v.* To mislead by lying; to lead into error. *I couldn't believe that my best friend told all those lies to* **deceive** *me.*
9. **derisive** (di · ri′ siv) *adj.* Mocking or jeering. *The* **derisive** *laughter of the class toward all student comments kept me from saying anything because I did not want to be ridiculed.*

10. **dermatologist** (dur · muh · tol' uh · jist) *n.* A doctor who deals with skin disorders. *When Sara broke out in a rash, she went to a **dermatologist** to find out what was wrong with her.*

11. **diagnose** (di· ig · nōsé') *v.* To determine what is wrong with someone after an examination. *It is very important for a doctor to be able to **diagnose** a person's illness correctly so that the doctor will know how to treat it.*

12. **epidermis** (ep · uh · dur' mis) *n.* Outermost layer of skin. *The **epidermis** is the layer of skin that is the most exposed.*

13. **exception** (ik · sep' shun) *n.* The act of taking out; something or someone that is taken out or left out; an objection. *In English spelling rules, there always seems to be an **exception** to which the rule does not apply.*

14. **extemporaneous** (ek · stem · puh · rā' nē · øus) *adj.* Done or spoken without special preparation. *When Rosa was called upon to express her views, her **extemporaneous** talk was so logical and well expressed that she couldn't have done better if she had spent hours preparing it.*

15. **gynecologist** (gī · nuh · kol' uh · jist) *n.* A doctor dealing with women's diseases, especially in reference to the reproductive organs. *Many women go to a **gynecologist** for an annual checkup even if they have no symptoms of anything wrong.*

16. **hypodermic** (hī · puh · dur' mik) *adj.* Referring to the area under the skin; used for injecting under the skin. *n.* A hypodermic injection; a hypodermic syringe or needle. *The doctor injected the **hypodermic** needle so far under Sara's skin that her arm hurt all day.*

17. **hypothesis** (hī · poth' uh · sis) *n.* (*pl.* **ses**) (sēz). An unproved scientific conclusion drawn from known facts; something assumed as a basis for argument; a possible answer to a problem that requires further investigation. *The **hypothesis** that was put forth as the solution to the problem seemed logical, but it required further investigation to prove whether it was correct.*

18. **intercept** (in · tur · sept') *v.* To stop or interrupt the course of. *When the ball was **intercepted** before a goal could be made, the home team audience screamed with delight.*

19. **misogynist** (muh · soj' uh · nist) *n.* Hater of women. *Although Tom is a misogamist, he isn't a **misogynist** because he likes women.*

20. **pedagogue** (ped' uh · gogúé) *n.* A teacher. *A **pedagogue** is a person who teaches students.*

21. **pediatrician** (pē · dē · uh · trish' un) *n.* A doctor who specializes in children's diseases. *I like to take my children to a **pediatrician** for a checkup because a pediatrician deals only with children's diseases.*

22. **perception** (pur · sep' shun) *n.* The act of becoming aware of something through the senses of seeing, hearing, feeling, tasting, and smelling. *If you have something wrong with your senses, your **perception** will be faulty.*

23. **perceptive** (pur · sep' tivé) *adj.* Being aware; having insight. *Being a **perceptive** individual, Yuki knew that this was not the right time to ask her father for use of the car.*

24. **prognosis** (prog · nō' sis) *n.* (*pl.* **ses**) (sēz) A prediction or conclusion regarding the course of a disease and the chances of recovery; a prediction. *Because the doctor's **prognosis** regarding Sara's illness was favorable, we knew that she would recover.*

25. **reception** (ri · sep′ shun) *n.* The act of receiving or being received; a formal social entertainment; the manner of receiving someone; the receiving of a radio or television broadcast. *I received a warm* **reception** *when I attended Carol's wedding* **reception,** *which was the social event of the year.*

26. **ridicule** (rid′ uh · kūlé) *n.* The language or actions that make a person the object of mockery or cause one to be laughed at or scorned. *v.* To mock or view someone in a scornful way; to hold someone up as a laughingstock; to make fun of. *I think it is cruel when someone* **ridicules** *another person and holds him or her up as a laughingstock.*

27. **ridiculous** (ruh · dik′ yuh · løus) *adj.* Unworthy of consideration; absurd (senseless); preposterous. *Rene's suggestion was so* **ridiculous** *that no one would even consider it.*

28. **susceptible** (suh · sep′ tuh · bul) *adj.* Easily influenced by or affected with. *When Stefan heard that he was* **susceptible** *to tuberculosis, he asked the doctor to help him to prevent the onset of the disease.*

29. **tempo** (tem′ pō) *n.* (*pl.* **tempi**) Rate of speed at which a musical composition is played; rate of activity. *The* **tempo** *of modern living is very fast.*

30. **temporary** (tem′ puh · rer · ē) *adj.* Lasting for a short period of time. *Maya was not upset when she was dismissed from her job because she had been told, when hired, that it was only a* **temporary** *position.*

31. **toxic** (tok′ sik) *adj.* Relating to poison. *All* **toxic** *materials should be clearly labeled and not stored near food.*

32. **toxicologist** (tok · si · kol′ uh · jist) *n.* One who specializes in the study of poisons. *A* **toxicologist** *was called in to help in the homicide investigation because all symptoms pointed to a possible death by poisoning.*

SPECIAL NOTES

1. The term *exception,* meaning "someone or something that is left out," has a special meaning when it is used in the phrase *to take exception. To take exception* means "to disagree," "to object." For example: *I take exception to what you are saying.*

2. *Hypothesis* is a term that is much used in the area of logic and science. A hypothesis may be defined as an unproved scientific conclusion drawn from known facts and used as a basis for further investigation. In science, a *hypothesis* is thus a possible explanation of observed facts and must be found true or false by more experiments.

3. You met the combining forms *ped, pod* in Lesson 10 of Chapter 5. *Ped, pod* means "foot" in such words as *biped, pedestrian, apodal, pseudopodia,* and *podiatrist. Ped, pedo* means "child" in such words as *pediatrician* and *pedagogue.*

4. *Capsule* can also mean "something extremely brief" such as an outline or survey. When *capsule* is used as an adjective, it means "extremely brief or small and very compact." When someone asks for a capsule report on something, he or she wants a very brief report.

Step IV. Practice

A **DIRECTIONS:** Each sentence has a missing word. Choose the word that *best* completes the sentence. Write the word in the blank. Each word is used once only as an answer.

Word List

capable	deceive	hypodermic	reception
capsule	dermatologist	hypothesis	ridicule
captive	diagnose	pediatrician	ridiculous
conceive	exception	perception	temporary
contemporary	gynecologist	prognosis	toxic

1. The political cartoonist holds someone or something up to _____ in each cartoon.

2. The scientists said that the _____ seems reasonable, but they would have to test it to see how good it is.

3. My _____ gave me medication to put on my rash.

4. When my sister's child had a very high fever, we took the baby to her _____.

5. Does that _____ contain the proper dose of medicine?

6. It is _____ to believe that a 90-year-old woman is attempting to run in the marathon.

7. After being a(n) _____ for five years, he had difficulty adjusting to a normal life.

8. The doctor said that the patient's _____ for recovery is excellent.

9. My boss is hiring a(n) _____ worker while his secretary is recovering in the hospital.

10. My doctor was not able to _____ my illness, so I went to another.

11. _____ materials are dangerous and should be clearly marked as poisonous.

12. It's a shame that someone who is as _____ as you are is not doing anything with his ability.

13. It is incredible that in _____ times, there are still people in the United States who do not have indoor bathrooms and other modern conveniences.

14. A(n) _____ to a rule is something that does not fit in.

15. The wedding _____ of the two wealthiest people in the world was held in the largest ballroom the reporters ever saw, and it was a spectacular affair.

16. Because the patient could not take any medicine by mouth, the doctor told the nurse to give the patient the medicine using a(n) _____ needle.

17. Nobody was able to _____ of a plan that was agreeable to all because everyone thought of a different one.

18. Some husbands or wives _____ their spouses by telling them lies.

19. Because I prefer a doctor who specializes in women's diseases, I go to a(n)

_____.

20. A person who is deaf has no _____ of what it is to hear.

STOP. Check answers at the end of the book (p. 348).

B **DIRECTIONS:** Each sentence contains an underlined vocabulary word. Write the
meaning of the underlined word in the space provided.

1. It is very difficult to keep up with the contemporary music scene because it is so
multifaceted and changes so quickly. _____

2. His comments were derisive and cruel although he veiled them with the appearance of good humor. _____

3. I take exception to your comments about the senator because I think she is doing
an excellent job of representing the state. _____

4. Ramona is usually very perceptive about people, but in this case she was completely wrong. _____

5. The plot of the opera revolved around an angry father's attempt to intercept a letter
from his daughter to her lover. _____

6. Children sometimes ridicule a person for the way he or she dresses, walks,
or talks, but adults should know better than to treat people scornfully.

_____

7. The conductor set such a rapid tempo that the soprano soloist could not keep up
with the orchestra. _____

8. I was surprised at your very cool reception of me and my friends, since I thought
you were looking forward to seeing us. _____

9. Professor Chan is an excellent scholar but he is so remote and formal in class that
he is not a very good pedagogue. _____

10. Even though Dr. Stein's talk was completely extemporaneous, he spoke so well
that it sounded as if he had written it all out in advance. _____

11. Even though Art says he is an agnostic, he acts as if he is sure of the existence of a
supreme being. _____

12. Irina is an extremely <u>capable</u> person, so I am sure she will be able to live on her own successfully. _____

13. The space <u>capsules</u> that the early astronauts rode in were incredibly tiny.

    _____

14. I was not trying to <u>deceive</u> you, but I didn't want to get into a big argument about using the car. _____

15. I think that if Carlos were a <u>misogynist</u> he would not have supported Senator Valerie Williams. _____

16. The next part of the experiment is to formulate a <u>hypothesis</u>, or an educated guess about this ecosystem. _____

17. Human <u>perception</u> is fairly limited: many animals can see, hear, or smell much more acutely than we can. _____

18. Sometimes it is fun to stop concentrating on the sensible or rational and focus instead on the <u>ridiculous</u>. _____

19. Evita is staying with her grandmother, but the situation is only <u>temporary</u>, because she will move into her new apartment next month. _____

20. Even though Frank has been mean to her in the past, Miranda is still highly <u>susceptible</u> to his charm and good looks. _____

STOP. Check answers at the end of the book (p. 348).

C **DIRECTIONS:** Write a sentence that makes sense using at least two words from this lesson. Illustrate the meanings of the words without actually defining them.

> ***Example***
> At the *reception,* the *dermatologist* said that it was not *ridiculous* to have food servers wear gloves.

_____

_____

_____

STOP. Check answers at the end of the book (p. 349).

D **DIRECTIONS:** Some of the words presented in Lesson 20 follow. Match each word with its meaning.

_____ 1. diagnose   a. having ability

_____ 2. prognosis   b. a small container that holds a dose of medicine

_____   3. pediatrician   c. the act of taking out

_____   4. gynecologist   d. to become pregnant with; to think

_____   5. toxic   e. a prisoner

_____   6. dermatologist   f. a formal social entertainment; act of
                                            receiving

_____   7. capable   g. to become aware of something through the
                                            senses

_____   8. captive   h. to mislead by lying

_____   9. deceive   i. referring to the area under the skin

_____   10. reception   j. an unproved scientific conclusion

_____   11. conceive   k. to mock or view someone in a scornful way

_____   12. perception   l. absurd; beyond belief

_____   13. exception   m. a doctor who specializes in skin diseases

_____   14. ridicule   n. referring to poison

_____   15. capsule   o. a doctor who specializes in children's diseases

_____   16. ridiculous   p. a prediction

_____   17. hypodermic   q. to determine what is wrong with someone
                                            after an examination

_____   18. hypothesis   r. a doctor who specializes in women's diseases

_____   19. temporary   s. of the same age; current

_____   20. contemporary   t. for a short time period

STOP. Check answers at the end of the book (p. 349).

EXTRA WORD POWER

de   Away; from; off; completely. *De* is found at the beginning of many words. For example: *deport*—to send someone away. *An alien who was involved in many holdups was **deported** to his own country.* Other words with *de*: *deflea*—to take off fleas; *delouse*—to free from lice; *decolor*—to take color away; *decode*—to change from code to plain language; *detoxify*—to take away poison; to destroy the poison; *decapitate*—to take off the head; to kill; *deprive*—to take something away from; *denude*—to strip the covering from completely. Can you supply more words with *ex, e,* or *de*?

(continued)

	Out of; from; lacking. When *ex* or *e* is placed at the beginning of a word, it means "out of" or "from." When *ex* is placed at the beginning of a word and a hyphen (-) is attached to the word, *ex* means "former" or "sometime." For example: *ex-president*—former president; *ex-wife*—former wife. Examples of *ex* meaning "out of" or "from": *exclude*—to keep from; *exit*—to go out of; *expect*—to look out for; *excuse*—to forgive; to apologize for; *exhale*—to breathe out.
e *ex*	

LESSON 21

Step I. Story in Context

DIRECTIONS: The following story includes several vocabulary words from this lesson. As you read the story, pay careful attention to the vocabulary words in boldface type, and try to figure out the meaning of each of these words. Put your answers in the blanks.

The Mysterious Crypt

Moses Hanes and Consuela Martinez had both majored in (1) **archaeology** _____ in the same school and had been in the college orchestra under the same (2) **conductor** _____. They had also been (3) **tenants** _____ in the same apartment building, but they met in Egypt while working on ancient ruins. On the dig, they discovered a strange (4) **crypt** _____, which had a (5) **cryptic** _____ inscription. After the (6) **crypt** _____ was brought to the surface, the **archaeologists** (7) **proceeded** _____ to open it. Just then, a strange little man dressed in an (8) **archaic** _____ costume jumped forth and yelled, "No! No! It is forbidden! Do so at great risk!" Before anyone could say anything, he disappeared as quickly as he had appeared. (9) **Subsequent** _____ to this, the sky clouded up, and a (10) **cyclone** _____ struck as if from nowhere. The whirlwinds were so forceful that no one was able to (11) **maintain** _____ his or her balance. Everyone (12) **conceded** _____ that what had happened was strange, but their (13) **deduction** _____ was that it was merely a coincidence; the (14) **cyclone** _____ was not a (15) **consequence** _____ of the little man's message. Everyone except Consuela was (16) **content** _____ that there was nothing to any of it.

The (17) **archaeologists** _____, therefore, (18) **proceeded** _____ to open the (19) **crypt** _____ to determine its (20) **contents** _____. Just as they began, another

(21) **cyclone** _____ hit the area. It was as if the (22) **cycle** _____ was starting all over again. The (23) **sequence** _____ was similar. The attempt to open the (24) **crypt** _____ (25) **preceded** _____ the (26) **cyclone** _____. "This is a bad omen!" said the guide. "I will not remain here anymore. The gods wish for you to return the (27) **crypt** _____ to its sacred burial grounds. You will never (28) **succeed** _____ in opening the (29) **crypt** _____. If you continue you will have (30) **chronic** _____ bad luck. This (31) **crypt** _____ was placed here thousands of years ago. The inscription is an (32) **abbreviation** _____ of the message contained inside. Everything is done in some kind of (33) **chronological** _____ order. You cannot disturb this order." With these words, the guide left the (34) **archaeologists** _____.

If you were them, would you have opened the (35) **crypt** _____?

STOP. Check answers at the end of the book (p. 349).

Step II. Combining Forms

A DIRECTIONS: A list of combining forms with their meanings follows. Look at the combining forms and their meanings. Concentrate on learning each combining form and its meaning. Cover the meanings, read the combining forms, and state the meanings to yourself. Check to see whether you are correct. Now cover the combining forms, read the meanings, and state the combining forms to yourself. Check to see whether you are correct.

Combining Forms	Meanings
1. archae, archaeo	ancient
2. brevi	short; brief
3. cede, ceed	go; give in; yield (give in)
4. chron, chrono	time
5. crypt, crypto	secret; hidden
6. cycl, cyclo	circle; wheel
7. duc	lead
8. sequi	follow
9. tain, ten, tent	hold

B DIRECTIONS: Cover the preceding meanings. Write the meanings of the following combining forms.

Combining Forms	Meanings
1. archae, archaeo	_____
2. brevi	_____

3. cede, ceed   _____

4. chron, chrono   _____

5. crypt, crypto   _____

6. cycl, cyclo   _____

7. duc   _____

8. sequi   _____

9. tain, ten, tent   _____

Step III. Vocabulary Words Derived from Combining Forms in Context

1. **abbreviation** (uh · brē · vē · ā′ shun) *n.* A shortened form of a word or phrase. *It is usual to give an **abbreviation** of the spelling of the states rather than writing them out completely because abbreviating is much faster and easier.*

2. **anachronism** (uh · nak′ ruh · niz · um) *n.* Something out of time order. *An example of an **anachronism** in a film would be to have an automobile present in a set representing the Middle Ages.*

3. **archaeology** (ar · kē · ol′ uh · jē) *n.* The study of the life and culture of ancient people, as by the digging up of old settlements, ruins from the past, and old human-made or other objects. *I knew that I would enjoy studying **archaeology** because I have always loved to dig in old places and hunt for things from the past so that I could learn more about ancient times.*

4. **archaic** (ar · kā′ ik) *adj.* Belonging to an earlier period; ancient; old-fashioned; no longer used. *It is surprising to find someone in our times who believes in such an **archaic** practice as bloodletting for curing disease.*

5. **chronic** (kron′ ik) *adj.* Continuing for a long time; prolonged; recurring. *Because he had a **chronic** cough, it lasted for a long period of time and always came back.*

6. **chronological** (kron · uh · loj′ i · kul) *adj.* Arranged in time order (earlier things or events precede later ones). *To arrange our outline on wars in the United States in **chronological** order, we needed to know the dates of the wars.*

7. **chronometer** (kruh · nom′ uh · tur) *n.* A very accurate clock; an instrument used to measure time. *Because the car's **chronometer** was always correct, I usually went by that time.*

8. **concede** (kun · sēde′) *v.* To give in; surrender; yield; grant; admit. *After a long discussion and debate on an issue, the union said that it would **concede** on this particular issue because the employers had given in on other issues.*

9. **concession** (kun · sesh′ un) *n.* An act of giving in. *To settle the strike, both sides had to make a number of **concessions.***

10. **conductor** (kun · duk′ tur) *n.* One who guides or leads; a guide or director; one who has charge of a railroad train; the director of an orchestra or chorus; any substance that conducts electricity, heat, and so on. *You could tell from the applause that the **conductor** of the orchestra was greatly admired by the large audience that had come to see him lead the orchestra.*

11. **consequence** (kon′ suh · kwensé) *n.* That which follows from any act; a result; an effect. *I had no idea what the **consequence** of my leaving home would be until I found out that my mother had become ill as a result of it.*

12. **content** (kon′ tent) *n.* What something holds (usually plural in this sense); subject matter; the material that something is made up of; the main substance or meaning. *The course **content** was supposed to deal with the earth's crust or makeup, but the instructor had not yet covered any subject matter related to geology.*

13. **content** (kun · tent′) *adj.* Satisfied; not complaining; not desiring something else. *It is obvious that Consuela is **content** with her life because she never complains and always seems free from worry.*

14. **crypt** (kript) *n.* An underground vault. *The **crypt** was buried fifty feet underground in a special cave.*

THE FAR SIDE® By GARY LARSON

"Mr. Bailey? There's a gentleman here who claims an ancestor of yours once defiled his crypt, and now you're the last remaining Bailey and ... oh, something about a curse. Should I send him in?"

15. **cryptic** (krip' tik) *adj.* Having a hidden or secret meaning; mysterious. *The **cryptic** message was very difficult to decode because no one was familiar with the meanings of the letters used in the code.*

16. **cycle** (sī' kul) *n.* A period that keeps coming back, in which certain events take place and complete themselves in some definite order; a round of years or ages; a pattern of regularly occurring events; a series that repeats itself. *We seem to be going through an economic **cycle** that is similar to one we had a decade ago.*

17. **cyclone** (sī' klōn*é*) *n.* A system of violent and destructive whirlwinds. *When the **cyclone** hit the small town, its winds were so strong that it destroyed everything in its path.*

18. **deduction** (di · duk' shun) *n.* The act of drawing a conclusion by reasoning that goes from the general to the particular; the subtraction of something; an inference or conclusion. *How much money are you able to get back by having so many **deductions** on your income tax?*

19. **detain** (di · tāin') *v.* To stop; to delay; to hold. *The man at the airport was **detained** by the police because they thought that he was a criminal attempting to flee the country.*

20. **induction** (in · duk' shun) *n.* Act of reasoning that goes from particular to general. *The scientists used the method of **induction** to conclude that their serum was effective.*

21. **maintain** (māin · tāin') *v.* To carry on or continue; to keep up; to keep in good condition. *When Mr. Singh lost his job, he found that he could not **maintain** his house because the needed repairs were too costly.*

22. **precede** (prē · sēd*é*') *v.* To go or come before. *In the circus parade, the clowns were to **precede** the others because, by entering first, the clowns would put the spectators in a good mood for the rest of the show.*

23. **proceed** (prō · sēed') *v.* To go on; to go forward; to carry on an action. *We will **proceed** the way we have been going unless someone knows some reason why we should not continue.*

24. **procession** (pruh · sesh' un) *n.* A parade. *The **procession** continued to move forward in an orderly manner even though it was raining very hard.*

25. **recession** (ri · sesh' un) *n.* Act of going back; in economics, the decline of business activity. *During a **recession,** when unemployment is high, economists try to figure out ways to stimulate the economy.*

26. **retentive** (ri · ten' tiv*é*) *adj.* Tenacious; ability to retain things; having a good memory. *Arthur has such a **retentive** memory that he can recall details from things he studied or read more than twenty years ago.*

27. **secede** (si · sēd*é*') *v.* To withdraw from. *During the Civil War, the South **seceded** from the Union.*

28. **sequence** (sē' kwens*é*) *n.* The following of one thing after another; order; a continuous or related series, with one thing following another. *The detectives investigating the suicide were trying to get the **sequence** of events, step-by-step and in order, to try to figure out why the man took his life.*

29. **subscription** (sub · skrip' shun) *n.* An agreement; an agreement to receive something and pay for it. *Each year when I take out a **subscription** for my favorite magazine, I sign a form promising to pay a certain amount of money for the delivery of the magazine.*

30. **subsequent** (sub' suh · kwent) *adj.* Following soon after; following in time, place, or order; resulting. *The **subsequent** chapter, which follows this one, is the last chapter in Part One of this book.*

31. **succeed** (suk · sēēd') *v.* To accomplish what is attempted; to come next in order; to come next after or replace another in an office or position. *The people who* **succeed** *seem to be those who do not stop until they have accomplished what they set out to do.*

32. **synchronize** (sin' kruh · nīzé) *n.* To take place at the same time; to agree in rate or speed. *We* **synchronized** *our watches to make sure that we all had the same time.*

33. **tenacious** (tuh · nā' shus) *adj.* Stubborn; tough; holding strongly to one's views. *He had such* **tenacious** *feelings on that issue that no one could change his mind.*

34. **tenant** (ten' unt) *n.* A person who holds property; one who lives in property belonging to another; one who rents or leases from a landlord; one who lives in a place. *The* **tenants** *told the landlord, who owned the building, that they would not pay the rent unless the landlord made the needed repairs to their apartments.*

35. **untenable** (un · ten' uh · bul) *adj.* Not able to be defended or held. *Her position on the issue was such an* **untenable** *one that we all agreed not to support her.*

SPECIAL NOTES

1. Note that the terms *content* (kon' tent) *n.* and *content* (kun · tent') *adj.* are spelled identically but are *pronounced differently* and have *different meanings*. Many of the words you have met have had more than one meaning. However, they were *pronounced identically*. Because *content* (kon' tent) *n.* and *content* (kun · tent') *adj.* are pronounced differently and each word has meanings different from those of the other, they are presented separately.

   a. **content** (kon' tent) *n.* What something holds (usually plural in this sense). *The* **contents** *of the box included all her childhood toys.*

   b. **content** (kon' tent) *n.* Subject matter. *The course* **content** *was so boring that I decided not to take any other courses in that subject.*

   c. **content** (kon' tent) *n.* The material that something is made up of. *When I checked the* **content** *of the ice cream I was eating, I found that it was made up almost completely of artificial products.*

   d. **content** (kun · tent') *adj.* Satisfied; not complaining; not desiring something else. *I am* **content** *with my job, so there is no need for me to look for another.*

2. The term *deduction* has a few meanings.

   a. **deduction.** A subtraction; something taken away. A *deduction* refers to your being able to subtract or take away a certain amount from something else. This meaning of *deduction* is much used in relation to income taxes. You can subtract or take away a certain amount of money from your income taxes on the basis of the number of *deductions* you have.

   b. **deduction.** Reasoning from the general to the particular or reasoning from given statements to conclusions. This meaning of *deduction* is used in *logic*, which is the *science of correct reasoning*. You met the term *logical*, which deals with correct reasoning, in Lesson 19. An example of deduction—going from the general to the specific—follows:

   > All men are good.
   > Arthur is a man.
   > Therefore, Arthur is good.

(continued)

In the preceding example, we can decide, on the basis of a general statement that all men are good, that a particular man, Arthur, must be good. (Note that on p. 233, the term *induction* is presented. Both *induction* and *deduction* are important parts of the scientific method, and both are reasoning processes used in logic. Inductive reasoning helps you arrive at general conclusions, whereas deductive reasoning helps you arrive at specific conclusions. Scientists collect sufficient data or evidence to make inductive conclusions.)

c. **deduction.** An inference; a conclusion. It is important for readers to be able to make *deductions* in reading because many times, writers do not directly state what they mean but present ideas in a more "roundabout" way, or *indirectly*.

In Lesson 19, you met the word *inference*. *Deduction* and *inference* have the same meaning. Remember that an *inference* is drawn from information that is not directly stated. The same is true of *deduction*. When all the information is given in statements but the information is given indirectly, you must make *deductions* or *inferences*. To get the information, you must "read between the lines." Mystery writers often use *inference* to make their stories more interesting and enjoyable. Following is an example of inference. Can you draw the proper inferences or make the correct deductions from the information given?

Read the following short selection, and answer the two questions.

> The six remaining boys were worn out from walking all day with such heavy knapsacks. They headed toward the mountain range, hoping to reach it before the sun finally set behind it. One-third of their original number had turned back earlier.

1. In what direction were the six boys headed?
2. How many boys had there been at the beginning of the trip?

To answer the first question, you must collect the following clues:

1. Boys walking toward mountain range.
2. Sun sets behind the mountain range.

From this information, you should conclude that the answer to the first question is "west" because the sun sets in the west and the boys were heading toward the setting sun.

To answer the second question, you must collect the following clues:

1. Six boys remaining.
2. One-third had turned back.

From this information, you should conclude that the answer to the second question is "nine" because if two-thirds of the boys equals six, one-third must be three, and six plus three equals nine.

Step IV. Practice

A **DIRECTIONS:** State the meaning of the word *deductions* in the cartoon. Then explain what makes the cartoon amusing.

Reprinted by permission of Tribune Media Services.

_____

_____

STOP. Check answers at the end of the book (p. 349).

B **DIRECTIONS:** A short story with missing words follows. Fill in the blanks with the words that *best* fit. Words are used only once. Note that *content* is given twice because it is used in two different ways.

Word List

abbreviation	corpse	homicide	proceed
chronic	cryptic	hypothesis	sequence
concede	cycle	illegal	subsequent
conductor	cyclone	local	succeed
consequence	deduction	maintain	television
content (n.)	description	morgue	tenant
content (adj.)			

I am a(n) (1)_____ in a large apartment building. I have been

(2)_____ living there and really had nothing much to complain about

until last month. A(n) (3)_____ of events took place that has made it

very difficult for me to (4)_____ my former way of living. What I am

saying is that as a(n) (5)_____ of one particular night, my whole life

has changed.

I remember the night very well for three reasons. First, we had such a violent (6)_____ during the day that some of my windows had been broken. Second, the night was very dark because the moon was completing its monthly (7)_____ just before the new moon. Third, a(n) (8)_____ took place right outside my broken window.

I should tell you that I live on the ground floor in a rather quiet neighborhood. My building is across the street from a large park, and during the summers, we have many famous (9)_____s leading orchestras in outdoor concerts. I live on the ground floor because I have a(n) (10)_____ back problem, and I never know when it will give me trouble.

Let me (11)_____ with my story of the murder. At about ten P.M., I thought I heard some sounds from outside, but I had the (12)_____ on, so I wasn't sure. The third time I thought I heard something, I went to my broken window to look outside. It was so dark that I saw nothing. However, on my floor, I found a paper attached to a broken piece of glass. Although I tried to read it, I did not (13)_____ in figuring out the (14)_____s of the paper. The paper contained a(n) (15)_____ message, which I could not decode. The only thing I could make out was *Dr.,* a(n) (16)_____ of the word *doctor.*

I immediately phoned the police. While waiting for the police, I again tried to decode the message. I finally had to (17)_____ to myself that I could not figure it out. The police arrived. I told them my story. They went out to investigate. It was then that they found the (18)_____. I was asked to look at the body. Frightened and trembling, I did. However, I had never seen the person before. The dead body was then taken to the (19)_____ because there was no identification on it. (20)_____ to that, the police came to question me. They wanted to know whether I had any (21)_____ that might be a possible explanation for the murder. I stated that I had none and that I knew nothing about it.

I told them that the only (22)_____ I could make or conclusion I could reach was that the person couldn't have died right away because he had time to pick up a piece of broken glass, attach some paper to it, and throw it through my already broken window.

The police were able to decode the message. The message gave such a good (23)_____of the murderer that the police were able to have a picture drawn of him. It turned out to be a(n) (24)_____ doctor from the neighborhood who was involved with the (25)_____ sale of drugs.

STOP. Check answers at the end of the book (p. 349).

C DIRECTIONS: Write a sentence that makes sense using at least two words from this lesson. Illustrate the meanings of the words without actually defining them.

Example

The *archaeologist* said that the *crypt* he had opened had a *cryptic, abbreviated* message, which he *deduced* had to do with materials in the *crypt*.

_____

_____

_____

_____

STOP. Check answers at the end of the book (p. 349).

D DIRECTIONS: Write the words from this lesson that go with the meanings.

1. Satisfied; not complaining _____

2. To continue; to keep up; to keep in good condition _____

3. A continuous series _____

4. A result; an effect _____

5. A person who rents or leases from a landlord _____

6. Following soon after _____

7. The study of the life and culture of ancient people _____

8. Referring to what is ancient _____

9. A round of years or ages _____

10. A violent, destructive whirlwind _____

11. Arranged in time order _____

12. To go forward _____

13. To give in _____

14. To go or come before _____

15. Continuing for a long time and coming back _____

16. To accomplish what is attempted; to come after _____

17. A shortened form of a word or phrase _____

18. One who guides or leads _____

19. The act of drawing a conclusion by reasoning; an inference _____

20. Having a hidden meaning _____

21. An underground vault _____

22. Subject matter _____

STOP. Check answers at the end of the book (p. 349).

EXTRA WORD POWER

dis	Away from; apart; not. When *dis* is placed in front of a word, it may give it the opposite meaning. It may result in undoing something that was done. It may take away some quality, power, rank, and so on. For example: *disrobe*—take off clothes; *disband*—break up the group; *disable*—make an object or someone not able to do something; *disloyal*—not loyal; *disapprove*—to not approve of; to regard as not worthy; *dishonest*—not honest; not to be trusted. How many more words with *dis* can you supply?
sub	Under; beneath; below; lower in rank. *Sub* is added to the beginning of many words. For example; *submarine*—undersea ship; *subfloor*—floor beneath; *subtraction*—the act of taking something away; *subset*—something that is under the larger set; *subcommittee*—committee under the original committee. Check your dictionary to find many more words beginning with *sub*.

QUESTION: In the following cartoon, the terms *tenacious* and *stubborn* are used. Even though *tenacious* and *stubborn* are synonyms, the child in the *Peanuts* cartoon gives an excellent comparison of the two terms. What is the comparison?

PEANUTS reprinted by permission of United Feature Syndicate, Inc.

ANSWER: Even though *tenacious* and *stubborn* are synonyms, the term *tenacious* is often used in a positive way, whereas the term *stubborn* is not. In other words, *tenacious* has a positive connotation, whereas *stubborn* has a negative connotation.

SPECIAL ACADEMIC WORDS

A **DIRECTIONS:** Here are some terms made up from combining forms that you met in this chapter and other chapters. State what field of science or study each is.

1. pediatrics _____

2. archaeology _____

3. logic _____

4. dermatology _____

5. toxicology _____

6. gynecology _____

B DIRECTIONS: Here are some combining forms that you met in this chapter. Without looking back, use these combining forms to see how many terms you remember from this chapter that are related to the fields of science or study in Practice A.

cap	derm	dia	fin	hypo	pro
chron	epi	fer	gnosi	log	tox

1. _____
2. _____
3. _____
4. _____
5. _____
6. _____
7. _____
8. _____
9. _____
10. _____
11. _____
12. _____
13. _____
14. _____
15. _____
16. _____
17. _____
18. _____

C DIRECTIONS: The answers to the following riddles are literature terms that you met in this chapter. See how well you do.

1. I always have the final say in a piece. _____

2. I'm always at the beginning. _____

3. You need two speakers conversing to create me. _____

4. You need only one of me, but I'm very long-winded. _____

5. I usually send you to another for information. _____

6. I don't tell you anything about what's inside a book, but I give you lots of information about the book. _____

7. I never give my name. _____

8. I never give my real name. _____

STOP. Check answers at the end of the book (pp. 349–350).

CHAPTER WORDS IN A PARAGRAPH

Write a paragraph on the given topic using at least two words from this chapter. The paragraph must make sense and be logically developed.

Topic: My Academic Goals

STOP. Check answers at the end of the book (p. 350).

GAINING WORD POWER ON THE INTERNET

1. Choose a search engine. Write the name of the chosen search engine:
   _____

2. Do a search of the following two terms: *hypothesis, archaeology.*

3. Choose one site or reference generated by your search for each term. Try to select sites that help you gain a better understanding of the terms you are researching. Write the chosen site for each term: _____ _____

4. Write a three-sentence paragraph on the site information for each term.

5. Log onto the Web site that accompanies this textbook for extra practice exercises at [http://www.ablongman.com/vocabulary].

STOP. Check answers at the end of the book (p. 350).

CROSSWORD PUZZLE

DIRECTIONS: The meanings of many of the combining forms from Lessons 19 to 21 follow. Your knowledge of these combining forms will help you solve the crossword puzzle. Note that *combining form* is abbreviated as *comb. f.*

Across

1. Meaning of comb. f. *deca*
4. Salespeople like to make lots of
   _____
6. Comb. f. for *poison*
7. Comb. f. for *skin*
10. Comb. f. for *other*
13. Sound a duck makes
15. Homonym of *two*
16. Comb. f. for *one who*
18. Rhymes with *ham*
20. Until, to
21. Comb. f. for *knowledge*
23. Comb. f. for *upon*
25. Homonym of *two*
26. Comb. f. for *lead*
28. Comb. f. for *down*
30. Comb. f. for *take*
31. Belonging to me
32. Comb. f. for *back*
33. Abbreviation for *railroad*
34. Comb. f. for *before*
36. Rule by the people

Down

1. You pay this on money you earn
2. Abbreviation for *elevated train*
3. Boy's name
4. Homonym of *sew*
5. Comb. f. for *follow*
8. You _____ faster than you walk
9. What a thing is made of
10. A preposition meaning "on" or "near"
11. Comb. f. for *speech; word*
12. Comb. f. for *state of, act of,* or *result of*
14. Home for chickens
16. Rhymes with *has*
17. Comb. f. for *laughter*
18. Comb. f. for *without*
19. Comb. f. for *measure*
22. On a nice day it shines
24. Way of saying *father*
27. Comb. f. for *go*
28. Roman numeral *100*
29. Comb. f. for *ancient*
30. Comb. f. for *secret*
31. Way of saying *mother*

42. Intention
43. Geometry is a _____ course
44. Comb. f. for *under*
46. Exclamation of surprise, suspicion, or triumph
47. A female actor
51. Used to express surprise, enthusiasm
52. Means *look*; _____ *and behold*
53. Comb. f. for *through*
54. A courageous man admired for his brave deeds
55. Sound made when laughing
56. Abbreviation for *New York*
57. Something small is a little _____
58. Comb. f. for *woman*
59. Comb. f. for *time*
62. Roman numeral *500*
63. Meaning of *uni*

34. Same as #24 Down
35. Comb. f. for *laughter*
37. Comb. f. for *in*
38. Way of saying *mother*
39. Meaning of *ali*
40. Sound made when surprised
41. Comb. f. for *circle*; *wheel*
45. Comb. f. for *one who*
48. Ending for the past tense of regular verbs
49. When you do wrong, you commit a _____
50. Meaning of *dict*
51. Rhymes with *let*
54. Refers to the rear
57. You say this when you leave
58. Abbreviation for a doctor who has a general practice
59. Same as #25 Across
60. Comb. f. for *in*
61. A pronoun

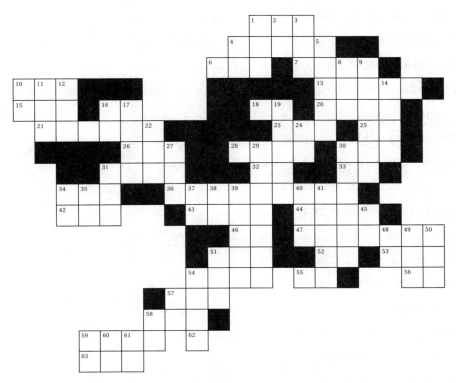

STOP. Check answers at the end of the book (p. 350).

ANALOGIES

DIRECTIONS: Find the word from the following list that *best* completes each analogy. There are more words listed than you need.

Word List

adult	contemporary	diameter	pediatrician
agnostic	content	epilogue	preface
ancient	cyclone	fertile	procession
archaic	deceive	finite	prognosis
bibliography	decimate	inference	reference
biography	deride	infinite	tenacious
captor	diagnosis	infinitesimal	toxicologist
catalogue	diagram	mouth	transparent
chronometer	dialect	pedagogue	visage
consequence	dialogue		

1. Clock : chronometer :: stubborn : _____.

2. Beginning : end :: prologue : _____.

3. Enthusiasm : apathy :: immeasurable : _____.

4. Deference : respect :: ridicule : _____.

5. Skin : dermatologist :: poison : _____.

6. Limp : wilted :: parade : _____.

7. Extemporaneous : prepared :: dissatisfied : _____.

8. Woman : gynecologist :: child : _____.

9. Lawyer : counselor :: teacher : _____.

10. Potentate : monarch :: current : _____.

11. Deportment : behavior :: effect : _____.

12. Snow: blizzard :: wind : _____.

13. Wrist : arm :: nose : _____.

14. Archaic : ancient :: bluff : _____.

15. Salary : employee :: ransom : _____.

16. Obese : plump :: eradicate : _____.

17. Sheer : opaque :: sterile : _____.

18. God : atheist :: knowing : _____.

19. Shawl : scarf :: deduction : _____.

20. Gait : trot :: speech : _____.

STOP. Check answers at the end of the book (p. 350).

MULTIPLE-CHOICE VOCABULARY TEST

DIRECTIONS: This is a test on words in Lessons 19 to 21. Vocabulary words are presented according to lessons. *Do all lessons before checking answers.* Underline the meaning that *best* fits the word.

Lesson 19

1. affinity
   a. end
   b. another
   c. close relationship
   d. finally

2. bibliography
   a. a list of books on a subject
   b. a note in a book
   c. refers to books
   d. the study of spelling

3. catalogue
   a. added to the end of a book
   b. an introduction
   c. conversation
   d. a listing of names, titles, and so on, in some order

4. circumference
   a. the distance across a circle
   b. refers to measurement
   c. the distance around a circle
   d. refers to a globe

5. conference
   a. a convention
   b. a friendly get-together
   c. a discussion or meeting on some important matters
   d. refers to science meetings

6. defer
   a. to postpone
   b. to detour
   c. to respect
   d. to carry forth

7. deference
   a. to delay
   b. to carry
   c. to put forth
   d. respect

8. definitive
   a. final
   b. to delay
   c. variety
   d. to respect

9. diagram
   a. divides circle in half
   b. conversation
   c. outline figure showing relationships
   d. introduction

10. dialect
    a. refers to speech
    b. language
    c. variety of speech
    d. respect

11. dialogue
    a. introduction
    b. conversation
    c. at the end of a book
    d. refers to reasoning

12. diameter
    a. line dividing a circle in half
    b. an outline showing relationships in a circle
    c. an outline
    d. a map

13. epilogue
   a. conversation
   b. a listing of books
   c. addition to the end of a book
   d. an introduction

14. fertile
   a. a producer
   b. able to produce a large crop
   c. refers to soil
   d. refers to children

15. fertilization
   a. a producer
   b. what one puts on soil
   c. union of sperm and egg
   d. refers to children

16. final
   a. able to produce
   b. limited number
   c. last
   d. refers only to tests

17. finale
   a. part in a play
   b. end
   c. a musical movement
   d. an entertainment

18. finite
   a. the end of a play
   b. at the end of a book
   c. added to a book
   d. having a limit or an end

19. inference
   a. to carry
   b. deduction
   c. something attractive
   d. very small

20. infinite
   a. ends in time
   b. endless
   c. ends
   d. certain number

21. infinitesimal
   a. final
   b. very small
   c. measured
   d. refers to size

22. logical
   a. relating to correct reasoning
   b. relating to an introduction
   c. a listing of names
   d. added to the end of a book

23. monologue
   a. refers to speech
   b. long speech by one person
   c. kind of speech
   d. a long speech

24. preference
   a. a note in a book
   b. a note in a book sending you for information
   c. a recommendation
   d. someone or something you choose over another

25. proficient
   a. an able person
   b. to know
   c. able to do something well
   d. to be aware

26. prologue
   a. added to the end of a book
   b. introduction to a play
   c. correct reasoning
   d. conversation

27. reference
   a. a person who sends things
   b. a chapter in a book
   c. a recommendation from a person
   d. a letter

28. suffer
   a. to be able to take pain
   b. to put up with pain
   c. to feel pain
   d. refers to pain

29. transfer
   a. to carry or send from one place to another
   b. a sender
   c. a carrier
   d. to cross

Lesson 20

30. capable   a. something for the head   c. refers to power
                  b. able to wear hats   d. having ability

31. contemporary a. referring to what is ancient c. referring to a short period of
                  b. referring to a time period   time
                                                   d. referring to what is modern

32. toxic   a. deadly   c. unsafe
                  b. poisonous   d. unclear

33. dermatologist a. a skin disease   c. a skin doctor
                  b. a doctor   d. refers to skin

34. hypodermic   a. a needle   c. area above the skin
                  b. referring to the area under   d. skin
                     the skin

35. hypothesis   a. any guess   c. an unproved conclusion
                  b. any idea   d. an unproved conclusion drawn
                                                      from known facts

36. temporary   a. referring to time   c. referring to a short time period
                  b. referring to a waiting period d. referring to a time period

37. capsule   a. a spaceship   c. an instrument
                  b. a rocket   d. a removable part of a rocket or
                                                      an airplane

38. ridiculous   a. funny   c. something not nice
                  b. unworthy of consideration   d. something not helpful

39. ridicule   a. to laugh   c. to make someone the object of
                  b. to joke   mockery
                                                   d. to be cruel

40. diagnose   a. to make a prediction   c. to give an examination
                  b. to make a prediction   d. to determine what is wrong
                     concerning someone's illness   with someone after an
                                                      examination

41. prognosis   a. refers to recovery   c. refers to knowing what is
                  b. refers to illness   wrong
                                                   d. a prediction concerning an
                                                      illness

42. pediatrician a. a woman who is a doctor   c. a doctor who specializes in foot
                  b. a doctor   diseases
                                                   d. a children's doctor

43. gynecologist a. a woman who is a doctor   c. a doctor who is a specialist
                  b. a doctor   d. a doctor who specializes in
                                                      women's diseases

44. captive
    a. a prisoner   c. a kidnapper
    b. a hunter   d. a searcher

45. conceive
    a. to learn   c. to teach
    b. to conceal   d. to think

46. deceive
    a. to believe   c. to mislead by lying
    b. to lead   d. to tell

47. reception
    a. to receive something   c. the manner of thinking
    b. the manner of receiving someone   d. the act of taking

48. exception
    a. something or one that is left out   c. being invited
    b. being included   d. refers to leaving

49. perception
    a. a sense   c. act of knowing something
    b. senses of seeing and hearing   d. act of becoming aware of something through the senses

50. derisive
    a. laughing   c. mockingbird
    b. refers to making fun of   d. to leave

51. epidermis
    a. refers to skin   c. layer of skin
    b. outermost layer of skin   d. refers to outermost

52. agnostic
    a. does not believe in God's existence   c. believes in God's existence
    b. is uncertain   d. refers to God

53. antitoxin
    a. poison   c. used against poison
    b. refers to poison   d. bacteria

54. misogynist
    a. refers to hatred   c. refers to women
    b. one who hates marriage   d. one who hates women

55. intercept
    a. to help   c. to finish
    b. interrupt the course of   d. to end

56. extemporaneous
    a. done immediately   c. not spoken
    b. speaking plainly   d. speaking without special preparation

57. pedagogue
    a. teacher   c. a ruler
    b. refers to children   d. a foot doctor

58. perceptive
    a. a human being   c. a being
    b. being aware   d. a rule

59. susceptible
    a. being aware   c. easily influenced by
    b. not being aware   d. not influenced by

60. tempo
    a. refers to rate   c. rate of activity
    b. musical composition   d. time

61. toxicologist
    a. a researcher   c. a scientist
    b. one who studies   d. one who studies poisons

Lesson 21

62. tenant
   a. one who takes care of apartments for a salary
   b. one who lives on property belonging to another
   c. one who takes care of buildings for a salary
   d. one who holds things

63. content
   a. subject matter
   b. refers to courses
   c. refers to teaching
   d. refers to learning

64. maintain
   a. to keep up in good repair
   b. to help someone
   c. to carry
   d. to hold

65. content
   a. worried
   b. unsure
   c. unhappy
   d. satisfied

66. sequence
   a. coming before
   b. coming after
   c. following
   d. the following of one thing after another

67. consequence
   a. an arrangement
   b. in order
   c. an effect
   d. following

68. subsequent
   a. in order
   b. following
   c. a result
   d. an arrangement

69. concede
   a. going before
   b. coming after
   c. to accomplish what one started out to do
   d. to give in

70. precede
   a. to go forward
   b. to come before
   c. to give in
   d. to accomplish things

71. proceed
   a. to come before
   b. to go forward
   c. to go back
   d. to give in

72. succeed
   a. to accomplish what one started out to do
   b. to give in
   c. to go forward
   d. to go back

73. abbreviation
   a. a short person
   b. a shortened form of a word or phrase
   c. refers to short
   d. a cutoff of something

74. conductor
   a. head of a company
   b. an orchestra leader
   c. one who takes
   d. one who takes away

75. deduction
   a. act of leading away
   b. act of leading
   c. a conclusion
   d. act of leading to

76. cryptic
   a. a hidden vault
   b. a mysterious vault
   c. an underground vault
   d. having a hidden or secret meaning

77. cycle
   a. refers to time
   b. refers to the wind
   c. refers to the mind
   d. a round of years or ages

78. cyclone
   a. a wind
   b. a rainstorm
   c. system of violent and destructive whirlwinds
   d. a round of years or ages

79. archaeology
   a. study of rocks
   b. study of rulers
   c. ancient life
   d. study of the life and culture of ancient people

80. archaic
   a. refers to rulers
   b. the study of ancient cultures
   c. ancient
   d. a time period

81. chronological
   a. referring to disease
   b. arranged in time order
   c. referring to an outline
   d. referring to an ancient time

82. chronic
   a. time
   b. time period
   c. continuing for a long time
   d. not returning

83. crypt
   a. having a hidden meaning
   b. having a secret meaning
   c. a vault
   d. an underground vault

84. anachronism
   a. refers to time
   b. a watch
   c. out of time order
   d. a means to measure

85. chronometer
   a. very accurate clock
   b. refers to time
   c. a measurement
   d. refers to a measurement

86. concession
   a. to hold
   b. a stand
   c. an act of giving in
   d. refers to food

87. detain
   a. to hold
   b. to put off doing
   c. refers to measuring
   d. to postpone

88. induction
   a. refers to reasoning
   b. an act
   c. reasoning from specific to general
   d. refers to logical order

89. procession
   a. parade
   b. yielding
   c. funeral
   d. before a parade

90. retentive
   a. memory
   b. refers to memory
   c. remembers odd things
   d. good memory

91. secede
   a. refers to the Civil War
   b. to withdraw from
   c. refers to withdraw
   d. a parade

92. subscription
   a. an agreement
   b. underwriting
   c. payment
   d. receiving something

93. synchronize
   a. to place
   b. to take place at the same time
   c. to set a time to meet
   d. refers to time

94. tenacious
   a. to have a position
   b. to have an opinion
   c. to be a pest
   d. stubborn

95. untenable
   a. not able to be defended
   b. to have a wrong opinion
   c. to defend
   d. to sway someone

96. recession
   a. relates to economics
   b. act of going back
   c. an act
   d. business activity

CHAPTER TRUE/FALSE TEST

DIRECTIONS: This is a true/false test on Lessons 19 to 21. Read each sentence carefully. Decide whether it is true or false. Put a *T* for *True* or an *F* for *False* in the blank. If the statement is false, change a word or words to make it true. The number after the sentence tells you in which lesson the word appears.

_____   1. <u>Archaic</u> and <u>chronic</u> are antonyms. 21

_____   2. A <u>procession</u> is a kind of parade. 21

_____   3. <u>Precede</u> and <u>secede</u> are antonyms. 21

_____   4. A <u>subsequent</u> event is the next one in a <u>sequence</u>. 21

_____   5. A <u>retentive</u> memory is an excellent one. 21

_____   6. To <u>concede</u> means to <u>succeed</u>. 21

_____   7. Eighteenth-century automobiles would be <u>anachronisms</u>. 21

_____   8. A <u>catalogue</u> contains <u>dialogue</u>. 19

_____   9. <u>Definitive</u> results are complete. 19

_____   10. <u>Fertile</u> soil would grow healthy crops. 19

_____   11. To show a <u>preference</u> is to show <u>deference</u>. 19

_____   12. Any <u>conference</u> will involve talking. 19

_____   13. A <u>captive</u> is someone who takes prisoners. 20

_____   14. <u>Conceive</u> is a synonym for *lie*. 20

_____   15. If you are <u>susceptible</u> to a disease, you should take an <u>antitoxin</u>. 20

_____   16. A male patient would go to a <u>gynecologist</u>. 20

_____   17. A physician would <u>diagnose</u> a disease before giving you a prognosis. 20

_____   18. A <u>dermatologist</u> treats problems of the feet. 20

_____   19. <u>Chronological</u> refers to time. 21

_____   20. A <u>conductor</u> drives a railroad train. 21

_____   21. Someone who was <u>content</u> would not complain. 21

_____   22. To <u>detain</u> someone is to assist him or her. 21

_____ 23. To <u>proceed</u> is to continue. 21

_____ 24. An <u>affinity</u> is a strong dislike. 19

_____ 25. To <u>defer</u> is to delay. 19

_____ 26. The <u>diameter</u> of a circle is the distance across it. 19

_____ 27. <u>Logical</u> arguments are not used in scientific reasoning. 19

_____ 28. A <u>finale</u> would come before a <u>prologue</u>. 19

_____ 29. Something that is <u>infinite</u> has no end. 19

_____ 30. <u>Derisive</u> laughter is sympathetic or kindly. 20

_____ 31. A child who is ill should see a <u>pediatrician</u>. 20

_____ 32. <u>Tempo</u> refers to speed. 20

_____ 33. Something that is <u>toxic</u> is good to eat. 20

_____ 34. An <u>extemporaneous</u> talk is one that is thoroughly prepared. 20

_____ 35. A <u>misogynist</u> would most likely be a man. 20

STOP. Check answers for both tests at the end of the book (p. 351).

SCORING OF TESTS

Multiple-Choice Vocabulary Test	
Number Wrong	*Score*
0–4	Excellent
5–9	Good
10–13	Weak
Above 13	Poor
Score _____	

True/False Test	
Number Wrong	*Score*
0–4	Excellent
5–7	Good
8–10	Weak
Above 10	Poor
Score _____	

1. If you scored in the excellent or good range on *both tests,* you are doing well. Go on to Chapter 9.
2. If you scored in the weak or poor range on either test, go to the next page and follow directions for Additional Practice. Note that the words on the tests are arranged so that you can tell in which lesson to find them. This arrangement will help you if you need additional practice.

ADDITIONAL PRACTICE SETS

A DIRECTIONS: Write the words you missed on the tests from the three lessons in the space provided. Note that the tests are presented so that you can tell to which lessons the words belong.

Lesson 19 Words Missed

1. _____   6. _____

2. _____   7. _____

3. _____   8. _____

4. _____   9. _____

5. _____   10. _____

Lesson 20 Words Missed

1. _____   6. _____

2. _____   7. _____

3. _____   8. _____

4. _____   9. _____

5. _____   10. _____

Lesson 21 Words Missed

1. _____   6. _____

2. _____   7. _____

3. _____   8. _____

4. _____   9. _____

5. _____   10. _____

B DIRECTIONS: Restudy the words that you have written down on this page. Study the combining forms from which those words are derived. Do Step I and Step II for those you missed. Note that Step I and Step II of the combining forms and vocabulary derived from these combining forms are on the following pages:

Lesson 19—pp. 212–219
Lesson 20—pp. 220–228
Lesson 21—pp. 229–239

C **DIRECTIONS:** Do Additional Practice 1 on this page and p. 255 if you missed words from Lesson 19. Do Additional Practice 2 on pp. 255–256 if you missed words from Lesson 20. Do Additional Practice 3 on pp. 256–257 if you missed words from Lesson 21. Now go on to Chapter 9.

Additional Practice 1 for Lesson 19

A **DIRECTIONS:** The combining forms presented in Lesson 19 follow. Match the combining form with its meaning.

_____	1. dia	a. end
_____	2. cata	b. down
_____	3. log, logo	c. through
_____	4. fin	d. book
_____	5. biblio	e. speech; word
_____	6. fer	f. before; forward
_____	7. epi	g. bring; bear; yield (give up)
_____	8. pro	h. upon; beside; among

STOP. Check answers at the end of the book (p. 351).

B **DIRECTIONS:** Some vocabulary words presented in Lesson 19 follow. Match the word with its meaning.

_____	1. prologue	a. to feel pain
_____	2. logical	b. outline figure showing relationships
_____	3. catalogue	c. last
_____	4. epilogue	d. someone or something chosen over another
_____	5. dialogue	e. a listing of books on a subject
_____	6. diagram	f. endless
_____	7. diameter	g. a discussion or meeting on an important matter
_____	8. bibliography	h. section added to the end of a book
_____	9. final	i. a listing of names, titles, and so on, in some order
_____	10. finite	j. distance around a circle
_____	11. infinite	k. having an end

_____ 12. fertile   l. the union of sperm and egg

_____ 13. reference   m. able to produce

_____ 14. fertilization   n. referring to correct reasoning

_____ 15. preference   o. a recommendation

_____ 16. transfer   p. introduction to a play

_____ 17. conference   q. to carry or send from one place to another

_____ 18. suffer   r. a line that divides a circle in half

_____ 19. circumference   s. conversation

STOP. Check answers at the end of the book (p. 351).

Additional Practice 2 for Lesson 20

A **DIRECTIONS:** The combining forms presented in Lesson 20 follow. Match the combining form with its meaning.

_____ 1. cap, cep   a. skin

_____ 2. gnosi, gnosis   b. laughter

_____ 3. ped, pedo   c. under

_____ 4. tox, toxo   d. take; receive

_____ 5. gyn, gyno   e. child

_____ 6. temp, tempo, tempor   f. woman

_____ 7. hypo   g. knowledge

_____ 8. derm, dermo   h. time

_____ 9. ri, ridi, risi   i. poison

STOP. Check answers at the end of the book (p. 351).

B **DIRECTIONS:** Some vocabulary words presented in Lesson 20 follow. Match the word with its meaning.

_____ 1. capable   a. to mock or view in a scornful way

_____ 2. captive   b. modern

_____ 3. conceive   c. a children's doctor

_____ 4. deceive   d. prediction concerning an illness

_____ 5. reception   e. poisonous

_____ 6. exception   f. having ability

_____ 7. perception   g. doctor who specializes in women's diseases

_____ 8. capsule   h. an unproved conclusion drawn from known facts

_____ 9. ridiculous   i. to think

_____ 10. ridicule   j. something or one that is left out

_____ 11. diagnose   k. to mislead by lying

_____ 12. prognosis   l. referring to the area under the skin

_____ 13. pediatrician   m. unworthy of consideration

_____ 14. gynecologist   n. a becoming aware of something through the senses

_____ 15. toxic   o. a prisoner

_____ 16. dermatologist   p. manner of receiving someone

_____ 17. hypodermic   q. lasting for a short period of time

_____ 18. hypothesis   r. to determine what is wrong with someone after an examination

_____ 19. temporary   s. a removable part of a rocket or airplane

_____ 20. contemporary   t. a skin doctor

STOP. Check answers at the end of the book (p. 351).

Additional Practice 3 for Lesson 21

A **DIRECTIONS:** The combining forms presented in Lesson 21 follow. Match the combining form with its meaning.

_____ 1. tain, ten, tent   a. short; brief

_____ 2. cede, ceed   b. ancient

_____ 3. sequi   c. hold

_____ 4. cycl, cyclo   d. lead

_____ 5. chron, chrono   e. circle; wheel

_____ 6. archae, archaeo   f. secret; hidden

_____ 7. crypt, crypto   g. follow

_____ 8. duc   h. go; give in; yield (give in)

_____ 9. brevi   i. time

STOP. Check answers at the end of the book (p. 352).

B **DIRECTIONS:** Some vocabulary words presented in Lesson 21 follow. Match the word with its meaning.

_____ 1. tenant

_____ 2. content

_____ 3. content

_____ 4. maintain

_____ 5. sequence

_____ 6. consequence

_____ 7. subsequent

_____ 8. cycle

_____ 9. cyclone

_____ 10. archaeology

_____ 11. archaic

_____ 12. chronological

_____ 13. chronic

_____ 14. concede

_____ 15. precede

_____ 16. proceed

_____ 17. succeed

_____ 18. abbreviation

_____ 19. conductor

_____ 20. deduction

_____ 21. cryptic

_____ 22. crypt

a. the study of the life and culture of ancient people

b. to go forward

c. to come before

d. to give in

e. one who lives on property belonging to another

f. a result

g. satisfied

h. a round of years or ages

i. the following of one thing after another

j. a system of violent and destructive whirlwinds

k. subject matter

l. to keep up

m. following

n. a shortened form of a word or phrase

o. ancient

p. having a hidden meaning

q. a conclusion

r. underground vault

s. continuing for a long time and returning

t. orchestra leader; one in charge of a train

u. arranged in time order

v. to accomplish what one started out to do

STOP. Check answers at the end of the book (p. 352).

Chapter 9

LESSON 22

Step I. Story in Context

DIRECTIONS: The following story includes several vocabulary words from this lesson. As you read the story, pay careful attention to the vocabulary words in boldface type, and try to figure out the meaning of each of these words. Put your answers in the blanks.

Politicians

The (1) **politicians** _____ in this election are more (2) **belligerent** _____ than usual. They must think that the best way to get the audience's (3) **attention** _____ is to be as vocal as possible and not very (4) **civil** _____ to one another. They speak so forcibly and loudly that they certainly don't need a (5) **megaphone** _____. Also, in one of the elections, it seemed as though the (6) **intention** _____ of the people running for office was to see how (7) **ambiguous** _____ they could be because they used (8) **vocabulary** _____ words that could be taken in more than one way. Furthermore, the (9) **tension** _____ between them was so great that the audience thought they might start swinging at one another. The moderator actually tried to (10) **pacify** _____ the two by saying, "People, people, we are all friends here. This is just a friendly debate." It didn't help. Each continued to be very (11) **intense** _____ when he spoke. In addition, each tried to make the audience feel that he was quite different from the other and that a vote for him would save our (12) **civilization** _____. It's funny because the two have such similar backgrounds. They are both (13) **civilians** _____ who went to the same school. They both have taken a number of (14) **civics** _____ courses, and they both chose the same (15) **vocation**_____; they both grew up in a (16) **metropolitan** _____ area; and they both went into (17) **politics** _____ at an early age. There is a (18) **postscript** _____ to this story. Neither one of them was elected.

STOP. Check answers at the end of the book (p. 352).

Step II. Combining Forms

A **DIRECTIONS:** A list of combining forms with their meanings follows. Look at the combining forms and their meanings. Concentrate on learning each combining form and its meaning. Cover the meanings, read the combining forms, and state the meanings to yourself. Check to see whether you are correct. Now cover the combining forms, read the meanings, and state the combining forms to yourself. Check to see whether you are correct.

Combining Forms	Meanings
1. ambi	both
2. belli, bello	war
3. civ, civis	citizen
4. mega	very large
5. pac, pax	peace
6. polis	city
7. post	after
8. tend, tens, tent	stretch; strain
9. voc, vox	voice; call

B **DIRECTIONS:** Cover the preceding meanings. Write the meanings of the following combining forms.

Combining Forms	Meanings
1. ambi	_____
2. belli, bello	_____
3. civ, civis	_____

4. mega _____

5. pac, pax _____

6. polis _____

7. post _____

8. tend, tens, tent _____

9. voc, vox _____

Step III. Vocabulary Words Derived from Combining Forms in Context

1. **ambidextrous** (am · bē · dek′ strøus) *adj.* Able to use both hands equally well. *Some **ambidextrous** people use their left hands for writing and their right hands for everything else.*

2. **ambiguous** (am · big′ ū · øus) *adj.* Having two or more meanings. *What Seth said was so **ambiguous** that I couldn't figure out whether he wanted to stay or go.*

3. **attention** (uh · ten′ shun) *n.* Mental concentration; care; a position of readiness; act of courtesy. *When children are tired, they cannot pay **attention** because they have lost their ability to concentrate.*

PEANUTS reprinted by permission of United Feature Syndicate, Inc.

4. **avocation** (av · uh · kā′ shun) *n.* A hobby; something one does in addition to his or her regular work, usually for enjoyment. *Stamp collecting is my father's **avocation.***

5. **belligerent** (buh · lij′ uh · runt) *adj.* Warlike. *n.* Any nation, person, or group engaged in fighting or war. *Because Ernesto has such a **belligerent** manner, he gets into a lot of fights.*

6. **civics** (siv′ iks) *n.* (Used in the singular.) The part of political science dealing with the study of civic affairs and the rights and responsibilities of citizenship. *In school, I took a course in **civics** because I wanted to learn more about the individual citizen's rights and responsibilities.*

7. **civil** (siv′ ul) *adj.* Of a citizen or citizens; relating to citizens and their government; relating to ordinary community life as distinguished from military or church affairs; courteous or polite. *Ernesto believes that **civil** liberties are the rights that individual citizens have.*

8. **civilian** (si · vil′ yun) *n.* One who is not in the military. *adj.* Of civilians; nonmilitary. *Ernesto feels good being a **civilian** again after spending three years in the army.*

9. **civilization** (siv′ uh · luh · zā · shun) *n.* A state of human society that has a high level of intellectual, social, and cultural development; the cultural development

of a specific people, country, or region. *In a **civilization,** a high level of intellectual, social, and cultural development is supposed to exist.*

10. **convocation** (kon · vuh · kā′ shun) *n.* An assembly; a group of people called together. *At the beginning of the college year, a **convocation** is held, at which time the president of the college gives his welcoming address.*

11. **detente** (dā · tant́é′) *n.* Easing of strained relations, especially between nations. *The President said that **detente** between the two nations would continue if each country lived up to its agreements.*

12. **detention** (di · ten′ shun) *n.* Confinement; the state of being detained in jail; a keeping back. *Ernesto was held in **detention** until bail was raised for him.*

13. **intense** (in · tenś́é′) *adj.* Having great or extreme force; very strong; existing or occurring to a high or extreme degree. *The heat was so **intense** from the fire that the firefighters could not enter the building.*

14. **intention** (in · ten′ shun) *n.* Aim; goal; purpose. *Although, as a child, her **intention** was to become a famous archaeologist, she never thought that she would achieve her goal.*

15. **megalopolis** (meg · uh · lop′ uh · lus) *n.* One very large city made up of a number of cities; a vast populous continuously urban area. *The area between Boston and Washington D.C, is considered one **megalopolis** because of the high density of population between these two cities.*

16. **megaphone** (meg′ uh · fōné) *n.* A device used to increase sound. *Ernesto uses a microphone rather than a **megaphone** when he wants to be heard by a large audience.*

17. **metropolitan** (met · ruh · pol′ i · tun) *adj.* Referring to a major city center and its surrounding area. *n.* A person who inhabits a metropolis or one who has the manners and tastes associated with a metropolis. *Ernesto lives in a **metropolitan** area so that he can be close to the kinds of stores, theaters, and restaurants that are found in large cities.*

18. **pacifist** (pas′ uh · fist) *n.* One against war; one who wants peace. *Because Ali was a **pacifist,** he would not join the armed forces or any other military organization.*

19. **pacify** (pas′ uh · fī) *v.* To bring peace to; to calm; to quiet. *Ernesto tried to **pacify** the mob, but he could not calm them down.*

20. **politician** (pol′ uh · tish · un) *n.* A person engaged in politics; a person involved in the science or art of government; a person who seeks advancement or power within an organization by dubious (doubtful) means. *Ernesto met with the **politicians** to determine whom he would support for office.*

21. **politics** (pol′ uh · tiks) *n.* (Although plural, it is usually looked upon as singular.) The science or art of government or of the direction and management of public or state affairs. *Ernesto is not interested in politics because he isn't interested in the management of public or state affairs.*

22. **posterior** (pō · stir′ ē · ur) *adj. n.* Located behind; in the rear; following after; succeeding; the buttocks. *This blueprint shows the **posterior** section of the new airplane our company is building.*

23. **posterity** (pos · ter′ uh · tē) *n.* Future generations; all of one's descendents (offspring). *Artists hope that their works will be admired by **posterity.***

24. **posthumously** (pos′ chū · møus · lē) *adv.* After death. *Many artists gain recognition **posthumously** rather than during their lifetime.*

25. **postmortem** (pōst mor′ tum) *adj. n.* Autopsy; examination of human body after death. *The doctor performed a* **postmortem** *examination on the victim in order to determine the cause of his death.*

26. **postscript** (pōst′ skript) *n.* Something added to a letter after the writer's signature; something added to written or printed legal papers. *The abbreviation of* **postscript,** *something added to a letter after the writer has signed his or her name, is P.S.*

27. **provoke** (pruh · vōke′) *v.* To irritate; to stir up anger or resentment. *The speaker's words so* **provoked** *some of the people in the audience that they stood up and booed.*

28. **rebel** (reb′ ul) *n.* (ri · bel′) *v.* One who opposes those in control or authority; to disobey those in authority. *The soldiers* **rebelled** *against their unjust commander.*

29. **rebellion** (ri · bel′ yun) *n.* Opposition to one in authority or dominance. *The* **rebellion** *against the commander resulted in many injuries.*

30. **tendon** (ten′ dun) *n.* A fibrous cord by which a muscle is attached. *When the athlete pulled the* **tendon** *in his leg, he was in great pain.*

31. **tension** (ten′ shun) *n.* The act of stretching or the condition of being stretched tight; mental strain. *The parents'* **tension** *was so great when their child was kidnapped that they did not know how long they could stand the mental strain.*

32. **vocabulary** (vō · kab′ · yuh · ler · ē) *n.* (*pl.* **ies**) A list of words and phrases, usually arranged alphabetically, that are defined or translated from another language; a stock of words possessed by an individual or a group. *You are gaining a larger* **vocabulary** *from doing the exercises involving lists of words and their definitions.*

33. **vocal** (vō′ kul) *adj.* Referring to the voice; having voice; oral; freely expressing oneself in speech, usually with force; speaking out. *When we strained our* **vocal** *cords from yelling at the basketball game, we could hardly use our voices the next day.*

34. **vocation** (vō · kā′ shun) *n.* A calling; a person's work or profession. *Carmen chose a* **vocation** *similar to her father's because she wanted to follow in his footsteps.*

35. **vociferous** (vō · sif′ ur · øus) *adj.* Of forceful, aggressive, and loud speech; clamorous. *The couple in the apartment above us were so* **vociferous** *that the neighbors called the police to complain about the noise.*

SPECIAL NOTES

1. The term *civilian,* which refers to someone who is not in the military, is used also by police and by others who wear special uniforms to refer to someone out of uniform.

2. The combining form *mega* also means "million."

Examples

megabuck = 1,000,000 dollars

megabit = 1,000,000 bits. (You met the terms *bit* and *byte* in Lesson 13.) A bit is a unit of computer information; one byte = 8 bits of data; usually 2 bytes = one word.)

megahertz = one million hertz (*hertz* = the international unit of frequency; it is equal to one cycle per second).

Step IV. Practice

A **DIRECTIONS:** Choose the word that *best* completes each sentence. Each word from the list below will be used no more than once, and not all words will be used.

Word List

ambidexterous	detention	posthumously	vocabulary
attention	intention	postmortem	vocal
avocation	megalopolis	provoke	vociferous
civil	pacifist	rebel	
convocation	posterior	rebellion	
detente	posterity	tendon	

1. I want to become a writer, but singing will always be my _____.

2. I sometimes think that your writing is simply too advanced for our times, but I am sure that _____ will appreciate it.

3. Maria is such a rule-abiding person that she never even got kept after school for _____ when she was in high school.

4. The speaker at the opening _____ always tries to give an address that will provide a theme for the academic year.

5. Doctors often use the word "anterior" when they mean "in front of" and "_____" when they mean "behind."

6. You know that Lou gets angry very quickly, so try not to _____ him.

7. During World War II, people who could prove that they had always been _____ were assigned to non-combat military duties.

8. After his computer died, Matt took it apart and performed a kind of _____ examination to see what had gone wrong.

9. After Abe finished speaking, several members of the committee voiced loud, strident, and _____ objections.

10. It's hard to believe, but there are many places just outside this huge, almost endless _____ where you can escape to beautiful natural areas.

11. Marian and Rob had been arguing for months, but now they seem to have entered a kind of _____.

12. Vladimir Nabokov's last novel is finally to be published _____, all these years after his death.

13. I'm not exactly _____, although I use my right hand for some tasks and my left hand for others.

14. Athletes often tear ligaments and _____, resulting in surgery and many months of physical therapy.

15. I am having a test today on Japanese _____ words and kanji symbols.

16. Umberto absolutely detests his in-laws, but he always tries to be _____ to them.

17. When Tilli suggested having sushi for the fourth night in a row, all her roommates rose up in _____.

18. I'm sorry you didn't enjoy the party, because my _____ in planning it was to make you happy.

19. Please pay careful _____ to my directions, since the format of your paper will be a large part of your grade.

20. Daniel has always been a _____, so I am not surprised that he is having trouble in boot camp.

STOP. Check answers at the end of the book (p. 352).

B **DIRECTIONS:** In the following sentences, give the meaning that *best* fits the underlined word.

1. During the president's speech, we paid very close <u>attention</u> to what was being said because we did not want to miss one word. _____

2. From his conflicting actions, I can't figure out what his <u>intentions</u> are. _____

3. There was considerable <u>tension</u> in the room after the instructor told the students that they needed to do more work. _____

4. The light was so <u>intense</u> that it hurt Gayle's eyes. _____

5. I avoid <u>belligerent</u> people because I am peaceful. _____

6. How do you feel now that you're out of uniform and a <u>civilian</u> again? _____

7. I think that courses in <u>civics</u> will help me because I want to become a politician. _____

8. Western <u>civilization</u> is different from Eastern civilization because the cultural development of the West and that of the East have been different. _____

9. There have been so many scandals in <u>politics</u> in the past decade that many people feel that elected officials are more concerned with selfish interests than with the proper management of public affairs. _____

10. It is sometimes difficult to be <u>civil</u> to persons who are rude and impolite. _____

11. As a <u>politician</u>, I intend to serve wisely the people who elected me to office. _____

12. What a change it was when Kim moved from a rural area, which is all farmland, to a metropolitan area. _____

13. The students were very vocal in their demands. _____

14. After studying so many words and their meanings, Martina has a larger vocabulary.

_____

15. My vocation is one that requires a lot of time, effort, and study. _____

16. The directions for the exam were so ambiguous that half the class did one thing and the other half did something else. _____

17. I needed to add a postscript to my letter because I thought of more things to say after I had already signed my letter. _____

18. The mother tried to pacify her screaming child by giving him a toy.

_____

STOP. Check answers at the end of the book (p. 352).

C DIRECTIONS: Write one sentence using at least two words from this lesson. Try to illustrate the meanings of the words without actually defining them. The sentence must make sense.

Example
The *politician* used a *megaphone* to try to *pacify* the *belligerent* crowd, but he could not get their *attention*.

_____

_____

_____

_____

STOP. Check answers at the end of the book (p. 352).

D DIRECTIONS: Underline the word that *best* fits the definition(s).

1. Mental concentration; act of courtesy
   a. tension   c. attention
   b. intense   d. intention

2. Aim; goal
   a. attention   c. tension
   b. intense   d. intention

3. Mental strain
   a. intense   c. attention
   b. tension   d. intention

4. Very strong
   a. tension   c. intention
   b. attention   d. intense

5. Warlike
   a. intense   c. belligerent
   b. tension   d. civil

6. One not in the military
   a. civil   c. civilian
   b. civilization   d. civics

7. Cultural development of a people
   a. civics   c. civilian
   b. civilization   d. civil

8. Polite; of a citizen or citizens
   a. civics   c. civilian
   b. politician   d. civil

9. Science of government dealing with the management of public affairs
   a. civilization   c. politics
   b. civics   d. civilian

10. The part of political science dealing with citizens' rights and responsibilities
    a. civics   c. civilization
    b. politics   d. civilian

11. A person involved in the science or art of government
    a. civilian   c. politics
    b. vocation   d. politician

12. Referring to a major city center and its surrounding area
    a. civilization   c. politics
    b. metropolitan   d. civilian

13. Something added to a letter after the signature
    a. vocabulary   c. metropolitan
    b. ambiguous   d. postscript

14. List of words that are defined
    a. vocation   c. vocal
    b. vocabulary   d. postscript

15. Referring to the voice
    a. vocal   c. vocabulary
    b. vocation   d. ambiguous

16. A person's work
    a. vocation   c. politics
    b. civilization   d. vocal

17. To calm
    a. civil   c. pacify
    b. vocal   d. postscript

18. Having two or more meanings
    - a. vocabulary
    - b. attention
    - c. vocal
    - d. ambiguous

19. Device to increase sound
    - a. vocal
    - b. intense
    - c. megaphone
    - d. telephone

STOP. Check answers at the end of the book (p. 352).

EXTRA WORD POWER

ance *ence*	Act of; state of; quality of. When *ance* is found at the end of a word, it means "act of," "state of," or "quality of." In an earlier lesson you met *tion,* which also means "state of" or "act of." If *ance* or *ence* is added to a word, the word changes to a noun. For example: **maintain.** To carry on or continue; to keep up. *I will **maintain** your car while you are away so that it will be in good working condition when you get home.* **maintenance.** The act of keeping up. *The **maintenance** of your car is important if it is to stay in good running condition.* Examples of words with *ance, ence; dependence*—act of trusting; act of relying on someone for support; *assistance*—act of helping; *sequence*—the state of following; *conference*—the act of meeting in a group. How many more words can you supply?
al	Relating to. When *al,* meaning "relating to," is added to the end of a word, the word is usually an adjective. For example: *vocal*—relating to the voice; *local*—relating to a place; *manual*—relating to the hand; *annual*—relating to the year; *universal*—relating to all; *legal*—relating to law; *apodal*—relating to being without feet; *nautical*—relating to sailing. How many more words can you supply?

LESSON 23

Step I. Story in Context

DIRECTIONS: The following story includes several vocabulary words from this lesson. As you read the story, pay careful attention to the words in boldface type, and try to figure out the meaning of these words. Put your answers in the blanks.

Analysis of A Novelist's Story

Recently, a writer for a widely read (1) **periodical** _____ did an

analysis of a well-known author's (2) **novels** _____. He wrote that

the author is a (3) **sophisticated** _____ and attractive woman, who is, however, very (4) **egocentric** _____. He said that her (5) **novels** _____ seem to (6) **consist** _____ primarily of (7) **circumstances** _____ from her own life and vividly reflect her (8) **philosophy** _____. She may have (9) **substituted** _____ different names and places, but the stories are nevertheless hers. For example, in one (10) **novel** _____, the main character is an attractive coed who is a (11) **sophomore** _____ at a (12) **distant** _____ college. While there, she goes through a number of difficult (13) **periods** _____. She is attacked in her (14) **dormitory** _____, and by the time someone comes to (15) **assist** _____ her, she has been brutally beaten. When the young woman is well enough to speak to the police, she is unable to help them find the attacker because he wore a (16) **translucent** _____ stocking on his face that distorted his facial features.

The coed finally recovers and goes back to school, but life is very difficult for her there. Wherever she goes, people point her out to others and start whispering. Also, she is always afraid. Wherever she goes, she feels that she is being watched. She has difficulty studying; she makes stupid (17) **errors** _____ on examinations; she can't give (18) **lucid** _____ explanations or remember even simple messages. At times, she feels that she is losing her mind. Other times, she feels as though she is having a heart attack. Her doctor tells her that she has developed (19) **hypertension** _____ since her attack and that she has to try to be more calm. This poor young coed seems to go from one disaster to another. Yet despite all these (20) **obstacles** _____, she (21) **persists** _____ at school and finally graduates.

Graduation seems to bring a major change in this young woman's life. It is as if she had been (22) **dormant** _____ and had finally awakened. Her awakening makes her sensitive to the needs of others around her. She goes to work at a research laboratory, which develops new devices or (23) **innovations** _____ that help others. Throughout her life, she is always influenced by what happened to her at school.

STOP. Check answers at the end of the book (p. 352).

Step II. Combining Forms

A DIRECTIONS: A list of combining forms with their meanings follows. Look at the combining forms and their meanings. Concentrate on learning each combining form and its meaning. Cover the meanings, read the combining forms, and state the meanings to yourself. Check to see whether you are correct. Now cover the combining forms, read the meanings, and state the combining forms to yourself. Check to see whether you are correct.

Combining Forms	Meanings
1. dorm	sleep
2. ego	I; me; the self
3. err	wander
4. hyper	over; above; excessive (very much)
5. luc, lum	light; clear
6. nov	new
7. peri	around
8. philo	love
9. sist, sta	stand
10. soph	wise

B **DIRECTIONS:** Cover the preceding meanings. Write the meanings of the following combining forms.

Combining Forms	Meanings
1. dorm	_____
2. ego	_____
3. err	_____
4. hyper	_____
5. luc, lum	_____
6. nov	_____
7. peri	_____
8. philo	_____
9. sist, sta	_____
10. soph	_____

Step III. Vocabulary Words Derived from Combining Forms in Context

1. **assist** (uh · sist′) *v.* To give help to. *n.* An act of helping. *Ali **assisted** his friend because his friend had always helped him.*
2. **circumstance** (sir′ kum · stansé) *n.* Something connected with an act, an event, or a condition; (*often pl.*): the conditions, influences, and so on surrounding and

influencing persons or actions; formal display, as in *pomp and circumstance. The* **circumstances** *of the suicide were so suspicious that a full-scale investigation was started.*

3. **consist** (kun · sist′) *v.* To be made up of. *Karin knows what the plan* **consists** *of because she made it up herself.*

4. **distant** (dis′ tint) *adj.* Separated or apart by space and/or time; away from; far apart; not closely related. *A* **distant** *relative came to visit us, but I had never met her before because I am not closely related to her and she lives in another state.*

5. **dormant** (dor′ munt) *adj.* Asleep or as if asleep; not active. *Bears are* **dormant** *during the winter.*

6. **dormitory** (dor′ muh · tor · ē) *n.* (*pl.* **ries**) A large room in which many people sleep; a building providing sleeping and living quarters, especially at a school, college, or resort (summer or winter hotel). *Our college* **dormitory** *houses one hundred students.*

7. **egocentric** (ē · gō · sen′ trik) *adj.* Self-centered; relating everything to oneself. *Simon is so* **egocentric** *that everything he says seems to start with* I, me, *or* my.

8. **egotistic** (ē · gō · tis′ tik) *adj.* Conceited; selfish; vain; very concerned with oneself. *I do not enjoy being in the company of* **egotistic** *people because they are too concerned with themselves.*

9. **erratic** (ir · rat′ ik) *adj.* Not stable; wandering; not regular. *Ali's behavior was so* **erratic** *that we wondered whether he was mentally ill.*

10. **error** (er′ rur) *n.* A mistake; something done, said, or believed incorrectly; a wandering from what is correct. *The* **error** *in judgment seemed like a very small mistake, but it caused a great deal of suffering for others.*

11. **hyperbole** (hī · per′ buh · lē) *n.* Overstatement; great exaggeration. *When Sharon said that she had walked a million miles today, she was using* **hyperbole.**

12. **hypertension** (hī · pur · ten′ shun) *n.* High blood pressure. *When someone is diagnosed as having* **hypertension,** *he or she should have his or her blood pressure checked frequently to make sure that it doesn't get too high.*

13. **illuminate** (il · lū′ muh · nāte) *v.* To light up; to make clear. *The lights so* **illuminated** *the room that everything could be seen clearly.*

14. **innovation** (in · nuh · vā′ shun) *n.* Something newly introduced; a new method; something new. *Angelo's* **innovation** *saved his company millions of dollars because his new method made it possible to manufacture the product more cheaply.*

15. **lucid** (lū′ sid) *adj.* Clear; easily understood; bright, shining. *When I ask a question about something I don't understand, I like to receive a* **lucid** *explanation.*

16. **novel** (nov′ ul) *n.* A work of fiction of some length. *adj.* New; strange; unusual. *It takes some people a while to get used to* **novel** *ideas because they do not like anything new or different.*

17. **novice** (nov′ ise) *n.* A beginner; a rookie; someone who is new at something. *Everyone thought that Hiroshi was an expert rather than a* **novice** *because of the way he handled himself on the tennis court.*

18. **obstacle** (ob′ stuh · kul) *n.* Something that stands in the way or opposes; something that stops progress; an obstruction. *There were many* **obstacles** *that stood in the way of my going to college, but I was able to overcome each of them.*

19. **obstinate** (ob′ stuh · nit) *adj.* Stubborn; tenacious. *My friend is so **obstinate** that once he makes up his mind, he will never change it.*

20. **perimeter** (puh · rim′ uh · tur) *n.* Boundary line of a closed plane figure; a measure of the outer part of a closed plane figure. *The **perimeter** of a circle would be its circumference.*

21. **period** (pir′ ē · od) *n.* A portion of time; a portion of time into which something is divided; a punctuation mark that signals a full stop at the end of a sentence, also used after abbreviations. *In my high school, the school day was divided into seven class **periods.***

22. **periodical** (pir · ē · od′ i · kul) *adj.* Referring to publications, such as magazines, that appear at fixed time intervals. *n.* A publication that appears at regular intervals. *I have a subscription to a **periodical** that is published every month.*

23. **periphery** (puh · rif′ ur · ē) *n.* The outer part or boundary of something. (*pl.* **eries**) **Periphery** *and* perimeter *are synonyms.*

24. **periscope** (per′ uh · skōpe) *n.* An instrument used by a submarine to see all around. *The sailor in the submarine used the **periscope** to view the approaching destroyer.*

25. **persist** (pur · sist′) *v.* To continue in some course of action even though it is difficult. *Even though Katya knew that it would be difficult to become an actress, she **persisted** in trying.*

26. **philosophy** (fi · los′ uh · fē) *n.* (*pl.* **phies**) The study of human knowledge; the love of wisdom and the search for it; a search for the general laws that give a reasonable explanation of something. *Students of **philosophy** seek to understand various ideas better.*

27. **sophisticated** (suh · fis′ tuh · kāt · id) *adj.* Not in a simple, natural, or pure state; worldly-wise; not naive; cultured; highly complicated; complex; experienced. *Because she has traveled quite a lot and is very cultured, she always acts in a **sophisticated** manner.*

28. **sophistry** (sof′ ist · rē) *n.* Faulty reasoning; unsound or misleading but clever argument. (*pl.* **ies**) *Some persons are so clever in presenting their illogical arguments that it is difficult to recognize that the arguments are filled with **sophistry.***

29. **sophomore** (sof′ uh · more) *n.* A second-year student in American high schools or colleges; an immature person; one who thinks he or she knows more than is the case. *As a college **sophomore,** I have two more years to go before I graduate.*

30. **stamina** (stam′ uh · nuh) *n.* Staying power; resistance to fatigue, illness, and the like. *Professional athletes need a lot of **stamina** in order to keep playing.*

31. **substitute** (sub′ sti · tūte) *v.* To put in place of another person or thing. *n.* One who takes the place of another person; something that is put in place of something else or is available for use instead of something else. *When our teacher was absent, a **substitute** took her place.*

32. **translucent** (trans · lū′ sent) *adj.* Permitting light to go through but not permitting a clear view of any object. *We had a **translucent** screen on our window that allowed light to go through, but persons looking through the screen could not get a clear view of what was in the room.*

SPECIAL NOTES

1. *Hyper,* meaning "over," "above," "excessive" (very much), is placed at the beginning of a great number of words. For example:

   hypersensitive—oversensitive.
   hyperactive—overactive.
   hyperproductive—overproductive.

   Check your dictionary for more words with *hyper.*

2. You met the term *geocentric,* which means "having or relating to the earth as the center," in Lesson 11. The term *heliocentric,* which is made up of the combining forms *helio* (sun) and *centric* (having [something specified] as its center), means "having or relating to the sun as the center." Our solar system is *heliocentric;* that is, the planets revolve around the sun.

Step IV. Practice

A DIRECTIONS: A number of sentences with missing words follow. Choose the word that *best* fits the sentence from the following words, and write it in the blank. All words are used.

Word List

assist	dormitory	innovation	period	sophisticated
circumstance	egocentric	lucid	periodical	sophomore
consist	error	novel	persist	substitute
distant	hypertension	obstacle	philosophy	translucent
dormant				

1. I make the most _____s when I am very excited about something because I don't stop to think.

2. He was not very _____ when he spoke, so we still do not know what took place.

3. I like the _____ glass we have in our living room because it allows light to come in, but people can't see clearly inside the room.

4. Some scientists may take courses in _____ because they are interested in general laws that give reasonable explanations that apply to the whole field of science.

5. Under what _____s would you consider taking this job?

6. Now that I'm a(n) _____, I have only two more years after this one to graduation.

7. Doctors have more _____ equipment today, which helps them to diagnose illnesses better.

8. We had a(n) _____ in our geometry class because our regular teacher was out ill.

9. The man needed a(n) _____ to get his car started, but no one seemed to want to stop to help.

10. In the not too _____ future, Adina intends to become a geologist.

11. Although I will probably meet many _____s in my life, I intend to overcome them.

12. I want to know what the medicine _____s of because I am allergic to some drugs.

13. In the past four decades, many _____s have been developed by humans that were never dreamed possible a century ago.

14. Ms. Montoya's _____s in teaching her biology course has helped her students enjoy new ways of learning.

15. The doctor said that the disease was _____ at the moment but it could become active at any time.

16. We have both males and females living in our college _____.

17. I am the kind of person who will _____ until I achieve what I started out to achieve.

18. Some people are so _____ that they talk only about themselves.

19. The doctor's prognosis for Nancy's mother was not too good because she suffers from _____ and has already had one stroke.

20. If this _____ of drought does not end, the farmers will not be able to produce the crops that are needed.

21. I receive a few _____s every month, but I don't always have time to read all the articles in them.

STOP. Check answers at the end of the book (p. 353).

B **DIRECTIONS:** Write the meaning for the underlined word in each sentence that *best* fits the context.

1. It was perhaps <u>hyperbole</u> to say that you are so hungry you could eat a horse.

   _____

2. Vic is a <u>novice</u> skier, so he will stick to the easiest slopes today.

   _____

3. Lawn grasses turn brown in summer because they become <u>dormant</u> in hot, dry weather. _____

4. Your argument seemed convincing at first, but now I realize that it is merely sophistry. _____

5. Running a marathon requires a great deal of stamina, but the triathlon takes much, much more. _____

6. We will illuminate the garden with Chinese lanterns to fit our Asian-inspired party theme. _____

7. Getting a job sometimes takes a while, but if you persist, you will eventually succeed. _____

8. Rick is so egotistic that no matter what the topic, he always manages to talk about himself. _____

9. It is good to be determined, but it is not good to be obstinate.

_____

10. Susan's behavior to me is very erratic: sometimes she is very friendly and other times, very cold. _____

11. The perimeter of the vegetable garden measures 48 feet. _____

12. If you plant tall shrubs all around the periphery of your yard, you will not be able to see your neighbors. _____

13. Her arguments were so lucid that I understood her point for the first time.

_____

14. Wendy has written many short stories, but she now has an idea that she wants to develop into a full-length novel. _____

15. All the windows of that house are so completely covered by thick foliage that I sometimes think the owners need a periscope to see people coming.

_____

16. The two sisters are such a contrast: Emily is so simple, and Louise is so sophisticated.

_____

17. It is hard to understand why Art reacted so strongly to his brother's arrival without knowing all the circumstances. _____

18. I can't go to the movies tonight because my sister needs me to assist her with her children. _____

19. "All people have equal rights" is a good basis for a personal philosophy.

_____

20. It is hard to know whether Lei's <u>innovation</u> will be a huge hit or a big flop.

    _____

21. If a person's life is divided into set <u>periods</u>, this is my "learning and growing" time.

    _____

STOP. Check answers at the end of the book (p. 353).

C **DIRECTIONS:** Write one sentence using at least two words from this lesson. Try to illustrate the meanings of the words without actually defining them. The sentence must make sense.

Example

The *sophisticated* man spoke about the *obstacles* he had to overcome to write his *novel* about an *egocentric* and *corrupt* politician.

_____

_____

_____

_____

STOP. Check answers at the end of the book (p. 353).

D **DIRECTIONS:** Write the words from this lesson that go with the meanings.

Meanings   *Words*

  1. Clear; easily understood   _____

  2. Permitting light to go through   _____

  3. A mistake   _____

  4. Worldly-wise   _____

  5. Second-year student   _____

  6. The study of human knowledge   _____

  7. Conditions or influences connected with an
     act or event   _____

  8. To put in place of   _____

  9. To be made up of   _____

10. Give help to   _____

11. Separated or apart by space and/or time   _____

12. Something in the way of   _____

13. Continue in some course even though
    it's difficult   _____

14. A new idea   _____

15. Strange; unusual; long work of fiction   _____

16. Large room in which many people sleep   _____

17. Asleep; not active   _____

18. Portion of time   _____

19. Referring to a publication that is put
    out at regular intervals   _____

20. High blood pressure   _____

21. Self-centered   _____

STOP. Check answers at the end of the book (p. 353).

QUESTION: In the following cartoon, the term *stamina* is used. How is the cartoon character using the term?

Reprinted by permission of Tribune Media Services.

ANSWER: Stamina has to do with staying power, the ability to endure, and it is usually used in relation to something difficult like physical endurance. The person in the cartoon uses the term in relation to the team he will be watching.

EXTRA WORD POWER

inter	Between; among. When *inter* comes at the beginning of a word, it means "between" or "among." Do *not* confuse *inter* with *intra*. For example: *interdepartmental*—between departments; *interdependent*—dependent upon one another; *interstate*—between states; *intercollegiate*—between colleges.
intra	Within; inside of. *Intra* comes at the beginning of a word. It means "within." Do not confuse *intra* with *inter*. For example: *intradepartmental*—within the department; *intracollegiate*—within the college; *intramural*—within a school or an institution. Can you supply more words that begin with *inter* and *intra*? Check your dictionary for long lists of such words.

LESSON 24

Step I. Story in Context

DIRECTIONS: The following story includes several vocabulary words from this lesson. As you read the story, pay careful attention to the words in boldface type, and try to figure out the meaning of each of these words.

The Firing of James Jefferson

When James Jefferson, not a very (1) **popular** _____ employee, was (2) **dismissed** _____ from his (3) **position** _____ at the (4) **federal** _____ government, he said that he would get even. It's too bad no one took his threat seriously. Let me explain. James Jefferson was suspected of stealing secrets and (5) **transmitting** _____ them to other governments. Our government did not have (6) **positive** _____ proof of this, so they decided to ask him to (7) **submit** _____ his resignation. James, however, refused to leave his (8) **post** _____. He felt that this would be an (9) **admission** _____ of guilt or (10) **equivalent** _____ to it. He came up with a (11) **proposal** _____ that he thought was (12) **magnificent** _____ and that would show that he was innocent. He said that he would give (13) **permission** _____ to anyone in the government to use (14) **hypnosis** _____ on him and ask him anything he or she wanted. The government officials said that even if James did pass the (15) **hypnosis** _____ test, it would be too risky to (16) **confide** _____ in him again. Too many people in the

(17) **population** _____ were at stake. They said that they had no (18) **animosity** _____ toward him, but they felt that he had to either resign or be (19) **dismissed** _____. James's (20) **innate** _____ stubborn (21) **nature** _____ would not allow him to resign, so he was (22) **dismissed** _____.

After his (23) **dismissal** _____, James's (24) **posture** _____ toward his innocence did not change. He became very belligerent; his one (25) **mission** _____ in life was to get even with "those" who had (26) **dismissed** _____ him. He had never been a (27) **magnanimous** _____ person, and his dismissal just (28) **magnified** _____ his (29) **animosity** _____. He had hatred toward everyone. He hated his mother, who had not given him good (30) **prenatal** _____ or (31) **postnatal** _____ care because she was an alcoholic, and he hated his father, who had walked out on his mother when James was born. As the days passed, James's (32) **animosity** _____ grew and grew. He was obsessed with getting even. He followed his former boss every day. One evening when his ex-boss was at a theater, James waited for the (33) **intermission** _____. During the (34) **intermission** _____, James started to approach his former boss. At that moment, security guards, who had been watching James, stepped forward and asked James to come with them for questioning.

STOP. Check answers at the end of the book (p. 353).

Step II. Combining Forms

A **DIRECTIONS:** A list of combining forms with their meanings follows. Look at the combining forms and their meanings. Concentrate on learning each combining form and its meaning. Cover the meanings, read the combining forms, and state the meanings to yourself. Check to see whether you are correct. Now cover the combining forms, read the meanings, and state the combining forms to yourself. Check to see whether you are correct.

Combining Forms	*Meanings*
1. anima, animus	spirit; mind; soul
2. equi	equal
3. feder, fid, fide	trust; faith
4. hypn, hypno	sleep
5. magna	great; large
6. miss, mitt	send
7. nasc, nat	born
8. pon, pos	place; set
9. pop	people

B **DIRECTIONS:** Cover the preceding meanings. Write the meanings of the following combining forms.

Combining Forms	Meanings
1. anima, animus	_____
2. equi	_____
3. feder, fid, fide	_____
4. hypn, hypno	_____
5. magna	_____
6. miss, mitt	_____
7. nasc, nat	_____
8. pon, pos	_____
9. pop	_____

Step III. Vocabulary Words Derived from Combining Forms in Context

1. **admission** (ad · mish′ un) *n.* Act of allowing to enter; entrance fee; a price charged or paid to be admitted; acknowledgment; a confession, as to a crime. *We did not know that we had to pay* **admission** *to enter the fair.*
2. **animate** (an′ uh · māte) *v.* To make alive; to move to action. *When Arthur tells a story, he becomes so* **animated** *that every part of him is alive and active.*
3. **animosity** (an · uh · mos′ uh · tē) *n.* (*pl.* **ties**) Hatred; resentment. *She felt great* **animosity** *toward the people who had attacked her father and beat him so badly that he had to go to the hospital.*
4. **confide** (kun · fīde′) *v.* To tell in trust; to tell secrets trustingly. *If you do not want others to know your secrets,* **confide** *only in people you can trust.*
5. **depose** (di · pōze′) *v.* To remove from a throne or high position; to let fall. *After some monarchs have been* **deposed,** *they have been executed.*
6. **dismiss** (dis · miss′) *v.* To tell or allow to go; to discharge, as from a job; to get rid of; to have done with quickly; to reject. *The class was* **dismissed** *when the period was over.*
7. **disposition** (dis · puh · zish′ un) *n.* One's usual frame of mind; a natural tendency. *Because Sunil has such a good* **disposition,** *I'm sure that he will he very nice to you.*
8. **emissary** (em′ uh · ser · ē) *n.* A person or agent sent on a specific mission. *Usually, an* **emissary** *is sent to another country to try to learn about the other country's plans and to try to influence the plans.*
9. **equivalent** (i · kwiv′ uh · lent) *adj.* Equal in value, meaning, force, and so on. *The amounts were* **equivalent,** *so that each person had exactly the same number.*
10. **equivocate** (i · kwiv′ uh · kāte) *v.* To use ambiguous language on purpose. *Noelle always seems to* **equivocate** *when she does not want to commit herself to giving an exact answer.*
11. **expound** (ik · spound′) *v.* To explain; to state in detail; to set forth. *Because the class had difficulty understanding the concept of intelligence, the professor* **expounded** *further on it.*

12. **federal** (fed′ ur · ul) *adj.* Of or formed by a compact relating to or formed by an agreement between two or more states, groups, and so on; relating to a union of states, groups, and so on in which central authority in common affairs is established by consent of its members. *All the states in the United States joined to form a* **federal** *government, that controls common affairs, such as foreign policy, defenses, and interstate commerce.*

13. **hypnosis** (hip · nō′ sis) *n.* (*pl.* **ses; sēz**) A sleeplike trance that is artificially brought about. *I can't believe that I was put in a state of* **hypnosis** *and did all those silly things, because I don't remember anything that took place.*

14. **infidelity** (in · fuh · del′ uh · tē) *n.* Adultery; breach of trust; unfaithfulness of a marriage partner. *Both spouses were suing for divorce on the grounds of* **infidelity** *because each had found that the other had been unfaithful.*

15. **innate** (in · nāte′) *adj.* Inborn; born with; not acquired from the environment; belonging to the fundamental nature of something; beginning in; coming from. **Innate** *characteristics are those that cannot be acquired after birth.*

16. **intercede** (in · tur · sēde′) *v.* To intervene; to come between. *The company's troubleshooter was called upon to* **intercede** *in the dispute that had hurt relations between the company and the town.*

17. **intermission** (in · tur · mish′ un) *n.* Time between events; recess. *The* **intermissions** *between acts in the play were each fifteen minutes long.*

18. **intermittent** (in · tur · mit′ tunt) *adj.* Not continuous; to start or stop at intervals. *Because the pain was* **intermittent,** *he had some pain-free moments.*

19. **intervene** (in · tur · vēne′) *v.* To come between; to intercede. *Because the strike had been going on for so long, the courts decided to* **intervene** *by asking for a cooling-off period for both sides.*

20. **magnanimous** (mag · nan′ i · møus) *adj.* Forgiving of insults or injuries; high-minded; great of soul. *The speaker was very* **magnanimous** *to overlook the insults that were yelled at him.*

21. **magnate** (mag′ nāte) *n.* A very important or influential person. *Bill Gates, a* **magnate** *of considerable wealth, has given billions of dollars to good causes.*

22. **magnificent** (mag · nif′ uh · sent) *adj.* Splendid; beautiful; superb. *The palace was so* **magnificent** *that it was difficult to find words to describe its splendor.*

23. **magnify** (mag′ nuh · fī) *v.* To increase the size of; to make larger; to enlarge. *The microscope* **magnifies** *very small objects so that they can be viewed easily.*

24. **malediction** (mal · uh · dik′ shun) *n.* Speaking badly of someone; slander; a curse. *The words* **malediction** *and benediction are antonyms.*

25. **malefactor** (mal′ uh · fak · tur) *n.* One who does something bad; a criminal; one who commits a crime. *A* **malefactor** *who is caught by the police is usually sent to jail.*

26. **missile** (mis′ sule) *n.* An object such as a weapon intended to be thrown or discharged as a bullet, arrow, or stone. *That big stone, which he used as a* **missile,** *hit its target.*

27. **mission** (mish′ un) *n.* Group or team of people who are sent some place to perform some work; the task, business, or responsibility that a person is assigned; the place where missionaries carry out their work; a place where poor people may go for assistance. *The astronauts were sent on a special* **mission** *to try to locate a missing spaceship.*

28. **nature** (nā′ chur) *n.* The necessary quality or qualities of something or someone; sort; kind; wild state of existence; uncivilized way of life; overall pattern or system; basic characteristic of a person; inborn quality; the sum total of all creation; the whole physical universe. *It seems to be his **nature** to behave in such a friendly manner all the time.*

29. **perfidious** (pur · fid′ ē · øus) *adj.* Deceitful; violating good trust; treacherous. *I did not know that I had a **perfidious** friend until I heard from others that my secrets had all been told.*

30. **permission** (pur · mish′ un) *n.* Act of allowing the doing of something; a consent. *I received **permission** from the instructor to audit her class.*

31. **popular** (pop′ yuh · lur) *adj.* Referring to the common people or the general public; approved of; admired; liked by most people. *Jack and Roberto were voted the most **popular** boys in their class because they were liked by the most people.*

32. **population** (pop · yuh · lā′ shun) *n.* Total number of people living in a country, city, or any area. *According to the various census figures, the **population** in the United States is increasing.*

33. **position** (puh · zish′ un) *n.* An act of placing or arranging; the manner in which a thing is placed; the way the body is placed, as in *sitting position;* the place occupied by a person or thing; the proper or appropriate place, as in *position;* job; a feeling or stand; social standing. *He had been sitting in that **position** for so long that if he hadn't moved a little, his legs would have fallen asleep.*

34. **positive** (poz′ i · tivé) *adj.* Being directly found to be so or true; real; actual; sure of something; definitely set; confident. *Kendra was **positive** that she could describe the men who kidnapped her because they hadn't bothered to blindfold her.*

35. **post** (pōst) *n.* A position or employment, usually in government service; an assigned beat; a piece of wood or other material to be used as a support; a place occupied by troops. *v.* To inform; to put up (as on a wall); to mail (as a letter). *Do you like the **post** you have with the government?*

36. **postnatal** (pōst · nāt′ ul) *adj.* Occurring after birth. *It is important that all infants receive good **postnatal** care.*

37. **postpone** (pōst · pōné′) *v.* To put off to a future time; to delay. *They had to **postpone** their annual reading convention for another month because many members could not come at the scheduled time.*

38. **posture** (pos′ chur) *n.* The placing or carriage of the body or parts of the body; a mental position or frame of mind. *Ryan's sitting **posture** is so poor that after a while, it may cause him to have back problems.*

39. **prenatal** (prē · nāt′ ul) *adj.* Being or taking place before birth. *A pregnant woman should take good care of herself so that her unborn child will be receiving good **prenatal** care.*

40. **proposal** (pruh · pō′ zul) *n.* An offer put forth to be accepted or adopted; an offer of marriage; a plan. *Because the governor's **proposal** for a tax plan was not acceptable to the people, the legislators voted against it.*

41. **proposition** (prop · uh · zish′ un) *n.* A plan set forth for consideration or acceptance. *His **proposition** sounded like a very sophisticated plan, so we decided to consider it at our next conference.*

42. **remission** (ri · mish' un) *n.* A pardon; temporary stopping or lessening of a disease. *The doctors were delighted that the disease had reached a state of **remission** and was now dormant.*

43. **submit** (sub · mit') *v.* To give in to another; to surrender; to concede; to present for consideration or approval; to present as one's opinion. *I will **submit** my manuscript to a publisher for possible publication.*

44. **transmit** (trans · mit') *v.* To send from one place to another; to pass on by heredity; to transfer; to pass or communicate news, information, and so on. *Certain diseases are **transmitted** from the parent to the child through heredity.*

Step IV. Practice

A **DIRECTIONS:** State the meaning of the word *position* in the first cartoon and the word *conscience* in the second. Then explain what makes each cartoon amusing.

1.

Reprinted by permission of Tribune Media Services.

2.

Reprinted by permission of Tribune Media Services.

1. _____

_____

2. _____

_____

STOP. Check answers at the end of the book (p. 353).

B **DIRECTIONS:** Choose the word that *best* completes each sentence. Each word from the list below will be used no more than once, and not all words will be used.

Word List

admission	expound	magnificent	permission
animate	infidelity	magnify	position
depose	innate	malediction	posture
dismiss	intercede	malefactor	proposition
disposition	intermittent	missile	remission
emissary	intervene	mission	submit
equivalent	magnanimous	perfidious	transmit
equivocate	magnate		

1. Her pleasant _____ makes it easy for her to get along with people.

2. Gabriela was sent overseas as a(n) _____, not a spy, although she carried out some espionage while on her mission.

3. The mother did not _____ in the dispute until her two small children began hitting one another.

4. Luckily the _____ missed the most heavily populated area near the center of the city, although it still caused a great deal of damage.

5. The senator put forth an interesting _____ about taxes for the finance committee to consider.

6. Several ideas about the _____ of income taxes for poor people have recently been discussed.

7. Your behavior is so untrustworthy that I might even call it _____ .

8. Singers must stand using proper _____ when they perform in order to support the voice well.

9. The term "_____" is perhaps a bit outmoded, but our town actually has a single person who owns the factory and a great deal of land and therefore exercises both political and financial influence.

10. Enrique's usual manner is extremely lively, vivacious, and _____ .

11. After the speaker _____ at great length about different varieties of trees, people began falling asleep all over the lecture hall.

12. Rod is having trouble choosing between two jobs, so he is finding it necessary to _____ when he speaks to either potential employer.

13. Some scientists now believe that humans as well as other animals have a(n) _____, inborn sense of morality.

14. The whole neighborhood knew that Mrs. Smith had been having an affair, but Mr. Smith did not seem to suspect her of _____ .

15. Our _____ is to identify and mark all the diseased trees in the park.

16. Dr. Swift has been _____ as head of the English department, but she keeps her job as dean of students.

17. I felt I had to _____ between my two brothers when they began to fight over who had bought our mother the best gift.

18. This was a day of very changeable weather, with _____ rain followed by sunshine.

19. The angry employee pronounced a _____ on his boss after she fired him.

20. The police caught and arrested the _____ only an hour after the crime was committed.

21. The news seemed to be instantaneously _____ throughout the campus community.

22. Your gift to the college was not only generous but also _____.

23. All classes were _____ early because the snowstorm threatened to turn into a blizzard.

24. Tasks were assigned fairly, so that all members of the team had _____ amounts of work.

25. The wedding was _____ and very costly, and the bride and groom went into debt to pay for it.

26. Jose is looking for a new _____ in which he can employ all of his skills and talents.

27. With your _____, I will come with you when you visit Sandra and Bernardo.

28. I _____ the song to the record label almost a year ago, but I just heard from them today.

STOP. Check answers at the end of the book (pp. 353–354).

C DIRECTIONS: Write one sentence using at least two words from this exercise. Try to illustrate the meanings of the words without actually defining them. The sentence must make sense.

Example

Mrs. Maple said that she was *positive* the *mission* had been *postponed* and a new *proposal* was being *submitted* by the person who was now in her former boss's *post*.

_____

_____

_____

_____

STOP. Check answers at the end of the book (p. 354).

D **DIRECTIONS:** A list of definitions follows. Give the word that *best* fits the definition. Try to relate the definition to the meanings of the combining forms.

Word List

admission	innate	permission	postpone
animosity	intermission	popular	posture
confide	magnanimous	population	prenatal
dismiss	magnificent	position	proposal
equivalent	magnify	positive	submit
federal	mission	post	transmit
hypnosis	nature	postnatal	

1. To send from one place to another _____

2. Sure of something _____

3. A piece of wood or other material to be used as a support _____

4. The manner in which a thing is placed _____

5. Forgiving of insults or injuries _____

6. The placing or carriage of the body _____

7. Time between events _____

8. A sleeplike trance that is artificially brought about _____

9. Splendid _____

10. An offer put forth to be accepted or adopted _____

11. Being before birth _____

12. Born with _____

13. Occurring after birth _____

14. The necessary qualities of something _____

15. Relating to or formed by an agreement between two or more states _____

16. To reveal in trust _____

17. To enlarge _____

18. Hatred _____

19. Total number of people living in a country _____

20. Entrance fee _____

21. Task or responsibility _____

22. Equal in value, meaning, and so on _____

23. Admired; liked by most people _____

24. To delay _____

25. To tell or allow to go _____

26. To give in to another _____

27. A consent _____

STOP. Check answers at the end of the book (p. 354).

EXTRA WORD POWER

mal	Bad; ill; evil; wrong; not perfect. *Mal* is found at the beginning of a great number of words. Examples: *malfunction*—to function badly; *malnourished*—badly nourished; *malformed*—abnormally formed; *maltreated*—treated badly. Check your dictionary for a list of words beginning with *mal*.
semi	Half; not fully; partly; occurring twice in a period. *Semi* is found at the beginning of a great number of words. For example: *semiblind*—partly blind; *semicircle*—half circle; *semiannual*—occurring twice in a year, occurring every half year; *semistarved*—partly starved; *semiwild*—partly wild. Check your dictionary for a long list of words beginning with *semi*.

SPECIAL ACADEMIC WORDS

A DIRECTIONS: Here are some civics terms made up from combining forms you met in this chapter. Without looking back at the chapter, see how well you can define them.

1. civics _____

2. politics _____

3. politician _____

4. civilian _____

5. civil _____

6. pacifist _____

7. detente _____

8. federal   _____

9. population   _____

10. megalopolis   _____

11. metropolitan   _____

12. civilization   _____

B **DIRECTIONS:** Choose the answers to the riddles from the civics terms presented in Practice A.

_____   1. I'm often ambiguous on purpose.

_____   2. I cover a very large area.

_____   3. I stay close to the city.

_____   4. You'll never catch me wearing a uniform.

_____   5. I avoid fights and arguments.

_____   6. I help to ease tension.

_____   7. I'm concerned about your rights.

_____   8. I was formed from many.

STOP. Check answers at the end of the book (p. 354).

CHAPTER WORDS IN A PARAGRAPH

Write a paragraph on the given topic using at least eight words from this chapter. The paragraph must make sense and be logically developed.

Topic: The Funniest Thing That Ever Happened To Me

STOP. Check answers at the end of the book (p. 354).

www GAINING WORD POWER ON THE INTERNET

1. Choose a search engine. Write the name of the chosen search engine: _____

2. Do a search of the following two terms: *politics, hypertension.*

3. Choose one site or reference generated by your search for each term. Try to select sites that help you gain a better understanding of the terms you are researching. Write the

    chosen site for each term: _____   _____

4. Write a three-sentence paragraph on the site information for each term.

5. Log onto the Web site that accompanies this textbook for extra practice exercises at [http://www.ablongman.com/vocabulary].

STOP. Check answers at the end of the book (p. 354).

CROSSWORD PUZZLE

DIRECTIONS: The meanings of many of the combining forms from Lessons 22 to 24 follow. Your knowledge of these combining forms will help you solve the crossword puzzle. Note that *combining form* is abbreviated as *comb. f.*

Across

1. Slang for a large crowd
3. A musical syllable
5. Same as #4 Down
6. Comb. f. for *equal*
7. Comb. f. for *out of; from; lacking*
8. Abbreviation of *mail*
9. Comb. f. for *sleep*
11. A friend
12. Ready to eat
15. Comb. f. for *spirit; mind*
19. You feel this way when you ache
21. Abbreviation of *masculine*
24. An insect
25. Antonym of *happy*
26. Comb. f. for *I; me*
27. An insect

Down

1. Way of saying *mother*
2. Comb. f. for *war*
3. Comb. f. for *faith*
4. Comb. f. for *without*
7. Comb. f. for *wander*
8. Meaning of *homo*
10. Comb. f. for *wrong*
11. Comb. f. for *peace*
13. Comb. f. for *after*
14. Time period
16. Comb. f. for *large*
17. Not required
18. Comb. f. for *stand*
20. Ending added to form past tense of regular verbs

(*continued*)

29. Rhymes with *hat*
30. Antonym of *bottom*
31. Meaning of *mono* and *uni*
32. Comb. f. for *one who*
34. Same as #32 Across
35. Eighth letter of the alphabet
36. Male equivalent of an actress
37. Comb. f. for *new*
39. Sixteenth letter of the alphabet
40. Same as #7 Across
41. Meaning of *hyper*
44. Meaning of *dorm*
48. Meaning of *cura*
49. On a nice day it shines
50. Antonym of *off*
52. Roman numeral *100*
53. A number rhyming with *fine*
55. The highest card is an ____
56. Another word for *clear*
58. Comb. f. for *one who*
59. Eighteenth letter of the alphabet
60. Roman numeral *1000*
61. Meaning of *en; em*
62. Same as #38 Down
64. Pronoun referring to *us*
65. Twenty-fifth letter of the alphabet
66. Antonym of *no*
67. Same as #61 Across
68. Same as #18 Down

21. A subway in Paris
22. Something that happened long ____
23. Comb. f. for *wise*
28. Homonym of *two*
29. Same as #4 Down
33. Abbreviation of *railroad*
34. Antonym of *off*
38. Comb. f. for *voice*
39. Comb. f. for *around*
42. A truck for moving
43. When you take the same books out of the library, you ____ them
45. Comb. f. for *clear; light*
46. Antonym of *friend*
47. Comb. f. for *city*
51. A woman who lives in a convent
52. Comb. f. for *citizen*
54. Poetic way of saying *before*
57. Contraction for *do not*
63. Same as #52 Across

STOP. Check answers at the end of the book (p. 355).

ANALOGIES

DIRECTIONS: Find the word from the following list that *best* completes each analogy. There are more words listed than you need.

Word List

active	avocation	content	fertilization
affect	civilian	convocation	impolite
agnostic	civilization	cyclone	inactive
aid	concession	decimate	infidelity
animosity	confide	dismiss	innate
antitoxin	consequence	expert	intense
attorney	contemporary	fertile	intention

knowledge	novel	politician	tense
lucid	novice	politics	toxicologist
magnificent	oral	procession	vacation
malediction	peace	proposal	visage
malefactor	persist	sequence	vocabulary
nature	polite	stubborn	vocation

1. Credible : incredible :: benediction : _____.

2. Uniform : same :: criminal : _____.

3. Hyper : hypo :: ambiguous : _____.

4. Admit : deny :: civil : _____.

5. Independent : dependent :: veteran : _____.

6. Intention : aim :: assembly : _____.

7. Quiet : vociferous :: relaxed : _____.

8. Entrance : exit :: dormant : _____.

9. Shy : bashful :: tenacious : _____.

10. Magnify : enlarge :: unfaithfulness : _____.

11. Belligerent : war :: pacifist : _____.

12. Content : dissatisfied :: love : _____.

13. Pine : tree :: banking : _____.

14. Infinite : finite :: military : _____.

15. Unpopular : popular :: weak : _____.

16. Error : mistake :: assist : _____.

17. Monotonous : changeless :: continue : _____.

18. Provoke : irritate :: unusual : _____.

19. Astronomer : stars :: philosopher : _____.

20. Position : post :: vocal : _____.

STOP. Check answers at the end of the book (p. 355).

MULTIPLE-CHOICE VOCABULARY TEST

DIRECTIONS: This is a test on words in Lessons 22 to 24. Words are presented according to lessons. *Do all lessons before checking answers.* Underline the meaning that *best* fits the word.

Lesson 22

1. civics
   a. cultural development
   b. not in uniform
   c. polite
   d. the study of the rights and responsibilities of citizenship

2. civilization
   a. dealing with citizens
   b. polite
   c. cultural development, as of a people
   d. not in the military

3. civil
   a. not in uniform
   b. polite
   c. cultural development
   d. the study of the rights and responsibilities of citizens

4. attention
   a. aim
   b. mental strain
   c. mental concentration
   d. very strong

5. intention
   a. mental concentration
   b. extreme force
   c. mental strain
   d. aim

6. tension
   a. mental strain
   b. aim
   c. mental concentration
   d. very strong

7. intense
   a. mental strain
   b. very strong
   c. mental concentration
   d. aim

8. belligerent
   a. aim
   b. very strong
   c. hatred
   d. warlike

9. civilian
   a. polite
   b. a state of human society
   c. refers to citizenship
   d. person not in the military

10. vocation
    a. one's work
    b. voice
    c. outspoken
    d. list of words

11. ambiguous
    a. referring to two
    b. having two or more meanings
    c. referring to many words
    d. referring to words with the same meanings

12. postscript
    a. a letter
    b. something written
    c. a signature
    d. something added to a letter after the writer's signature

13. pacify
    a. an agreement
    b. to calm
    c. to help
    d. to work with

14. politics
    a. science or art of government
    b. cultural development
    c. rule by people
    d. refers to a city

15. politician
    a. science or art of government
    b. refers to citizens
    c. refers to the city
    d. person engaged in the science or art of government

16. metropolitan
    a. surrounding area of a city
    b. a person involved in city government
    c. city government
    d. referring to a major city center and its surrounding area

17. vocal
    a. manner of speaking   c. referring to a person's work
    b. referring to the voice   d. referring to peace

18. vocabulary
    a. refers to work   c. refers to new words
    b. refers to the voice   d. list of words that are defined

19. ambidextrous
    a. an able person   c. refers to hands
    b. able to write very well   d. able to use both hands equally well

20. avocation
    a. hobby   c. refers to a job
    b. work   d. a vacation

21. convocation
    a. parade   c. refers to group
    b. refers to vacation   d. an assembly

22. detente
    a. refers to strained relations   c. refers to nations
    b. easing of strained relations   d. refers to a tent

23. detention
    a. refers to jail   c. confinement
    b. easing of relations   d. refers to tents

24. megalopolis
    a. a city   c. refers to an urban area
    b. a large city made up of a number of cities   d. refers to a large population

25. pacifist
    a. one who wants peace   c. one who likes to swim in the Pacific Ocean
    b. refers to the Pacific Ocean   d. one who likes to surf

26. posterior
    a. refers to a body part   c. in the rear
    b. refers to someone   d. coming before

27. posterity
    a. refers to coming after   c. the buttocks
    b. future generations   d. in the rear

28. posthumously
    a. after   c. coming after
    b. refers to the buttocks   d. after death

29. postmortem
    a. refers to after death crime   c. refers to after death party
    b. autopsy   d. an examination

30. provoke
    a. to make people sad   c. to call people
    b. to irritate   d. refers to calling forth

31. rebel
    a. refers to control   c. arms
    b. refers to arms   d. taking arms against authority

32. rebellion
    a. refers to arms   c. opposition to one in authority
    b. opposition   d. a dominant person

33. tendon
    a. a fibrous cord   c. a muscle
    b. an attachment   d. refers to cord

34. vociferous
    a. clamorous   c. a loud person
    b. refers to voice   d. refers to speech

Lesson 23

35. lucid
   a. a light
   b. clear
   c. permitting light to go through
   d. to view

36. translucent
   a. a clear view
   b. light
   c. permitting light to go through but not allowing a clear view
   d. light can go through and permits a very clear view

37. error
   a. to walk around
   b. to wander off walking
   c. a mistake
   d. to lie

38. obstacle
   a. something helpful
   b. something harmful
   c. something that stands in the way
   d. a large rock

39. persist
   a. to stand around
   b. to move on
   c. to stand for
   d. to continue in some course even when it is difficult

40. innovation
   a. a book
   b. a strange idea
   c. something newly introduced
   d. an immunization

41. novel
   a. refers to a nonfiction book
   b. new
   c. something done over
   d. refers to a biography

42. dormitory
   a. a house
   b. a room
   c. resort
   d. a building providing sleeping and living quarters at a school

43. dormant
   a. active
   b. inactive
   c. awake
   d. referring to door

44. period
   a. a circle
   b. time
   c. portion of time
   d. portion of something

45. sophisticated
   a. worldly-wise
   b. very knowledgeable
   c. not clever
   d. to know how to dress

46. sophomore
   a. third-year student
   b. immature person
   c. someone who is knowledgeable
   d. someone not too smart

47. philosophy
   a. refers to knowledge
   b. wise man
   c. the study of human knowledge
   d. charity

48. circumstances
   a. the conditions surrounding an act
   b. the acts
   c. the events
   d. aims

49. substitute
   a. to put in place of
   b. to place
   c. to set
   d. to take

50. consist
   a. to place
   b. to stand
   c. to put together
   d. to be made up of

51. assist
   a. to stand by
   b. to stand off
   c. to help
   d. to place

52. distant
   a. separated by time and/ or space
   b. a relation
   c. refers to space
   d. to stand by

53. hypertension
   a. mental strain
   b. very strong force
   c. very tired
   d. high blood pressure

54. egocentric
   a. not concerned with self
   b. self-centered
   c. self-sufficient
   d. able to help self

55. egotistic
   a. vain
   b. concerned about
   c. refers to others
   d. refers to people

56. erratic
   a. a stable
   b. an error
   c. wandering
   d. crazy

57. hyperbole
   a. refers to anything excessive
   b. great exaggeration
   c. any plane figure
   d. gross

58. illuminate
   a. to help
   b. firecrackers
   c. to make clear
   d. any lights

59. novice
   a. a baby
   b. a beginner
   c. a child
   d. a soldier

60. obstinate
   a. a rookie
   b. to light up
   c. help
   d. stubborn

61. perimeter
   a. refers to a measure
   b. measure of the outer part of a closed plane figure
   c. refers to a triangle
   d. to measure a closed plane figure

62. periphery
   a. refers to a boundary
   b. used on a submarine
   c. a rectangle
   d. a measurement

63. periscope
   a. an instrument
   b. instrument on a submarine
   c. an instrument to see things
   d. instrument on submarine to see all around

64. sophistry
   a. reasoning
   b. clever arguments
   c. faulty reasoning
   d. arguments

65. stamina
   a. refers to disease
   b. great runner
   c. resistance
   d. staying power

Lesson 24

66. mission
   a. the task or responsibility a person is assigned
   b. a vacation trip
   c. a house
   d. atomic particles

67. permission
   a. weekly allowance
   b. a consent
   c. to give in to
   d. to give

68. dismiss
    a. to leave
    b. to let alone
    c. to tell to go
    d. to go

69. postpone
    a. to mail
    b. to delay
    c. to put away
    d. to stay

70. positive
    a. the manner of sitting
    b. to put off
    c. sure of
    d. not confident

71. posture
    a. a place
    b. a setting
    c. the manner of carrying the body
    d. mental strain

72. post
    a. a government job
    b. government
    c. to put off
    d. to serve

73. proposal
    a. to put off
    b. to send away
    c. an acceptance
    d. an offer

74. magnanimous
    a. large
    b. highly spirited
    c. forgiving of insults
    d. splendid

75. magnify
    a. to see from
    b. something large
    c. to help
    d. to enlarge

76. admission
    a. act of allowing to enter
    b. allow to do
    c. refers to money
    d. an allowance

77. submit
    a. to allow to do
    b. to let go
    c. to give in to
    d. to help

78. transmit
    a. to send away
    b. to give in
    c. to let go
    d. to send from one place to another

79. intermission
    a. a space
    b. time period
    c. a responsibility
    d. time between events

80. position
    a. place occupied by a thing
    b. to put off
    c. something proper
    d. to put away

81. magnificent
    a. forgiving of insults
    b. large of spirit
    c. splendid
    d. large

82. animosity
    a. full of spirit
    b. refers to the mind
    c. hatred
    d. large of soul

83. hypnosis
    a. sleep
    b. put to sleep
    c. a sleeplike trance artificially brought on
    d. a drug

84. federal
    a. government
    b. relating to states
    c. faith in government
    d. relating to an agreement between two or more states to join into a union

85. confide
    a. faith in
    b. to tell in trust
    c. to tell everything
    d. to give information

86. innate
   a. not born
   b. acquired after birth
   c. birth
   d. born with

87. postnatal
   a. refers to nose condition
   b. occurring before birth
   c. born with
   d. occurring after birth

88. prenatal
   a. refers to birth
   b. born with
   c. occurring before birth
   d. occurring after birth

89. nature
   a. outside
   b. flowers
   c. the necessary qualities of something
   d. a person

90. popular
   a. people
   b. approved of
   c. the number of people
   d. lots of people

91. population
   a. people
   b. total number of people living in an area
   c. liked by people
   d. an area in which people live

92. equivalent
   a. equal to
   b. unlike
   c. a comparison
   d. a mathematical sign

93. equivocate
   a. refers to speech
   b. ambiguous language
   c. language
   d. unsure of oneself

94. expound
   a. to explain
   b. to confuse
   c. to help
   d. refers to English money

95. infidelity
   a. refers to faithfulness
   b. unfaithful
   c. refers to divorce
   d. a trusting person

96. intercede
   a. to help
   b. to intervene
   c. to set straight
   d. to murder

97. intermittent
   a. refers to the theatre
   b. continuous
   c. refers to intervals in a theatre
   d. not continuous

98. intervene
   a. to come between
   b. to aid
   c. between consenting people
   d. to mourn

99. magnate
   a. refers to someone
   b. people
   c. someone very important
   d. refers to large

100. malediction
   a. the opposite of good
   b. refers to speaking
   c. to speak ill of someone
   d. refers to bad

101. malefactor
   a. speaking ill of someone
   b. someone famous
   c. a criminal
   d. refers to a doer

102. animate
   a. to make
   b. refers to animals
   c. to explain
   d. to make alive

103. emissary
   a. a person
   b. refers to mission
   c. an agent sent on a mission
   d. refers to an agent

104. perifidious   a. treacherous   c. trusting
                     b. speaking ill of someone   d. faithful

105. missile   a. an object   c. a weapon
                b. an object in space   d. a space ship

106. proposition   a. a position   c. a plan
                    b. something unsettling   d. a wedding announcement

107. remission   a. refers to disease   c. an agent sent on a mission
                  b. a pardon   d. refers to temporary

108. depose   a. to remove   c. to pose
               b. to remove from a   d. a high position
                  high position

109. disposition   a. a job   c. tendency
                    b. someone's mind   d. a natural tendency

CHAPTER TRUE/FALSE TEST

DIRECTIONS: This is a true/false test on Lessons 22 to 24. Read each sentence carefully. Decide whether it is true or false. Put a *T* for *true* or an *F* for *false* in the blank. If the answer is false, change a word or part of the sentence to make it true. The number after the sentence tells you whether the word is from Lesson 22, 23, or 24.

_____   1. When you pay <u>attention</u> to something, you do not need to concentrate. 22

_____   2. A <u>pacifist</u> is <u>belligerent</u>. 22

_____   3. A <u>civilian</u> is a member of the armed forces. 22

_____   4. *Intense* and *tension* are synonyms. 22

_____   5. If you live in a <u>metropolitan</u> area, you are in or near a major city. 22

_____   6. If you <u>postpone</u> something, you are putting it off. 24

_____   7. A <u>proposal</u> is something you must accept. 24

_____   8. All <u>intermissions</u> are at least ten minutes. 24

_____   9. A <u>sophisticated</u> plan is a complex plan. 23

_____   10. You can clearly see through something <u>translucent</u>. 23

_____   11. <u>Politics</u> is the science of people. 22

_____   12. <u>Civilization</u> can exist in the wilderness without people. 22

_____   13. Your <u>vocation</u> is what you are called. 22

_____   14. A <u>postscript</u> is the last paragraph of your essay. 22

_____   15. When you are <u>ambiguous</u>, what you say can be taken in two ways. 22

_____ 16. The way you dress would be due to innate factors. 24

_____ 17. *Equivalent* and *equal* are synonyms. 24

_____ 18. An egocentric person is concerned with himself or herself. 23

_____ 19. To persist in a course means that you need an assist. 23

_____ 20. *Civil* and *rude* are antonyms. 22

_____ 21. An innovation is an archaic plan. 23

_____ 22. A dormant disease is in remission. 23, 24

_____ 23. To transmit information means that you send it from one place to another. 24

_____ 24. *Hypnosis* and *dormant* are synonyms. 23, 24

_____ 25. *Animosity* and *love* are antonyms. 24

_____ 26. *Submit* and *concede* are synonyms. 24

_____ 27. A person who behaves like a sophomore is someone who is worldly-wise. 23

_____ 28. Federal refers to all unions. 24

_____ 29. Astronauts can go on missions. 24

_____ 30. A novel can be an autobiography. 23

STOP. Check answers for both tests at the end of the book (pp. 355–356).

SCORING OF TESTS

Multiple-Choice Vocabulary Test	
Number Wrong	*Score*
0–4	Excellent
5–10	Good
11–14	Weak
Above 14	Poor
Score _____	

True/False Test	
Number Wrong	*Score*
0–3	Excellent
4–6	Good
7–9	Weak
Above 9	Poor
Score _____	

1. If you scored in the excellent or good range on *both tests,* you are doing well. You have now completed the work in this text.
2. If you scored in the weak or poor range on either test, go to the next page and follow directions for Additional Practice. Note that the words on the tests are arranged so that you can tell in which lesson to find them. This arrangement will help you if you need additional practice.

ADDITIONAL PRACTICE SETS

A **DIRECTIONS:** Write the words you missed on the tests from the three lessons in the space provided. Note that the tests are presented so that you can tell to which lessons the words belong.

Lesson 22 Words Missed

1. _____ 6. _____

2. _____ 7. _____

3. _____ 8. _____

4. _____ 9. _____

5. _____ 10. _____

Lesson 23 Words Missed

1. _____ 6. _____

2. _____ 7. _____

3. _____ 8. _____

4. _____ 9. _____

5. _____ 10. _____

Lesson 24 Words Missed

1. _____ 6. _____

2. _____ 7. _____

3. _____ 8. _____

4. _____ 9. _____

5. _____ 10. _____

B **DIRECTIONS:** Restudy the words that you have written down on this page. Study the combining forms from which those words are derived.

Do Step I and Step II for those you missed. Note that Step I and Step II of the combining forms and vocabulary derived from these combining forms are on the following pages:

Lesson 22—pp. 258–267
Lesson 23—pp. 267–277
Lesson 24—pp. 277–286

C **DIRECTIONS:** Do Additional Practice 1 on this page and the next if you missed words from Lesson 22. Do Additional Practice 2 on pp. 301–302 if you missed words from Lesson 23. Do Additional Practice 3 on pp. 302–303 if you missed words from Lesson 24. You have now finished *Gaining Word Power*.

Additional Practice 1 for Lesson 22

A **DIRECTIONS:** The combining forms presented in Lesson 22 follow. Match the combining form with its meaning.

_____ 1. tend, tens, tent   a. war

_____ 2. belli, bello   b. city

_____ 3. civ, civis   c. stretch; strain

_____ 4. polis   d. after

_____ 5. pac, pax   e. both

_____ 6. voc, vox   f. very large

_____ 7. post   g. voice; call

_____ 8. ambi   h. citizen

_____ 9. mega   i. peace

STOP. Check answers at the end of the book (p. 356).

B **DIRECTIONS:** Some vocabulary words presented in Lesson 22 follow. Match the word with its meaning.

_____ 1. attention   a. aim

_____ 2. intention   b. person not in the military

_____ 3. tension   c. cultural development, as of a people

_____ 4. intense   d. mental concentration

_____ 5. belligerent   e. the science or art of government

_____ 6. civilian   f. referring to a major city center and its surrounding area

_____ 7. civics   g. warlike

_____ 8. civilization   h. referring to the voice

_____ 9. civil   i. job; profession

_____ 10. politics   j. able to be taken in two or more ways

_____ 11. politician   k. having extreme force

_____ 12. metropolitan

l. person engaged in the science or art of government

_____ 13. vocal

m. the study of the rights and responsibilities of citizenship

_____ 14. vocabulary

n. to calm

_____ 15. vocation

o. something written after the signature

_____ 16. ambiguous

p. polite; relating to ordinary community life

_____ 17. postscript

q. a list of words with definitions

_____ 18. pacify

r. mental strain

_____ 19. megaphone

s. a device used to increase sound

STOP. Check answers at the end of the book (p. 356).

Additional Practice 2 for Lesson 23

A DIRECTIONS: The combining forms presented in Lesson 23 follow. Match the combining form with its meaning.

_____ 1. luc, lum

a. wise

_____ 2. err

b. love

_____ 3. soph

c. stand

_____ 4. sist, sta

d. light; clear

_____ 5. nov

e. I; me; the self

_____ 6. dorm

f. over; above; excessive

_____ 7. peri

g. wander

_____ 8. hyper

h. around

_____ 9. ego

i. new

_____ 10. philo

j. sleep

STOP. Check answers at the end of the book (p. 356).

B DIRECTIONS: Words presented in Lesson 23 follow. Match the word with its meaning.

_____ 1. lucid

a. second-year student

_____ 2. translucent

b. to put in place of

_____ 3. error

c. separated by time and/or space

_____ 4. sophisticated

d. work of fiction of some length

_____ 5. sophomore

e. clear

_____ 6. philosophy   f. something newly introduced

_____ 7. circumstances   g. inactive

_____ 8. substitute   h. to continue in some course even when it is
                                                 difficult

_____ 9. assist   i. the study of human knowledge

_____ 10. consist   j. mistake

_____ 11. distant   k. to help

_____ 12. obstacle   l. worldly-wise

_____ 13. persist   m. something in the way of

_____ 14. innovation   n. something connected with an act

_____ 15. novel   o. portion of time

_____ 16. dormitory   p. self-centered

_____ 17. dormant   q. permitting light to go through but not
                                                 allowing a clear view

_____ 18. period   r. high blood pressure

_____ 19. periodical   s. a building providing sleeping quarters

_____ 20. hypertension   t. to be made up of

_____ 21. egocentric   u. a publication that appears at regular intervals

STOP. Check answers at the end of the book (p. 356).

Additional Practice 3 for Lesson 24

A DIRECTIONS: The combining forms presented in Lesson 24 follow. Match the combining form with its meaning.

_____ 1. miss, mitt   a. spirit; mind; soul

_____ 2. pon, pos   b. born

_____ 3. anima, animus   c. place; set

_____ 4. magna   d. people

_____ 5. hypn, hypno   e. trust; faith

_____ 6. feder, fid, fide   f. great; large

_____ 7. nasc, nat   g. equal

_____ 8. equi   h. sleep

_____ 9. pop   i. send

STOP. Check answers at the end of the book (p. 356).

B **DIRECTIONS:** Words presented in Lesson 24 follow. Match the word with its meaning.

_____ 1. mission	a. place occupied by a thing
_____ 2. dismiss	b. sure of
_____ 3. admission	c. time between events
_____ 4. permission	d. the manner of carrying the body
_____ 5. submit	e. to enlarge
_____ 6. transmit	f. referring to agreement of two or more states to join into a union
_____ 7. intermission	g. the task or responsibility of a person
_____ 8. position	h. sleeplike trance artificially brought on
_____ 9. postpone	i. occurring after birth
_____ 10. positive	j. necessary qualities of something or someone
_____ 11. posture	k. to give in to
_____ 12. post	l. to tell to go
_____ 13. proposal	m. splendid
_____ 14. magnanimous	n. total number of people in an area
_____ 15. animosity	o. occurring before birth
_____ 16. magnify	p. forgiving of insults
_____ 17. magnificent	q. liked by many people
_____ 18. hypnosis	r. government job
_____ 19. federal	s. act of allowing to enter
_____ 20. confide	t. to send from one place to another
_____ 21. innate	u. to tell in trust
_____ 22. postnatal	v. hatred
_____ 23. prenatal	w. equal to
_____ 24. nature	x. a consent
_____ 25. popular	y. born with
_____ 26. population	z. to delay
_____ 27. equivalent	aa. an offer

STOP. Check answers at the end of the book (p. 356).

GLOSSARY

Combining Forms Presented in *Gaining Word Power*

The number after the meaning refers to the page on which the combining form is presented as the main entry for the combining form.

A. Without. 145
Able. Can do; able. 140
Age. Condition, state of; action; collection of; place for. 72
Agog. Leading; directing; inciting. 141
Agogue. Leading; directing; inciting. 141
Al. Relating to. 267
Ali. Other. 141
Ambi. Both. 259
Ance. Act of; state of; quality of. 267
Anima. Spirit; mind; soul. 278
Animus. Spirit; mind; soul. 278
Anni. Year. 98
Annu. Year. 98
Ante. Before. 46
Anthrop. Mankind; man; human. 147
Anthropo. Mankind; man; human. 147
Anti. Against. 192
Aqua. Water. 169
Aqui. Water. 169
Ar. One who; that which. 110
Arch. Rule; chief; ruler. 141
Archae. Ancient. 230
Archaeo. Ancient. 230
Archy. Rule; government. 141
Astro. Star. 169
Aud. Hear. 185
Audi. Hear. 185
Aut. Self. 98
Auto. Self. 98

Belli. War. 259
Bello. War. 259
Bene. Good. 185

Bi. Two. 98
Biblio. Book. 213
Bio. Life. 98
Brevi. Short; brief. 230

Cap. Take; receive. 221
Capit. Head. 177
Cata. Down. 213
Cede. Go; give in; yield. 230
Ceed. Go; give in; yield. 230
Cent. Hundred; hundredth part. 135
Centi. Hundred; hundredth part. 135
Centr. Center. 272
Centri. Center. 272
Centric. Having (something specified) as its center. 272
Cep. Take; receive. 221
Chron. Time. 230
Chrono. Time. 230
Cide. Murder; kill. 177
Civ. Citizen. 259
Civis. Citizen. 259
Co. Together; with. 176
Col. Together; with. 176
Com. Together; with. 176
Con. Together; with. 176
Contra. Against; opposite. 111
Cor. Together; with. 176
Corp. Body. 177
Corpor. Body. 177
Cracy. Rule; government. 141
Crat. A supporter or participant of a form of government; ruler. 141
Cred. Believe. 135

Crypt. Secret; hidden. 230
Crypto. Secret; hidden. 230
Cura. Care. 185
Cyber. Computer. 138
Cycl. Circle; wheel. 230
Cyclo. Circle; wheel. 230

De. Away; from; off; completely. 228
Dec. Ten. 135
Deca. Ten. 135
Deci. Tenth part. 135
Dem. People. 141
Demo. People. 141
Derm. Skin. 221
Dermo. Skin. 221
Dia. Through. 213
Dic. Say; speak. 111
Dict. Say; speak. 111
Dis. Away from; apart; not. 239
Dom. State or condition of being; rank; total area of. 25
Dorm. Sleep. 269
Duc. Lead. 230

E. Out of; from; lacking. 229
Ec. Environment. 119
Eco. Environment. 119
Ego. I; me; the self. 269
Em. In; into. 177
En. In; into. 177
Ence. Act of; state of; quality of. 267
Enni. Year. 98
Epi. Upon; beside; among. 213
Equi. Equal. 278
Er. One who; that which. 110
Err. Wander. 269
Ex. Out of; from; lacking; former. 229

Fac. Make; do. 185
Fect. Make; do. 185
Feder. Trust; faith. 278
Fer. Bring; bear; yield. 213
Fic. Make; do. 185
Fid. Trust; faith. 278
Fide. Trust; faith. 278
Fin. End. 213
Frater. Brother. 177
Fratr. Brother. 177
Ful. Full of; characterized by; having the qualities of. 30

Gamy. Marriage. 147
Gen. Kind; race; descent. 147
Geno. Kind; race; descent. 147
Geo. Earth. 104
Giga. One billion. 138
Glot. Language. 141
Gnosi. Knowledge. 221
Gnosis. Knowledge. 221
Gon. Figure; having (a specified number of) angles. 147
Gram. Something written or drawn; a record. 111
Graph. Something written; machine. 98
Graphy. Writing; drawing; writing in or on a specified field; science. 98
Greg. Herd; flock; crowd; group. 19
Gyn. Woman. 221
Gyno. Woman. 221

Hect. Hundred. 138
Hecto. Hundred. 138
Helio. Sun. 272
Hem. Blood. 119
Hema. Blood. 119
Hemo. Blood. 119
Heter. Different; other. 147
Hetero. Different; other. 147
Hexa. Six. 152
Hom. Same; man; human. 147
Homo. Same; man; human. 147
Hyper. Over; above; excessive. 269
Hypn. Sleep. 278
Hypno. Sleep. 278
Hypo. Under. 221

Ible. Can do; able. 140
Ic. Relating to; like. 81
Il. Not; into. 219
Im. Into; not. 219
In. Into; not. 219
Inter. Between; among. 277
Intra. Within; inside of. 277
Ion. State of; act of; result of. 119
Ir. Not; into. 219
Ish. Belonging to; like or characteristic of; tending to; somewhat or rather; about. 81
Ism. Act of, practice of, or result of, condition of being; action or quality of. 76
Ist. One who. 151

Ive.   Of; relating to; belonging to; having the nature or quality of; tending to. 267

Kilo.   Thousand. 135

Leg.   Law. 147
Legis.   Law. 147
Less.   Without. 176
Lex.   Law. 147
Loc.   Place. 185
Loco.   Place. 185
Log.   Speech; word. 213
Logo.   Speech; word. 213
Logy.   Study of; science of. 104
Luc.   Light; clear. 269
Lum.   Light; clear. 269

Magna.   Great; large. 278
Mal.   Bad; ill; evil; wrong; not perfect. 286
Man.   Hand. 185
Manu.   Hand. 185
Mega.   Very large; million. 259
Meter.   Measure. 104
Micro.   Very small. 104
Milli.   Thousand; thousandth part. 135
Mis.   Wrong; hate. 147
Miso.   Wrong; hate. 147
Miss.   Send. 278
Mitt.   Send. 278
Mon.   One. 141
Mono.   One. 141
Morph.   Form. 147
Morphic.   Having a (specified) form or shape. 147
Mors.   Death. 177
Mort.   Death. 177

Nano.   One billionth. 135
Nasc.   Born. 278
Nat.   Born. 278
Naut.   Sailor. 169
Nomin.   Name. 185
Non.   Not. 192
Nov.   New. 269

Octa.   Eight. 152
Olig.   Few. 141
Oligo.   Few. 141
Ology.   Study of; science of. 104
Omni.   All. 169
Onym.   Name. 185
Or.   One who; that which. 110
Osteo.   Bone. 119

Pac.   Peace. 259
Pathy.   Feeling; suffering. 177
Pax.   Peace. 259
Ped.   Foot; child. 98, 221
Pedo.   Child. 221
Penta.   Five. 152
Peri.   Around. 269
Philo.   Love. 269
Phob.   Fear. 111
Phobo.   Fear. 111
Phon.   Sound. 104
Phono.   Sound. 104
Pod.   Foot. 98
Polis.   City. 259
Poly.   Many. 147
Pon.   Place; set. 278
Pop.   People. 278
Port.   Carry. 135
Pos.   Place; set. 278
Post.   After. 259
Poten.   Powerful. 169
Pre.   Before. 183
Pro.   Before; forward. 213
Pseudo.   False. 185

Re.   Again; back. 103
Ri.   Laughter. 221
Ridi.   Laughter. 221
Risi.   Laughter. 221

Sci.   Know. 169
Scio.   Know. 169
Scope.   A means for seeing; watching or viewing. 104
Scrib.   Write. 104
Scrip.   Write. 104
Semi.   Half; not fully; partly; occurring twice in a period. 286
Septa.   Seven. 152
Sequi.   Follow. 230
Ship.   State; condition or quality of; office, rank, or dignity; art or skill. 51
Sion.   State of; act of; result of. 119
Sist.   Stand. 269
Soph.   Wise. 269
Spect.   See; view; observe. 111
Sta.   Stand. 269
Sub.   Under; beneath; below; lower in rank. 239
Super.   Above in position, over; above or beyond; greater than or superior to;

extra; in the highest degree; in excessive degree. 56

Syl.   Same; with; together; along with. 177
Sym.   Same; with; together; along with. 177
Syn.   Same; with; together; along with. 177

Tain.   Hold. 230
Tele.   From a distance. 104
Temp.   Time. 221
Tempo.   Time. 221
Tempor.   Time. 221
Ten.   Hold. 230
Tend.   Stretch; strain. 259
Tens.   Stretch; strain. 259
Tent.   Hold; stretch; strain. 230, 259
Tetra.   Four. 152
Theo.   God. 141
Tion.   Act of; state of; result of. 119
Tox.   Poison. 221
Toxo.   Poison. 221

Trans.   Across; beyond; through; on the other side of; over. 220
Tri.   Three. 152

Un.   Not. 183
Uni.   One. 111
Ure.   Act; result of an action; agent of action; state of. 72

Ven.   Come. 169
Veni.   Come. 169
Vent.   Come. 169
Vid.   See. 169
Vis.   See. 169
Voc.   Voice; call. 259
Vox.   Voice; call. 259

Y.   Having; full of; tending to; like; somewhat. 21

Zo.   Animal; animal kingdom or kind. 119
Zoo.   Animal; animal kingdom or kind. 119

Vocabulary Words Presented in *Gaining Word Power*

Abbreviation.   A shortened form of a word or phrase.

Abridge.   To shorten; to curtail; to give the substance of in fewer words.

Accreditation.   Act of bringing into favor; a vouching for; a giving authority to.

Acquisition.   The act of obtaining or acquiring; something obtained or gained, as property, knowledge, and so on.

Acreage.   Collection of acres.

Acrophobia.   An extreme fear of high places.

Adaptation.   The act of fitting or suiting one thing to another; an adjusting to fit new conditions; a change for a new use.

Adept.   Highly skilled; proficient; expert.

Admission.   Act of allowing to enter; entrance fee; a price charged or paid to be admitted; acknowledgment; a confession, as to a crime.

Advantage.   Any condition, state, or circumstance favorable to success.

Adversary.   One who opposes another, as in battle or debate; one who acts against something or someone; enemy; antagonist; opponent.

Aesthetic.   Referring to beauty; sensitive to art and beauty; showing good taste; artistic.

Affect.   To act upon or to cause something; to influence; to produce an effect or change in.

Affinity.   Close relationship; attraction to another.

Affirm.   To declare or state positively; to say or maintain that something is true.

Affirmative.   Having the quality of a positive statement.

Affluent.   Having an abundance of goods or riches; wealthy; flowing freely.

Affront.   To insult; an insult; an open and intentional insult.

Agnostic.   Professing uncertainty; one who is not for or against; one who doubts that the ultimate cause (God) and the essential nature of things are knowable.

Agoraphobia.   An extreme fear of being in open spaces or fear of leaving one's house.

Ailurophobia.   An extreme fear of cats.

Alias.   Another name taken by a person, often a criminal.

Alien.   A foreigner; a person from another country; foreign.

Alienate.   To make others unfriendly to one; to estrange (to remove or keep at a distance).

Allocate.   To set apart for a special purpose; to divide up something; to divide and distribute something.

Allot.   To divide or distribute by lot; to distribute or parcel out in portions; to appoint.

Alternative.   A choice between two or more things; a remaining choice; a choice.

Ambidextrous.   Able to use both hands equally well.

Ambiguous.   Having two or more meanings.

Americanism.   Practice of values characteristic of Americans.

Amnesty.   A pardon from the government; act of letting someone off.

Amoral.   Without morals; without a sense of right or wrong.

Amortize.   The gradual extinction of a debt such as a mortgage or a bond issue by payment of a part of the principal at the time of each periodic interest payment.

Anachronism.   Something out of time order; an error in chronology in which a person, an object, or an event is assigned an incorrect date or period.

Anarchist.   One who believes that there should be no government.

Anarchy.   The absence of government; no rule; a state of disorder; chaos.

Anecdote.   A short, entertaining account of some happening, usually personal or biographical.

Animate.   To make alive; to move to action.

Animosity.   Hatred; resentment.

Anniversary.   Yearly return of a date marking an event or an occurrence of some importance; returning or recurring each year.

Annual.   Occurring once a year; yearly.

Annuity.   An investment that yields a fixed sum of money, payable yearly.

Anonymous.   Lacking a name; of unknown authorship.

Antacid.   Something that acts against acid.

Antagonize.   To make unfriendly; to make an enemy of; to oppose; to act against.

Ante meridiem.   Before noon (the abbreviation is A.M.).

Antebellum.   Before the war.

Antecedent.   Going before in time; prior; preceding; previous; the word, phrase, or clause to which a pronoun refers.

Antedate.   To date before.

Antediluvian.   Relating to the period before the flood described in the Bible.

Anteroom.   Waiting room; a lobby.

Anthropoid.   A person who resembles an ape in either stature, walk, or intellect; resembling man, used especially of apes such as the gorilla, chimpanzee, and orangutan; resembling an ape.

Anthropologist.   One who is in the field of anthropology.

Anthropology.   The study of humankind; the study of the cultures and customs of people.

Anthropomorphic.   Giving human shape or characteristics to gods, objects, animals, and so on.

Antigambling.   Against gambling.

Antilabor.   Against labor.

Antimachine.   Against machines.

Antimen.   Against men.

Antipathy.   A dislike for someone.

Antitoxin.   Something used against bacterial poison; a substance formed in the body that counteracts a specific toxin; the antibody formed in immunization with a given toxin, used in treating certain infectious diseases or in immunizing against them.

Antiwar.   Against war.

Antiwomen.   Against women.

Antonym.   A word opposite in meaning to some other word.

Apathy.   Lack of feeling; indifference.

Apodal.   Having no feet.

Apprehensive.   Fearful, expecting evil, danger, or harm; anxious.

Aquanaut.   One who travels underwater; a person trained to work in an underwater chamber.

Aquarium. A pond, a glass bowl, a tank, or the like, in which aquatic animals or plants are kept; a place in which aquatic collections are shown.

Aquatic. Living or growing in or near water; performed on or in water.

Arachnophobia. An extreme fear of spiders.

Archaeology. The study of the life and culture of ancient people, as by the digging up of old settlements, ruins from the past, and old manmade or other objects.

Archaic. Belonging to an earlier period; ancient; old-fashioned; no longer used.

Archetype. The original pattern or model from which something is made or developed; the original model or pattern of which all things of the same kind are representations or copies.

Arrogant. Full of pride and self-importance; overbearing; haughty.

Asset. Anything owned that has value; any valuable or desirable thing that serves as an advantage.

Assist. To give help to; an act of helping.

Assistance. Act of helping.

Astraphobia. An extreme fear of lightning.

Astrology. The art or practice that claims to tell the future and interpret the influence of the heavenly bodies on the fate of people; a reading of the stars.

Astronaut. One who travels in space; a person trained to travel in outer space.

Astronomy. The science that deals with stars, planets, and space.

Atheist. One who does not believe in the existence of God.

Attention. Mental concentration; care; a position of readiness; acts of courtesy.

Attitude. A way of acting, thinking, or feeling that shows one's disposition (one's frame of mind) or opinion; the feeling itself; posture.

Attrition. A gradual wearing down or weakening; a rubbing out or grinding down.

Audible. Capable of being heard.

Audience. An assembly of listeners or spectators at a concert, play, speech, and so on.

Audiology. The study of hearing.

Audiometer. An instrument used to measure hearing.

Audiovisual. Of, pertaining to, involving, or directed at both hearing and sight.

Audit. To examine or check such things as accounts; to attend class as a listener; an examination of accounts to report the financial state of a business.

Audition. A trial hearing, as of an actor or singer; the act of hearing; to try out for a part in an audition.

Auditorium. A building or hall for speeches, concerts, public meetings, and so on; the room in a building occupied by an audience.

Author. One who writes.

Autobiography. Life story written by oneself.

Autocracy. A form of government in which one person rules absolutely.

Autocrat. A ruler who has absolute control of a country.

Autograph. Signature; written by a person's own hand: an *autograph* letter; containing autographs: an *autograph* album; to write one's name on or in.

Automaton. A person or an animal acting in an automatic or mechanical way.

Autonomous. Self-governing; functioning independently of other parts.

Avocation. Something a person does in addition to his or her regular work, usually for enjoyment; a hobby.

Barbarism. The condition of being primitive or brutal.

Beautiful. Having the qualities of beauty.

Beggar. One who begs.

Belligerent. Warlike; any nation, person, or group engaged in fighting war.

Benediction. A blessing; the expression of good wishes.

Benefactor. One who gives help or confers a benefit; a patron.

Beneficiary. One who receives benefits or advantages; the one to whom an insurance policy is payable.

Benefit. That which is helpful; advantage; a payment; a performance given to raise funds for a worthy cause; to aid.

Biannual.   Occurring twice a year; (loosely) occurring every two years.

Bibliography.   A listing of books on a subject by an author (the description includes author's name, title, publisher, date of publication, and so on).

Bicentennial.   Pertaining to or in honor of a two hundredth anniversary; consisting of or lasting two hundred years; occurring once in two hundred years; a two hundredth anniversary.

Biennial.   Occurring once every two years; lasting for two years.

Bifocals.   Pair of glasses with two-part lenses.

Bigamist.   One who is married to two spouses at the same time.

Bigamy.   Marriage to two spouses at the same time.

Bilateral.   Involving two sides.

Bilingual.   Able to use two languages equally well; a bilingual person.

Bimonthly.   Occurring every two months; occurring twice a month.

Binary.   Made up of two parts; twofold; relating to base two.

Biographer.   A person who writes biographies.

Biography.   Person's life story.

Biologist.   One who is in the field of biology.

Biology.   Science of life.

Biopsy.   In medicine, the cutting out of a piece of living tissue for examination.

Biped.   Two-footed animal.

Bisexual.   Of both sexes; having both male and female organs, as is true of some plants and animals; a person who is sexually attracted to both sexes.

Bit.   A unit of computer information.

Biweekly.   Occurring every two weeks; occurring twice a week.

Blameless.   Without blame; without fault.

Bland.   Mild; soft; gentle; balmy; kindly; soothing.

Bluish.   Rather blue.

Bookish.   Inclined to books; involved with books.

Boyish.   Like or characteristic of a boy.

Byte.   Eight bits of data.

Candid.   Honest; outspoken; frank.

Capable.   Able to be affected; able to understand; having ability; having qualities that are able to be developed.

Capital.   City or town that is the official seat of government; money or wealth; first letter of a word at the beginning of a sentence; excellent.

Capitalism.   The economic system in which all or most of the means of production, such as land, factories, and railroads, are privately owned and operated for profit.

Capital punishment.   The death penalty.

Capitol.   The building in which a legislative body meets.

Capitulate.   To give up; surrender.

Capsule.   A small container made of gelatin (or other material that melts) that holds a dose of medicine; a special removable part of an airplane or rocket; can also mean "something extremely brief."

Caption.   The heading of a chapter, section, or page in a book; the title or subtitle of a picture.

Captive.   One who is taken prisoner; one who is dominated.

Captor.   One who holds someone a prisoner.

Castigate.   To correct or subdue by punishing; criticize with drastic severity; to rebuke.

Catalogue.   A listing of names, titles, and so on in some order; a book containing such a list; to make a catalog.

Centennial.   Pertaining to a period of one hundred years; lasting one hundred years; a one hundredth anniversary.

Centimeter.   In the metric system, a unit of measure equal to 1/100 meter (0.3937 inch).

Centipede.   Wormlike animal with many legs.

Century.   Period of one hundred years.

Characteristic.   Marking the peculiar quality or qualities of a person or thing; distinctive; special; a special trait, feature, or quality; individuality.

Christendom.   The Christian world.

Chronic. Continuing for a long time; prolonged; recurring.

Chronological. Arranged in time order (earlier things or events precede later ones).

Chronometer. A very accurate clock or watch; an instrument used to measure time.

Circumference. The distance around a circle; a boundary line of any rounded area.

Circumstance. Something connected with an act, event, or condition; (often pl.) the conditions, influences, and so on surrounding and influencing persons or actions; formal display, as in *pomp and circumstance.*

Citizenship. State or quality of being a citizen.

Civics. (Used in the singular.) The part of political science dealing with the study of civic affairs and the rights and responsibilities of citizenship.

Civil. Of a citizen or citizens; relating to citizens and their government; relating to ordinary community life as distinguished from military or church affairs; polite.

Civilian. One who is not in the military; of civilians; nonmilitary.

Civilization. A state of human society that has a high level of intellectual, social, and cultural development; the cultural development of a specific people, country, or region.

Claustrophobia. An extreme fear of being confined, as in a room or a small place.

Coincidence. The occurrence of things or events at the same time by chance.

Collateral. The pledging of property by a borrower to protect the interests of the lender.

Colleague. A fellow worker in the same profession.

Collect. To gather together.

Combine. To join together; unite.

Concede. To give in; surrender; yield; grant; admit.

Conceive. To become pregnant with; to form in the mind; to understand; to think; to believe; to imagine; to develop mentally.

Concession. An act of giving in; a right granted by the government or other authority for a specific purpose.

Concise. Brief; terse.

Conductor. One who guides or leads; a guide or director; one who has charge of a railroad train; the director of an orchestra or a chorus; any substance that conducts electricity, heat, and so on.

Conference. A discussion or meeting on some important matter.

Confide. To tell in trust; to tell secrets trustingly.

Conscience. The sense of the moral goodness of one's own conduct with the feeling of obligation to do right or be good.

Consequence. That which follows from any act; a result; an effect.

Conservative. Tending to maintain established traditions and to resist or oppose any change in these; cautious; moderate; traditional in style or manner; avoiding showiness; one who clings to traditional or long-standing methods, beliefs, and so on.

Consist. To be made up of.

Constraint. Confinement; the act of restricting; the act of using force; compulsion; coercion; restriction.

Contagious. Spreading by contact; spreading or tending to spread from person to person.

Contemporary. Belonging to the same age; living or occurring at the same time; current; one living in the same period as another or others; a person or thing of about the same age or date or origin.

Content.[1] Satisfied; not complaining; not desiring something else.

Content.[1] What something holds (usually plural in this sense); subject matter; the material that something is made up of; the main substance or meaning.

Contradiction. Something (such as a statement) consisting of opposing parts.

Contrary. Opposite.

Contrast. Difference between things; use of opposites for a certain result.

Convene. To come together; to assemble.

---

[1]*Content* and *content* are presented because they are pronounced differently.

Convenient. Well suited to one's purpose, personal comfort, or ease.

Convention. A formal meeting of members for political or professional purposes; accepted custom, rule, or opinion.

Convocation. A group of people called together; an assembly.

Corporal punishment. Bodily punishment; a beating.

Corporation. A group of people who get a charter granting them as a body certain of the powers, rights, privileges, and liabilities (legal responsibilities) of an individual, separate from those of the individuals who make up the group.

Corpse. Dead body.

Corpulent. Fat; fleshy; obese.

Correspond. To be equivalent; to write letters to one another.

Corroborate. To confirm (to strengthen; to make firm; to affirm); to make more certain.

Covert. Secret; concealed; covered over; sheltered.

Covet. To desire very much what another has; to crave; to long for.

Co-worker. Someone working with you.

Crafty. Sly; skillful in deceiving; cunning.

Creative. Tending to be able to create.

Credential. Something that entitles one to credit or confidence; something that makes others believe in a person; (pl.) testimonials entitling a person to credit or to exercise official power.

Credible. Believable.

Credit. Belief in something; trust; faith; good name; in an account, the balance in one's favor; a unit of academic study; to supply something on credit to.

Creditor. One to whom a sum of money or other thing is due.

Creed. A statement of religious belief; a statement of belief; principles.

Criterion. A standard of judging; any established law, rule, or principle by which a correct judgment may be formed.

Crypt. An underground vault.

Cryptic. Having a hidden or secret meaning; mysterious.

Curator. Head of a department of a museum; one in charge.

Curtail. To shorten; to lessen; to cut off the end or a part; to cut back on; to reduce.

Cybermate. Computer pal.

Cyberphobia. An extreme fear of working with computers.

Cyberspace. Digital information on the computer network.

Cycle. A period that keeps coming back, in which certain events take place and complete themselves in some definite order; a round of years or ages; a pattern of regularly occurring events; a series that repeats itself.

Cyclone. A system of violent and destructive whirlwinds.

Cynophobia. Extreme fear of dogs.

Danish. Belonging to Denmark.

Datum. (*Data*, the plural of *datum*, is usually used.) Information given, granted, or admitted; a premise upon which something can be argued; material used as a basis for calculations.

Decade. Period of ten years.

Decagon. A ten-sided figure with ten angles.

Decameter. In the metric system, a measure of length containing 10 meters, equal to 393.70 inches or 32.81 feet.

Decapitate. To take off the head; to kill.

Deceive. To mislead by lying; to lead into error.

Decimal. Numbered by tens; based on ten; pertaining to tenths or the number 10; a decimal fraction.

Decimate. To take or destroy a tenth part of; to destroy but not completely; to destroy a great number or proportion of.

Decimeter. In the metric system, a unit of length equal to 1/10 meter.

Decode. To change from code to simple language.

Decolor. To take color away.

Deduction. The act of drawing a conclusion by reasoning or reasoning that goes from the general to the particular; the taking away or subtraction of something; an inference or a conclusion.

Defer. To leave to another's opinion or judgment; to delay; to postpone.

Deference. Respect; a giving in to another's opinion or judgment.

Definitive. Conclusive, final; most nearly complete or accurate.

Deflea. To take off fleas.

Delete. To take out or remove a letter, word, and so on; to erase.

Delouse. To free from lice.

Demagogue. A person who stirs up the emotions of people in order to become a leader and achieve selfish ends.

Democracy. A form of government in which there is rule by the people either directly or through elected representatives.

Democrat. A person who believes in rule by the people.

Demography. The statistical study of human populations, including births, deaths, marriages, population movements, and so on.

Denude. To strip the covering from completely.

Dependence. Act of trusting; act of relying on someone for support.

Deport. To send someone away.

Deportment. Manner of conducting or carrying oneself; behavior; conduct.

Depose. To remove from a throne or other high position; to let fall.

Deprive. To take something away from.

Derisive. Mocking; jeering.

Dermatologist. A doctor who deals with skin disorders.

Derogative. Tending to belittle.

Derogatory. Tending to make less well regarded; tending to belittle someone or something; disparaging; belittling.

Description. An account that gives a picture of something in words.

Destructive. Tending to cause destruction or the tearing down of things.

Detain. To stop; to hold; to keep from proceeding; to delay.

Detente. Easing of strained relations, especially between nations.

Detention. A keeping or holding back; confinement; the state of being detained in jail.

Detoxify. To take away poison; to destroy the poison.

Devilish. Like or characteristic of a devil.

Diagnose. To determine what is wrong with someone after an examination.

Diagram. An outline figure that shows the relationship between parts or places; a graph or chart.

Dialect. A variety of speech; a regional form of a standard language.

Dialogue. A conversation in which two or more take part; the conversation in a play.

Diameter. A straight line passing through the center of a circle.

Dictaphone (a trademark). A machine for recording and reproducing words spoken into its mouthpiece (differs from a tape recorder because it has controls that allow it to be used in transcription).

Dictation. The act of speaking or reading aloud to someone who takes down the words.

Dictator. A ruler who has absolute power.

Dictatorship. Office or rank of a head of government who has absolute control of the government.

Diction. Manner of speaking; choice of words.

Dictionary. A book for alphabetically listed words in a language, giving information about their meanings, pronunciations, and so forth.

Dictum. An authoritative statement; a saying.

Dilemma. Any situation that necessitates a choice between equally unfavorable or equally unpleasant alternatives; an argument that presents two equally unfavorable alternatives.

Diligent. Applying oneself in whatever is undertaken, working in a constant effort to accomplish something; industrious.

Dirty. Full of dirt.

Disable. To make an object or someone not able to do something.

Disapprove. Not to approve of; not to regard as worthy.

Disband. To break up (a group).

Discreet. Careful about what one says or does; prudent; cautious.

Disdain.   To regard as unworthy; the feeling of scorn or despisal; expression of scorn (contempt).

Dishonest.   Not honest; not to be trusted.

Disloyal.   Not loyal.

Dismiss.   To tell or allow to go; to discharge, as from a job; to get rid of; to have done with quickly; to reject.

Disposition.   One's usual frame of mind or one's usual way of reacting; a natural tendency.

Disrobe.   To take off clothes.

Distant.   Separated or apart by space and/or time; away from; far apart; not closely related.

Docile.   Easy to teach; easy to discipline; obedient.

Dormant.   Asleep or as if asleep; not active.

Dormitory.   A large room in which many persons sleep; a building providing sleeping and living quarters, especially at a school, college, or resort (summer or winter hotel).

Dukedom.   The rank or title of a duke; the area governed by a duke.

Ecology.   The study of the relationship between living organisms and their environment.

Economize.   To use or manage with thrift or prudence; to avoid waste or needless spending; to reduce expenses.

Ecstasy.   Great joy.

Effect.   Something brought about by some cause; the result; consequence.

Effective.   Producing or having the power to bring about an intended result; producing results with the least amount of wasted effort.

Egocentric.   Self-centered; relating everything to oneself.

Egotistic.   Conceited; very concerned with oneself; selfish; vain.

Emancipate.   To set free from servitude or slavery; to set free.

Emissary.   A person or agent sent on a specific mission.

Empathy.   The imaginative putting of oneself into another person's personality or skin; ability to understand how another feels because one has experienced it firsthand or otherwise.

Enjoyable.   Able to be enjoyed.

Enthusiastic.   Relating to enthusiasm or a lively interest in something.

Envision.   To imagine something; to picture in the mind.

Epidemic.   Relating to the rapid spread of a disease or something else that spreads like an epidemic disease.

Epidermis.   Outermost layer of skin.

Epilogue.   A short section added at the end to a book, poem, and so on; a short speech added to a play and given at the end.

Equivalent.   Equal in value, meaning, force, and so on.

Equivocate.   To use ambiguous language on purpose.

Eradicate.   To destroy completely; to pull out by the roots; to wipe out; to exterminate.

Erratic.   Wandering; not regular, not stable.

Error.   A mistake; something done, said, or believed incorrectly; a wandering from what is correct.

Euphemism.   The substitution of a word or phrase that is less direct, milder, or vaguer for one thought to be harsh, offensive, or blunt; a word or phrase considered less distasteful or less offensive than another.

Euphemistic.   Relating to euphemism or a milder way to say something.

Evidence.   That which serves to prove or disprove something.

Evident.   Obvious; clearly seen; plain.

Exception.   The act of taking out; something or one that is taken out or left out; an objection.

Exclude.   To keep from.

Excuse.   To forgive.

Exhale.   To breathe out.

Exit.   To go out of.

Exonerate.   To relieve, as of a charge or blame resting on one; to clear of a charge of guilt; to relieve of a debt or duty.

Exotic.   Foreign, charmingly unfamiliar; not native; strangely beautiful.

Expect. To look out for.

Expedite. To hasten; to speed up the progress of.

Export. To carry away; to carry or send some product to some other country or place; something that is exported.

Exposure. State of being exposed.

Expound. To state in detail; to set forth; to explain.

Ex-president. Former president.

Extemporaneous. Done or spoken without special preparation; makeshift; done or spoken as if without special preparation. (In speech classes, spoken with preparation but delivered without notes.)

Ex-wife. Former wife.

Facsimile. An exact copy; to make an exact copy of; the transmission of graphic matter by electronic means.

Faction. A number of persons in an organization, group, government, party, and so on, having a common goal, often self-seeking.

Factory. A building or buildings in which things are manufactured.

Famish. To make or be very hungry; starve.

Famished. Very hungry.

Fatal. Resulting in or capable of causing death; deadly; bringing ruin or disaster; having decisive importance.

Fatherless. Without a father.

Fatigue. Physical or mental tiredness; weariness; to tire out.

Federal. Of or formed by a compact; relating to or formed by an agreement between two or more states, groups, and so on; relating to a union of states, groups, and so on, in which central authority in common affairs is established by consent of its members.

Fertile. Able to produce a large crop; able to produce; capable of bearing offspring, seeds, fruit, and so on; productive in mental achievements; inventive; having abundant resources.

Fertilization. The act of making something able to produce; in biology, the union of a male and female germ cell; impregnation.

Fictitious. Imaginary; not real; made up; fabricated.

Final. Last; coming at the end; conclusive.

Finale. The last part; end; the concluding movement of a musical composition; the last scene of an entertainment.

Finite. Having a limit or end; able to be measured.

Foliage. Collection or mass of leaves.

Formidable. Dreaded; causing awe or fear; hard to handle; of discouraging or awesome strength, size, difficulty, and so on.

Fraternity. A group of men joined together by common interests for fellowship; a brotherhood; a Greek letter college organization.

Fratricide. Killing of a brother; may also refer to the killing of a sister.

Freedom. Condition of being free.

Friendship. State of being a friend.

Frugal. Thrifty; not spending freely; avoiding waste.

Frustrate. To defeat; to bring to nothing.

Frustrated. Filled with a sense of discouragement and dissatisfaction as a result of defeated efforts, inner conflicts, or unresolved problems.

Futile. Useless; ineffectual; trifling; unimportant.

Genealogy. The science or study of one's descent; a tracing of one's ancestors.

General. Referring to all; in the U.S. Army and Air Force, an officer of the same rank as an admiral in the U.S. Navy.

Generate. To produce; to cause to be; to bring into existence.

Generic. Referring to all in a group or class.

Genocide. The systematic and deliberate killing of a whole group or a group of people bound together by customs, language, politics, and so on.

Genus. A class, kind, or group marked by shared characteristics or by one shared characteristic.

Geocentric. Having or relating to the earth as the center.

Geography. A descriptive science that deals with the earth, its division into continents and countries, the climate, plants, animals, natural resources, inhabitants, and industries of the various divisions.

Geologist. One who is in the field of geology.

Geology. Study of earth's physical history and makeup.

Geometry. Branch of mathematics dealing with the measurement of points, lines, planes, and so on.

Gigabyte. One billion bytes; a unit of storage capacity in a computer.

Governorship. Rank or office of governor.

Grammar. That part of the study of language that deals with the forms and structure of words (morphology) and their arrangement in phrases and sentences (syntax); the study or description of the way language is used.

Graphic. Marked by realistic and vivid detail.

Gregarious. Fond of the company of others; sociable; characteristic of a flock, herd, or crowd.

Gynecologist. A doctor who deals with women's diseases, especially in reference to reproductive organs.

Harmless. Without harm; without hurting.

Haughty. Having or showing great pride in oneself and contempt (disrespect) or scorn for others; overbearing; snobbish; arrogant.

Haulage. Act of hauling.

Healthy. Full of health.

Hectometer. A unit of measure equal to 100 meters.

Heliocentric. Having or relating to the sun as the center.

Hematology. A branch of biology that deals with the study of blood.

Heroic. Like a hero.

Hertz. The international unit of frequency; equal to one cycle per second.

Heterogeneous. Consisting of different ingredients or unlike things; mixed.

Hexagon. Six-sided figure with six angles.

Historic. Relating to history, which is an account of what has happened; famous in history.

Homicide. Any killing of one human being by another.

Homogeneous. Being the same throughout; being uniform.

Homograph. A word that is spelled the same way as another but has a different meaning. It may also have a different pronunciation.

Homonym. A word that agrees in pronunciation with some other word but differs in meaning and may differ in spelling.

Homophone. Words that are pronounced the same but have different spellings and meanings.

Homosexual. Referring to the same sex or to sexual desire for those of the same sex; a homosexual individual.

Horsy. Like a horse.

Hostile. Unfriendly; referring to an enemy.

Hydrophobia. An extreme fear of water; rabies, a viral infectious disease of the central nervous system whose symptoms include an inability to swallow. (Because of the association of water with the act of swallowing, the term *hydrophobia* is used for rabies.)

Hyperactive. Overactive.

Hyperbole. Great exaggeration; an overstatement.

Hyperbolic. Relating to a hyperbole or a great exaggeration.

Hyperproductive. Overproductive.

Hypersensitive. Oversensitive.

Hypertension. High blood pressure.

Hypnosis. A sleeplike trance that is artificially brought about.

Hypocrite. A person who pretends to be what he or she is not; one who pretends to be better than he or she really is.

Hypodermic. Referring to the area under the skin; used for injecting under the skin; a hypodermic injection; a hypodermic syringe or needle.

Hypothesis. An unproved scientific conclusion drawn from known facts; something assumed as a basis for argument; a possible answer to a problem that requires further investigation.

Illegal. Not legal; not lawful.

Illuminate. To give light to; to make clear; to light up.

Illustrate. To make clear.

Imminent. About to happen; threatening (said especially of danger).

Immoral. Not moral; knows difference between right and wrong but chooses to do wrong.

Immortal. Referring to a being who never dies; undying; one who never dies.

Imperfect. Not perfect; having a fault.

Import. To carry in; bring in goods from another country; something that is imported.

Important. Deserving of notice.

Impotent. Without power to act; physically weak; incapable of sexual intercourse (said of males).

Inclination. A personal leaning or bent; a liking; a bending, slanting, or sloping; a slope.

Incorporate. To unite; combine.

Incredible. Not believable.

Indictment. A charge; an accusation.

Induction. The act of reasoning that goes from the particular to general or the act of drawing a conclusion from specific data or facts; initiation; an introduction; an installation.

Ineffectual. Not being able to bring about results.

Infamous. Having a bad reputation; notorious.

Inference. Something derived by reasoning; something that is not directly stated but suggested in the statement; a logical conclusion that is drawn from statements; deduction.

Infidelity. Breach of trust; lack of faith in a religion; unfaithfulness of a marriage partner; adultery.

Infinite. Having no limit or end; not able to be measured.

Infinitesimal. Too small to be measured; very minute.

Initiate. To introduce by doing or using first; to bring into practice or use; to admit as a member into a fraternity, sorority, club, and so on, especially through use of a secret ceremony.

Innate. Inborn; born with; not acquired from the environment; belonging to the fundamental nature of something.

Innovation. Something newly introduced; a new method, something new.

Inquisitive. Given to asking many questions; prying; curious.

Inscription. Something written or engraved on a surface; a brief or informal dedication in a book to a friend.

Inspection. The act of looking into something.

Integrate. To unite; to make whole or complete by adding together parts.

Intense. Having great or extreme force; very strong; existing or occurring to a high or extreme degree.

Intention. Aim; goal; purpose.

Intercede. To come between; to come between as an influencing force; to intervene.

Intercept. To stop or interrupt the course of.

Intercollegiate. Between colleges.

Interdepartmental. Between departments.

Interdependent. Dependent upon one another.

Intermission. Time between events; recess.

Intermittent. Starting or stopping again at intervals; not continuous; coming and going at intervals.

Interrogate. To ask questions of formally; to examine by questioning.

Interstate. Between states.

Intervene. To come between; to act as an influencing force; to intercede.

Intimidate. To make timid; to cause fear; to scare; to discourage by threats or violence.

Intracollegiate. Within the college.

Intradepartmental. Within the department.

Intramural.   Within a school or an institution.

Intricate.   Complicated; difficult to follow or understand; complex.

Invincible.   Impossible to overcome; not able to be conquered.

Invisible.   Not able to be seen.

Irish.   Belonging to Ireland.

Irregular.   Not uniform; not the same.

Irrigate.   To wet.

Isolate.   To set apart from others; to place alone; to separate.

Jeopardy.   Risk; danger; peril.

Joyful.   Full of joy.

Killer.   One who kills.

Kilobyte.   A unit of storage capacity in a computer system; loosely 1,000 bytes.

Kilometer.   In the metric system, a unit of length equal to 1,000 meters.

Kingdom.   Area controlled by a king.

Kingship.   Dignity or rank of king.

Laudable.   Worthy of praise; commendable.

Laughable.   Able to be laughed at.

Leadership.   Skill as a leader.

Legal.   Referring to law; lawful.

Legislative.   Relating to the body of lawmakers.

Legislature.   Body of people who are responsible for lawmaking.

Lethal.   Causing death; deadly.

Liability.   A debt; legal obligation to make good any loss or damage that occurs in a transaction (a business deal); something that works to one's disadvantage.

Liberal.   Giving freely; generous; large or plentiful; tolerant of views differing from one's own; broad-minded; favoring reform or progress.

Listless.   Spiritless; indifferent; inactive; apathetic.

Local.   Referring to a relatively small area, region, or neighborhood; limited.

Location.   A place or site; exact position or place occupied; a place used for filming a motion picture or a television program.

Logical.   Relating to the science concerned with correct reasoning.

Lucid.   Clear; easily understood; bright; shining.

Magnanimous.   Forgiving of insults or injuries; high-minded; great of soul.

Magnate.   A very important or influential person.

Magnificent.   Splendid; beautiful; superb.

Magnify.   To increase the size of; to make larger; to enlarge.

Maintain.   To carry on or to continue; to keep up; to keep in good condition.

Maintenance.   The act of keeping up.

Malediction.   A speaking badly of someone; slander; a curse.

Malefactor.   Someone who does something bad; a criminal.

Malformed.   Abnormally formed.

Malfunction.   To function badly.

Malnourished.   Badly nourished.

Maltreated.   Treated badly.

Manageable.   Able to be managed.

Manicure.   Care of the hands and fingernails; to care for the hands; to cut evenly.

Manipulation.   The act of handling or operating; the act of managing or controlling skillfully or by shrewd use of influence; the act of changing or falsification for one's own purposes or profit.

Manual.   Referring to the hand; made, done, or used by the hands; a handy book used as a guide or source of information.

Manufacture.   To make goods or articles by hand or by machinery; to make something from raw materials by hand or machinery; the act of manufacturing.

Manuscript.   Written by hand or typed; not printed; a document written by hand; a book written by hand or typed and usually sent in for publication; style of penmanship in which letters are not joined together.

Marriage.   State of being wed.

Massive.   Having the quality of being very large.

Megabit.   1,000,000 bits.

Megabuck.   1,000,000 dollars.

Megahertz.   One million hertz.

Megalopolis. One very large city made up of a number of cities; a vast, populous, continuously urban area.

Megaphone. A device used to increase sound.

Meter. In the metric system, a unit of length equal to approximately 39.37 inches; an instrument for measuring the amount of something (as water, gas, electricity); an instrument for measuring distance, time, weight, speed, and so forth; a measure of verse.

Metropolitan. Referring to a major city center and its surrounding area; a person who inhabits a metropolis or one who has the manners and tastes associated with a metropolis.

Microbe. A very small living thing; a microorganism.

Microfilm. Film on which documents are photographed in a reduced size for storage convenience.

Micrometer.[1] A unit of length equal to one millionth of a meter, also called micron.

Micrometer.[1] An instrument used to measure accurately very small distances, angles, and diameters.

Microorganism. An organism so small that it can be seen only under a microscope.

Microscope. Instrument used to make very small objects appear larger so that they can be seen.

Millennium. Period of 1,000 years; a one thousandth anniversary; a period of great happiness (the millennium).

Millimeter. In the metric system, a unit of length equal to 1/1,000 meter (0.03937 inch).

Million. A thousand thousands (1,000,000); a very large or indefinitely large number; being one million in number.

Misanthrope. Hater of humankind.

Miscellaneous. Mixed; consisting of several kinds; various.

Misnomer. A name wrongly applied to someone or something; an error in the naming of a person or place in a legal document.

Misogamist. Hater of marriage.

Misogynist. Hater of women.

Missile. An object, especially a weapon, that is intended to be thrown or discharged, as a bullet, arrow, stone, and so on.

Mission. Group or team of people sent somewhere to perform some work; the task, business, or responsibility that a person is assigned; the place where missionaries carry out their work; a place where poor people may go for assistance.

Modify. To change slightly or make minor changes in character, form, and so on; to change or alter; to limit or reduce; in grammar, to limit or restrict a meaning.

Monarchy. A government or state headed by a king, a queen, or an emperor; called absolute (or despotic) when there is no limitation on the monarch's power and constitutional (or limited) when there is such limitation.

Monogamist. One who believes in or practices monogamy.

Monogamy. Marriage to one spouse at one time.

Monoglot. A person who knows, speaks, or writes only one language; speaking and writing only one language.

Monologue. A long speech by one person; a dramatic sketch performed by one actor.

Monophobia. An extreme fear of being alone.

Monopoly. Exclusive control of a commodity or service in a given market; control that makes possible the fixing of prices and the elimination of free competition.

Monorail. A single rail serving as a track for trucks or cars suspended from it or balanced on it.

Monosyllable. A word consisting of one syllable.

Monotone. Speech that has no change in pitch; speech in an unvaried tone.

Monotonous. Changeless; dull; uniform; having no variety.

---

[1]*Micrometer* and *micrometer* are presented separately because they are pronounced differently and have different meanings.

Morgue.   Place where dead bodies (corpses) of accident victims and unknown persons found dead are kept; for reporters, it refers to the reference library of old newspaper articles, pictures, and so on.

Mortal.   Referring to a being who must eventually die; causing death; ending in death; a human being.

Mortality.   The state of having to die eventually; proportion of deaths to the population of the region; death rate; death on a large scale, as from disease or war.

Mortgage.   The pledging of property to a creditor (one to whom a sum of money is owed) as security for payment; to pledge.

Mortician.   A funeral director; undertaker.

Mortify.   To cause to feel shame; to punish (one's body) or control (one's physical desires or passions) by self-denial, fasting, and the like, as a means of religious or ascetic (severe) discipline.

Motherless.   Without a mother.

Mundane.   Referring to everyday things; referring to that which is routine or ordinary; referring to worldly things rather than more high-minded or spiritual things.

Naive.   Foolishly simple; childlike; unsophisticated.

Nanosecond.   One-billionth of a second.

Nationalism.   Devotion to one's nation.

Native.   Belonging to a country by birth.

Nature.   The necessary quality or qualities of something; sort; kind; wild state of existence; uncivilized way of life; overall pattern or system; basic characteristic of a person; inborn quality; the sum total of all creation.

Nautical.   Pertaining to seamen, ships, or navigation; relating to sailing.

Non-Arab.   Not an Arab.

Nonbeliever.   Not a believer.

Noncapitalist.   One who is not a capitalist.

Non-Catholic.   Not a Catholic.

Non-Communist.   One who is not a Communist.

Noncriminal.   Not criminal.

Noneffective.   Not effective.

Non-English.   Not English.

Nostalgic.   Homesick; longing to go back to one's home, hometown, and so on; longing for something far away or long ago.

Novel.   A work of fiction of some length; new; strange; unusual.

Novice.   Someone new at something; a rookie; a beginner.

Obfuscate.   To darken; to confuse; to obscure.

Obstacle.   Something that stands in the way or opposes; an obstruction.

Obstinate.   Stubborn; tenacious.

Octagon.   Eight-sided figure with eight angles.

Oligarchy.   A form of government in which there is rule by a few (usually a privileged few).

Omission.   Anything left out or not done; failure to include.

Omnibus.   A large motor vehicle designed to carry a number of people as passengers; an *omnibus* bill is a legislative bill that carries a mixture of provisions.

Omnipotent.   All-powerful.

Omnipresent.   Being present everywhere at all times.

Omniscient.   All-knowing.

Optimist.   One who is hopeful; a cheerful person; one who tends to take the most hopeful view or expects the best outcome.

Orphanage.   Place for orphans or collection of orphans.

Orthography.   The part of language study that deals with correct spelling.

Osteology.   The study of bones.

Outage.   State of being interrupted.

Overt.   Open to view; public; apparent; able to be seen.

Pacifist.   One who is against war; one who is against conflict; one who wants peace.

Pacify.   To bring peace to; to calm; to quiet.

Paradox.   Contradiction; a self-contradictory statement that is false; a statement that seems absurd, contradictory, or unbelievable but may be true.

Passage.   Act of passing.

Passive.   Not acting; acted upon; unresisting; not opposing; unenthusiastic.

Patriotism.   Quality of being a patriot.

Pauperism.   Condition of being very poor.

Peaceful.   Characterized by peace.

Pedagogue.   A teacher.

Pedestal.   A base or bottom support.

Pedestrian.   One who goes on foot.

Pediatrician.   A doctor who specializes in children's diseases.

Pediatrics.   Branch of medicine dealing with children's care and diseases.

Pedicure.   Care of the feet, toes, and nails.

Penmanship.   Art or skill of handwriting.

Pentagon.   Five-sided figure with five angles.

Perception.   The act of becoming aware of something through the senses of seeing, hearing, feeling, tasting, and/or smelling.

Perceptive.   Being aware; having insight, understanding, or intuition, as a perceptive analysis of the problems involved.

Perfidious.   Violating good trust; treacherous; deceitful; deliberately faithless.

Perimeter.   A measure of the outer part or boundary of a closed plane figure; boundary line of a closed plane figure.

Period.   A portion of time; a portion of time into which something is divided; a punctuation mark that signals a full stop at the end of a sentence; used after abbreviations.

Periodic.   Taking place, occurring or appearing at regular intervals.

Periodical.   Referring to publications, such as magazines, that appear at fixed time intervals; a publication that appears at regular intervals.

Periphery.   The outer part or boundary of something.

Periscope.   An instrument used by a submarine to see all around.

Permission.   Act of allowing the doing of something; a consent.

Persevere.   To persist; to continue doing something in spite of difficulty.

Persist.   To continue in some course or action even though it is difficult.

Personification.   A figure of speech in which a nonliving thing or idea is made to appear as having the qualities of a person.

Pertinent.   Relevant; relating to or bearing upon the matter in hand; being to the point.

Peruse.   To read carefully; to inspect closely.

Pessimist.   One who expects the worst to happen in any situation; one who looks on the dark side of things; a gloomy person.

Phenomenon.   Any fact, circumstance, or experience that is apparent to the senses and that can be scientifically described; something extremely unusual.

Philosophy.   The study of human knowledge; the love of wisdom and the search for it; a search for the general laws that give a reasonable explanation of something.

Phobia.   Extreme fear.

Phonetics.   A study dealing with speech sounds and their production.

Phonics.   Study of the relationship between letter symbols of a written language and the sounds they represent.

Player.   One who plays.

Podiatrist.   One specializing in the care and treatment of feet, especially foot disorders.

Podium.   A raised platform for the conductor of an orchestra; a dais.

Poetic.   Like poetry.

Politician.   A person engaged in politics; a person involved in the science or art of government; a person who seeks advancement or power within an organization by dubious (doubtful) means.

Politics.   (Although plural, it is usually looked upon as singular.) The science or art of government or of the direction and management of public or state affairs.

Polyandry.   The marriage of one woman to two or more men at the same time.

Polygamist.   One who is married to many spouses at the same time.

Polygamy.   Marriage to many spouses at the same time.

Polyglot.   A person who knows, speaks, or writes many languages; speaking or writing many languages.

Polygon.   A closed plane figure with several angles and sides.

Polygyny.   The marriage of one man to two or more women at the same time.

Popular.   Approved of; admired; liked by most people; referring to the common people or the general public.

Population.   Total number of people living in a country, city, or any area.

Port.   Place to or from which ships carry things; place where ships may wait.

Portable.   Can be carried; easily or conveniently transported.

Porter.   A person who carries things; one who is employed to carry baggage at a hotel or transportation terminal.

Position.   An act of placing or arranging; the manner in which a thing is placed; the way the body is placed; the place occupied by a person or thing; the proper or appropriate place; job; a feeling or stand; social standing.

Positive.   Being directly found to be so or true; real; actual; sure of something; definitely set; confident.

Post.   A position or employment, usually in government service; an assigned beat; a piece of wood or other material to be used as a support; a place occupied by troops; to inform; to put up (as on a wall); to mail (as a letter).

Posterior.   In the rear; later; following after; coming after in order; succeeding; located behind; the buttocks.

Posterity.   Future generations; all of one's descendants (offspring).

Posthumously.   After death.

Postmortem.   Happening or performed after death; referring to an examination of a human body after death; autopsy.

Postnatal.   Occurring after birth.

Postpone.   To put off to a future time; to delay.

Postscript.   Something added to a letter after the writer's signature; something added to written or printed legal papers.

Posture.   The placing or carriage of the body or parts of the body; a mental position or frame of mind.

Potent.   Physically powerful; having great authority; able to influence; strong in chemical effects.

Potentate.   A person possessing great power; a ruler; a monarch.

Potential.   The possible ability or power one may have; having force or power to develop.

Precede.   To go or come before.

Precedent.   Something done or said that may serve as an example; in law, a legal decision serving as an authoritative rule in future similar cases.

Pre-Christian.   Referring to the time before there were Christians.

Predict.   To say before; to foretell; to forecast; to tell what will happen.

Preference.   The choosing of one person or thing over another; the valuing of one over another; a liking better.

Preheat.   To heat before.

Prehistoric.   Referring to the time before history was recorded.

Prejudge.   To judge or decide before.

Prejudice.   An opinion or judgment made beforehand.

Premature.   Ripened before.

Prenatal.   Being or taking place before birth.

Prerevolutionary.   Referring to time before a revolution.

Prescription.   A doctor's written directions for the preparation and use of medicine; an order; direction; rule.

Preset.   To set before.

Preunite.   To join together before.

Prisoner.   One who is kept in prison.

Proceed.   To go on; to go forward; to carry on an action.

Procession.   A parade, as a funeral *procession*; any continuous course.

Procrastinate.   To put off doing something until a future time; to postpone taking action.

Proficient.   Knowing something very well; able to do something very well.

Prognosis. A prediction or conclusion regarding the course of a disease and the chances of recovery; a prediction.

Prologue. An introduction, often in verse (poetry), spoken or sung before a play or opera; any introductory or preceding event; a preface.

Proposal. An offer put forth to be accepted or adopted; an offer of marriage; a plan.

Proposition. A plan or something put forth for consideration or acceptance.

Provision. The act of being prepared beforehand; something made ready in advance; a part of an agreement referring to a specific thing.

Provoke. To stir up anger or resentment; to irritate.

Prudent. Capable of using sound judgment in practical matters; wisely cautious; sensible; not rash.

Pseudonym. False name, especially used by an author to conceal his or her identity; pen name.

Pseudopodium. False foot.

Pseudoscience. A false science.

Public. Relating to the public or people at large.

Question. The act of asking.

Rebel. One who opposes or takes arms against those in authority or control; to disobey those in authority or control; opposing or taking arms against a ruler or government.

Rebellion. Opposition to one in authority or dominance.

Reception. The act of receiving or being received; a formal social entertainment; the manner of receiving someone.

Recession. The act of going back; in economics, the decline of business activity.

Recomb. To comb again.

Redo. To do again.

Reference. A referring or being referred; the giving of a problem to a person, committee, or authority for settlement; a note in a book that sends the reader for information to another book; the name of another person who can offer information or recommendation; the mark or sign, as a number or letter, directing the reader to a footnote and so on; a written statement of character, qualification, or ability; testimonial.

Relevant. Applying to the matter in question; suitable; relating to.

Reliable. Dependable; trustworthy.

Reluctant. Unwilling; opposed.

Remission. A temporary stopping or lessening of a disease; a pardon.

Repay. To pay back.

Repent. To feel pain, sorrow, or regret for something left undone or done; to feel remorse.

Replenish. To supply or fill again.

Replete. Well filled or supplied.

Reporter. A person who gathers information and writes reports for newspapers, magazines, and so on.

Rerun. To run again.

Retentive. Having the ability to retain or keep in things; tenacious, as a retentive memory; having a good memory.

Return. To go back.

Rework. To work again.

Rewrite. To write again.

Ridicule. Language or actions that make a person the object of mockery or cause one to be laughed at or scorned; to mock or view someone in a scornful way; to hold someone up as a laughingstock; to make fun of.

Ridiculous. Unworthy of consideration; absurd (senseless); preposterous.

Rupture. The act of something breaking apart.

Salty. Full of salt.

Salvage. Act of saving.

Satiate. To fill; to satisfy the appetite completely; to supply with anything to excess; to glut (overindulge).

Science. Any area of knowledge in which the facts have been investigated and presented in an orderly manner.

Scientific. Relating to science.

Scotophobia. Extreme fear of darkness.

Scribe.   A writer, author; a public writer or secretary; in Scripture and Jewish history, a man of learning.

Script.   Writing that is either cursive, printed, or engraved; a piece of writing; a prepared copy of a play for the use of actors.

Scripture.   Books of the Old and New Testament; a text or passage from the Bible; the sacred writings of a religion.

Scrutinize.   To observe closely; to examine or inquire into critically; to investigate.

Secede.   To withdraw from.

Sedate.   Calm; composed; quiet; serene; sober; to put under sedation.

Segregate.   To set apart from others; to separate.

Semiannual.   Occurring twice yearly; occurring every half year.

Semiblind.   Partly blind.

Semicircle.   Half circle.

Semistarved.   Partly starved.

Semiwild.   Partly wild.

Sentimental.   Having or showing tenderness, emotion, feeling, and so on, influenced more by feeling or emotion than by reason; having or showing exaggerated or superficial emotion.

Septagon.   Seven-sided figure with seven angles.

Sequence.   The following of one thing after another; order; a continuous or related series, with one thing following another.

Shrinkage.   Act of shrinking; amount of decrease.

Significant.   Having or expressing meaning; full of meaning; important.

Socialism.   The principle whereby the ownership and operation of the means of production are by society or the community rather than by private individuals, with all members of the community sharing in the work and the products.

Sophisticated.   Not in a simple, natural, or pure state; worldly-wise; not naive; cultured; highly complicated; complex; experienced.

Sophistry.   Faulty reasoning; unsound or misleading but clever and plausible (appearing real) argument or reasoning.

Sophomore.   A second-year student in American high schools or colleges; an immature person; one who thinks he or she knows more than he or she does.

Spanish.   Belonging to Spain.

Spectacle.   Something showy that is seen by many (the public); an unwelcome or sad sight.

Spectacles.   Eyeglasses.

Spectacular.   Relating to something unusual, impressive, exciting, or unexpected.

Spectator.   An onlooker; one who views something.

Speculate.   To think about something by viewing it from all sides; to take part in any risky business venture.

Spillage.   The act of spilling; amount spilled.

Stagnant.   Lacking motion or current; not flowing or moving; foul (dirty and bad-smelling) from lack of movement; lacking in activity; sluggish; dull.

Stamina.   Staying power; resistance to fatigue, illness, and the like.

Stardom.   Status of being a star.

Stethoscope.   A hearing instrument used in examining the heart, lungs, and so on.

Sticky.   Tending to stick.

Subcommittee.   A committee under the original committee.

Subfloor.   Floor beneath.

Submarine.   Ship undersea.

Submit.   To give in to another; to surrender; to concede; to present for consideration or approval; to present as one's opinion.

Subscription.   An agreement; a promise in writing to pay some money; an agreement to receive something and pay for it.

Subsequent.   Following soon after; following in time, place, or order; resulting.

Subset.   Something that is under the larger set.

Substitute.   To put in place of another person or thing; one who takes the place of another person; something that is put in place of something else or is available for use instead of something else.

Subtraction.   The act of taking something away.

Succeed.   To accomplish what is attempted; to come next in order; to come next after or replace another in an office or position.

Suffer.   To feel pain or distress.

Suicide.   Killing of oneself.

Superabundance.   Abundance in excess.

Superacid.   Excessively acid.

Superb.   Very fine.

Supercritical.   Highly critical.

Superintendent.   One who has charge of a building, office, institution, and so on.

Superior.   Of higher degree.

Superlative.   Of the highest degree.

Superpower.   Excessive or superior power.

Supersafe.   Safe in the highest degree.

Superstitious.   Having beliefs that are not consistent with the known laws of science.

Supersweet.   Sweet in the highest degree.

Supervision.   The act of overseeing others.

Susceptible.   Easily influenced by or affected with; especially liable to.

Sustain.   To maintain; to keep in existence; to keep going; to uphold; to support.

Syllable.   A vowel or a group of letters with one vowel sound.

Symbol.   Something that stands for or represents another thing; an object used to represent something abstract.

Symmetry.   Balanced form or arrangement; balance on both sides.

Sympathy.   Sameness of feeling with another; ability to feel pity for another.

Symphony.   A large-scale musical composition for full orchestra; harmony of sound, especially of instruments; harmony of any kind.

Symptom.   In medicine, a condition that results from a disease and serves as an aid in diagnosis; a sign or token that indicates the existence of something else.

Synchronize.   To cause to agree in rate or speed; to occur at the same time.

Synonym.   A word that has the same meaning as some other word.

Synthesis.   A putting together of two or more things to form a whole.

Tacit.   Unspoken; not expressed openly but implied.

Tactful.   Considerate; conscientiously inoffensive; skillful in dealing with people or difficult situations.

Tallish.   Rather tall.

Tearful.   Full of tears.

Telecommunication.   Communication from a distance.

Telegram.   Message sent from a distance.

Telegraph.   Instrument for sending a message in code at a distance; to send a message from a distance.

Telemeter.   An instrument that measures distance; instrument that sends information to a distant point.

Telephone.   Instrument that sends and receives sound, such as the spoken word, over distance; to send a message by telephone.

TelePrompTer (a trademark).   A device for unrolling an enlarged script in front of a speaker on television.

Telescope.   Instrument used to view distant objects.

Television.   An electronic system for the transmission of visual images from a distance; a television receiving set.

Temerity.   Rash boldness; foolhardiness.

Temperate.   Moderate in everything; avoiding extremes or excesses.

Temperature.   Degree of hotness or coldness of something.

Tempo.   The rate of speed at which a musical composition is supposed to be played; rate of activity.

Temporary.   Lasting for a short period of time.

Tenacious.   Stubborn; tough; holding or tending to hold strongly to one's views, opinions, rights, and so on; retentive, as a tenacious memory.

Tenant.   A person who holds property; one who lives on property belonging to another; one who rents or leases from a landlord; one who lives in a place.

Tendon.   A fibrous cord by which a muscle is attached.

Tenet.   Any opinion, doctrine, principle, dogma, and the like held as true; belief.

Tension. The act of stretching or the condition of being stretched tight; mental strain.

Tentative. Done on trial or experimentally; not final; uncertain.

Tenure. The right to hold or possess something; length of time something is held; status assuring an employee of permanence in his or her position or employment (tenure protects employees such as teachers from being dismissed except for serious misconduct or incompetence).

Terminate. To end.

Terrorism. Practice of terror; use of fear to frighten or intimidate.

Terse. Brief; concise.

Tetragon. Four-sided figure with four angles.

Theocracy. A form of government in which there is rule by a religious group.

Theology. The study of religion.

Thirtyish. About thirty.

Thrifty. Clever at managing one's money; economical; not spending money unnecessarily.

Torture. Act of causing severe pain.

Toxic. Relating to poison.

Toxicologist. One who specializes in the study of poisons.

Tragic. Like a tragedy, in which something is very sad or there is disaster.

Transatlantic. Across the Atlantic Ocean.

Transcript. A written or typewritten copy of an original; a copy or reproduction of any kind.

Transfer. To carry or send from one person or place to another; to cause to pass from one person or place to another; an act of transferring or being transferred.

Transhuman. Beyond human limits.

Translucent. Permitting light to go through but not permitting a clear view of any object.

Transmit. To send from one place to another; to pass on by heredity; to transfer; to pass or communicate news, information, and so on.

Transparent. Able to be seen through.

Transport. To carry from one place to another.

Trigon. Three-sided figure with three angles.

Triskaidekaphobia. An extreme fear of the number thirteen.

Trite. Used so often as to be too common; made commonplace by repetition; lacking freshness or originality.

Turmoil. Confused motion or state; disturbance; tumult.

Unable. Not able.

Unaided. Not helped.

Unanimous. Agreeing completely; united in opinion; being in complete agreement; being of one mind.

Uncarpeted. Not carpeted.

Uncaught. Not caught.

Unclaimed. Not claimed.

Uncooked. Not cooked.

Uniform. Being always the same; special form of clothing.

Unify. To make or form into one.

Unilateral. Occurring on one side only; done by one only; one-sided.

Union. A joining; a putting together.

Unique. Being the only one of its kind.

Unison. A harmonious agreement; a saying of something together.

Universal. Applying to all.

Universe. Everything that exists.

Unloved. Not loved.

Untenable. Not able to be held or defended.

Unwed. Not married.

Valid. Sound; well grounded on principles or evidence; having legal force.

Variable. Changeable; something that may or does vary.

Venture. A risky or dangerous undertaking.

Verbose. Wordy.

Versatile. Turning with ease from one thing to another; able to do many things well; many-sided; having many uses.

Vestige. A trace, mark, or sign of something that once existed but doesn't anymore.

Vindicate.   To clear from criticism, accusation, or suspicion.

Vindictive.   Revengeful in spirit; spiteful.

Virile.   Manly; masculine; forceful; able to procreate (to produce or reproduce).

Visa.   Something stamped or written on a passport that grants an individual entry to a country.

Visage.   The face; the appearance of the face or its expression.

Visible.   Able to be seen; evident; apparent; on hand.

Vision.   The sense of sight.

Visionary.   A person who sees visions.

Visor.   The projecting front brim of a cap for shading the eyes.

Vital.   Necessary to life; essential; energetic.

Vocabulary.   A list of words and phrases, usually arranged alphabetically, that are defined or translated from another language; a stock of words possessed by an individual or group.

Vocal.   Referring to the voice; having voice; oral; freely expressing oneself in speech, usually with force; speaking out.

Vocation.   A calling; a person's work or profession.

Vociferous.   Of forceful, aggressive, and loud speech; clamorous.

Wastage.   Amount wasted.

Wattage.   Amount of electric power; total number of watts needed.

Wavy.   Like a wave.

Wisdom.   The state of having knowledge.

Zoology.   The study of animals.

A N S W E R   K E Y

Chapter 2

Lesson 1 (pp. 17–21)

Story in Context (pp. 17–18)

(1) unspoken, (2) separate, (3) unite, (4) unsophisticated, (5) prying, (6) concise, (7) wordy, (8) maintains, (9) unsophisticated, (10) frank, (11) discouraged, (12) end, (13) reads carefully, (14) apathetic, (15) temporary.

Practice A (pp. 19–20)

(1) curious, (2) happy, (3) combine, (4) read; unspoken, (5) defeated, (6) unsophisticated; frank, (7) wordy, (8) inattentive, (9) end, (10) brief; initial, (11) keep up, (12) separate

Practice B (pp. 20–21)

(1) segregate, (2) naive, (3) candid, (4) inquisitive, (5) frustrate, (6) verbose, (7) tacit, (8) terse, (9) sustain, (10) integrate.

Practice C (p. 21)

Sentences will vary.

Lesson 2 (pp. 22–25)

Story in Context (p. 22)

(1) unfriendly, (2) imaginary, (3) lessen, (4) wealthy, (5) pardons, (6) secret, (7) open, (8) deadly, (9) deadly, (10) suitable.

Practice A (p. 24)

(1) verbose, (2) covert, (3) lethal, (4) amnesty, (5) overt, (6) curtail, (7) hostile, (8) naive, (9) candid, (10) relevant, (11) fictitious, (12) temerity, (13) crafty, (14) tenet.

Practice B (p. 24–25)

(1) job security, (2) boldness, (3) apparent, (4) wealthy, (5) made up, (6) reduce, (7) related, (8) many-sided, (9) decisively important, (10) hidden

Practice C (p. 25)

Sentences will vary.

Lesson 3 (pp. 26–30)

Story in Context (p. 26)

(1) homesick, (2) marked by emotion, (3) difficult to overcome, (4) everyday, (5) starved, (6) very tired, (7) choice, (8) looking on the bright side, (9) looking on the dark side, (10) brief, (11) restrictions, (12) confuse, (13) considerate.

Practice A (pp. 28–29)

(1) amnesty, (2) concise, (3) nostalgic, (4) tactful, (5) variable, (6) optimist, (7) obfuscate, (8) formidable, (9) constraints, (10) crafty, (11) sentimental, (12) fatigued, (13) mundane, (14) expedite, (15) pessimist, (16) hostile, (17) alternative, (10) tenets

Practice B (p. 29)

(1) sentimental, (2) fatigued, (3) formidable, (4) famished, (5) optimist, (6) pessimist, (7) mundane, (8) alternative, (9) concise, (10) nostalgic.

Practice C (p. 30)

Sentences will vary.

Fun with Cartoons (p. 30)

Sustain—to maintain. The humor in the cartoon is that the senator tries to give a long political speech on why he is quitting the race, but the translator gives the reason very concisely by saying that they are broke. In other words, there is no more money.

Special Academic Words (pp. 30–31)

Practice A (pp. 30–31)

1. The act of uniting.
2. The act of separating.
3. A pardon from the government; the act of letting off.
4. Unfriendly.
5. Applying to the matter in question; suitable.
6. Open to view.
7. Secret; concealed.
8. Imaginary; not real; made up.
9. Any opinion, doctrine, principle, dogma, and the like held as true; belief
10. Sly; skillful in deceiving.

Practice B (p. 31)

(1) crafty, (2) overt, (3) covert, (4) tenet, (5) relevant, (6) segregation, (7) integration, (8) fictitious, (9) hostile, (10) amnesty.

Chapter Words in a Paragraph (p. 31)

Paragraphs will vary.

Gaining Word Power on the Internet (p. 32)

Answers will vary.

Crossword Puzzle (pp. 32–33)

Analogies (pp. 33–34)

(1) naive, (2) integrate, (3) famished, (4) defeat, (5) obfuscate, (6) mundane, (7) steady, (8) concise, (9) spiritless, (10) optimist, (11) ecstasy, (12) temerity, (13) posterior, (14) terminate, (15) amnesty, (16) tenet, (17) prying, (18) vociferous, (19) curtail, (20) tacit.

Multiple-Choice Vocabulary Test (pp. 34–37)

Lesson 1

(1) c, (2) d, (3) b, (4) c, (5) b, (6) c, (7) b, (8) a, (9) b, (10) a, (11) c, (12) b, (13) b, (14) a, (15) d.

Lesson 2

(16) c, (17) d, (18) b, (19) c, (20) d, (21) a, (22) c, (23) b, (24) b, (25) a, (26) c, (27) a, (28) b, (29) d, (30) a.

Lesson 3

(31) b, (32) b, (33) b, (34) c, (35) d, (36) c, (37) d, (38) c, (39) c, (40) a, (41) b, (42) a, (43) b, (44) c, (45) c.

Chapter True/False Test[1] (p. 37)

(1) F; to *integrate* means to bring together, (2) F; a *listless* person is lacking in energy, (3) T, (4) T, (5) T, (6), F; if you *peruse* a document, you read it carefully, (7) T, (8) T, (9) F; something that is

---

[1]False answers may vary

relevant is applicable, (10) F; a *fatal* shooting is one in which someone is killed, (11) T, (12) T, (13) F; you feel *famished* if you haven't eaten for a long time, (14) T, (15) T, (16) F; to *obfuscate* means to confuse, (17) F; an *optimist* always expects the best, (18) T

STOP. Turn to page 38 for the scoring of the tests.

Additional Practice Sets (pp. 38–41)

Additional Practice 1

(1) honest, (2) prying, (3) unsophisticated, (4) unite, (5) separate, (6) maintain, (7) unspoken, (8) brief, (9) filled with a sense of discouragement, (10) wordy.

Additional Practice 2

(1) affluent, (2) covert, (3) overt, (4) fatal, (5) fictitious, (6) amnesty, (7) curtail, (8) hostile, (9) lethal, (10) relevant.

Additional Practice 3

(1) choice, (2) brief, (3) discouragingly difficult, (4) starved, (5) tired, (6) ordinary, (7) filled with tenderness, emotional, (8) person who looks at the bright side of things, (9) person who looks at the bad or gloomy side of things, (10) homesick.

Chapter 3
Lesson 4 (pp. 42–46)

Story in Context (pp. 42–43)

(1) a choice between two equally unfavorable alternatives, (2) industrious, (3) the occurrence of things at the same time, by chance, (4) asserted, (5) arrogant, (6) scorn, (7) wipe out, (8) take out, (9) relevant, (10) separated, (11) fill up, (12) haughty, (13) sign.

Practice A (pp. 44–45)

(1) scorn, (2) industrious, (3) proud, (4) eliminate, (5) two things happening at once, (6) choice, (7) refill, (8) economical, (9) state, (10) overbearing

Practice B (pp. 45–46)

(1) coincidence, (2) dilemma, (3) pertinent, (4) affirm, (5) arrogant, (6) isolate, (7) eradicate, (8) delete, (9) disdain, (10) diligent.

Practice C (p. 46)

Answers will vary.

---

[1]As a sentimental person is filled with emotion, he or she would not be apathetic. An apathetic person is without feelings.

Lesson 5 (pp. 46–51)

Story in Context (pp. 46–47)

(1) unwilling, (2) fellow workers, (3) dependable, (4) question, (5) complicated, (6) prior, (7) important, (8) example, (9) persist, (10) modify.

Practice A (p. 49)

(1) delay, (2) complicated, (3) practical, (4) major, (5) change, (6) opposed, (7) prior example, (8) dependable, (9) preceding events, (10) persist

Practice B (p. 50)

(1) colleague, (2) precedent, (3) persevere, (4) reliable, (5) interrogate, (6) reluctant, (7) significant, (8) intricate, (9) antecedent, (10) adaptation.

Practice C (p. 51)

Sentences will vary.

Lesson 6 (pp. 51–56)

Story in Context (pp. 51–52)

(1) traditional person, (2) broad-minded person, (3) broad-minded person, (4) economically wise, (5) advantage, (6) be thrifty, (7) debt, (8) parceled, (9) foul, (10) desiring, (11) change, (12) necessary, (13) rebuking, (14) commendable.

Practice A (p. 54)

(1) vindicate, (2) sedate, (3) conservative, (4) castigated, (5) economize, (6) vital, (7) covet, (8) assets, (9) frugal, (10) laudable, (11) allot, (12) modify

Practice B (pp. 54–55)

(1) avoid waste, (2) a person who is open-minded, (3) thrifty, (4) something of value, (5) parcel out or set aside, (6) opposed to change, (7) longs for, (8) foul from not moving, (9) alter, (10) disadvantage.

Practice C (p. 55)

Sentences will vary.

Fun with Cartoons (pp. 56–57)

1. Colleague—a fellow worker, usually in the same profession. The student doesn't know the definition of the word *colleague*. He guesses that it's a collie—the kind of dog used in the Lassie films.
2. Procrastination—the putting off for later whatever you have to do. The cartoon is amusing because only a procrastinator would leave reading a book until the last moment. It is also amusing because if Jeremy, the boy in the cartoon, doesn't comprehend what he is reading, he is not reading.

Special Academic Words (p. 57)

Practice A (p. 57)

1. To use or manage with thrift or prudence; to avoid waste or needless spending.
2. To divide or distribute by lot; to distribute or parcel out in portions.
3. Clever at managing one's money; economical.
4. Anything owned that has value; any valuable or desirable thing that serves as an advantage.
5. A debt; legal obligation to make good any loss or damage that occurs in a business deal; something that works to one's disadvantage.

Practice B (p. 57)

(1) liability, (2) asset, (3) economize or thrifty, (4) allot, (5) thrifty or economize.

Chapter Words in a Paragraph (p. 58)

Paragraphs will vary.

Gaining Word Power on the Internet (p. 58)

Answers will vary.

Crossword Puzzle (pp. 58–59)

Analogies (pp. 59–60)

(1) manly, (2) scorn, (3) question, (4) conservative, (5) replenish, (6) affirm, (7) persevere, (8) intricate, (9) associate, (10) isolate, (11) commendable, (12) delete, (13) covet, (14) sensible, (15) alter, (16) diligent, (17) vital, (18) postpone, (19) eradicate, (20) save.

Multiple-Choice Vocabulary Test (pp. 60–63)

Lesson 4

(1) c, (2) c, (3) b, (4) a, (5) c, (6) c, (7) b, (8) d, (9) d, (10) c, (11) a, (12) b, (13) c, (14) d, (15) a.

Lesson 5
(16) d, (17) c, (18) a, (19) d, (20) c, (21) b, (22) a, (23) b, (24) c, (25) d, (26) c, (27) a, (28) a, (29) c, (30) d.

Lesson 6
(31) d, (32) c, (33) d, (34) c, (35) d, (36) c, (37) d, (38) b, (39) a, (40) c, (41) d, (42) a, (43) c, (44) a, (45) b.

Chapter True/False Test 2[1] (pp. 63–64)

(1) T, (2) T, (3) T, (4) F; come before, not after; (5) F; work with, (6) F; relevant, (7) F; to rebuke, (8) T, (9) T, (10) F; to satisfy it, (11) F; complicated, (12) T, (13) T, (14) T, (15) F; ask many questions, (16) F; unforgiving, (17) F; innocent, (18) T.

STOP. Turn to pp. 64–67 for the scoring of the tests.

Additional Practice Sets (pp. 64–65)

Additional Practice 1
(1) diligent, (2) dilemma, (3) delete, (4) eradicate, (5) pertinent, (6) isolate, (7) affirm, (8) coincidence, (9) haughty, (10) disdain.

Additional Practice 2
(1) adaptation, (2) intricate, (3) significant, (4) colleagues, (5) reluctant, (6) reliable, (7) precedent, (8) interrogate, (9) persevere, (10) antecedent.

Additional Practice 3
(1) allot, (2) asset, (3) conservative, (4) frugal, (5) economize, (6) liability, (7) covet, (8) stagnant, (9) liberal, (10) modify.

Chapter 4

Lesson 7 (pp. 68–72)

Story in Context (pp. 68–69)
(1) insulted, (2) a personal leaning, (3) a particular trait, (4) belittling, (5) feeling, (6) unfriendly, (7) pretending to be other than what they really are, (8) mild phrases, (9) scare, (10) artistic.

Practice A (pp. 70–71)
(1) attitude, (2) aesthetic, (3) affront, (4) characteristic, (5) antagonize, (6) inclination, (7) euphemism, (8) hypocrite, (9) intimidate, (10) derogatory.

Practice B (pp. 71–72)
(1) belittling, (2) personal liking, (3) feeling, (4) artistic, (5) feel remorse, (6) distinctive, (7) substitution, (8) pretender, liar, (9) oppose, (10) confirm, (11) insult, (12) clear

Practice C (p. 72)
Sentences will vary.

---

[1]Answers for *false* are suggested answers.

Lesson 8 (pp. 73–76)

Story in Context (p. 73)
(1) fearful, (2) cautious, (3) begin, (4) mild, (5) being left out, (6) observe closely, (7) everyone agrees, (8) mixed, (9) notorious, (10) obedient.

Practice A (pp. 74–75)
(1) discreet, (2) apprehensive, (3) docile, (4) infamous, (5) bland, (6) scrutinize, (7) omission, (8) unanimous, (9) miscellaneous, (10) initiate.

Practice B (pp. 76–77)
(1) apprehensive, (2) criterion, (3) bland, (4) invincible, (5) miscellaneous, (6) scrutinized, (7) unanimous, (8) valid, (9) infamous, (10) data, (11) omission, (12) docile

Practice C (p. 76)
Sentences will vary.

Lesson 9 (pp. 77–81)

Story in Context (p. 77)
(1) tumult, (2) outgoing, (3) opponents, (4) inactive, (5) strange, (6) skilled, (7) commonplace, (8) acquiring, (9) spreading, (10) short, personal stories.

Practice A (p. 79)
(1) abridge, (2) adept, (3) phenomenon, (4) trite, (5) contagious, (6) anecdotes, (7) imminent, (8) gregarious, (9) exotic, (10) turmoil, (11) acquisition, (12) passive

Practice B (pp. 79–80)
(1) enemy, (2) unenthusiastic or inactive, (3) disturbance, (4) commonplace, (5) short, entertaining accounts of some happenings, (6) spreading by contact, (7) foreign or strange, (8) fond of the company of others, (9) act of obtaining something, (10) highly skilled.

Practice C (pp. 80–81)
(1) acquiring, (2) skilled, (3) strange; commonplace, (4) skilled; short entertaining stories, (5) inactive, (6) opponent, (7) tumult, (8) spreading.

Practice D (p. 81)
Sentences will vary.

Fun with Cartoons (p. 82)

The cartoon is amusing because of what you expect to take place. It's ridiculous that Professor Fishhawk has such a jumble of data for his IRS audit. You would expect some kind of order to the professor's documents. Instead, the professor shows the IRS agent a messy pile of documents that the professor must have left exposed to the elements, since he claims that whatever is missing is due to a natural wearing down by wind, rot, or an occasional brushfire.

Special Academic Words (pp. 82–83)

Practice A (pp. 82–83)

1. To relieve, as of a charge or blame resting on one; to clear of a charge.
2. To confirm; to make more certain.
3. Risk; danger.
4. To feel pain, sorrow, or regret for something left undone or done; to feel remorse.
5. Careful about what one says or does; prudent; cautious.
6. To make unfriendly; to make an enemy of; to oppose.

7. A way of acting, thinking, or feeling that shows one's disposition or opinion; the feeling itself.
8. Marking the peculiar quality or qualities of a person or thing; distinctive; a special trait.
9. To make timid; to cause fear.
10. Contradiction.
11. Tending to make less well regarded; tending to belittle someone or something.
12. A personal leaning or bent; a liking; a bending; slanting.
13. Agreeing completely; united in opinion.
14. Having a bad reputation; notorious.
15. To observe closely; to examine or inquire into critically.
16. Sound; well grounded on principles or evidence; having legal force.
17. One who opposes another, as in battle or debate; one who acts against something or someone; enemy; antagonist; opponent.

Chapter Words in a Paragraph (p. 83)
Paragraphs will vary.

Gaining Word Power on the Internet (p. 83)
Answers will vary.

Crossword Puzzle (pp. 83–85)

Across/Down solution grid:

- 1 A H A
- 4 R I N G
- 6 S I R — 7 D I S
- 10 M E — 11 I R E
- 12 L A G — 13 S E E S — 15 D A M
- 18 S T A T E — 21 S C — 22 D O C I L E
- 24 D E R O G A T O R Y — 27 S H E — E
- 28 I — 29 O — 30 R E E L — 32 A — 33 A T
- 34 S O S — 36 T E S T — 37 R U N
- 39 C U T — 40 P A S T — 42 W A S
- 43 B A S E — 44 A N — 45 D I C E
- 46 P E R — 47 A S S E T — 50 A I N T
- 51 A G E — 52 M I S C E L L A N E O U S
- 55 I D A — 56 E R — 57 N O
- 58 V O C A L — 60 R I
- E T H A — S
- E — T — T
- E — I
- C

Analogies (pp. 85–86)

(1) compliment, (2) fearful, (3) terminate, (4) commonplace, (5) unskilled, (6) ally, (7) standard, (8) inclination, (9) spreading, (10) unmanageable, (11) disturbance, (12) exonerate, (13) bland, (14) notorious, (15) exotic, (16) passive, (17) careful, (18) gregarious, (19) scrutinize, (20) over-indulgent.

Multiple-Choice Vocabulary Test (pp. 86–89)

Lesson 7

(1) c, (2) a, (3) c, (4) a, (5) c, (6) a, (7) b, (8) d, (9) c, (10) d, (11) b, (12) a, (13) d, (14) b, (15) a.

Lesson 8

(16) b, (17) c, (18) a, (19) a, (20) d, (21) b, (22) b, (23) d, (24) b, (25) c, (26) a, (27) d, (28) c, (29) a, (30) d.

Lesson 9

(31) b, (32) d, (33) c, (34) c, (35) d, (36) d, (37) c, (38) b, (39) c, (40) b, (41) c, (42) c, (43) c, (44) d, (45) b.

Chapter True/False Test[1] (pp. 89–90)

(1) F; opponent, (2) T, (3) T, (4) F; legal, (5) T, (6) F; insult, (7) F; synonym, (8) T, (9) F; careful, (10) F; unsuccessful, (11) T, (12) T, (13) F; a contradiction, (14) F; unlikely to argue, (15) T, (16) T, (17) T, (18) T, (19) F; shorten, (20), T, (21) F; commonplace.

STOP. Turn to p. 90 for the scoring of the tests.

Additional Practice Sets (pp. 90–93)

Additional Practice 1

(1) affront, (2) attitude, (3) euphemism, (4) intimidate, (5) inclination, (6) characteristic, (7) hypocrites, (8) antagonize, (9) aesthetic, (10) derogatory.

Additional Practice 2

(1) omission, (2) bland, (3) miscellaneous, (4) scrutinize, (5) unanimous, (6) infamous, (7) docile, (8) initiate, (9) discreet, (10) apprehensive.

Additional Practice 3

(1) trite, (2) turmoil, (3) adversary, (4) passive, (5) contagious, (6) gregarious, (7) adept, (8) acquisition, (9) exotic, (10) anecdote.

---

[1]Answers for true/false test are suggested answers.

Chapter 5
Lesson 10 (pp. 97–103)

Story in Context (pp. 97–98)

(1) able to speak and write two languages, (2) signature, (3) life stories, (4) life story written by oneself, (5) every two months, (6) every two weeks, (7) yearly return of a date, (8) walkers, (9) foot doctor, (10) yearly, (11) twice a year, (12) every two years, (13) yearly payment of money, (14) humans.

Practice A (pp. 98–101)

(1) **autobiography**—Life story written by oneself; (2) **biography**—life story written by someone else. The first is when you write your own life story; the second is when someone else writes your life story. Amusing commentaries will vary.

Practice B (pp. 101–102)

(1) autobiography, (2) biographies, (3) autographs, (4) anniversary, (5) biweekly, (6) bimonthly, (7) biped, (8) pedestrian, (9) annual, (10) biennial.

Practice C (pp. 102–103)

(1) spelling, (2) yearly, (3) vivid, (4) platform, (5) twice a month, (6) two-legged animals, (7) walkers, (8) machine, (9) self-governing (10) bifocals, (11) stand, (12) foot doctor, (13) fluent in two languages, (14) tissue sample, (15) fixed yearly payment

Practice D (p. 103)

Sentences will vary.

Lesson 11 (pp. 104–110)

Story in Context (p. 104)

(1) instrument for transmitting sound, (2) descriptive science of the earth, (3) medical instrument, (4) a picture in words, (5) a very small living thing, (6) an organism that cannot be seen with the naked eye, (7) instrument for looking at very small things, (8) doctor's written directions, (9) cursive handwriting, (10) study of living things.

Practice A (pp. 107–108)

(1) biography, (2) autobiography, (3) script, (4) biology, (5) microscope, (6) description, (7) telescope.

Practice B (pp. 108–109)

(1) description, (2) biographer, (3) telephone, (4) geography, (5) autobiographies, (6) scripts, (7) telescope, (8) microscope, (9) geometry, (10) geology.

Practice C (pp. 109–110)

(1) believing the earth is at the center of the universe, (2) branch of math that deals with measurement, points, lines, and planes (3) metric unit of length that equals 3.3 feet, (4) engraved writing,

(5) method of preserving documents in reduced size on film, (6) study of speech sounds, (7) instrument for viewing distant objects, (8) written records, (9) sacred writings, (10) instrument for transmitting code, (11) relationships between letters and sounds, (12) study of the earth

Practice D (p. 110)

Sentences will vary.

Lesson 12 (pp. 111–113)

Story in Context (p. 111)

(1) everything that exists, (2) a joining, (3) message sent from a distance, (4) being one of a kind, (5) a ruler who has absolute power, (6) opposite, (7) act of speaking to someone who takes down the words, (8) a special form of clothing, (9) together, (10) manner of speaking, (11) impressive, (12) a book of alphabetically listed words in a language, (13) differences, (14) extreme fear, (15) showy sight, (16) onlookers, (17) complete, (18) something consisting of opposing parts.

Practice A (pp. 115–116)

(1) dic, dict—say; speak, (2) phob, phobo—fear.
The first cartoon is humorous because one does not expect to see a goat acting as a secretary. It is also ridiculous that the professor asks the goat whether it takes dictation.

Practice B (p. 117)

(1) dictator, (2) union, (3) universe, (4) contrary, (5) phobia, (6) contradiction, (7) dictionary, (8) spectacular, (9) unique, (10) uniforms.

Practice C (pp. 117–118)

(1) machine for recording and playing words, (2) fear of small spaces, (3) difference, (4) way of speaking, (5) fear of water, (6) message sent by wires, (7) thinks, (8) forms and structures of words in a language, (9) charge, (10) writing down what someone says, (11) audience, (12) fear of heights.

Practice D (p. 118)

Answers will vary.

Special Academic Words (p. 119)

Practice A (p. 119)

(1) the study of bones, (2) the study of animals, (3) the study of the relationship between living organisms and their environment, (4) a branch of biology that deals with the study of blood.

Practice B (p. 119)

(1) biology, (2) orthography, (3) geometry, (4) geography, (5) geology, (6) phonetics.

Chapter Words in a Paragraph (p. 120)

Paragraphs will vary.

Gaining Word Power on the Internet (p. 120)

Answers will vary.

Crossword Puzzle (pp. 120–121)

¹O	²R				
³H	A	⁴D			
	⁵P	E	⁶D		
	⁷B	I	O	⁸	
	⁹T	E	L	¹⁰E	
		O	¹¹R	■	¹²C
		¹³G	R	A	¹⁴P	¹⁵H
¹⁶D	¹⁷A	Y	■	¹⁸H	A	¹⁹M
²⁰I	■	²¹S	²²C	O	P	E
²³C	²⁴A	²⁵B	■	²⁶O	N	
²⁷A	T	■	²⁸A	²⁹U	T	O
	³⁰I	N	■			
	³¹L	I	³²N	³³E		
	³⁴O	H				

Analogies (pp. 122–123)

(1) pedestrian, (2) telescope, (3) hydrophobia, (4) spectacle, (5) biweekly, (6) spectacular, (7) unique, (8) uniform, (9) podium, (10) autograph, (11) automaton, (12) phobia, (13) contradict, (14) bifocals, (15) unite, (16) orthography, (17) transcript, (18) indictment, (19) biennial, (20) microbe.

Multiple-Choice Vocabulary Test (pp. 123–128)

Lesson 10

(1) c, (2) a, (3) a, (4) c, (5) a, (6) c, (7) d, (8) b, (9) a, (10) b, (11) c, (12) b, (13) c, (14) b, (15) c, (16) a, (17) a, (18) d, (19) c, (20) a, (21) b, (22) a, (23) a, (24) b.

Lesson 11

(25) c, (26) d, (27) c, (28) b, (29) a, (30) a, (31) d, (32) b, (33) b, (34) c, (35) c, (36) b, (37) b, (38) b, (39) c, (40) c, (41) d, (42) a, (43) b, (44) c, (45) a, (46) a, (47) b.

Lesson 12

(48) a, (49) c, (50) d, (51) c, (52) a, (53) c, (54) a, (55) a, (56) c, (57) a, (58) c, (59) c, (60) c, (61) a, (62) c, (63) c, (64) b, (65) d, (66) a, (67) c, (68) a, (69) a, (70) b, (71) c, (72) a, (73) c.

Chapter True/False Test[1] (p. 128)

(1) T; (2) F, geology to biology; (3) F, agreement to disagreement; (4) F, autobiography to biography; (5) F, goes on a bicycle to walks; (6) F, same to different or unique to uniform or universal; (7) T; (8) F, twice a year to every two years or biennially to biannually; (9) T; (10) F, telescope to microscope; (11) T; (12) T; (13) T; (14) F, a play script to the Bible; (15) F, life story to signature; (16) F, is not to is.

STOP. Turn to p. 129 for the scoring of the tests.

Additional Practice Sets (pp. 129–133)

Additional Practice 1

A. (1) b, (2) g, (3) c, (4) a, (5) d, (6) f, (7) e.
B. (1) c, (2) b, (3) j, (4) e, (5) i, (6) h, (7) d, (8) g, (9) a, (10) f, (11) k.

Additional Practice 2

A. (1) g, (2) a, (3) d, (4) f, (5) c, (6) e, (7) b, (8) h.
B. (1) h, (2) f, (3) g, (4) d, (5) c, (6) a, (7) i, (8) e, (9) b, (10) j.

Additional Practice 3

A. (1) f, (2) c, (3) d, (4) e, (5) a, (6) b.
B. (1) l, (2) m, (3) g, (4) i, (5) h, (6) b, (7) c, (8) e, (9) f, (10) k, (11) o, (12) d, (13) p, (14) r, (15) a, (16) j, (17) q, (18) n.

Chapter 6

Lesson 13 (pp. 134–140)

Story in Context (pp. 134–135)

(1) one hundred years, (2) believable, (3) unbelievable, (4) thousand years, (5) behavior, (6) beliefs (7) sending to other countries, (8) easily carried, (9) very brief period of time, (10) ten-year periods, (11) one thousand times one thousand, (12) believe in, (13) one hundred years

Practice A (p. 138)

credit—praise or approval; You do not expect the student, who cannot answer a question which he obviously is supposed to be able to answer, to naively say that he should be rewarded or praised for being honest. The concept is silly, it is ridiculous.

Practice B (p. 139)

(1) decade, (2) credential, (3) incredible, (4) million, (5) credit, (6) incredible, (7) credential, (8) credible, (9) credential, (10) portable, (11) port, (12) export, (13) import, (14) million.

Practice C (pp. 139–140)

Sentences will vary.

---

[1]Answers for *false* are suggested answers.

Lesson 14 (pp. 140–145)

Story in Context (pp. 140–141)

(1) form of government in which one person possesses unlimited power, (2) rule by one, (3) a person who has absolute control, (4) a person who stirs up people for his or her own selfish ends, (5) disorder, (6) a form of government where there is rule by the people through elected representatives, (7) foreigner, (8) estranged, (9) another name, (10) does not believe in the existence of God, (11) the study of religion, (12) estranged, (13) government by a religious group.

Practice A (p. 144)

(1) alias, (2) autocrat, (3) monarchies, (4) archetype, (5) theology, (6) monotonous, (7) oligarchy, (8) monoglots, (9) atheists, (10), alienating, (11) monorail, (12) anarchy

Practice B (pp. 144–145)

(1) anarchy, (2) demagogue, (3) democracy, (4) autocracy, (5) monarchy, (6) atheist, (7) autocrat, (8) alias, (9) aliens, (10) alienate, (11) theocracy.

Practice C (p. 145)

Sentences will vary.

Lesson 15 (pp. 146–151)

Story in Context (p. 146)

(1) people who are responsible for lawmaking, (2) people who are sexually attracted to the same gender, (3) marriage to one spouse at one time, (4) marriage to two spouses at the same time, (5) marriage to many spouses at the same time, (6) marriage to many spouses at the same time, (7) marriage to two spouses at the same time, (8) lawful, (9) hater of humankind, (10) referring to all, (11) marriages to two people at the same time, (12) being the same, (13) marriage to many spouses at the same time, (14) study of humankind, (15) general, (16) words spelled the same but having different meanings or pronunciations, (17) married to many spouses at the same time.

Practice A (p. 150)

(1) general, (2) The T-shirts have a general saying—they refer to any saying.

Practice B (pp. 150–151)

(1) homosexual, (2) genus, (3) bisexual, (4) anthropology, (5) generate, (6) polyglot (7) legal, (8) heterogeneous, (9) anthropomorphic, (10) genealogy, (11) legislature, (12) general

Practice C (p. 151)

Sentences will vary.

Special Academic Words (p. 152)

Practice A (p. 152)

(1) three-sided figure with three angles, (2) four-sided figure with four angles, (3) five-sided figure with five angles, (4) six-sided figure with six angles, (5) seven-sided figure with seven angles, (6) eight-sided figure with eight angles.

Practice B (p. 152)

(1) decameter, (2) decimeter, (3) centimeter, (4) millimeter, (5) hectometer, (6) kilometer.

Chapter Words in a Paragraph (p. 152)
Paragraphs will vary.

Crossword Puzzle (pp. 153–154)

Gaining Word Power on the Internet (p. 154)
Answers will vary.

Analogies (pp. 154–155)
(1) podiatrist, (2) polyglot, (3) decameter, (4) reporter, (5) polygon, (6) deca, (7) alien, (8) decimal, (9) export, (10) incredible, (11) millennium, (12) decimate, (13) century, (14) anarchy, (15) anthropology, (16) archetype, (17) bigamy, (18) creditor, (19) alienate, (20) credential.

Multiple-Choice Vocabulary Test (pp. 155–160)

Lesson 13

(1) b, (2) b, (3) d, (4) d, (5) d, (6) a, (7) c, (8) d, (9) a, (10) c, (11) a, (12) a, (13) a, (14) c, (15) a, (16) d, (17) a, (18) b, (19) d, (20) d, (21) c, (22) b, (23) c, (24) d, (25) a, (26) b, (27) c, (28) b.

Lesson 14

(29) c, (30) a, (31) b, (32) b, (33) d, (34) c, (35) c, (36) b, (37) a, (38) b, (39) d, (40) c, (41) b, (42) c, (43) c, (44) d, (45) c, (46) c, (47) b, (48) c, (49) a, (50) d.

Lesson 15

(51) c, (52) b, (53) a, (54) c, (55) b, (56) b, (57) a, (58) a, (59) b, (60) a, (61) c, (62) c, (63) c, (64) c, (65) b, (66) d, (67) c, (68) c, (69) c, (70) c, (71) a, (72) d.

Chapter True/False Test[1] (pp. 160–161)

(1) F; an animal that has many legs and crawls, (2) T, (3) T, (4) F; demography is the study of human populations, (5) T, (6) T, (7) F, (8) F; homonyms, (9) T, (10) F; passes laws, (11) T, (12) F; dictatorship or autocracy, (13) T, (14) F; one track, (15) F; no competitors, (16) T, (17) T, (18) T, (19) F; trust, (20) F; from other countries, (21) F; would probably not get married, (22) T, (23) T, (24) F; afraid of being alone

STOP. Turn to p. 160 for the scoring of the tests.

Additional Practice Sets (pp. 162–167)

Additional Practice 1

A. (1) b, (2) e, (3) d, (4) f, (5) c, (6) a.
B. (1) incredible, (2) century, (3) port, (4) centennial, (5) millennium, (6) credible, (7) credits, (8) million, (9) credentials, (10) billionth second (very short time), (11) portable, (12) reporter, (13) export, (14) bicentennial, (15) imports, (16) decade.

Additional Practice 2

A. (1) d, (2) a, (3) b, (4) g, (5) f, (6) c, (7) h, (8) e.
B. (1) alienate, (2) alias, (3) alien, (4) monarchy, (5) autocrat, (6) autocracy, (7) democracy, (8) anarchy, (9) atheist, (10) theocracy, (11) theology, (12) demagogue.

Additional Practice 3

A. (1) k, (2) h, (3) j, (4) g, (5) c, (6) f, (7) i, (8) b, (9) e, (10) a, (11) d.
B. (1) g, (2) s, (3) l, (4) c, (5) m, (6) r, (7) f, (8) t, (9) q, (10) h, (11) j, (12) n, (13) a, (14) b, (15) o, (16) i, (17) d, (18) p, (19) k, (20) e.

Chapter 7

Lesson 16 (pp. 168–175)

Story in Context (pp. 168–169)

(1) reading of the stars, (2) information to either prove or disprove something, (3) sense of sight, (4) those who sail through space, (5) those who sail underwater, (6) powerless, (7) area of knowledge in which something has been investigated in an orderly manner, (8) ability, (9) powerful, (10) obvious, (11) ability, (12) bring together, (13) preparations, (14) formal meetings, (15) handy, (16) at all places at the same time, (17) study of space, stars, and planets, (18) water, (19) glass bowl for aquatic animals, (20) able to be seen, (21) not able to be seen.

Practice A (p. 173)

Evidence—information that can prove or disprove something.
Answer will vary.

Practice B (pp. 173–174)

(1) decade, (2) anniversary, (3) evident, (4) convenient, (5) scientists, (6) convention, (7) convention, (8) astronauts, (9) aquatic, (10) aquanauts, (11) astrologer, (12) convention, (13)

---

[1]Answers for *false* are suggested answers.

incredible, (14) visible (or evident), (15) evident, (16) omnipresent, (17) incredible, (18) impotent, (19) astronauts, (20) aquanauts, (21) invisible, (22) visible, (23) provision, (24) evidence.

Practice C (p. 174)

Sentences will vary.

Practice D (p. 175)

(1) aquarium, (2) astronaut, (3) envisioned, (4) evidence, (5) scientist, (6) nautical (7)aquanaut, (8) potential, (9) visionary, (10) evident, (11) omnipotence, (12) omnipresent

Lesson 17 (pp. 176–183)

Story in Context (pp. 176–177)

(1) the killing of oneself, (2) the killing of one human by another, (3) Greek letter college organization of men, (4) indifference, (5) dead body, (6) place where dead bodies of accidents and unknown persons are kept, (7) undertaker, (8) pity, (9) putting oneself imaginatively in another's place and knowing what that person feels, (10) the killing of oneself, (11) the killing of oneself, (12) bodily, (13) the death penalty, (14) the killing of a group of people bound together by custom, (15) human being, (16) unable to die, (17) death, (18) a group of people who get a charter to give them certain rights of an individual, but not separately liable, (19) an economic system in which almost all the means of production are privately owned and operated for profit, (20) pledging of properties, (21) combine.

Practice A (p. 181)

Prediction—it means to foretell the future. Answers will vary.

Practice B (pp. 181–182)

(1) capital, (2) captions, (3) corpulent, (4) empathizing, (5) fraternity, (6) suicide, (7) mortified, (8) symbol, (9) sympathy, (10) corporation, (11) mortgage, (12) symptom, (13) apathetic, (14) incorporate, (15) synthesized

Practice C (p. 183)

Answers will vary.

Lesson 18 (pp. 184–191)

Story in Context (pp. 184–185)

(1) neighborhood, (2) buildings in which things are manufactured, (3) made by machines, (4) buildings in which things are manufactured, (5) by hand, (6) the one to whom an insurance policy is payable, (7) result, (8) able to be heard, (9) gain advantage, (10) divide up, (11) powerful, (12) written scripts, (13) written script, (14) alias, (15) unknown authorship, (16) influenced, (17) unknown authorship, (18) examination, (19) sound and sight, (20) tryout, (21) a building in which various things are held, (22) people assembled to listen or watch, (23) wrong names, (24) words usually spelled differently and have different meanings but sound the same, (25) words similar in meaning, (26) words opposite in meaning, (27) written script, (28) care of hands, (29) one who gives to another.

Practice A (p. 190)

Audible—means "able to be heard." The cartoon is amusing because the quarterback, who is much smaller than the opposing team's football players, realizes that his only course of action is to cry for "help" after the opposing team "shifts into a new defense." We get the idea that the quarterback is scared.

Practice B (pp. 190–191)

(1) manual, (2) benefit, (3) factory, (4) manufacture, (5) benefactor, (6) beneficiary, (7) factory, (8) location, (9) audience, (10) effective, (11) effect, (12) audible, (13) local, (14) audition, (15) manicure, (16) audition, (17) location, (18) audible, (19) manicure, (20) pseudonym.

Practice C (p. 191)

Answers will vary.

Crossword Puzzle (pp. 192–193)

Special Academic Words (p. 194)

(1) mortgage, (2) factory, (3) manufacture, (4) incorporate, (5) corporation, (6) capital, (7) amortized, (8) capitalism.

Chapter Words in a Paragraph (p. 194)

Paragraphs will vary.

Gaining Word Power on the Internet (p. 194)

Answers will vary.

Analogies (p. 195)

(1) underwater, (2) omnipresent, (3) impotent, (4) convene, (5) pseudoscience, (6) pseudopodal, (7) mortify, (8) caption, (9) visage, (10) facsimile, (11) audiology, (12) homicide, (13) corpulent, (14) antipathy, (15) convenient, (16) apathy, (17) creed, (18) effect, (19) anonymous, (20) capitulate.

Multiple-Choice Vocabulary Test (pp. 196–202)

Lesson 16

(1) a, (2) d, (3) a, (4) a, (5) a, (6) a, (7) d, (8) c, (9) c, (10) c, (11) b, (12) a, (13) c, (14) b, (15) b, (16) a, (17) d, (18) b, (19) c, (20) c, (21) c, (22) c, (23) a, (24) a, (25) c, (26) d, (27) a, (28) d, (29) b, (30) d.

Lesson 17

(31) c, (32) d, (33) d, (34) b, (35) d, (36) a, (37) b, (38) d, (39) b, (40) c, (41) a, (42) c, (43) d, (44) a, (45) b, (46) b, (47) a, (48) b, (49) d, (50) d, (51) b, (52) c, (53) d, (54) b, (55) c, (56) d, (57) c, (58) a, (59) b, (60) c, (61) c, (62) a, (63) b.

Lesson 18

(64) b, (65) d, (66) d, (67) a, (68) b, (69) d, (70) b, (71) d, (72) d, (73) c, (74) d, (75) a, (76) a, (77) d, (78) c, (79) c, (80) d, (81) b, (82) c, (83) a, (84) d, (85) b, (86) c, (87) d, (88) d, (89) c, (90) d, (91) b, (92) d, (93) a, (94) c, (95) c, (96) d, (97) c, (98) c, (99) a.

Chapter True/False Test[1] (pp. 203–204)

(1) F; it can be practiced anywhere, (2) T, (3) T, (4) F; someone who cares for objects in a museum, (5) T, (6) F; to be vanquished, (7) T, (8) T, (9) F; to open it, (10) F; who travels in space, (11) T, (12) T, (13) F; the words neither mean the same nor the opposite, (14) F; it means "all," (15) T, (16) F; to hand out, (17) T, (18) F; help, (19) F; to describe as a person, (20) T, (21) T, (22) T, (23) F; it means "not potent," (24) F; a group of people, (25) T, (26) F; a loan, (27) T, (28) F; death penalty vs. a beating.

STOP. Turn to p. 204 for the scoring of the tests.

Additional Practice Sets (pp. 204–211)

Additional Practice 1

A. (1) c, (2) h, (3) g, (4) b, (5) f, (6) a, (7) e, (8) d.
B. (1) vision, (2) invisible, (3) visible,[2] (4) provisions, (5) science, (6) evidence, (7) evident,[7] (8) astrology, (9) astronauts, (10) aquanauts, (11) astronomy, (12) aquatic, (13) aquarium, (14) convene, (15) conventions, (16) convenient, (17) potent, (18) impotent, (19) potential, (20) omnipresent.

Additional Practice 2

A. (1) b, (2) f, (3) d, (4) e, (5) c, (6) g, (7) h, (8) a.
B. (1) homicide, (2) genocide, (3) empathy, (4) apathy, (5) sympathy, (6) suicide, (7) fraternity, (8) corporation, (9) capitalism, (10) incorporate, (11) mortals, (12) immortals, (13) corpse, (14) capital punishment, (15) corporal punishment, (16) mortality, (17) morgue, (18) mortgage, (19) mortician, (20) capital.

Additional Practice 3

A. (1) h, (2) a, (3) b, (4) f, (5) g, (6) c, (7) d, (8) e.
B. (1) manicure, (2) manuscript, (3) factory, (4) benefactor, (5) Manual, (6) audible, (7) audit, (8) audition, (9) audiovisual, (10) effective, (11) auditorium, (12) manufacture, (13) effect, (14) beneficiary, (15) benefit, (16) audience, (17) affect, (18) homonyms, (19) synonyms, (20) antonyms, (21) pseudonyms, (22) misnomer, (23) anonymous, (24) local, (25) allocate, (26) location, (27) manipulated, (28) pseudoscience, (29) pedicure.

---

[1]Answers for *false* are suggested answers.
[2]Although *visible* and *evident* are synonyms, *visible* is the more specific and therefore *better* answer for number 3; *evident* is the *better* answer for number 7.

Chapter 8

Lesson 19 (pp. 212–219)

Story in Context (pp. 212–213)

(1) productive, (2) send from one place to another, (3) endless, (4) feel distress, (5) last, (6) liking, (7) introduction, (8) ending, (9) conversation, (10) reasonable, (11) names of persons who could corroborate what we wrote, (12) a listing of books on a subject with author's name, title, publisher, date of publication, and so on, (13) a listing of names, titles, and so on in some order, (14) meeting, (15) limited, (16) chart, (17) a straight line passing through the center of a circle, (18) boundary line around a circle, (19) impregnation.

Practice A (pp. 216–217)

(1) infinitesimal, (2) dialect, (3) monologue, (4) epilogue, (5) inference, (6) finite, (7) circumference, (8) deference, (9) affinity, (10) bibliography, (11) proficient, (12) suffered, (13) transfer, (14) diagram, (15) finale

Practice B (pp. 217–218)

(1) prologue, (2) dialogue, (3) epilogue, (4) diagram, (5) bibliography, (6) final, (7) finite, (8) infinite, (9) conference, (10) diameter, (11) circumference, (12) transfer, (13) logical, (14) catalogue, (15) fertile, (16) reference, (17) preference, (18) suffer, (19) fertilization.

Practice C (p. 218)

Sentences will vary.

Practice D (p. 219)

(1) infinite, (2) bibliography, (3) final, (4) suicide, (5) prologue, (6) incredible, (7) illegal, (8) fertile, (9) finite, (10) logical, (11) catalogue, (12) dialogue, (13) fertilization, (14) circumference, (15) diameter, (16) epilogue, (17) diagram, (18) suffer, (19) reference, (20) preference, (21) conference, (22) transfer.

Lesson 20 (pp. 220–228)

Story in Context (pp. 220–221)

(1) current, (2) absurd, (3) poisonous, (4) doctor who treats children, (5) determined what's wrong after an examination, (6) imagine or understand, (7) prisoners, (8) mislead, (9) awareness, (10) doctor of women's diseases, (11) short term, (12) able, (13) objection, (14) skin doctor, (15) able, (16) social entertainments, (17) make fun of, (18) possible answer to a problem, (19) prediction, (20) containers of medicine, (21) under the skin.

Practice A (pp. 225–226)

(1) ridicule, (2) hypothesis, (3) dermatologist, (4) pediatrician, (5) capsule, (6) ridiculous, (7) captive, (8) prognosis, (9) temporary, (10) diagnose, (11) Toxic, (12) capable, (13) contemporary, (14) exception, (15) reception, (16) hypodermic, (17) conceive, (18) deceive, (19) gynecologist, (20) perception.

Practice B (pp. 226–227)

(1) current, (2) mocking, (3) objection, (4) insightful, (5) stop, (6) make fun of, (7) speed, (8) way of greeting, (9) teacher, (10) unprepared, (11) doubter, (12) able, (13) removable part of a space vehicle, (14) mislead, (15) hater of women, (16) unproved conclusion, (17) sensory ability, (18) absurd, (19) for a short time, (20) strongly affected

Practice C (p. 227)

Sentences will vary.

Practice D (pp. 227–228)

(1) q, (2) p, (3) o, (4) r, (5) n, (6) m, (7) a, (8) e, (9) h, (10) f, (11) d, (12) g, (13) c, (14) k, (15) b, (16) l, (17) i, (18) j, (19) t, (20) s.

Lesson 21 (pp. 229–239)

Story in Context (pp. 229–230)

(1) study of life and culture of ancient people, (2) director of an orchestra, (3) rented from a landlord, (4) underground vault, (5) mysterious, (6) underground vault, (7) went on, (8) ancient, (9) following soon after, (10) system of violent and destructive whirlwinds, (11) to keep, (12) admitted, (13) reasoning, (14) system of violent and destructive whirlwinds, (15) result, (16) satisfied, (17) those who study the life and culture of ancient people, (18) went on, (19) underground vault, (20) what it held, (21) system of violent and destructive whirlwinds, (22) pattern, (23) order, (24) underground vault, (25) came before, (26) system of violent and destructive whirlwinds, (27) underground vault, (28) accomplish, (29) underground vault, (30) prolonged, (31) underground vault, (32) shortened form, (33) time order, (34) those who study the life and culture of ancient people, (35) underground vault.

Practice A (p. 236)

(1) deduction—the subtraction of something. (2) The cartoon is amusing because you don't expect someone to use something such as cinderblocks as an expense and then use the cinderblocks for paperweights.

Practice B (pp. 236–238)

(1) tenant, (2) content, (3) sequence, (4) maintain, (5) consequence, (6) cyclone, (7) cycle, (8) homicide, (9) conductor, (10) chronic, (11) proceed, (12) television, (13) succeed, (14) content, (15) cryptic, (16) abbreviation, (17) concede, (18) corpse, (19) morgue, (20) subsequent, (21) hypothesis, (22) deduction, (23) description, (24) local, (25) illegal.

Practice C (p. 238)

Sentences will vary.

Practice D (pp. 238–239)

(1) content, (2) maintain, (3) sequence, (4) consequence, (5) tenant, (6) subsequent, (7) archaeology, (8) archaic, (9) cycle, (10) cyclone, (11) chronological, (12) proceed, (13) concede, (14) precede, (15) chronic, (16) succeed, (17) abbreviation, (18) conductor, (19) deduction, (20) cryptic, (21) crypt, (22) content.

Special Academic Words (pp. 240–241)

Practice A (p. 240)

(1) medicine—children's doctor, (2) study of life and culture of ancient people, (3) science of reasoning, (4) medicine—study of the skin, (5) study of poisons, (6) medicine—study of women's diseases, especially those related to the reproductive organs.

Practice B (p. 241)

(1) hypodermic, (2) epidermis, (3) dermis, (4) dermatologist, (5) pediatrician, (6) toxicologist, (7) antitoxin, (8) toxic, (9) logical, (10) inference, (11) hypothesis, (12) induction, (13) fertile, (14) fertilization, (15) conceive, (16) diagnose, (17) prognosis, (18) gynecologist.

Practice C (p.241)

(1) epilogue, (2) prologue, (3) dialogue, (4) monologue, (5) reference, (6) bibliography, (7) anonymous, (8) pseudonym.

Chapter Words in a Paragraph (p. 241)

Paragraphs will vary.

Gaining Word Power on the Internet (p. 242)

Answers will vary.

Crossword Puzzle (pp. 242–243)

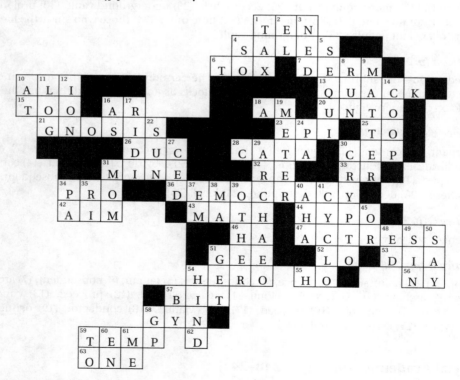

Analogies (pp. 244–245)

(1) tenacious, (2) epilogue, (3) finite, (4) deride, (5) toxicologist, (6) procession, (7) content, (8) pediatrician, (9) pedagogue, (10) contemporary, (11) consequence, (12) cyclone, (13) visage, (14) deceive, (15) captor, (16) decimate, (17) fertile, (18) agnostic, (19) inference, (20) dialect.

Multiple-Choice Vocabulary Test (pp. 245–250)

Lesson 19

(1) c, (2) a, (3) d, (4) a, (5) c, (6) a, (7) d, (8) a, (9) c, (10) c, (11) b, (12) a, (13) c, (14) b, (15) c, (16) c, (17) b, (18) d, (19) b, (20) b, (21) b, (22) a, (23) b, (24) d, (25) c, (26) b, (27) c, (28) c, (29) a.

Lesson 20

(30) d, (31) d, (32) b, (33) c, (34) b, (35) d, (36) c, (37) d, (38) b, (39) c, (40) d, (41) d, (42) d, (43) d, (44) a, (45) d, (46) c, (47) b, (48) a, (49) d, (50) b, (51) b, (52) b, (53) c, (54) d, (55) b, (56) d, (57) a, (58) b, (59) c, (60) c, (61) d.

Lesson 21

(62) b, (63) a, (64) a, (65) d, (66) d, (67) c, (68) b, (69) d, (70) b, (71) b, (72) a, (73) b, (74) b, (75) c, (76) d, (77) d, (78) c, (79) d, (80) c, (81) b, (82) c, (83) d, (84) c, (85) a, (86) c, (87) a, (88) c, (89) a, (90) d, (91) b, (92) a, (93) b, (94) d, (95) a, (96) b.

Chapter True/False Test[1] (pp. 251–252)

(1) F; archaic means ancient and chronic means continuing, (2) T, (3) F; precede means to go before and secede means to withdraw, (4) T, (5) T, (6) F; it means to admit defeat, (7) T, (8) F; it contains entries and information, (9) T, (10) T, (11) F; one means to choose and the other means to show respect, (12) T, (13) F; it means a prisoner, (14) F; it means to get an idea or become pregnant, (15) T, (16) F; a gynecologist treats women, (17) T, (18) F; skin, (19) T, (20) F; sells a ticket or shows you to your seat, (21) T, (22) F; to stop the person, (23) T, (24) F; an attraction, (25) T, (26) T, (27) F; they are used, (28) F; a finale is the very end of a piece, a prologue the very beginning, (29) T, (30) F; mocking, (31) T, (32) T, (33) F; poisonous, (34) F; without preparation, (35) T

STOP. Turn to p. 252 for the scoring of the tests.

Additional Practice Sets (pp. 253–257)

Additional Practice 1

A. (1) c, (2) b, (3) e, (4) a, (5) d, (6) g, (7) h, (8) f.
B. (1) p, (2) n, (3) i, (4) h, (5) s, (6) b, (7) r, (8) e, (9) c, (10) k, (11) f, (12) m, (13) o, (14) l, (15) d, (16) q, (17) g, (18) a, (19) j.

Additional Practice 2

A. (1) d, (2) g, (3) e, (4) i, (5) f, (6) h, (7) c, (8) a, (9) b.
B. (1) f, (2) o, (3) i, (4) k, (5) p, (6) j, (7) n, (8) s, (9) m, (10) a, (11) r, (12) d, (13) c, (14) g, (15) e, (16) t, (17) l, (18) h, (19) q, (20) b.

---

[1]Answers for *false* are suggested answers.

Additional Practice 3

A. (1) c, (2) h, (3) g, (4) e, (5) i, (6) b, (7) f, (8) d, (9) a.
B. (1) e, (2) g (or k), (3) k (or g), (4) l, (5) i, (6) f, (7) m, (8) h, (9) j, (10) a, (11) o, (12) u, (13) s, (14) d, (15) c, (16) b, (17) v, (18) n, (19) t, (20) q, (21) p, (22) r.

Chapter 9

Lesson 22 (pp. 258–267)

Story in Context (pp. 258–259)

(1) persons engaged in politics, (2) aggressive, (3) concentration, (4) polite, (5) a device used to increase sound, (6) aim, (7) words with more than one meaning, (8) words, (9) mental strain, (10) calm, (11) very strong, (12) human society, (13) not in the military, (14) dealing with citizenship, (15) profession, (16) major city center, (17) the science of government, (18) something written after.

Practice A (pp. 263–264)

(1) avocation, (2) posterity, (3) detention, (4) convocation, (5) posterior, (6) provoke, (7) pacifists, (8) postmortem, (9) vociferous, (10) megalopolis, (11) detente, (12) posthumously, (13) ambidextrous, (14) tendons, (15) vocabulary, (16) civil, (17) rebellion, (18) intention, (19) attention, (20) rebel

Practice B (pp. 264–265)

(1) mental concentration, (2) aims, (3) mental strain, (4) very strong, (5) warlike, (6) one not in the military, (7) the part of political science dealing with the rights and responsibilities of citizens, (8) cultural development of a people, (9) the science or art of government, (10) polite, (11) one who is in politics, (12) referring to a major city center and surrounding area, (13) freely expressive of opinions, (14) stock of words, (15) work, (16) having two or more meanings, (17) addition to a letter after signature, (18) calm.

Practice C (p. 265)

Sentences will vary.

Practice D (pp. 265–267)

(1) c, (2) d, (3) b, (4) d, (5) c, (6) c, (7) b, (8) d, (9) c, (10) a, (11) d, (12) b, (13) d, (14) b, (15) a, (16) a, (17) c, (18) d, (19) c.

Lesson 23 (pp. 267–277)

Story in Context (pp. 267–268)

(1) publication, (2) works of fiction, (3) worldly-wise, (4) vain, (5) works of fiction, (6) be made up, (7) situations, (8) love of wisdom and search for it, (9) put in place, (10) work of fiction, (11) 2nd year student, (12) far away, (13) times, (14) sleeping quarters, (15) help, (16) light can go through, but you cannot see clearly, (17) mistakes, (18) clear, (19) high-blood pressure, (20) obstructions, (21) continues, (22) asleep, (23) new methods.

Practice A (pp. 272–273)

(1) error, (2) lucid, (3) translucent, (4) philosophy, (5) circumstance, (6) sophomore, (7) sophisticated, (8) substitute, (9) assist, (10) distant, (11) obstacle, (12) consist, (13) innovation, (14) novel, (15) dormant, (16) dormitory, (17) persist, (18) egocentric, (19) hypertension, (20) period, (21) periodical.

Practice B (pp. 273–275)

(1) exaggeration, (2) beginner, (3) inactive, (4) unsound but clever reasoning, (5) staying power, (6) light up, (7) keep trying, (8) self-centered, (9) stubborn, (10) irregular, (11) measure of the outside of a closed figure, (12) outer part, (13) clear, (14) long work of fiction, (15) device for seeing outside, (16) complicated, not simple, (17) prior conditions, influences, and events, (18) help, (19) general law, (20) new idea, (21) portion of time

Practice C (p. 275)

Sentences will vary.

Practice D (pp. 275–276)

(1) lucid, (2) translucent, (3) error, (4) sophisticated, (5) sophomore, (6) philosophy, (7) circumstances, (8) substitute, (9) consist, (10) assist, (11) distant, (12) obstacle, (13) persist, (14) innovation, (15) novel, (16) dormitory, (17) dormant, (18) period, (19) periodical, (20) hypertension, (21) egocentric.

Lesson 24 (pp. 277–286)

Story in Context (pp. 277–278)

(1) admired, (2) discharged, (3) job, (4) union of states, (5) passing, (6) actual, (7) give, (8) position, (9) confession, (10) equal, (11) offer, (12) splendid, (13) a consent, (14) a sleeplike trance artificially brought about, (15) a sleeplike trance artificially brought about, (16) tell secrets to him, (17) total number of people, (18) hatred, (19) discharged, (20) inborn, (21) quality, (22) discharged, (23) dischargement, (24) attitude, (25) task, (26) discharged, (27) forgiving of insults, (28) enlarged, (29) hatred, (30) before birth, (31) after birth, (32) hatred, (33) time between events, (34) time between events.

Practice A (pp. 282–283)

(1) Position—job; (2) conscience—the feeling one has when he or she does something right or wrong. The first cartoon is amusing because when someone refers to a key position, you expect the person to get a high position, but in the cartoon, the term *key* is taken literally. The character in the Shoe cartoon got the position of janitor, in which he has lots of keys to open doors. It's funny because of what you don't expect. The second cartoon is humorous because you don't expect the person whose paper is being copied to claim that he doesn't want the other person to copy his paper because he didn't want to feel badly about two people rather than one getting an F.

Practice B (pp. 283–284)

(1) disposition, (2) emissary, (3) intervene, (4) missile, (5) proposition, (6) remission, (7) perfidious, (8) posture, (9) magnate, (10) animated, (11) expounded, (12) equivocate, (13) innate, (14) infidelity, (15) mission, (16) deposed, (17) intercede, (18) intermittent, (19) malediction,

(20) malefactor, (21) transmitted, (22) magnanimous, (23) dismissed, (24) equivalent, (25) magnificent, (26) position, (27) permission, (28) submitted

Practice C (pp. 284–285)

Sentences will vary.

Practice D (pp. 285–286)

(1) transmit, (2) positive, (3) post, (4) position, (5) magnanimous, (6) posture, (7) intermission, (8) hypnosis, (9) magnificent, (10) proposal, (11) prenatal, (12) innate, (13) postnatal, (14) nature, (15) federal, (16) confide, (17) magnify, (18) animosity, (19) population, (20) admission, (21) mission, (22) equivalent, (23) popular, (24) postpone, (25) dismiss, (26) submit, (27) permission.

Special Academic Words (pp. 286–287)

Practice A (pp. 286–287)

1. The part of political science dealing with the study of civic affairs and the rights and responsibilities of citizenship.
2. The science or art of government or of the direction and management of public or state affairs.
3. A person involved in the science or art of government.
4. One who is not in the military.
5. Relating to citizens and their government; relating to ordinary community life as distinguished from military or church affairs; polite.
6. One who is against war; one who is against conflict.
7. Easing of strained relations, especially between nations.
8. Relating to or formed by an agreement between two or more states, groups, and so on, in which central authority in common affairs is established by consent of its members.
9. Total number of people living in a country, city, or any area.
10. One very large city made up of a number of cities; a vast, populous, continuously urban area.
11. Referring to a major city center and its surrounding area; a person who inhabits a metropolis or one who has the manners and tastes associated with a metropolis.
12. A state of human society that has a high level of intellectual, social, and cultural development.

Practice B (p. 287)

(1) politician, (2) megalopolis, (3) metropolitan, (4) civilian, (5) pacifist, (6) detente, (7) civics, (8) federal.

Chapter Words in a Paragraph (p. 287)

Paragraphs will vary.

Gaining Word Power on the Internet (p. 287)

Answers will vary.

Crossword Puzzle (pp. 288–289)

Analogies (pp. 289–290)

(1) malediction, (2) malefactor, (3) lucid, (4) impolite, (5) novice, (6) convocation, (7) tense, (8) active, (9) stubborn, (10) infidelity, (11) peace, (12) animosity, (13) vocation,[1] (14) civilian, (15) intense, (16) aid, (17) persist, (18) novel, (19) knowledge, (20) oral.

Multiple-Choice Vocabulary Test (pp. 290–291)

Lesson 22

(1) d, (2) c, (3) b, (4) c, (5) d, (6) a, (7) b, (8) d, (9) d, (10) a, (11) b, (12) d, (13) b, (14) a, (15) d, (16) d, (17) b, (18) d, (19) d, (20) a, (21) d, (22) b, (23) c, (24) b, (25) a, (26) c, (27) b, (28) d, (29) b, (30) b, (31) d, (32) c, (33) a, (34) a.

Lesson 23

(35) b, (36) c, (37) c, (38) c, (39) d, (40) c, (41) b, (42) d, (43) b, (44) c, (45) a, (46) b, (47) c, (48) a, (49) a, (50) d, (51) c, (52) a, (53) d, (54) b, (55) a, (56) c, (57) b, (58) c, (59) b, (60) d, (61) b, (62) a, (63) d, (64) c, (65) d.

Lesson 24

(66) a, (67) b, (68) c, (69) b, (70) c, (71) c, (72) a, (73) d, (74) c, (75) d, (76) a, (77) c, (78) d, (79) d, (80) a, (81) c, (82) c, (83) c, (84) d, (85) b, (86) d, (87) d, (88) c, (89) c, (90) b, (91) b, (92) a, (93) b,

---

[1] *Vocation* is the answer because the relationship between *pine* and *tree* is one of *classification*.

(94) a, (95) b, (96) b, (97) d, (98) a, (99) c, (100) c, (101) c, (102) d, (103) c, (104) a, (105) c, (106) c, (107) b, (108) b, (109) d.

Chapter True/False Test[1] (pp. 297–298)

(1) F, do not to do; (2) F, is to is not or belligerent to peaceful; (3) F, is to is not; (4) F, are to are not; (5) T; (6) T; (7) F, must to need not or something you must accept to a plan; (8) F, are to are not or at least ten minutes to time between events; (9) T; (10) F, can to cannot; (11) F, is to is not or people to government; (12) F, can to cannot; (13) F, is to is not or what you are called to your profession; (14) F, is to is not or last paragraph of your essay to something added to a letter after the signature; (15) T; (16) F, would be to would not be; (17) T; (18) T; (19) F, means to does not mean or you need an assist to you continue in what you are doing; (20) T; (21) F, is to is not or an archaic plan to a new plan; (22) T; (23) T; (24) F, are to are not or Hypnosis to Inactive[2]; (25) T; (26) T; (27) F, is to is not or worldly-wise to immature; (28) F, refers to does not refer or all unions to a union of states; (29) T; (30) F, can to cannot.

STOP. Turn to p. 298 for the scoring of the tests.

Additional Practice Sets (pp. 299–303)

Additional Practice 1

A. (1) c, (2) a, (3) h, (4) b, (5) i, (6) g, (7) d, (8) e, (9) f.
B. (1) d, (2) a, (3) r, (4) k, (5) g, (6) b, (7) m, (8) c, (9) p, (10) e, (11) l, (12) f, (13) h, (14) q, (15) i, (16) j, (17) o, (18) n, (19) s.

Additional Practice 2

A. (1) d, (2) g, (3) a, (4) c, (5) i, (6) j, (7) h, (8) f, (9) e, (10) b.
B. (1) e, (2) q, (3) j, (4) l, (5) a, (6) i, (7) n, (8) b, (9) k, (10) t, (11) c, (12) m, (13) h, (14) f, (15) d, (16) s, (17) g, (18) o, (19) u, (20) r, (21) p.

Additional Practice 3

A. (1) i, (2) c, (3) a, (4) f, (5) h, (6) e, (7) b, (8) g, (9) d.
B. (1) g, (2) l, (3) s, (4) x, (5) k, (6) t, (7) c, (8) a, (9) z, (10) b, (11) d, (12) r, (13) a, (14) p, (15) v, (16) e, (17) m, (18) h, (19) f, (20) u, (21) y, (22) i, (23) o, (24) j, (25) q, (26) n, (27) w.

---

[1]Answers for *false* are suggested answers.
[2]Persons can be active while under *hypnosis*. Also, *hypnosis* is a noun and *dormant* is an adjective.